Essays on Language and Usage

Essays on Language and Usage SECOND EDITION

EDITED BY

LEONARD F. DEAN
UNIVERSITY OF CONNECTICUT

AND

KENNETH G. WILSON
UNIVERSITY OF CONNECTICUT

New York   OXFORD UNIVERSITY PRESS   1963

© 1959, 1963 by Oxford University Press, Inc.
Library of Congress Catalogue Card Number: 63–7866
Printed in the United States of America
Second Printing, June, 1963

Preface

From the early grades through the first year of college, the text-books and lessons in grammar and usage scarcely change. The repetition is well meant and apparently necessary: if they won't learn what's good for them, make them do it again. Certainly habits are formed and re-formed by repetitive drill, but it is clear from the record that repetition is not enough.

This book is based on the conviction that knowledge must be added to drill so that repetition may open into growth. Everyone aims at this, at confidence and pleasure in the use of language rather than at anxiety about being correct; the problem has been to get the liberating knowledge, which is scattered through books and journals, into the hands of the students. We have tried to solve that problem by bringing together here a generous number of readable, authoritative essays on language and usage. These essays put the usual handbooks in perspective, and they provide a proper linguistic foundation for the study of rhetoric and composition. They have been arranged in an order which we hope will be useful for the teacher of composition and his students.

We are indebted to colleagues, students, and former teachers; to critics, known and anonymous; and to the authors and publishers of the essays reprinted here.

Storrs, Connecticut   LEONARD F. DEAN
February 1959   KENNETH G. WILSON

Prefatory Note to the Second Edition

In revising *Essays on Language and Usage* we have made changes intended to help express more fully and effectively the original purposes of the book. To make it more practically useful, we nearly doubled the suggestions for study, incorporated a number of entries from various kinds of dictionaries, and added essays which bring the reader close to the living history of the language, from Elizabethan efforts to enrich the vocabulary to very recent discussions of usage and dictionary-making. Finally, a new section on style has been added to clarify the relation between the study of language and the practice of writing.

We are grateful to the many teachers and students who have made suggestions for revision from their experience with the first edition. Such a response renews one's sense of the generous spirit and intelligence that unify the great diversity of our schools and colleges when they concern themselves with a liberal subject.

We wish to thank the following publishers and institutions for their help and for their kind permission to reprint dictionary entries which appear in this book: The G. & C. Merriam Company, publishers of the *Webster's New International Dictionary*, Second Edition, and of the *Webster's Third New International Dictionary*; The World Publishing Company, publishers of *Webster's New World Dictionary*; The Rare Book Division of the New York Public Library; Appleton-Century-Crofts, successors to The Century Company, publishers of *The Century Dictionary and Cyclopedia*; and The Clarendon Press, Oxford, publishers of *The Oxford English Dictionary*.

Storrs, Connecticut   L. F. D.
December 1962   K. G. W.

Contents

IV   Usage, 249

V   Style, 313

Aids to Study and Topics for Writing, 355

PART ONE

Dictionaries, Words, and Meanings

Our language is all around us. In studying it, we can enter anywhere, and one thing will lead to another. The ten essays making up this section have been placed first for the practical reason that they are an introduction to dictionaries, the books about language to which we turn every day for help in reading and writing.

The first essay is a brief history of dictionaries by Harold Whitehall, professor of English linguistics at Indiana University. A knowledge of this history is part of a liberal education: it liberates us from the false notion of *the* dictionary. Whitehall reminds us that there have been different kinds of dictionaries to serve different users and different needs, that dictionaries vary in quality, and that dictionaries must change as the language grows and changes.

Dictionaries contain much more accurate and useful information than many of us may realize in our haste to check a spelling or a meaning. Mitford Mathews, editor of *A Dictionary of Americanisms* (1951) and author of the next two essays in this section, proves this by leading us into the fine print in four kinds of modern dictionaries: abridged, unabridged, encyclopedic, and historical. The fascinating information in an historical dictionary, one which traces the changing meanings of words, is the subject of the fourth essay by Stuart Robertson, revised by Frederic G. Cassidy, professor of English at the University of Wisconsin. This essay shows through examples how meanings shift over the years between special and general, respectable and disreputable. In the fifth essay the late H. L. Mencken describes in humorous detail how the names of things change because of our genteel use of euphemisms, words chosen or invented to prettify and ennoble the appearance of life. In the sixth essay Margaret Schlauch, formerly professor of English at New York University and now at the University of Warsaw, gives examples of the re-creation offered by writers who deliberately recover the lost or faded meanings of words.

The notion that any dictionary of a living, changing language can be a permanent and final authority has been promoted in modern times by exploiting through advertising our latent fears of being "incorrect" in writing and speaking. Samuel Johnson's *Dictionary of the English Language* (1755) carries only the old-fashioned meaning of *advertise:* to inform. In the Preface to that *Dictionary*, the seventh essay in this section, Johnson informs us with refreshing candor that he had dreamed of permanently purifying and regulating the language but that he finally found it impossible to embalm something which was living and changing. Words are the daughters of the earth, as he puts it, and even with the most modern methods they cannot be completely brought to book.

The most modern methods were used in the making of the latest unabridged Webster's Dictionary, which is discussed in the last three essays in this section by Dwight Macdonald, editor and reviewer, and James Sledd and Bergen Evans, professors of English and linguistics at Northwestern University. Their discussions point up the fact that we are fortunate to experience the publication of a major unabridged dictionary because such an event helps to make us aware of the extraordinary complexity and richness of our language.

HAROLD WHITEHALL

The Development of the English Dictionary

The evolution of the English dictionary is rooted in the general evolution of the English language. In this development the chief pressures were exerted by the steady increase in the word stock of English from the 50,000–60,000 words of Anglo-Saxon through the 100,000–125,000 words of the Middle-English vocabulary to the huge total of some 650,000 words which could theoretically be recorded in an exhaustive dictionary of contemporary English. Such an overall increase as this made the dictionary *necessary*. The pressure of vocabulary, however, has always been influenced and reinforced by the intellectual climate of each successive period of the language. A dictionary is not exactly a work of art, yet it bears as strongly as an artistic production the impress of the age that bore it. For that reason, the history of the dictionary is a fascinating chapter in the history of ideas.

The beginnings of dictionary history are neither national nor concerned with any of the national languages. They are concerned with the international language of medieval European civilization: Latin. Our first word books are lists of relatively difficult Latin terms, usually those of a Scriptural nature, accompanied by glosses in easier or more familiar Latin. Very early in the Anglo-Saxon period, however, we find glosses containing native English (i.e., Anglo-Saxon) equivalents for the hard Latin terms, and it may be that two of these—the *Leiden* and *Erfurt Glosses*—represent the earliest written English we possess. Such glosses, whether Latin-Latin or Latin-English, continued to be compiled during the entire Anglo-Saxon and most of the Middle-English period.

The next stage of development, attained in England around 1400, was the collection of the isolated glosses into what is called a *glossarium*, a

From the Introduction to *Webster's New World Dictionary of the American Language.* College Edition, © 1958 by The World Publishing Company. Reprinted by permission of the publisher.

3

kind of very early Latin-English dictionary. As it chances, our first example of the glossarium, the so-called *Medulla Grammatica* written in East Anglia around 1400, has never been printed; but two later redactions were among our earliest printed books, and one of these, the *Promptorium Parvulorum sive Clericorum,* issued by Wynkyn de Worde in 1499, was the first work of a dictionary nature ever to be printed on English soil. Significantly enough, this version of the *Medulla* places the English term first and its Latin equivalent second.

The first onset of the Renaissance worked against rather than in favor of the native English dictionary. The breakdown of Latin as an international language and the rapid development of international trade led to an immediate demand for foreign-language dictionaries. The first of such works, Palsgrave's *Lesclaircissement de la Langue Francoyse* (1523), was rapidly followed by Salesbury's Welsh-English dictionary (1547), Percival's English-Spanish dictionary (1591), and finally, by the best known of all such works, Florio's Italian-English dictionary (1599). Meanwhile, the first great classical dictionary, Cooper's *Thesaurus* (1565), had already appeared. The history of dictionaries is larded with strange occurrences: we are not surprised, therefore, that the publication of Cooper's work was delayed five years because his wife, fearing that too much lexicography would kill her husband, burned the first manuscript of his magnum opus. It should be noted, in passing, that none of these various word books of the 16th century actually used the title *dictionary* or *dictionarium.* They were called by various kinds of fanciful or half-fanciful names, of which *hortus* "garden," and *thesaurus* "hoard" were particularly popular.

During the late 16th century, the full tide of the Renaissance had been sweeping a curious flotsam and jetsam into English literary harbors. Constant reading of Greek and Latin bred a race of Holofernes pedants who preferred the Latin or Greek term to the English term. Their principle in writing was to use Latino-Greek polysyllabics in a Latino-English syntax. Their strange vocabulary—studded with what some critics call "inkhorn" terms—eventually affected English so powerfully that no non-Latinate Englishman could ever hope to read many works in his own language unless he was provided with explanations of elements unfamiliar to him. The "Dictionary of Hard Words," the real predecessor of the modern dictionary, was developed to provide precisely such explanations. It is significant that the first English word book to use the name *dictionary,* Cokeram's *The English Dictionary* (1623), is subtitled "An Interpreter of Hard Words." Among those explained on its first few pages are *Abequitate, Bulbulcitate,* and *Sullevation.* In point of time, the first "dictionary of hard words" was Robert Cawdrey's *Table Alphabeticall of Hard*

Words (1604). Of the various works of the same class appearing after this date may be mentioned John Bullokar's *English Expositor* (1616) and Edward Phillip's *New World of Words* (1658), both of which reveal a strong interest in the reform of spelling, Blount's *Glossographia* (1656) containing the first etymologies ever to appear in a printed English dictionary, and Thomas Kersey's *Dictionarium Anglo-Brittanicum* (1708), which also includes legal terms, provincialisms, and archaisms. If the 16th was the century of the foreign-language dictionary, the 17th was the century of the dictionary of hard words.

Between 1708 and 1721, hard-word dictionaries began to be replaced by word books giving ever-increasing attention to literary usage. The Latino-Greek borrowings of the earlier century had been either absorbed into the language or sloughed away. The French influence, from 1660 onwards, had replaced Renaissance stylistic ideas with notions of a simple elegance in syntax and a quiet effectiveness in vocabulary. These stylistic virtues were actually achieved in the works of Swift, Addison, Steele, and lesser writers. The literary mind of the early 18th century, therefore, was convinced that English had finally attained a standard of purity such as it had never previously known; it was also convinced that the brash outgrowth of mercantile expansionism, later to be reinforced by the infant Industrial Revolution, might very well destroy this hard-won standard of literary refinement. What more natural than that the standard should be enshrined in a dictionary for the admiration and guidance of posterity?

The first word book to embody the ideals of the age was Nathaniel Bailey's *Universal Etymological Dictionary of the English Language,* originally published in 1721, and then, in a beautiful folio volume with illustrations by Flaxman, in 1731. This, one of the most revolutionary dictionaries ever to appear, was the first to pay proper attention to current usage, the first to feature etymology, the first to give aid in syllabification, the first to give illustrative quotations (chiefly from proverbs), the first to include illustrations, and the first to indicate pronunciation. An interleaved copy of the 1731 folio edition was the basis of Samuel Johnson's *Dictionary* of 1755; through Johnson, it influenced all subsequent lexicographical practice. The position of dictionary pioneer, commonly granted to Johnson or to Noah Webster, belongs in reality to one of the few geniuses lexicography ever produced: Nathaniel Bailey.

Johnson's *Dictionary* (1755) enormously extends the techniques developed by Bailey. Johnson was able to revise Bailey's crude etymologies on the basis of Francis Junius' *Etymologicon Anglicanum* (first published in 1743), to make a systematic use of illustrative quotations, to fix the spelling of many disputed words, to develop a really discriminating system of definition, and to exhibit the vocabulary of English much more fully than had ever been attempted before. In his two-volume work, the age and following ages found their ideal word book. Indeed, a good deal of the importance of the book lies in its later influence. It dominated English letters for a full century after its appearance and, after various revisions, continued in common use until 1900. As late as the '90's, most Englishmen used the word *dictionary* as a mere synonym for Johnson's *Dictionary;* in 1880 a Bill was actually thrown out of Parliament because a word in it was not in "the Dictionary."

One of the tasks taken upon himself by Johnson was to remove "improprieties and absurdities" from the language. In short, he became a linguistic legislator attempting to perform for English those offices performed for French by the French Academy. From this facet of his activities we get the notion, still held by many dictionary users, and fostered by many dictionary publishers, that the dictionary is a "supreme authority" by which to arbitrate questions of "correctness" and "incorrectness." The dictionaries of the second half of the 18th century extended this notion particularly to the field of pronunciation. By 1750, the increasing wealth of the middle classes was making itself felt in the social and political worlds. Those who possessed it, speakers, for the most part, of a middle-class dialect, earnestly desired a key to the pronunciations accepted in polite society. To provide for their needs, various pronunciation experts—usually of Scottish or Irish extraction—edited a series of pronunciation dictionaries. Of these, the most important are James Buchanan's *New English Dictionary* (1769), William Kenrick's *New Dictionary of the English Language* (1773), Thomas Sheridan's *General Dictionary of the English Language* (1780), and, above all, John Walker's *Critical Pronouncing Dictionary and Expositor of the English Language* (1791). In such works, pronunciation was indicated by small superscript numbers referring to the "powers" of the various vowel sounds. Despite the legislative function exercised by the authors of almost all of these works, we must admit that they did indicate contemporary pronunciation with great accuracy, and when Walker's pronunciations were combined with Johnson's definitions the result was a dictionary which dominated the word-book field, both in England and the United States, until well after 1850.

If the chief contributions of the 18th century to dictionary making were (1) authoritative recording of literary vocabulary and (2) accurate recording of pronunciation, those of the 19th were unmistakably (1) the recording of word history through dated quotations and (2) the development of encyclopedic word books. Already in 1755, Samuel Johnson had hinted in his preface that the sense of a word "may easily be collected entire from the examples." During the first twenty-five years of the century, the researches of R. K. Rask, J. L. C. Grimm, and F. Bopp clearly defined the historical principle in linguistic. It was only a question of time, therefore, before someone combined Johnson's perception with the findings of the new science of historical linguistics. That person was Charles Richardson, who, in his *New Dictionary of the English Language* (1836), produced a dictionary completely lacking definitions but one in which both the senses and the historical evolution of the senses were accurately indicated by dated defining quotations. Richardson's work leads directly to the great *New English Dictionary on Historical Principles*, first organized in 1858, begun under Sir James Murray in 1888, and completed under Sir William Craigie in 1928. With its supplement (1933), the *New English Dictionary* or *Oxford English Dictionary* (N.E.D. or O.E.D.) covers the vocabulary of English with a completeness of historical evidence and a discrimination of senses unparalleled in linguistic history. No other language has ever been recorded on anything approaching this scale, and no dictionary of English since the *New English Dictionary* was completed has failed to reveal a profound debt to this monumental work. As compared with the effort represented by the N.E.D., the attempt to record the technological vocabularies of the language as first seen in John W. Ogilvie's *Universal Dictionary of the English Language* (1850) seems to be of minor importance, although it has had great practical effect on subsequent American dictionaries.

Since the publication of the O.E.D., the only important British dictionary has been Henry Cecil Wyld's *Universal Dictionary of the English Language* (1932), a work of somewhat restricted vocabulary coverage but one which may well point the way to the dictionary of the future. Wyld has discarded the older logical definitions for definitions of a more functional nature; his examples delve deeply into idiom; his etymologies are of a completeness and modernity unparalleled until this present dictionary in any medium-sized word book. The failure of Wyld's book to achieve much popularity on this side of the Atlantic underlines the fact that the typical American dictionary of the English language is a work *differing in kind* from any of those so far mentioned. It differs because the conditions of American life and culture differ from those of English life and culture.

The modern American dictionary is typically a single compact volume published at a relatively modest price containing: (1) definitive American spellings, (2) pronunciations indicated by diacritical markings, (3) strictly limited etymologies, (4) numbered senses, (5) some illustrations, (6) selective treatment of synonyms and antonyms, (7) encyclopedic inclusion of scientific, technological, geographical, and biographical items. It owes its development, within the general framework of the evolution sketched above, to the presence of a large immigrant population in this country, to the elaborate American system of popular education, and to the vast commercial opportunities implicit in both of these.

The first American dictionaries were unpretentious little schoolbooks based chiefly on Johnson's *Dictionary* of 1755 by way of various English abridgments of that work. The earliest of these were Samuel Johnson Junior's *School Dictionary* (1798), Johnson and Elliott's *Selected Pronouncing and Accented Dictionary* (1800), and Caleb Alexander's *Columbian Dictionary* (1800). The most famous work of this class, Noah Webster's *Compendious Dictionary of the English Language* (1806) was an enlargement of Entick's *Spelling Dictionary* (London, 1764), distinguished from its predecessors chiefly by a few encyclopedic supplements and emphasis upon its (supposed) Americanism. The book was never popular and contributed little either to Webster's own reputation or to the development of the American dictionary in general.

The first important date in American lexicography is 1828. The work that makes it important is Noah Webster's *An American Dictionary of the English Language* in two volumes. Webster's book has many deficiencies—etymologies quite untouched by the linguistic science of the time, a rudimentary pronunciation system actually inferior to that used by Walker in 1791, etc.—but in its insistence upon American spellings, in definitions keyed to the American scene, and in its illustrative quotations from the Founding Fathers of the Republic, it provided the country with the first *native* dictionary comparable in scope with that of Dr. Johnson. It was not, as is often claimed, the real parent of the modern American dictionary; it was merely the foster-parent. Because of its two-volume format and its relatively high price it never achieved any great degree of popular acceptance in Webster's own lifetime. Probably its greatest contribution to succeeding American dictionaries was the style of definition writing—writing of a clarity and pithiness never approached before its day.

The first American lexicographer to hit upon the particular pattern that distinguishes the American dictionary was Webster's lifelong rival, Joseph E. Worcester. His *Comprehensive Pronouncing, and Explanatory Dictionary of the English Language* (1830), actually a thoroughly revised abridgment of Webster's two-volume work of 1828, was characterized by the additions of new words, a more conservative spelling, brief, well-phrased definitions, full indication of pronunciation by means of diacritics, use of stress marks to divide syllables, and lists of synonyms. Because it was compact and low priced, it immediately became popular—far more popular, in fact, than any of Webster's own dictionaries in his own lifetime. As George P. Krapp, in his *The English Language in America*, says:

"If one balances the faults of the Webster of 1828 against the faults of the Worcester of 1830, the totals are greatly in the favor of Worcester." One might feel the same about its merits as compared with those of Webster's own revision of his *American Dictionary* (1841), which featured the inclusion of scientific terms compiled by Professor W. Tully. The first Webster dictionary to embody the typical American dictionary pattern was that of 1847, edited by Noah Webster's son-in-law, Chauncey A. Goodrich, and published by the Merriams.

Temperamentally the flamboyant Noah Webster and the cautious Joseph Worcester were natural rivals. Their rivalry, however, was as nothing compared with that which developed between the rival publishers of the Webster and Worcester dictionaries. By 1845, the great flood of immigration and the vast extension of the school system had suddenly lifted dictionary making into the realm of big business. In a "war of the dictionaries" that reflects the rudimentary business ethics of the period, the rival publishers used every device of advertisement and every stratagem of high-powered salesmanship to drive each other off the market. Unsavory as this war appears in retrospect, it certainly helped to force rapid improvement of the dictionaries that these publishers controlled. Worcester's initial advantages were surpassed in the Merriam-Webster of 1847; the innovations in Worcester's edition of 1860 were more than paralleled in the Merriam-Webster of 1864, one of the best dictionaries ever to appear, but one from which almost everything really characteristic of Noah Webster himself was deleted. The battle was finally decided in favor of the Webster dictionaries, chiefly because the popularity of Webster's "Little Blue Back Speller" had put their name in every household, partly because of the death of Joseph Worcester, and partly because of the merit of the Merriam product from 1864 onwards.

Since about 1870, the climate of American dictionary making has been much more peaceful. In the field of unabridged dictionaries, the most important accretion is the *Century Dictionary* (1889), edited by the great American linguist, William Dwight Whitney, and issued in six volumes. Unfortunately, this magnificent work, considered by many authorities to be basically the finest ever issued by a commercial publisher, has lost much of its popularity because of inadequate subsequent revision. The fact that it was not in a one-volume format undoubtedly also worked against its popular success. The only other new unabridged dictionaries that have appeared in the period are Webster's *Imperial Dictionary of the English Language* (1904), and Funk and Wagnalls *New Standard Dictionary* (1893). The first of these, the only unabridged dictionary ever published west of the Appalachians, was issued in Chicago by George W. Ogilvie, a publisher who carried on his own private guerrilla "war of the dictionaries" against the Merriam Company between 1904 and circa 1917. At the moment, the most important advances in lexicography are taking place in the field of the abridged collegiate-type dictionaries.

Meanwhile the scholarly dictionary has not been neglected. Once the *New English Dictionary* was published, scholarly opinion realized the need to supplement it in the various periods of English and particularly in American English. The first of the proposed supplements, edited by Sir William Craigie and Professor J. R. Hulbert, is the *Dictionary of American English on Historical Principles,* completed in 1944. This was followed by a *Dictionary of Americanisms,* edited by Mitford M. Mathews and published in 1951. A *Middle English Dictionary,* a *Dictionary of the Older Scottish Tongue,* and a *Dictionary of Later Scottish* are in preparation, and work on the *American Dialect Dictionary* of the American Dialect Society is now finally under way.

MITFORD M. MATHEWS

Meanings and Etymologies

In a single written sentence, a hundred elusive meanings obscurely palpitate.
GILES LYTTON STRACHEY

There is an old saying that the same man never crossed the same river twice. The man is bound to be a little different on his second crossing. He is at least a little older and more experienced. For one thing, he knows more about crossing rivers. Also, the river is not quite the same. It may be much higher, or lower, than it was when the man crossed it before. It would be impossible for the man to find and pass through or over just the same water he crossed earlier.

This old saying occurs to one who contemplates the manifold meanings words have. No word is ever used twice in just the same sense. The matter is perplexing in the extreme, and we need not go into it here, but it is a well-known fact that many words, especially those that are old in the language, have more than one clearly recognizable meaning.

One of the most important things a lexicographer has to do is to record the meanings of words. He has the task of arranging these meanings in the order he thinks will be of most help to those who use his work.

Different editors solve this problem of arrangement in different ways. In the prefatory part of your dictionary you will find some indication of the plan that has been followed in arranging the meanings. In the Merriam-Webster dictionaries, the meanings are arranged, as far as possible, in the order in which they arose. In those dictionaries, the first meanings given are the earliest a word is known to have had, and the more modern meanings come later.

The arrangement of meanings is difficult, no matter what plan is used. Students not instructed about this aspect of dictionaries sometimes suppose that the first meaning given for a word is the most common one, but that is not always the case. The only safe course is to examine the forematter of your dictionary to see what plan has been followed.

Many of those who consult a dictionary search through the meanings, often in haste, hoping to find the one in which they are interested or one that will satisfy their immediate need. Such a method is not to be recommended. Such flutterings about leave only a meager residue of information and interest in the mind of the searcher. The most fruitful way to approach the meanings is by way of etymologies. Many times the etymology will illuminate not only a particular meaning but all the meanings a word has, and will show the way to related words and their meanings.

For example, *nausea* is a classical Greek word in English dress. It is based upon another Greek word meaning a ship. The Greeks were acquainted with the miseries of sea-sickness, which their word *nausia* meant, but in thinking of this distress they focused attention on a ship rather than on the sea. Dictionaries in their etymologies point out that *nausea* is closely related to *nave* (of a church or cathedral), *nautical*, *naval*, each of them having this basic idea of a ship.

Clinic is from a Greek word meaning a bed, and the meanings of the word and those of its derivatives and combinations stem from this significance. *Longitude* is based upon a Latin word for *long*, and this sense colors all its meanings. The same is true of *latitude*, from a Latin word for *broad*, and, indeed, of an avalanche of others.

Sometimes the original meaning of a word is markedly different from some of its later ones. *Scene* started out in classical Greek meaning a tent and later a booth before which actors played and into which they retired to change their costumes. As the art of acting became more elaborate, the scene of a Greek theater became the permanent structure forming the background of the stage (cf. our expression "to look behind the scene"). The extension of the meaning of the word has continued until it now means anything that lies open to view. The idea of a tent is not felt at all.

One who does not pay attention to etymologies misses surprising and fascinating information about word relationships. For example, *hyena* is a Greek word in modern English form. It was the name the Greeks applied to the animal still so called. Dictionaries dismantle this Greek name for the hyena and show that it was the feminine form of the Greek word for hog and consequently meant sow. When the Greeks called a hyena a sow, they no doubt did so in allusion to its pronounced mane, suggesting the bristling arched mane of a wild sow.

The Greek word *hys*, without any feminine suffix, meant hog or swine. Latin had the same word with the same meaning but spelled it *sus*. The Greek word, with its feminine suffix, appears now in English as *hyena,* and the Latin *sus* accounts for our *sow. Hyena* and *sow* certainly do not at first glance appear to be cognates, but they are. Similarly *six* and the first part of *hexagon* are cognates, *six* being from the Germanic *sex,* and *hex-* coming from Greek *hex* meaning six.

Let us now look carefully at some dictionary entries in an effort to secure from them all the information they contain. We shall begin by looking closely at the entry *anecdote* in the College Edition of *Webster's New World Dictionary.*[1]

> **an·ec·dote** (an′ik-dōt′), *n.* [Fr.; ML. *anecdota;* Gr. *anekdota,* neut. pl. of *anekdotos,* unpublished; *an-,* not + *ekdotos* < *ekdidonai; ek-,* out + *didonai,* to give], 1. *pl.* originally, little-known, entertaining facts of history or biography; hence, 2. a short, entertaining account of some happening, usually personal or biographical. —*SYN.* see story.

This dictionary makes etymology one of its strong features and so serves exceptionally well for our purpose.

The following things about this entry are of interest.

1. The entry word, printed in boldface to give it more prominence, is divided by periods into its three syllables. This form of division not only helps out with the pronunciation of a word, but it also gives assistance to one who has to divide a word at the end of a line of writing or printing. In such cases, words should be divided with respect to their syllables.

2. Then, within curves, the word is rewritten, this time in symbols that show pronunciation. A heavy accent mark,′ immediately follows the syllable which receives most stress, and a lighter mark indicates the syllable getting minor stress. A syllable, here *ik,* which gets no stress is followed by a hyphen.

Following the indication of pronunciation comes the abbreviation of the part of speech to which the word belongs. It is the conventional practice to give these abbreviations in italics.

3. It is well-accepted dictionary procedure to place etymologies in square brackets just after the indication of the part of speech of the word involved. The etymologies are perhaps the parts of dictionaries least often looked at, especially by younger students who are in such a hurry to get an education that they often miss fine opportunities to learn something. How much is missed by those who fail to give attention to etymologies may be seen by examining somewhat closely the one given here.

To show in a simpler way what it means, let us write the etymology in a much more expanded form, making no use of the abbreviations with which it is generously provided and with which we have become familiar on previous pages, and retaining the transliterated forms of the Greek words that occur. It may make this expanded version of the etymology easier to follow if we begin at the very end of it and proceed back to its beginning, just as it is sometimes easier to follow a stream from its source to its mouth than it is to explore it beginning at the mouth.

> In Greek there was a verb, *didonai,* meaning to give. A common prefix, *ek-,* was often used before this verb and it then became *ekdidonai* to give out. From this expanded form of the verb, Greek formed an adjective, *ekdotos,* given out. In Greek it was customary to prefix *an-* to adjectives beginning with a vowel and thus reverse or negate their meanings. So the Greeks formed *anekdotos,* not given out.
>
> Greek adjectives had masculine, feminine, and neuter forms. The neuter plural of *anekdotos* was *anekdota,* unpublished things, that is, things not given out. Latin, during the medieval period, borrowed *anekdota* in the form *anecdota.* This Latin term passed into French, where it was spelled *anecdote.* From French the word, unchanged in form, passed into English.

The etymology we began with has about twenty words in it; the expanded form above has many times as many. It is easy, however, for anyone who looks at the etymology in the dictionary to see that *anecdote* comes from French, which derived it from Latin, which obtained it from Greek, and that the basic meaning of it is things not published or given out. Anyone who considers this etymology thoughtfully may well be puzzled over the fact that *anecdote* began its career with such an odd meaning. A fuller account of the word is needed before this puzzle can be cleared up.

4. The definitions are numbered and begin with small letters. The numbering is of course a great convenience. The use of small letters at the beginnings of the definitions is a mere stylistic device, those charged with producing this dictionary feeling that the looks of the page justified the use of the small letters rather than capitals in such cases. The meanings are given in the order of their ages, the oldest meaning being given first. Observe how the original meaning led on to sense 2, the one which nowadays the word usually has.

5. At the very end of the entry there is a reference to *story* for a presentation of the synonyms of *anecdote.* English abounds in words that mean about the same thing. Dictionaries perform a useful service by giving such groups of words and distinguishing between such terms as *anecdote, narrative, tale, story.*

Of course, the larger a dictionary is, the more information one can obtain from it. Here is the entry *anecdote* as it appears in the current large unabridged *Webster's New International Dictionary, Second Edition.*[2] *

an'ec·dote (ăn'ĕk·dōt; ăn'ĭk-), *n.* [F., fr. Gr. *anekdotos* not published, fr. *an-* not + *ekdotos* given out, fr. *ekdidonai* to give out, to publish, fr. *ek* out + *didonai* to give. See DATE point of time.] **1.** *pl.* Literally, unpublished items; narratives of secret or private details of history; — often in book titles. *Now Rare.*
2. A narrative, usually brief, of a separable incident or event of curious interest, told without malice and usually with intent to amuse or please, often biographical and characteristic of some notable person, esp. of his likable foibles.
  Some modern *anecdotes* aver, He nodded in his elbow chair. *Prior.*
  Syn. — See STORY.
an'ec·dote, *v. i.* To tell anecdotes. — *v. t.* To use as a subject for anecdotes. *Both Rare.*

The attention already given to *anecdote* as it appears in a smaller dictionary makes it unnecessary to do more here than to point out some features of the present entry not taken account of in the one previously examined.

Notice that the etymology here ends with a reference to the entry DATE, meaning a point of time. An inspection of the etymology given of that entry reveals that *anecdote* belongs to a group of words that are related because they all trace their ancestry, in whole or in part, back to the same IE root that is seen in the Greek verb *didonai,* meaning to give. Here is the list of words Webster cites as being related in the manner indicated: *anecdote, condone, dado, damn, dative, datum, die, n., donate, dose, dower, edit, pardon, render, sacerdotal.*

All these words have in them the basic idea of giving. In some of them this primary notion is quite obvious, as it clearly is in *donate* and *dose.* In some of the words, other ideas are involved along with that of giving, and it is interesting to work these out by looking at a good dictionary. For example, the first syllable of *condone* adds the idea of "altogether" to that of giving and suggests giving entirely. The first syllable in *pardon* has nearly the same significance, and the word suggests giving thoroughly or completely. The case is different with *render.* Here the *re-* suggests "back" or "again." To *render* something is to give it back. The *e-* in *edit* imparts the idea of "out" to that of *give.* To *edit* a thing is to give it out.

It should not be supposed that these are all the English words that are related because they all have in them this idea of giving. Even in a large dictionary, space is limited. Words suggested by those in the list are left out. For example, *antidote* is omitted. The first element, *anti-,* is easily recognized as having in it the idea of "against." An *antidote* is something given against something, usually a poison.

One of the unique and highly valuable features of the unabridged Merriam-Webster is that it often groups words basically related because they, or parts of them, go back to a common ancestor word. No other English dictionary gives so much of this kind of information. Some of the commonest words in the language have a surprisingly large number of relatives. Here is a list of a few words related to *stand, v.:*

assist, circumstance, consist, constant, contrast, cost, desist, destine, distant, exist, extant, instant, obstacle, obstinate, persist, stage, stalwart, stamen, standard, state, station, statue, steed, stool, subsist, substance, superstition, system, vassal

The entry *stand, v.* in *Webster's New International Dictionary, Second Edition,* should be seen for the full list.

Those interested in becoming acquainted with a large number of words should cultivate the habit of considering them as related to other words. Making the acquaintance of words by mastering them in isolation is slow and laborious, to be done only when absolutely necessary.

The next dictionary in which we shall examine the word *anecdote* is the *Century* [3] in which the entry is as follows:

> **anecdote** (an′ek-dōt), *n.* [<F. *anecdote*, first in pl. *anecdotes,* M.L. *anecdota,* < Gr. ἀνέκδοτα, pl., things unpublished, applied by Procopius to his memoirs of Justinian, which consisted chiefly of gossip about the private life of the court; prop. neut. pl. of ἀνέκδοτος, unpublished, not given out, < Gr. ἀν- priv. + ἔκδοτος, given out, verbal adj. of ἐκδιδόναι, give out, publish, < ἐκ, out (= L. *ex:* see ex-), + διδόναι, give, = L. *dare,* give: see *dose* and *date.*] **1.** *pl.* Secret history; facts relating to secret or private affairs, as of governments or of individuals: often used (commonly in the form *anecdota*) as the title of works treating of such matters.—**2.** A short narrative of a particular or detached incident or occurrence of an interesting nature; a biographical incident; a single passage of private life. =Syn.   *Anecdote, Story.* An *anecdote* is the relation of an interesting or amusing incident, generally of a private nature, and is always reported as true. A *story* may be true or fictitious, and generally has reference to a series of incidents so arranged and related as to be entertaining.

In this treatment of the word there are some things not observed before.

1. As is often done in dictionaries, the sign < is used freely in the sense of "from." One instance of its use is seen in the etymology above.

2. According to the etymology given here, the form which *anecdote* had in French was the plural, a form to be expected from the word's being derived from a plural in Latin and in Greek. With this information, it is easier to understand why it was in its plural form that the word made its first appearance in English.

3. The fuller meaning of the source word, *anecdota,* is here made clear —"applied by Procopius to his memoirs of Justinian, which consisted chiefly of gossip about the private life of the court." What is needed now is some information about Procopius and Justinian. In 1894 the *Century*

was completed by a *Cyclopedia of Names*. By referring to this volume we find that Procopius (?490–565 A.D.) was a historian in the old city of Byzantium, now Istanbul, during the time (527–565 A.D.) Justinian was emperor there.

Without letting the ruler find out about it, Procopius wrote the gossip about the goings-on at the court. The historian did not like Justinian, and he knew his head would roll if his manuscript came to the attention of the emperor. He selected a title for his collection of choice scandal that would indicate that the work was not designed for giving out or publishing.

4. The remainder of the *Century* entry is easily understood with the possible exception of the abbreviation "priv." for *privative,* a word used in grammar in connection with those prefixes which change the sense of a word from a positive to a negative one, as do *un-, il-, in-, ir-,* in English. Compare such words as *lawful, unlawful; legal, illegal; tolerant, intolerant; regular, irregular.* On page 14 we mentioned that Greek made use of a prefix of this kind, *a-,* which might also appear as *an-.* In Greek grammars this prefix is referred to as "alpha privative."

It may appear to the beginner that by this time we have certainly found out all there is to know about *anecdote,* but we have not. Here is how the entry looks in the *Oxford English Dictionary.*[4]

> **Anecdote** (æ·nèkdoᵘt). [a. Fr. *anecdote,* or ad. its source, med. L. *anecdota* (see sense I), a. Gr. ἀνέκδοτα things unpublished, f. ἀν priv. + ἔκδοτ-ος published, f. ἐκδιδόναι to give out, publish: applied by Procopius to his 'Unpublished Memoirs' of the Emperor Justinian, which consisted chiefly of tales of the private life of the court; whence the application of the name to short stories or particulars.]
>
> **1.** *pl.* Secret, private, or hitherto unpublished narratives or details of history. (At first, and now again occas. used in L. form *anecdota* (ăne·kdotă.)
>
> 1676 MARVEL *Mr. Smirke* Wks. 1875 IV. 71 A man . . might make a pleasant story of the *anecdota* of that meeting. 1686 F. SPENCE (*title*) Anecdotes of Florence, or the secret History of the House of Medicis [a translation of Varillas' *Anecdotes de Florence*]. 1727 SWIFT *Gulliver* III. viii. 230 Those who pretend to write anecdotes, or secret history. 1727–51 CHAMBERS *Cycl., Anecdotes, Anecdota,* a term used by some authors, for the titles of Secret Histories; that is, of such as relate the secret affairs and transactions of princes; speaking with too much freedom, or too much sincerity, of the manner and conduct of persons in authority, to allow of their being made public. 1769 BURKE *State Nat.* Wks. II. 157 Professing even industriously, in this publick matter, to avoid anecdotes, I say nothing of those famous reconciliations and quarrels which weakened the body. 1882 *Pall Mall G.* 23 Oct. 5 To dispel by means of 'anecdota' the common impression that Mdme. de Staël and her mother did not get on very well together.
>
> **2.** The narrative of a detached incident, or of a single event, told as being in itself interesting or striking. (*At first,* An item of gossip.)
>
> 1761 YORKE in Ellis *Orig. Lett.* II. 483 IV. 429 Monsieur Coccei will tell you all the anecdotes of London better than I can. 1769 *Junius Lett.* xxix. 133 The anecdote was referred to, merely to show how ready a man, etc. 1789 BOSWELL *Lett.* (1857) 311 It [life of Johnson] will certainly be . . full of literary and characteristic anecdotes (which word, by the way, Johnson always condemned, as used in the sense that the French, and we from them, use it, as signifying particulars). 1806 MAR. EDGEWORTH *Forester*

(1832) 160 Telling little anecdotes to his disadvantage. **1832** HT. MAR-
TINEAU *Demerara* i. 12 He told some anecdotes of Alfred's childhood. *Mod.*
An after-dinner anecdote.

 b. *collect.*

 1826 DISRAELI *Viv. Grey* III. ii. 95 A companion who knew everything,
everyone, full of wit and anecdote.

 3. *Comb.*, as *anecdote-book, -loving;* **anecdote-monger** a retailer
of anecdotes.

 1862 BURTON *Bk.-hunter* II. 125 Irish bulls . . manufactured for the . .
anecdote-books betray their artificial origin. **1836** *Edin. Rev.* LXIII. 364 By
no means so explanatory as his anecdote-loving master could desire. **1807**
Ibid. X. 43. The large tribe of anecdote-mongers. **1850** MAURICE *Mor. Philos.*
164 The gossiping anecdote-mongers of later Greece.

1. With the information already given, it is easy to understand the etymology of this entry. It should be observed that according to it, *anecdote* may not have come into English from French, but directly from medieval Latin. That this source is likely is suggested by the spelling the word has in the earliest example found of its use in English. Had it come from the French *anecdotes,* it is not easy to see why Marvell in 1676 spelled it *anecdota.* Of course, it may have come into English both from French and from Latin.

2. The most noteworthy feature of this entry, and of the dictionary from which it comes, is that the definitions are followed by examples of the use of the word in the senses given. These examples all follow the same pattern. First comes the date, then the author's name in small capitals, then the title of the work cited, usually abbreviated, followed by the number of the page. Some sources are cited in a manner slightly different from this, as is seen in the last quotation given under 1. The use of illustrative quotations is a marked feature of historical dictionaries. They are given generously in the *OED,* there being about 1,827,306 of them in that great work.

It would be a mistake, however, to conclude that the earliest example given in the *OED* for a word in a particular sense is really the first time the word occurs in print. The *OED* is a remarkable dictionary, but it would be much more so if those who collected material for it had been able to find the very first printed uses of all the words with which the dictionary deals. It is extremely useful to have such dates as are given, but they should not be misinterpreted.

3. Under 3 in the above entry there are given combinations into which *anecdote* has entered. The first two of these, *anecdote-book,* and *anecdote-loving,* are illustrated by only one example each. Neither of the expressions appears to have been much used. The same may be said of *anecdote-monger,* which is treated slightly differently because two examples of its use were available.

NOTES

1. This entry is reproduced here by permission of The World Publishing Co.

2. By permission. From *Webster's New International Dictionary, Second Edition,* copyright, 1934, 1939, 1945, 1950, 1953, 1954, by G. & C. Merriam Co.

2.* [Editors' note; Since the Mathews book first appeared the G. & C. Merriam Co. has published its Third Edition (1961); for purposes of comparison and currency, we reprint the new edition's entry for *anecdote.*

an·ec·dote \'anik,dōt *also* -nək-; *usu* -ōd·+V\ *n, pl* **anecdotes**
\-ts\ *or* anecdo·ta \,ᶻᵃ'dōd·ə, -ōtə\ *see numbered senses* [F
& Gk; F, fr. Gk *anekdotos* unpublished, fr. *an-* + *ekdotos*
given out, fr. *ekdidonai* to give out, publish, fr. *ek* out, out of
+ *didonai* to give — more at EX-, DATE] **1** *pl* anecdota *also*
anecdotes **:** items of unpublished or secret history or biography
2 *pl* anecdotes **:** a usu. short narrative of an interesting, amusing, or curious incident often biographical and generally
characterized by human interest — an·ec·dot·ism \'ᶻᵃ
,dōd·,izəm,-ō,tiz-\ *n* -s — an·ec·dot·ist \-ōd·əst, -ōtə-\ *n* -s

From *Webster's New International Dictionary,* Third Edition, copyright © 1961 by G. & C. Merriam Co.]

3. This entry is reproduced here with the permission of Appleton-Century-Crofts, Inc., successors to The Century Co., publishers of *The Century Dictionary and Cyclopedia.*

4. This entry is reproduced here with the permission of The Clarendon Press, Oxford, England, publishers of the *Oxford English Dictionary.*

MITFORD M. MATHEWS

Dictionaries Contain Surprises

> Neither is a dictionary a bad book to read. There is no cant in it, no excess of explanation, and it is full of suggestion,—the raw material of possible poems and histories.
>
> RALPH WALDO EMERSON

Our explanation of *anecdote* as it appears in a good desk-size dictionary, a good unabridged one, in the encyclopedic *Century Dictionary,* and in the historical *Oxford English Dictionary* has afforded a glimpse of four distinct types of general dictionaries. Very little, of course, can be found out about a dictionary from looking up one word in it. Unabridged dictionaries contain about a half-million entries, so it is difficult in a brief space to give a good characterization of their chief features.

It is remarkable how much information about words is packed into such a dictionary as the current *Webster's New International, Second Edition.* Any entry in it is likely to be a revelation. Those who never examine words in dictionaries until they are confronted with some kind of problem about them, never know what they are missing in the way of intriguing information about words they have known all their lives. For example, here is the treatment which the *New International* gives the very common verb *sit:* [1]

sit (sĭt), *v.; past tense* SAT (săt), *Archaic* SATE (săt, rarely săt); *past part.* SAT, *Obs.* SIT'TEN (sĭt'ⁿn); *pres. part. &* *verbal n.* SIT'TING. [ME. *sitten,* fr. AS. *sittan;* akin to OS. *sittian,* OFris. *sitta,* D. *zitten,* G. *sitzen,* OHG. *sizzan,* ON. *sitja,* Sw. *sitta,* Dan. *sidde,* Goth. *sitan,* Lith. *sedéti,* L. *sedēre* to sit, *sedes* seat, Gr. *hezesthai* to sit, *hedra* seat, Skr. *sadas* a seat, *sīdati* he sits. Cf. ASSIDUOUS, ASSIZE, CEDE, CHAIR, DISSIDENT, INSIDIOUS, NEST, OBSESS, POLYHE-DRON, POSSESS, PRESIDENT, RESIDENCE, SADDLE, SANHEDRIN, SÉANCE, SEAT, SEDATE, SEDENTARY, SEDIMENT, SEE, *n.,* SESSION, SET, SEWER servant, SIEGE, SIZAR, SOOT, SUBSIDY, SUPERSEDE.] *Intransitive:* **1.** To rest upon the haunches, or the lower or posterior extremity of the trunk; to occupy a seat; as, to *sit* by the fire, in a chair, on a bench, at table, to work; to *sit* cross-legged, erect, close. **2.** Hence: a *Obs. exc. Dial.* To kneel. **b** To perch or roost with the body drawn up close, as birds. **c** To squat, as a hare or a toad. **3.** To occupy a place or seat as a member of an official body; as, to *sit* in Congress.

From *Words: How To Know Them.* © 1956 by Holt, Rinehart and Winston, Inc. Reprinted by permission of the publisher.

4. To hold a session; to be in session for official business; — said of legislative assemblies, courts, etc.

5. To cover and warm eggs for hatching, as a fowl; to brood; to incubate; as, a *sitting* hen.

6. a To take a position for a certain purpose as for one's picture or bust; as, to *sit* to or for a painter. **b** To pose as a model; figuratively, to serve as the original of, as a character.

7. To be a candidate at an examination. *Chiefly Brit.*

8. To remain in the same state; to remain inactive or quiescent; to rest in any condition Now figurative.

> Night *sits* monarch yet in the mid sky. *Milton.*

9. a *Archaic.* To have one's abiding place; remain; dwell. **b** To remain as a tenant.

10. a To be located or situated. "Love *sits* in her smile." *Burns.* **b** To be supported; lie, rest, or bear; — with *on* or *upon.* **c** To affect one as with a certain weight; press; weigh, as food on the stomach or grief at the heart.

11. To be adjusted; to fit; as, a coat *sits* well or ill.

> This new and gorgeous garment, majesty,
> *Sits* not so easy on me as you think. *Shak.*

12. To suit one well or ill; to become; befit. *Obs.*

13. To hold a relative position; to have direction; — chiefly of the wind. "*Sits* the wind in that quarter?" *Scott.*

14. *Mil.* To maintain a stationary position, as in besieging.

——, *Transitive:* **1.** To seat (oneself); also, to settle; — often with *down.*

2. To cause to be seated; to seat or place in position.

> He *sat* me down in a chair. *Somerset Maugham.*

3. To keep one's seat upon; to sit upon.

> Hardly the muse can *sit* the headstrong horse. *Prior.*

4. To sit, or cause to sit, upon (eggs); — of a hen bird.

5. To remain in company with.

6. a *Obs.* To weigh or press upon; to oppress; beset; also, to stand (as an expense); to cost. **b** *Rare.* To fit; to be adjusted to or fitted for. **c** *Obs. exc. Dial.* To suit (well or ill); to become; befit. **d** *Obs.* To pay no heed to; to disregard; disobey. **e** *Now Rare.* To abide through; endure; stand.

7. *Rowing.* To trim by the poise of the body, or by the use of the oars, or by both.

Syn. — Squat; roost; weigh, press.

sit at meat or *at table.* To be at table for eating.

sit at one's feet. To follow one as a pupil, disciple, or enthusiastic admirer.

sit down. **a** To place oneself on a chair or other seat; also, to become seated accidentally. **b** To settle; to fix a permanent abode. **c** To begin a siege; encamp; as, the enemy *sat down* before the town. **d** To rest; to cease as satisfied.

> Here we cannot *sit down*, but still proceed in our search. *Rogers.*

sit down on or *upon.* To sit on; to repress. *Slang.*

sit down on one's knees. To kneel. *Obs.*

sit in. To assume a seat or place as a participant; — originally with reference to games, esp. at cards. *Colloq.*

sit loose. To be heedless or indifferent. *Colloq.*

sit on or *upon.* **a** To hold deliberations concerning, as in a court. **b** To hold a seat as a member of. **c** *Slang.* To repress; squelch.

sit on brood. To ponder. *Poetic.* *Shak.*

sit on, or *upon, one's knee.* To kneel. *Obs.*

sit on the fence. To be on the fence. See *on the fence,* under FENCE.

sit on the lid. To keep down agitation that might cause disturbance. *Colloq.*

sit on the splice. *Cricket.* To play solely on the defense; to stonewall.

sit on the throne. To reign.

sit out. **a** To remain to the conclusion of; as, to *sit out* a stupid play. **b** To outstay in a social call; as, he *sat out* his rival. **c** To remain aloof, esp. seated, during the progress of (a game or dance). **d** To sit or remain apart during the progress of a game, dance, etc.

sit over. **a** To move sidewise on a seat, esp. to make room. **b** To be preoccupied with while sitting.

sit pretty. To be placed in a highly favorable situation, esp. as when holding a good hand at cards. *Slang, U.S.*

sit tight. *Colloq.* **a** To hold fast, as in a saddle; hence, to maintain one's position without change; often, to maintain silence. **b** To remain quiet in or as in hiding.

sit under. To attend religious service under the instruction or ministrations of; also, to attend the classes or lectures of (some teacher).

sit up. **a** To rise from a recumbent posture; to sit with the body upright; hence, *Colloq.*, to exhibit interest or surprise. **b** To stay up after the accustomed hour of retiring; — often with *for* or *with.* **c** *Colloq., U.S.* To assume one's seat at table. **d** *Anglo-Indian.* Formerly, to receive company.

> **sit up and take notice.** To show marked interest.
> *Colloq., U.S.*
> **sit upon.** See *sit on*, above.
> **sit upon one's knee.** See *sit on one's knee*, above.
> **sit** (sĭt), *n.* **1.** Act, period, or manner of sitting; specif.,
> the manner in which a garment, or part of one, rests in
> fitting.
> **2.** *Coal Mining.* A settling or falling of the roof; — often
> in *pl.*

Following the etymology and enumeration of terms related to *sit* comes a long list of meanings of the word and explanations of its use in more than a dozen phrases.[1] *

But the *New International* with its more than 3,000 pages cannot give as full treatment to terms as that given by the *Oxford English Dictionary* with its more than 15,000 pages. One of the outstanding characteristics of this dictionary is that it gives information about how words have been spelled throughout their history. Under the entry *thief* that word is shown to have had a perfect welter of spellings, a few of them being *thef, thif, theyf, thefe, theef, thife, theyff, theaf, theiff.*

Often interesting things have happened to the spellings of words. For example, *abominable* came into English from Old French which had taken it from Latin *abominabilis*. It was not immediately apparent that *abominable* is based ultimately on the two Latin terms, *ab* off, away and *omen* sign, token. The erroneous impression became widespread that the word was from the Latin *ab homine,* signifying away from man, inhuman, beastly. Therefore a new spelling, *abhominable* became current. The word occurs in this spelling 18 times in the first folio of Shakespeare. In *Love's Labour's Lost* Holophernes speaks contemptuously of the "rackers of ortagriphie" who were beginning to write *abominable* for the time-honored *abhominable.*

From this it is seen that the present spelling of this word is recent and came in over the sarcastic protest of Shakespeare and no doubt others. Inquisitiveness about words is amply rewarded by the *OED*. Here is the story of *cobalt.*[2]

> a. Ger. *kobalt,* formerly also *kobald, -olt, -old, -elt, -el,* app. the
> same word as *kobold,* etc., goblin or demon of the mines; the ore
> of cobalt having been so called by the miners on account of the
> trouble which it gave them, not only from its worthlessness (as
> then supposed), but from its mischievous effects upon their own
> health and upon silver ores in which it occurred, effects due mainly
> to the arsenic and sulphur with which it was combined. From the
> miners of the Harz or Erzgebirge the name became common Ger-
> man, and thence passed into all the European langs., F. *cobalt,* It.,
> Sp., Pg. *cobalto,* Du., Da., Russ., Pol., Boh., etc., *kobalt,* Sw. *kobolt.*

In order to demonstrate more fully some of the characteristic features of this dictionary, we reproduce with the publisher's permission a some-what longer entry from it.

horns or antlers, and by the presence of spots on the young: the various genera and species being distinguished as *rein-deer, moose-deer, red deer, fallow deer;* the Musk Deer belong to a different family, *Moschidæ.*

A specific application of the word, which occurs in OE. only contextually, but became distinct in the ME. period, and by its close remained as the usual sense.

[*c* 893 K. Ælfred Oros. I. i. (Sw.) 18 He [Ohthere] hæfde þa ჳyt ða he þone cyningc sohte, tamra deora unbebohtra syx hund. þa deor hi hatað hranas.] *a* 1131 [see *der fald* in 4]. *c* 1205 Lay. 2586 To huntien after deoren [*c* 1275 after deores]. 1297 R. Glouc. (Rolls) 9047 He let [make] þe parc of Wodestoke, & der þer inne do. *c* 1325 *Song on Passion* 59 (*O. E. Misc.*) He was todrawe so dur islawe in chace. 1375 Barbour *Bruce* VII. 497 [He] went..to purchase venysoun, For than the deir war in sesoun. *c* 1420 *Anturs of Arth.* (Camden) iv, Thay felle to the female dure, feyful thyk fold. 1464 *Mann. & Househ. Exp.* 195 A payr breganderys cueryd wyth whyte deris leder. 1470–85 Malory *Arthur* x. lxi, He chaced at the reed dere. 1538 Starkey *England* I. iii. 98 A dere louyth a lene barren..ground. 1601 Shaks. *Jul. C.* III. i. 209 Like a Deere, strocken by many Princes. 1611 Coryat *Crudities* 10 A goodly Parke..wherein there is Deere. 1774 Goldsm. *Nat. Hist.* (1776) III. 80 An hog, an ox, a goat, or a deer. 1855 Longf. *Hiaw.* III. 169 Where the red deer herd together.

b. occasional plural *deers.*

c 1275 [see 1205 in prec.] 1674 N. Cox *Gentl. Recreat.* II. (1677) 58 The reasons why Harts and Deers do lose their Horns yearly. 1769 Home *Fatal Discov.* III, Stretch'd on the skins of deers. *c* 1817 Hogg *Tales & Sk.* II. 89. The place of rendezvous, to which the deers weer to be driven.

† c. *Deer of ten:* a stag of ten, i. e. one having ten points or tines on his horns; an adult stag of five years at least, and therefore 'warrantable' or fit to be hunted. *Obs.*

1631 Massinger *Emp. of East* IV. ii, He will make you royal sport, He is a deer Of ten, at the least.

3. *Small deer:* a phrase originally, and perhaps still by Shakspere, used in sense **1**; but now humorously associated with sense **2**.

14... *Sir Beues* (1885) p. 74/2 (MS.C.) Ratons & myse and soche smale dere, That was hys mete that vii yere. 1605 Shaks. *Lear* III. iv. 144 But Mice, Rates, and such small Deare, Haue bin Toms food, for seuen long yeare. 1883 G. Allen in *Colin Clout's Calender* 14 Live mainly upon worms, slugs, and other hardy small deer.

transf. 1857 H. Reed *Lect. Eng. Poets* x. II. 17 The small deer that were herded together by Johnson as the most eminent of English poets.

4. *attrib.* and *Comb.,* as *deer bed, herd, -hide, -keeper, kind, life, -sinew, -snaring,* etc.; *deer-like, deer-loved* adjs. [Several already in OE., as *déor-fald* an enclosure or cage for wild beasts in the amphitheatre, or for beasts of the chase, a deer-park, *déor-edisc* deer-park, *déor-net* net for wild animals, etc.]

1835 W. Irving *Tous Prairies* xi, The tall grass was pressed down into numerous ° 'deer beds', where those animals had couched. *a* 1000 Ags. Gloss. in Wr.-Wülcker 201 *Causea, domus in theatro,* °deorfald. *a* 1131 *O. E. Chron.* an. 1123 Se king rad in his der fald [æt Wudestoke]. 1860 G. H. K. *Vac. Tour.* 123 Peaks..where the scattered remnants of the great °deer herds can repose in security. 1814 Scott *Ld. of Isles* III. xix, Goat-skins or °deer-hides o'er them cast. 1849 James *Woodman* vii, I have got my °deer-keepers watching. 1875 Lyell *Princ. Geol.* II. III. xxxix. 359 Animals of the °deer kind. 1860 G. H. K. *Vac. Tour.* 122 The shepherds..see a good deal of °deer life. 1840 Mrs. Norton *Dream* 127 The dark, °deer-like eyes. 1876 Geo. Eliot *Dan. Der.* IV. liv. 114 Deer-like shyness. 1831 Lytton *Godolph.* 23 The °deer-loved fern. *c* 1000 Ælfric *Voc.* in Wr.-Wülcker 167 *Cassis,* °deornet. 1856 Kane *Arct. Expl.* II. vii. 79 To walk up Mary River Ravine until we reach the °deer-plains. 1866 Kingsley *Herew.* I. vi. 178 Sea-bows of horn and °deer-sinew. 1862 S. St. John *Forests Far East* II. 34, I have been out °deer-snaring in this neighbourhood.

b. Special comb.: **deer-brush,** an American shrub in Arizona; **deer-cart,** the covered cart in which a tame stag to be hunted is carried to the meet; **deer-dog** = Deer-hound; **deer-drive,** a shooting expedition in which the deer are driven past the sportsman; so

In examining the *Deer* entry, notice that immediately after the
of the word comes the respelling for pronunciation in a system n(
in American dictionaries. Next there is a full display of the spellin;
has had throughout its history. In this presentation, numbers ar
to denote centuries, 1 standing for "before the year 1100 A.D.," 2
twelfth century (*i.e.* 1100 to 1200), 3 for the thirteenth century, etc.
that in the fourteenth century the modern spelling became do
though after that time such spellings as *dere, dur, deere* and oth
found. From the beginning, the plural form has been the same
singular, though sporadic plurals such as *deore, deoran, deers*
been used.

Next, within square brackets the etymology is given, in which ab
use is made of abbreviations. It is instructive to look at this etyi
closely. It begins by pointing out that *deer* is common to the Teuto
Germanic languages. The etymological treatment then enumera
forms of spellings *deer* had in some of these Germanic languag
omitting to give the word as it now exists in Dutch, German, Ice
Swedish, and Danish. It is difficult to see how more information
have been given in such a small space.

Deer (dīeɪ) Forms: 1 díor, déor, 2–3 deor, (2 dær), 2–4 der,
(2–3 dor, 3 dier, 3–4 duer, 4 dur, 5 dure, deure), 4–6 dere, (4–7
deere, 5, 7 diere, 5– (*Sc.*) deir, 6–7 deare), 4– deer, (5 theer).
Pl. 1–9 normally same as sing.; also 2 deore, deoran, 2–3 -en; 3–4
deores, dueres, 7–9 *occas.* deers. [A Comm. Teut. sb.: OE., *díor,
déor* = OS. *dier,* OFris. *diar, dier* (MDu. and Du. and LG. *dier*),
OHG. *tior* (MHG. *tier,* Ger. *tier, thier*):—WG. *dior,* ON. °*djúr*
(Icel. *dýr,* Sw. *djur,* Da. *dyr*); Goth. *dius, diuz-*:—OTeut. *deuzo*ᵐ:
—pre-Teut. *dheuso•m.*
Generally referred to a root *dhus* to breathe (cf. *animal* from *anima*), and
thought by some etymologists to be the neuter of an adj. used subst. Cf. Dear
a.² (Not connected with Gr. θηρ wild beast.)]

†1. A beast: usually a quadruped, as distinguished from birds and
fishes; but sometimes, like *beast,* applied to animals of lower orders.
Obs.

c 950 *Lindisf. Gosp.* Luke xviii. 25 Se camal þæt *micla dear. a* 1000
Boeth. Metr. xxvii. 24 Swa swa fuðl oððe dior. *c* 1000 Ælfric *Voc.* in Wr.-
Wülcker 118/31 *Fera,* wild deor. *Bellua, reðe deor* . . *Unicornis,* anhyrne
deor. 1154 *O. E. Chron.* (Laud MS.) an. 1135 Pais he makede men & dær.
c 1200 Ormin 1176 Shep iss . . stille der. *Ibid.* 1312 Lamb iss soffte &
stille deor. *a* 1250 *Owl & Night.* 1321 Al swo deth mani dor and man. *c* 1250
Gen. & Ex. 4025 Also leun is miðful der. 1482 Caxton *Reynard* (Arb.) 18
The rybaud and the felle diere here I se hym comen.

B. plural.

c 1000 Ælfric *Gen.* i. 25 And he sið ofer þa deor. *c* 1175 *Lamb. Hom.*
43 Innan þan ilke sea weren un-aneomned deor, summe feðerfotetd, summe
al bute fet. *Ibid.* 115 þene bið his erd ihened . . on wilde deoran. *c* 1200
Trin. Coll. Hom. 177 Oref, and deor, and fishshes, and fugeles. *Ibid.* 209 Hie
habbeð geres after wilde deore. *Ibid.* 224 Of wilde diere. *c* 1350 *Gen. & Ex.*
4020 On ilc brend eft twin der. *Ibid.* 4032 Efte he sacrede deres mor. *a* 1310
in Wright *Lyric P.* xiii. 44 Deores with huere derne rounes. *Ibid.* xiv 45 In
dounes with this dueres plawes. *c* 1340 *Gaw. & Gr. Kt.* 1151 Der drof in þe
dale . . bot heterly þay were Restayed with þe stablye.

2. The general name of a family (*Cervidæ*) of ruminant quadrupeds, distinguished by the possession of deciduous branching

deer-driving; **deer-eyed** *a.,* having eyes like deer, having soft or languid eyes; **deer-fence,** a high railing such as deer cannot leap over; **deer-flesh,** venison; **deer-forest,** a 'forest' or extensive track of unenclosed wild land reserved for deer; † **deer-goat,** an old name for the capriform or caprine antelopes; **deer-grass,** species of Rhexia (N.O. *Melastomaceæ*); **deer-leap,** a lower place in a hedge or fence where deer may leap; **deer-meat** = *deer-flesh;* **deer-neck,** a thin neck (of a horse) resembling a deer's; **deer-park,** a park in which deer are kept; † **deer-reeve,** a township officer in New England in the colonial days, whose duty it was to execute the laws as to deer; **deer-plain,** a plain inhabited by deer; **deer-saddle,** a saddle on which a slain deer is carried away; **deer's-eye** = BUCK-EYE (the tree); **deer's foot** (*grass*), the fine grass *Agrostis setacea;* **deer's hair** = DEER-HAIR; **deer's milk,** a local name of the wood spurge, *Euphorbia amygdaloides;* **deer's tongue,** deer-tongue, a N. American Cichoraceous plant, *Liatris odoratissima;* **deer-tiger,** the puma or cougar; **deer-yard,** an open spot where deer herd, and where the ground is trodden by them.

1883 W. H. BISHOP in *Harper's Mag.* Mar. 502/2 The °'deer brush' resembles horns. 1840 HOOD *Up the Rhine* 186 The hearse, very like a °deer-cart. 1814 SCOTT *Ld. of Isles* v. xxiii, Many a °deer-dog howl'd around. 1882 *Society* 21 Oct. 19/1 Setting out for a °deer-drive. 1860 G. H. K. *Vac. Tour.* 143 Mr. Scrope..was a great hand at °deer-driving. 1884 Q. VICTORIA *More Leaves* 14 The gate of the °deer-fence. *a* 1300 *Cursor M.* 3603 (Cott.) If þou me °dere flesse [*v. r. venisun*] ani gete. 1854 *Act* 17–8 *Vict.* c. 91 § 42 Where such shootings or °deer forests are actually let. 1892 E. WESTON BELL *Scot. Deerhound* 80 Probably not more than twenty deer forests, recognized as such, were in existence prior to the beginning of the present century. 1607 TOPSELL *Four-f. Beasts* (1658) 93 Of the first kinde Tragelaphvs which may be called a °Deer-goat. 1693 SIR T. P. BLOUNT *Nat. Hist.* 30 The Deer-Goat ..being partly like a deer partly like a Goat. 1866 *Treas. Bot.* 972/2 Low perennial often bristly herbs, commonly called °Deer-grass, or Meadow-beauty, [with] large showy cymose flowers. 1540–2 *Act* 31 *Hen. VIII, c.* 5 To make °dere leapes and breakes in the sayde hedges and fences. 1838 JAMES *Robber* i, In front appeared a °deer-park. 1860 G. H. K. *Vac. Tour.* 172 It is no light business to get our big stag..on the °deer saddle. 1762 J. CLAYTON *Flora Virginica* 57 *Æsculus floribus octandris* Linn . . . °Dear's Eye, and Bucks Eyes. 1883 *Century Mag.* XXVI. 383 Among the lily-pads, °deer-tongue, and other aquatic plants. 1880 *7th Rep. Surv. Adirondack Reg. N. Y.* 159 We reached an open forest plateau on the mountain, where we were surprised to find a °'deer-yard.' Here the deep snow was tramped down by deer into a broad central level area.

Then, still within the brackets, there comes a note in smaller type, from which we learn that *deer* is believed to go back to a root, *i.e.* the earliest ideal form that can be inferred from existing words, and that this root had in it the sense "to breathe." A reference is then made to *animal* as being related to *anima,* the Latin word for air, breath, life. The basic meaning of *animal* therefore is something living. Similarly, as some scholars think, *deer* may have in it the idea of breathing, and mean, basically, anything that lives or breathes.

The etymology, in conclusion, warns us not to think that the Greek word meaning a wild beast is the source of *deer.*

Only advanced students are likely ever to need such detailed information about the early forms and etymological history and connections of words shown in this treatment of *deer.* But it is well for anyone to know that such information is available and where it may be found. Look at the etymology of *deer* in your desk dictionary and see how brief it necessarily is.

The enumeration of senses follows. Sense 1 is preceded by a dagger, (†), to indicate that it is now obsolete. We no longer use *deer* in the general sense of a beast, especially a quadruped as distinguished from birds and fishes. Note however that this sense has remained in the German *Tier* to this day. It may well be, however, that *deer* in the early sense of an animal is preserved in our word *wilderness*. See what your dictionary says about the make-up of this word.

To illustrate this first sense, a quotation of about the year 950 is given from the *Lindisfarne Gospels,* the book of Luke in the New Testament being cited, Chapter 18, Verse 25, "The camel that large animal." The passage is the familiar one about the camel's going through the eye of a needle, but only so much of it is quoted as shows that a camel was, in Old English, called a deer.

The latest example of this original sense is from a work by Caxton, famous for the role he played in English printing. Then come nearly a dozen passages written from about 1000 A.D. to about 1340 A.D., showing early plural forms of the word.

Sense 2 shows the narrowing down of the meaning of *deer* to an animal of a particular family of "ruminant quadrupeds." Among the quotations given to illustrate this sense of the word, notice that the last one, of 1855, is from a well-known American work, Longfellow's *Hiawatha.* Under Sense 2 there are subdivisions marked b. and c. which are self-explanatory.

Attributive and combinative uses are given under 4. Among the authors drawn upon in this section there are two Americans, Irving and Kane. A little further, under 4. b., special combinations are given and defined. These differ from the ones under 4 in being better established as fixed expressions. The first of them is *deer-brush,* pointed out as an American name for a shrub found in Arizona. Notice that further down in this list *deer-reeve* occurs as an obsolete term once used in New England for "a township officer . . . whose duty it was to execute the laws as to deer." *Deer's tongue, deer tongue* is listed as a North American plant and the supporting evidence is from American sources. The last combination, *deeryard,* is also an American term and is illustrated by American evidence.

A close examination of such an entry as this—and it is among the simpler ones in the *OED*—is likely to surprise one not accustomed to such fullness of treatment of terms. Students often go through college, and even much beyond, without ever becoming aware of the richness of treatment of words in this dictionary.

NOTES

1. By permission. From *Webster's New International Dictionary, Second Edition*, copyright, 1934, 1939, 1945, 1950, 1953, 1954, by G. & C. Merriam Co.

1.° [Editors' note: Herewith a reprint of the entry *sit* from the Third Edition.

¹sit \(¦)sit, *usu* -id‧+V; *before a vowel-initial adverb with primary stress often* ‚səd‧ *or* ‚sət; *before "down" often* ‚sə *or* (¦)si\ *vb* sat \(¦)sat, -ad‧, *before "down" often* (¦)sa\ *also chiefly dial* sot \(¦)sä|t, |d‧\ *or archaic* sate \(¦)sā|t, (¦)sa|, |d‧\ sat *also chiefly dial* sot \(¦)sä|t, |d‧\ *or archaic* sit‧ten \¦sit'n\ sitting; sits [ME *sitten*, fr. OE *sittan*; akin to OHG *sizzen* to sit, ON *sitja*, Goth *sitan*, L *sedēre*, Gk *hezesthai* to sit, *hedra* seat, Skt *sīdati* he sits] *vi* 1 : to rest in a position in which the body is essentially vertical and supported or balanced chiefly on the buttocks or thighs or both ⟨~ on a stool⟩ ⟨~ in a chair⟩ ⟨~ cross-legged⟩ 2 a *obs* : KNEEL b *of an animal* : to assume a position with the hindquarters at rest on a supporting surface ⟨a dog trained to stand and ~ at command⟩ c *of a bird* : to perch or rest esp. with the feet drawn up close or with the body touching the ground 3 : to occupy a place as a member of an official body ⟨~ in Congress⟩ ⟨~ on the board of directors⟩ ⟨~ as a member of a committee⟩ 4 : to hold a session : be in session for official business ⟨magistrate ... may ~ in any place convenient —F.T.Giles⟩ ⟨the legislature is still *sitting*⟩ ⟨official committee ... *sitting* on the question of the ultimate size and organization —Roy Lewis & Angus Maude⟩ 5 : to have or continue in an occupation or function ⟨gamblers dealt or *sat* lookout with their sombreros on —W.N.Burns⟩ 6 *of a hen* : to cover eggs for hatching : BROOD, SET 7 a : to take a position for having one's portrait painted or for being photographed ⟨~ for a painter⟩ b : to serve as the original of a painted or sculptured figure or of a fictional character 8 a *archaic* : to have one's dwelling place : DWELL b *obs* : to remain as a tenant 9 : to lie in wait ⟨anyone *sitting* at the entrance to the pass, they'll see us if we go through the field —Norman Mailer⟩ 10 a *of clothing* : to lie or hang relative to the wearer ⟨the collar *sits* awkwardly at the back⟩ ⟨trying to see how the new coat ~s behind⟩ b : LIE, REST — used with *on* or *upon* ⟨author's assumed regionalism ~s uneasily on his verse —W.M.Maidment⟩ ⟨great triumvirate of Edwardian novelists ... that label ~s comfortably on these three —P.M.Fulcher⟩ c : to affect one with or as if with a certain weight : PRESS, WEIGH ⟨her years *sat* lightly upon her⟩ ⟨the pie *sat* heavily on his stomach⟩ 11 : to float in a specified manner ⟨load so that the ship ~s several feet deeper in the water aft⟩ ⟨the boat ~s practically on top of the water⟩ 12 a : to have a location ⟨thy rapt soul *sitting* in thine eyes —John Milton⟩ ⟨cottage *sitting* on the edge of a cliff⟩ ⟨house ~s well back from the road⟩ b *of wind* : to blow from a certain direction ⟨when the wind ~s one way I can hear the steam train —Christopher Morley⟩ ⟨always rains when the wind ~s in the west⟩ 13 : to please or agree with one — used with *with* and an adverb ⟨setting an example that may not ~ well with the more obedient Communist leaders —N.Y. Times⟩ 14 : to remain in the same state ⟨left the dishes *sitting* on the table⟩ : remain inactive or quiescent ⟨the car ~s in the garage unused all week⟩ ⟨do something, don't just ~ there⟩ ⟨*sitting* behind prison bars⟩ 15 : to be a candidate for a degree, certificate, or award : take or prepare to take an examination — used with *for* ⟨was *sitting* for a scholarship at Newton College —Angela Thirkell⟩ ⟨*sat* for his examinations ... as a river pilot —N.Y. Herald Tribune⟩ 16 : to act as a relief for a parent or nurse in watching over a child or an invalid ⟨~ with a friend's baby⟩ ~ *vt* 1 : to cause (oneself) to be seated — usu. used with *down* ⟨*sat* him down to write a letter⟩ 2 : to cause to be seated : place on or in a seat : put in a sitting position ⟨let me ~ you on the sofa ... and talk over small matters —F.D.Roosevelt⟩ ⟨a ·story that *sat* me up straight —S.H.Holbrook⟩ 3 *of a hen* : to sit upon (eggs) 4 a : to keep one's seat upon ⟨~ a horse⟩ b : to trim (a boat) by the poise of the body or by the use of oars 5 *chiefly dial* : SUIT, BECOME, BEFIT 6 : to provide seats or seating room for ⟨the car will ~ six people comfortably⟩ 7 *Brit* : to answer the questions of (an examination) in writing — sit at one's feet : to listen to or follow as a pupil, disciple, or admirer — sit at table : to be at table for eating : DINE — sit loose : to be heedless or indifferent ⟨scholars ... who *sit loose* to the obligations and responsibilities of church membership —Alan Richardson⟩ — sit on 1 : to hold deliberations concerning ⟨several judges have *sat on* this case⟩ 2 : REPRESS, SQUELCH 3 : to delay action or decision concerning : keep quiet or out of sight : SUPPRESS ⟨he had *sat on* stories before, like some other newsmen — Time⟩ ⟨*sat on* appropriations plans until they were certain which way winds ... were blowing —Newsweek⟩ — sit on one's hands

1 : to withhold applause **:** fail to show approval or enthusiasm **2** : fail to take expected or appropriate action **:** sit by — **sit on the lid** : to keep down agitation **:** hold in check forces of protest or rebellion — **sit on the splice** *cricket* **:** STONEWALL — contrasted with *lay on the wood* — **sit on the throne** **:** REIGN — **sit pretty** **:** to be in a highly favorable situation ⟨*sitting pretty* with a full house against a flush and a straight⟩ ⟨Americans ... had a virtual monopoly of piston-engined air transports, and they were *sitting pretty* —Charles Gardner⟩ — **sit tight** **1** : to maintain one's position without change ⟨preferred to *sit tight* with his present investments⟩ ⟨colonel decided to *sit tight* and send out patrols —Walter Bernstein⟩ **2** : to remain quiet in or as if in hiding — **sit under** : to attend religious service under the instruction or ministrations of; *also* **:** to attend the classes or lectures of (a teacher) **²sit** \'sit, *usu* -id·+V\ *n* -s **1'** : an act or period of sitting ⟨a long ~ at the station between trains⟩ **2** : the manner in which a garment fits ⟨~ of a coat around the shoulders⟩ **3** : a settling or falling of the roof of a mine — usu. used in pl. **4** : an entire mature celery plant

From *Webster's New International Dictionary, Third Edition*, copyright © 1961 by G. & C. Merriam Co.]

2. This part of the entry *Cobalt* and the following entry *Deer* are reproduced by permission of The Clarendon Press, Oxford, England, publishers of the *Oxford English Dictionary*.

STUART ROBERTSON AND FREDERIC G. CASSIDY

Changing Meanings and Values of Words

Even though it is generally recognized that meanings change, many people still cling, curiously enough, to the quite contradictory notion that
words all have "true" meanings, that changes somehow take us away
from the "true" meaning, and that the way to find out what a word "really
means" is to find out what it once meant. This is particularly true in
respect to borrowed words in English, the belief evidently being that
the meaning of the word in contemporary English and the meaning of the
Latin or Greek word from which the English word is derived must be one
and the same. A little reflection should show that an appeal to etymology
in order to establish the present meaning of the word is as untrustworthy
as an appeal to spelling in order to establish its present pronunciation.
And for a reason that is almost exactly parallel: change of *meaning* is
likely to have altered the etymological sense, which is thereby rendered
archaic or obsolete, just as change of *sound* is likely to be unrecorded
in the "antiquarian" spelling that so frequently characterizes Modern
English. The study of etymology has great value and interest—a point to
which we shall later return—but its usefulness in settling the question of
what a word means is subject to considerable qualification.

Let us see what results when one ignores the idea that a word may
change its meaning, and appeals to its etymology in order to determine
its present meaning. A handbook of only twenty-odd years ago on "correct
English" [1] sets forth the following dictum: "*Dilapidated* . . . Said of a
building or other structure. But the word is from the Latin *lapis,* a stone,
and cannot properly be used of any but a stone structure." One might
just as reasonably argue that because *candidate* is related to the Latin
candidus (white), it cannot properly be used of an aspirant for political

office unless he is clothed in a suit of white material. More clearly even, one might protest that *holiday* properly describes Christmas or Easter, but should never be used of Independence Day or Labor Day; or that *bonfire* should not be applied except where the combustible material is bone. These arguments are not much more grotesque than some that have been seriously maintained in defense of an etymological crotchet, while ignoring the fact of change of meaning. Indeed, one who argues on this basis is a victim of the "etymological fallacy."

The fact is that what a word once meant is not necessarily what it now means; the etymological meaning has often died out, and a quite new development is the living descendant. This is particularly true of words in common or popular use. Words, after all, are for the most part purely conventional symbols. They mean only what those who are using them agree to make them mean. Exactly the same principles apply to "learned" words, but because their traditional users have generally known the language from which they were borrowed, or of whose elements they were composed, they have tended to preserve the etymological meaning —indeed, it is conventional to use such words with an eye to their source; thus they are less prone to alterations of meaning than are popular words. It is in this way, incidentally, that a cultural tradition holds in check, to some extent, the constant tendency of language to change.[2]

Change of meaning, however, though usually unpredictable, is not utterly arbitrary; as we shall see in a moment, it often proceeds along familiar paths. Furthermore, though it takes place in all languages, it does not proceed at the same rate even in related ones. If we look at cognate words in English and German, for example, which might have been expected to have the same meaning, we often find them widely different, and the difference is most commonly the result of some radical change of sense in the English word. Opposite instances can be found, admittedly, in which the English word has stood still and the German one changed; yet it is usually the latter which is conservative. Examples of this characteristic English shift in meaning are the following: *Schlagen* and *slay* are originally the same word, but the German word retains the general meaning of "smite" or "strike" while the English word has become narrowed to mean "strike with fatal consequences" or "kill."[3] *Knabe* is the cognate in German of Old English *cnapa* or *cnafa,* and has the same meaning, "boy"; but Modern English *knave* has a radically different one; the German *Tier* means any kind of animal, as did the cognate Old English *deor,* but in Modern English *deer* means one particular kind of animal.

GENERALIZATION AND SPECIALIZATION. One very common type of change is that in which the "area" of the meaning is changed. When a word that has referred broadly or inclusively begins instead to refer narrowly or exclusively, this is an example of "specialization" of meaning; the contrary is called "generalization." Interestingly enough, the same word may undergo both processes at different stages of the development of its meaning. *Go*, for example, is a verb of motion that seems as general as possible in meaning, and presumably this is also the basic meaning; early in its history in English, however, it must have specialized, for Old English *gān* sometimes means "walk," and in Middle English *ryde or gon* (ride or walk) is a familiar formula. Although the present meaning is the generalized one, the specialization "walk" was still possible in the late seventeenth century, as we see in these phrases from Bunyan: "I am resolved to run when I can, to go when I cannot run, and to creep when I cannot go." [4]

Borrowed words are quite as likely as native ones to undergo such transformations in meaning. *Virtue* [5] is connected with Latin *vir* (man). Thus, *virtue* first meant "manliness" in general; but its meaning later specialized to stand for the manly quality most in demand in the military state, namely "fortitude" or "warlike prowess"—the meaning familiar in Caesar's *Commentaries*. But a still later Latin meaning is more comprehensive, and it was this very general meaning that was attached to *virtue* when it was borrowed in English through French. One possible specialization was "power," as in "Virtue had gone out of him," or even "magical power," as in "the virtue of the spell" or Milton's "virtuous ring and glass." More commonly, however, the word in English retained a general sense of "noble quality"—though more and more with reference to moral rather than to mental or physical characteristics. But another specialization limits its application to women; for example, "All the sons were brave, and all the daughters virtuous," where *virtuous* is equivalent to "chaste." "A woman's virtue" will today be interpreted in only the last sense. A curious evolution, indeed, when one recalls that the etymological meaning is "manliness."

The foregoing are particularly striking examples, but hundreds of others could be cited. We find generalization in such everyday words as *picture*, once restricted, as the etymology would suggest (compare: the *Picts*, "painted ones"), to a *painted* representation of something seen, but now applicable to photograph, crayon drawing, and so forth; *butcher*, who once slew one animal only, the goat (French *bouc*); the verb *sail*, which has been transferred to *steam* navigation, just as *drive* has been transferred to self-propelled vehicles; *injury*, which once was limited to "injustice"; *zest*, which meant "bit of lemon-peel"; *chest*, which usually meant "coffin"—"He is now deed and nayled in his cheste"; [6] *pen*, which meant "feather," but which is now much more likely to mean a writing implement tipped with metal than a quill; *quarantine*, from which the original meaning of a "forty" days' isolation has quite disappeared; and *companion*, which has likewise lost the etymological sense of "one who (shares) bread with" another.

But generalization of meaning does not always stay within bounds; under some conditions the meaning becomes so broad that, in extreme cases, there is hardly any meaning left. We have a whole set of words, used conversationally when we either do not know, or cannot remember, or perhaps will not take the trouble to search for a more precise term: the *what-you-may-call-it* kind of word—*thingumabob, doohickie, jigger,* and so on.[7] Not so long ago *gadget* was imported into the U. S. from England, and has found a very hearty welcome into this company.

Another type, in which generalization goes even farther, has aroused strong opposition from guardians of literary style, who realize that emptiness and "jargon" result from the indiscriminate use of "words that mean little or nothing, but may stand for almost anything":[8] such words are *thing, business, concern, condition, matter, article, circumstance.* As we all recognize at once, these are words that have a fairly exact sense, but which also have acquired the ability to fit into a wide variety of everyday contexts, in which their meaning becomes extremely vague—in fact, almost wholly dependent on the context. The word *deal* is the current American favorite in this group, its gamut of meaning running all the way from perfectly favorable ("Your job sounds like a pretty fine deal") to thoroughly unfavorable ("I won't take part in any of his deals"). This word serves the purpose, and is going through the same general sort of development, that *proposition* did a generation ago.

Even more frequent than generalization, and even more readily illustrated in numberless familiar instances, is the opposite process of specialization. *Steorfan* is an Old English word, cognate with the German *sterben*, which meant "die"; but the standard Modern English meaning ("starve") is a specialized one, namely "die from hunger." Another specialization, "die from cold," is found in certain Modern English dialects: "[he] . . . bid her come . . . sit close by the fire: he was sure she was starved" is from the Yorkshire dialect of *Wuthering Heights* (Chapter XXX). The older meaning of *meat* was "food" in general, as one might suspect from the archaic phrase *meat and drink* and from the compound *sweetmeat*. For the meaning "meat," the older term was *flesh* or *flesh meat*. It is interesting to observe, incidentally, that the German cognate for *flesh*, *Fleisch*, suggests first of all the specialized sense of "meat"; this is the present meaning, too, of French *viande*, while the English *viands* retains the general sense of "food." *Coast* is a borrowing, through French, from a

Latin word for "side" or "rib" (compare Modern English *intercostal*), and once meant "border" or "frontier"—the "coast of Bohemia" was not always an absurdity. But *coast* in present use not only has the usual specialization "seashore"; as employed in the eastern United States, it means specifically "Pacific coast." *Shore,* on the other hand, means, in parts of the east at any rate, "Atlantic shore." [9] In some of the same localities, however, "eastern shore" means what elsewhere would have to be expanded into "eastern shore of the Chesapeake in Maryland," just as in part of New England "the cape" means definitely "Cape Cod." *Token* formerly had the broad meaning "sign," but was long ago specialized to mean a physical thing that is a sign (of something)—as in *love token,* or the metal tokens used on streetcars or buses.

An *undertaker* once could undertake to do anything; nowadays he only undertakes to manage funerals. So, to people in general, *doctor* stands only for *doctor of medicine. Liquor,* which once was synonymous with *liquid,* is now definitely specialized. *Reek,* like the German *rauchen,* once had the broad meaning "smoke," as it still has in the Scotch dialect; but the standard Modern English use limits it quite definitely to unpleasant exhalations. *Disease* meant "discomfort"—"lack of ease" in general. *Girl* meant "young person (of either sex)." The limitation of *corpse* to "*dead body*" made it necessary to re-borrow the word in its Modern French form *corps* for another possible meaning of "body," and to make occasional use of the original Latin, *corpus,* for still another sense, "complete collection of writings." *Corn,* in general American use, will be immediately understood as "Indian corn" or "maize." But the word itself once meant simply "grain," and so, in other parts of the English-speaking world, it is differently specialized [10]—in Scotland, to mean "oats," and in England "wheat." Keats's allusion to "Ruth amid the alien corn" probably calls up, to many American readers, a very different picture from what the poet had in mind.

What are the factors that account for specialization of meaning? One is, of course, that localities and groups of people have their own specialized associations for words that otherwise may convey a broader meaning. It has been well remarked that "every man is his own specializer." [11] *Pipe,* for example, calls up different ideas in the mind of the smoker, the plumber, and the organist. *Ring* may be thought of in connection with jewelry, opera, politics, or pugilism—even though, in the last connection, the "squared circle" has long since superseded the original truly circular shape. Quite apart from particular or local specializations, however, there are a great many words whose meaning has become specialized for nearly everybody. A second factor that helps to account for both generalization and specialization is the fading of the etymological significance of the word. Thus, to illustrate the one point, *arrive* [< Lat. *ad* (to) + *ripa* (shore)] originally applied to the end of a voyage only, and was used without the preposition, since this was included in the word. Milton's "ere he arrive the happy isle" illustrates a use that is in strict accord with the etymology of the word. When, however, consciousness of the Latin parts that made up the word was weakened, it was no longer used transitively, but in the phrase "arrive at," and with the more generalized application to the end of any journey.

Yet another factor is the competition among synonymous words. The borrowing of the Latin *animal* and the French *beast* meant that, with the native *deer*, English would have possessed three exactly synonymous terms for one idea; it is obviously in the interests of economy that *deer* should have specialized to mean one particular species of animal rather than "animal" in general, and that *beast* should have acquired connotations that limit its sphere. *Bird* and *fowl*, *dog* and *hound*, *boy* and *knave*, *chair* and *stool* are further instances of words that were once synonyms but that have been differentiated in meaning here by the specialization of the second term of each pair.

A further remark about generalization and specialization is suggested by some of the words just alluded to. The degree of specialization which a language exhibits seems to depend on cultural need. In a culture in which the coconut is essential—as in Polynesia—an extremely complex vocabulary is said to have grown up, with different terms for many stages or ripeness of the fruit. So also, the Eskimos have different terms for falling snow, snow on the ground, snow packed hard like ice, slushy snow, wind-driven flying snow, and other kinds.[12] Many similar examples could be cited, for the languages of peoples of undeveloped culture appear to be particularly rich in specialized terms. At one time in the course of the English language it must have seemed desirable to speakers to make verbal distinctions in connection with groups of animals—mostly those of interest to farmers and hunters. An elaborate set of what are called "company terms" was accordingly developed, some (but by no means all) of which survive today. The better known ones include a *herd* or a *drove* of cattle, but a *flock* of sheep (or birds), a *school* of fish, a *pack* of wolves (or hounds), a *covey* of partridges, and a *swarm* of bees. But there are others far more esoteric,[13] such as *nye* of pheasants, *cete* of badgers, *sord* of mallards, *wisp* of snipe, *doylt* of tame swine, *gaggle* of geese, *harras* of horses, and *kennel* of raches. There is a similar profusion of names for the same animal (*cow, heifer, bull, calf, steer,* and *ox*), the young of various animals (*puppy, kitten, kid, calf, colt, lamb,* and so forth), and the male and female of the same species (*gander* and *goose, drake* and *duck, horse* and *mare, cock* and *hen, dog* and *bitch*).[14] The need for a generic term is of course particularly felt here, and it is supplied, not quite satisfactorily, by the convention of making either the name of the male (*horse* and *dog*) or of the female (*cow, duck,* and *goose*), or even that of the young of the species (*chicken* and *pig*), perform a larger duty.

ELEVATION AND DEGRADATION. If generalization and specialization may be said to involve a change in the "area" of meaning, elevation and deg-radation [15] involve the rising or falling of meaning in a scale of values. Thus a word which once denominated something bad (or at least neutral) but comes to refer to something good, has undergone *elevation* of mean-ing; the reverse of this process, obviously, represents a *degradation* of meaning.

And here a word of warning: we must not confuse the linguistic signal with the thing it stands for, though that error is too often made. It is not the word as such which is bad or good, or which becomes elevated or degraded, but only the meaning which society chooses to put upon it. As we shall see, society often reverses itself in the course of time, and words which were once disapproved may become "respectable," while others that had social favor may lose it. This would not be possible if the value were inherent in the word. With this in mind, then, let us illustrate degradation of meaning.

Many terms that are now descriptive of moral depravity were once quite without this suggestion. *Lust,* for example, meant simply "pleasure," as in German; *wanton* was "untaught"; *lewd* was merely "ignorant," "lerned and lewed" being a phrase commonly standing for "clergy and laity"; *immoral* was "not customary"; *vice* "flaw"; *hussy,* "housewife"; *wench,* "young girl"; and *harlot,* "fellow" (of either sex). In a similar way, words that impute rascality have often been thoroughly innocent labels: *villain,* for example, was "farm laborer"; *counterfeiter,* "imitator" or "copy-ist"; *pirate* (at least in its earlier Greek sense), "one who adventures or tries"; *buccaneer,* "one who smokes meat"; *ringleader,* simply "leader" (in a good or a neutral sense); *varlet, knave,* and *imp* meant merely "boy"; and *sly, crafty,* and *cunning* all implied the compliment "skilful." A peren-nial form of humor—the city man's ridicule of the countryman—is wit-nessed in the degradation of such nouns as *peasant, boor* (compare German *Bauer* and Dutch *Boer*), and *churl,* and in the frequent implica-tion of such adjectives as *bucolic, rural, rustic,* and *provincial.*

When a word may be applied in two possible ways, one favorable or complimentary and the other reverse, it is extremely likely that it will specialize in the less desirable sense. Thus, *suggestive* is likely to mean only "evilly suggestive," though it *may* still mean "informative" or "illuminating," and though the noun *suggestion* has escaped any such specialization—just as the verb *to harbor* is limited to unworthy or illegal concealment (as in "harboring a criminal" or "harboring thoughts of revenge"), while the noun *harbor* retains the old broad and literal meaning of "haven." *Asylum*, through association with the idea of "refuge for the insane," has followed a course like that of the verb *harbor*. A *libel*, in Middle English and early Modern English, was simply a "brief bit of writing" (from Lat. *libellum*, little book); now it is definitely limited to something malicious or defamatory. *Doom* once meant "judgment"; now it means only "condemnation." *Reek*, as we have seen, can now stand only for unpleasant distillations; *stink* and *stench* have specialized in the same way from a formerly neutral meaning, and *smell* and even *odor* seem likely to follow their lead. A *smirk* was once merely a smile, without the suggestion of affectation. One could formerly *resent* benefits as well as injuries, and *retaliate* for favors as well as slights; compare with the present meanings of these words the ordinary implications of the phrase "get even with" or "get square with."

On the other hand, instances of words that have traveled an opposite path, from the humble to the exalted, or from the base to the refined, are not far to seek. The institution of chivalry brought about the elevation of *knight* (youth) and *squire* (shield-bearer); and *chivalry* itself was invested by the Romantic Revival with a glamor that the word (as we see from its source, Fr. *cheval*, horse) did not originally possess. "Romantic" ideas in the late eighteenth and early nineteenth centuries were similarly responsible for the gain in dignity of such words as *bard,* once a term of contempt like *vagabond; minstrel,* once applicable to juggler and buffoon as well as musician; and *enthusiasm,* in the earlier eighteenth century akin to *fanaticism.* Like *knight,* other terms for rank or position have had the good fortune to take on added prestige when the offices for which they stood changed their character, and when their own etymological meanings were forgotten. Such is the history of *marshal* (originally, "horse-servant"), *chamberlain* (room-attendant), *minister* (servant), *constable* (stable-attendant), *governor* (pilot), and *steward* (sty-guardian). It is true that in a number of these words the extent of the elevation fluctuates: *marshal* is a less dignified title when it is applied to the lone policeman of an American village than when it is applied to the highest ranking officers of the English or the French army; there is a similar variation between the American and the British connotations for *constable,* just as *steward* may suggest a club attendant as well as the Lord High Steward of England, or even the royal dynasty of the *Stewarts* (or Stuarts); [16] likewise, *governor* may mean the warden of an English prison or the chief administrative officer of one of our American states. On the whole, however, the fact that any present implication of these words represents a gain in dignity over the etymological one is patent enough.

So too it is with a number of political and religious labels: *Tory, Whig, Puritan, Quaker,* and *Methodist* are well-known examples of names that were originally applied in contempt but that have taken on dignified associations (though, to some, *Puritan* and perhaps *Tory* still convey a derisive significance). Archbishop Trench long ago pointed out that the influence of Christianity elevated *angel* from merely "messenger," *martyr* from "witness," and *paradise* from "park," through the Biblical application to the abode of our first parents (as in *Paradise Lost* and "*earthly* paradise") to the "blisful waiting-place of faithful departed spirits." [17] Miscellaneous further illustrations of elevation are *pretty* from an early meaning "sly," through "clever," to something approaching "beautiful"; *nice* from an etymological meaning "ignorant," through its earliest English sense "foolish," and later ones like "particular," to its present broad and vague colloquial meaning of "pleasant" or "acceptable"; and *fond* from "foolish" to "affectionate."

The usual view of degradation and elevation has been that the downward path is far the more common. Despite McKnight's protest to the effect that elevation has been less noticed simply because it is less dramatic,[18] there seems to be every reason to agree with the general verdict. Examples of elevation, after all, are far less easy to find than examples of degradation, which indeed meet us at every turn. Besides, most of the words that have been cited as undergoing elevation fall into a few obvious categories, while the types of degradation are extremely various. The truth of the matter would appear to be that degradation has been more noticed not because it is more spectacular but simply because it is omnipresent, as elevation is not. Why should this be so, and why should the use of words be made difficult by a lurking leer, a hint of unpleasant connotation that makes a word that appears to be absolutely right in denotation impossible for a given occasion? It is hard to escape the conclusion that there is a disagreeable commentary on human nature here. How difficult it is for superlatives to retain their superlative force—because the general tendency is to apply them on light occasion and hence to weaken their meaning! So *fair* comes to mean "passable," and indeed is often equivalent to "not good"; and *quite* has passed, in its usual American application at least, from "entirely" or "completely" to "moderately." The tendency to procrastinate finds illustration in a whole series of words or phrases—*by and by, presently, anon, immediately, directly,* and *soon* itself—that have "slowed up," changing their meaning from "now" or "at once" to "soon" or "after a time." It is scarcely a far-fetched interpretation to see in the narrowing of *demure* to apply to *mock* modesty, of *genteel* to *spurious* gentility, of *sophistication* to *worldly* wisdom, of *egregious* to notoriety rather than fame, of *sanctimonious* to *pretended* holiness, and of *grandiose* to *tinsel* (itself an example of degradation) grandeur—to see in all these, and dozens of others that might be mentioned, the workings of human motives like suspicion, contempt, and general pessimism.

NOTES

1. *Write It Right,* by Ambrose Bierce, New York (Neale), 1928. The work is well worth investigating as a striking demonstration of what pedantry, combined with ignorance of linguistic processes, will do for one. To much of it, a witty definition of Bierce's own is curiously applicable: "*positive*—mistaken at the top of one's voice."

2. Some of this holding in check is unconscious, some conscious; we shall have to postpone to a later chapter the question of the values and judgments upon which conscious attempts to control language are based.

3. The Latin word *caedere,* though unrelated to English *slay,* has undergone exactly the same specialization of meaning.

4. Quoted by Bradley, *The Making of English,* p. 182.

5. This history is given in greater detail in Greenough and Kittredge, *Words and Their Ways in English Speech,* pp. 241–242.

6. Chaucer's clerk, speaking of Petrarch (*Clerk's Prologue,* line 30).

7. Louise Pound has collected more than 100 such terms now current in popular speech: "American Indefinite Names," *American Speech,* Vol. VI, No. 4 (April 1931), pp. 257–259.

8. Greenough and Kittredge, *op. cit.,* p. 235.

9. In Philadelphia it is often used in a still more specific sense, "southern New Jersey shore"; it sometimes bears a yet more localized signification: "Atlantic City," which occurs repeatedly in the headlines of Philadelphia newspapers.

10. In other Germanic languages, the cognate word has still different specializations in various places: "barley" in Sweden, "rye" in north Germany, and "spelt" in south Germany. (Jespersen, *Mankind, Nation, and Individual,* p. 212.)

11. Quoted by Greenough and Kittredge, *op. cit.,* p. 251.

12. See B. L. Whorf, "Science and Linguistics," *The Technology Review,* Vol. XLII, No. 6 (April 1940), reprinted in *Four Articles on Metalinguistics,* Washington, D.C. (Foreign Service Institute), 1950, p. 6. For further examples see Jespersen, *Language,* pp. 429–431.

13. These, and many others, are mentioned in an editorial comment in *The New York Times* for November 20, 1930. All but *doylt* are recorded in the *Oxford Dictionary.*

14. McKnight, *English Words and Their Background,* p. 239, calls attention

in greater detail to the lack of generalizing terms in the animal kingdom, and suggests further that the variety of names for sea craft (*sloop, schooner, brig, ship, boat, dinghy, bark,* and so on) is a similar survival of primitive habits of thought.

15. Elevation is also called *aggradation* or *amelioration,* and degradation is also called *degeneration* or *pejoration.*

16. Greenough and Kittredge, *op. cit.,* p. 296.

17. Archbishop Richard Chevenix Trench, *On the Study of Words,* New York (Armstrong), 20th ed. (no date), p. 114.

18. *English Words and Their Background,* p. 292; cf. also Janet Aiken, *English Present and Past,* p. 112, and G. A. Van Dongen, *Amelioratives in English.*

H. L. MENCKEN

Euphemisms

The American, probably more than any other man, is prone to be apologetic about the trade he follows. He seldom believes that it is quite worthy of his virtues and talents; almost always he thinks that he would have adorned something far gaudier. Unfortunately, it is not always possible for him to escape, or even for him to dream plausibly of escaping, so he soothes himself by assuring himself that he belongs to a superior section of his craft, and very often he invents a sonorous name to set himself off from the herd. Here we glimpse the origin of a multitude of characteristic American euphemisms, e.g., *mortician* for *undertaker, realtor* for *real-estate agent, electragist* for *electrical contractor, aisle manager* for *floor-walker, beautician* for *hairdresser, exterminating engineer* for *rat-catcher,* and so on. *Realtor* was devised by a high-toned real-estate agent of Minneapolis, Charles N. Chadbourn by name. He thus describes its genesis:

> It was in November, 1915, on my way to a meeting of the Minneapolis Real Estate Board, that I was annoyed by the strident peddling of a scandal sheet: "All About the Robbery of a Poor Widow by a Real Estate Man." The "real estate man" thus exposed turned out to be an obscure hombre with desk-room in a back office in a rookery, but the incident set me to thinking. "Every member of our board," I thought, "is besmirched by this scandal article. Anyone, however unworthy or disreputable, may call himself a real estate man. Why do not the members of our board deserve a distinctive title? Each member is vouched for by the board, subscribes to its Code of Ethics, and must behave himself or get out." So the idea incubated for three or four weeks, and was then sprung on the local brethren.[1]

As to the etymology of the term, Mr. Chadbourn says:

Real estate originally meant a royal grant. It is so connected with land in the public mind that *realtor* is easily understood, even at a first hearing. The suffix *-or* means a doer, one who performs an act, as in *grantor, executor, sponsor, administrator.*

The Minneapolis brethren were so pleased with their new name that Mr. Chadbourn was moved to dedicate it to the whole profession. In March, 1916, he went to the convention of the National Association of Real Estate Boards at New Orleans, and made a formal offer of it. It was accepted gratefully, and is now defined by the association as follows:

> A person engaged in the real estate business who is an active member of a member board of the National Association of Real Estate Boards, and as such, an affiliated member of the National Association, who is subject to its rules and regulations, who observes its standards of conduct, and is entitled to its benefits.[2]

In 1920 the Minneapolis Real Estate Board and the National Association of Real Estate Boards applied to Judge Joseph W. Molyneaux of Minneapolis for an injunction restraining the Northwestern Telephone Exchange Company from using *realtor* to designate some of its hirelings, and on September 10 the learned judge duly granted this relief. Since then the National Association has obtained similar injunctions in Virginia, Utah and other States. Its general counsel is heard from every time *realtor* is taken in vain, and when, in 1922, Sinclair Lewis applied it to George F. Babbitt, there was an uproar. But when Mr. Chadbourn was appealed to he decided that Babbitt was "fairly well described," for he was "a prominent member of the local board and of the State association," and one could scarcely look for anything better in "a book written in the ironic vein of the author of 'Main Street.'" [3] Mr. Chadbourn believes that *realtor* should be capitalized, "like *Methodist* or *American*," [4] but so far it has not been generally done. In June, 1925, at a meeting of the National Association of Real Estate Boards in Detroit, the past presidents of the body presented him with a gold watch as a token of their gratitude for his contribution to the uplift of their profession. On May 30, 1934, the following letter from Nathan William MacChesney, general counsel of the National Association, appeared in the *New Republic:*

> [*Realtor*] is not a word, but a trade right, coined and protected by law by the National Association of Real Estate Boards, and the term is a part of the trade-mark as registered in some forty-four States and Canada. Something over $200,000 has been spent in its protection by the National Association of Real Estate Boards in attempting to confine its use to those real estate men who are members of the National Association of Real Estate Boards, subject to its code for ethics and to its

discipline for violation. It has been a factor in making the standards of the business generally during the past twenty years, and the exclusive right of the National Association of Real Estate Boards has been sustained in a series of court decisions, a large number of injunctions having been issued, restraining its improper use.

In 1924 the *Realtor's Bulletin* of Baltimore reported that certain enemies of realtric science were trying to show that *realtor* was derived from the English word *real* and the Spanish word *toro*, a bull, and to argue that it thus meant *real bull*. But this obscenity apparently did not go far; probably a hint from the alert general counsel was enough to stop it. During the same year I was informed by Herbert U. Nelson, executive secretary of the National Association, that "the real-estate men of London, through the Institute of Estate Agents and Auctioneers, after studying our experience in this respect, are planning to coin the word *estator* and to protect it by legal steps." This plan, I believe came to fruition, but *estator* never caught on, and I can't find it in the Supplement to the Oxford Dictionary. *Realtor,* however, is there—and the first illustrative quotation is from "Babbitt"! In March, 1927, J. Foster Hagan, of Ballston, Va., reported to *American Speech* that he had encountered *realtress* on the window of a real-estate office there, but this charming derivative seems to have died a-bornin'. In 1925 or thereabout certain ambitious insurance solicitors, inflamed by *realtor,* began to call themselves *insurors,* but it, too, failed to make any progress.

Electragist, like *realtor,* seems to be the monopoly of the lofty technicians who affect it: "it is copyrighted by the Association of Electragists International, whose members alone may use it." [5] But *mortician* is in the public domain. It was proposed by a writer in the *Embalmers' Monthly* for February, 1895, but the undertakers, who were then *funeral-directors,* did not rise to it until some years later. On September 16, 1916, some of the more eminent of them met at Columbus, O., to form a national association, on the lines of the American College of Surgeons, the American Association of University Professors, and the Society of the Cincinnati, and a year later they decided upon National Selected *Morticians* as its designation.[6] To this day the association remains so exclusive that, of the 24,000 undertakers in the United States, only 200 belong to it. But any one of the remaining 23,800 is free to call himself a *mortician,* and to use all the other lovely words that the advance of human taxidermy has brought in. *Mortician,* of course, was suggested by *physician,* for undertakers naturally admire and like to pal with the resurrection men, and there was a time when some of them called themselves *embalming surgeons*. A *mortician* never handles a *corpse;* he *prepares* a *body* or *patient*. This business is carried on in a *preparation-room* or *operating-room,* and when it is achieved the patient is put into a *casket* [7] and stored in the *reposing-room* or *slumber-room* of a *funeral-home*. On the day of the funeral he is moved to the *chapel* therein for the last exorcism, and then hauled to the cemetery in a *funeral-car* or *casket-coach*.[8] The old-time shroud is now a *négligé* or *slumber-shirt* or *slumber-robe*, the mortician's worktruck is an *ambulance*, and the cemetery is fast becoming a *memorial-park*. In the West cemeteries are being supplanted by public mausoleums, which sometimes go under the names of *cloisters, burial-abbeys,* etc.[9] To be laid away in one runs into money. The vehicle that morticians use for their expectant hauling of the ill is no longer an *ambulance*, but an *invalid-coach*. *Mortician* has been a favorite butt of the national wits, but they seem to have made no impression on it. In January, 1932, it was barred from the columns of the Chicago *Tribune*. "This decree goes forth," announced the *Tribune*, "not for lack of sympathy with the ambition of undertakers to be well regarded, but because of it. If they haven't the sense to save themselves from their own lexicographers, we shall not be guilty of abetting them in their folly." [10] But *mortician* not only continues to flourish; it also begets progeny, e.g., *beautician, cosmetician, radiotrician* and *bootician*.[11] The barbers, so far, have not devised a name for themselves in *-ician*, but they may be trusted to do so anon. In my youth they were *tonsorial artists*, but in recent years some of them have been calling themselves *chirotonsors*.[12] Practically all American press-agents are now *public relations counsel, contact-managers* or *publicists*, all tree-trimmers are *tree-surgeons*, all milk-wagon and bakery-wagon drivers have become *salesmen*, nearly all janitors are *superintendents*, many gardeners have become *landscape-architects* (in England even the whales of the profession are simple *landscape-gardeners*), cobblers are beginning to call themselves *shoe-rebuilders*,[13] and the corn-doctors, after a generation as *chiropodists*, have burst forth as *podiatrists*. The American fondness for such sonorous appellations arrested the interest of W. L. George, the English novelist, when he visited the United States in 1920. He said:

> Business titles are given in America more readily than in England. I know one *president* whose staff consists of two typists. Many firms have four *vice-presidents*. In the magazines you seldom find merely an *editor;* the others need their share of honor, so they are *associate* (not *assistant*) *editors*. A dentist is called a *doctor*. I wandered into a university, knowing nobody, and casually asked for the *dean*. I was asked, "Which *dean?*" In that building there were enough deans to stock all the English cathedrals. The master of a secret society is *royal supreme knight commander*. Perhaps I reached the extreme at a theatre in Boston, when I wanted something, I forgot what, and was told that

I must apply to the *chief of the ushers.* He was a mild little man, who had something to do with people getting into their seats, rather a come-down from the pomp and circumstance of his title. Growing interested, I examined my programme, with the following result: It is not a large theatre, but it has a *press-representative,* a *treasurer* (box-office clerk), an *assistant treasurer* (box-office junior clerk), an *advertising-agent,* our old friend the *chief of the ushers,* a *stage-manager,* a *head-electrician,* a *master of properties* (in England called *props*), a *leader of the orchestra* (pity this—why not *president?*), and a *matron* (occupation unknown).[14]

George might have unearthed some even stranger magnificoes in other playhouses. I once knew an ancient bill-sticker, attached to a Baltimore theatre, who boasted the sonorous title of *chief lithographer.* Today, in all probability, he would be called a *lithographic-engineer.* For a number of years the *Engineering News-Record,* the organ of the legitimate engineers, used to devote a column every week to just such uninvited invaders of the craft, and some of the species it unearthed were so fantastic that it was constrained to reproduce their business cards photographically in order to convince its readers that it was not spoofing. One of its favorite exhibits was a bedding manufacturer who first became a *mattress-engineer* and then promoted himself to the lofty dignity of *sleep-engineer.* No doubt he would have called himself a *morphician* if he had thought of it. Another exhilarating specimen was a tractor-driver who advertised for a job as a *caterpillar-engineer.* A third was a beautician who burst out as an *appearance-engineer.* In an Atlanta department-store the *News-Record* found an *engineer of good taste*—a young woman employed to advise newly-married couples patronizing the furniture department, and elsewhere it unearthed *display-engineers* who had been lowly window-dressers until some visionary among them made the great leap, *demolition-engineers* who were once content to be house-wreckers, and *sanitary-engineers* who had an earlier incarnation as garbage-men. The *wedding-engineer* is a technician employed by florists to dress churches for hymeneal orgies. The *commence-ment-e.* arranges college and high-school commencements; he has lists of clergymen who may be trusted to pray briefly, and some sort of fire-alarm connection, I suppose, with the office of Dr. John H. Finley, the champion commencement orator of this or any other age. The *packing-e.* is a scientist who crates clocks, radios and chinaware for shipment. The *correspondence-e.* writes selling-letters guaranteed to pull. The *income-e.* is an insurance solicitor in a new false-face. The *dwelling-e.* replaces lost keys, repairs leaky roofs, and plugs up rat-holes in the cellar. The *vision-e.* supplies spectacles at cut rates. The *dehorning-e.* attends to bulls who grow too frisky. The *Engineering News-*

Record also discovered a *printing-e.*, a *furniture-e.*, a *photographic-e.*, a *financial-e.* (a stock-market tipster), a *paint-e.*, a *clothing-e.*, a *wrapping-e.* (a dealer in wrapping-paper), a *matrimonial-e.* (a psychoanalyst specializing in advice to the lovelorn), a *box-e.* (the *packing-e.* under another name), an *automotive-painting-e.*, a *blasting-e.*, a *dry-cleaning-e.*, a *container-e.*, a *furnishing-e.*, a *socio-religious-e.* (an uplifter), a *social-e.* (the same), a *feed-plant-e.*, a *milk-e.*, a *surface-protection-e.*, an *analyzation-e.*, a *fiction-e.*, a *psychological-e.* (another kind of psychoanalyst), a *casement-window-e.*, a *shingle-e.*, a *fumigating-e.*, a *laminated-wood-e.*, a *package-e.* (the *packing-e.* again), a *horse-e.*, a *podiatric-e.* (a corn-doctor), an *ice-e.*, a *recreation-e.*, a *tire-e.*, a *paint-maintenance-e.*, a *space-saving-e.*, a *film-e.* (or *film-gineer*), a *criminal-e.* (a criminologist), a *diet-kitchen-e.*, a *patent-e.*, an *equipment-e.*, a *floor-covering-e.*, a *society-e.*, a *window-cleaning-e.*, a *dust-e.*, a *hospitalization-e.*, a *baking-e.*, a *directory-e.*, an *advertising-e.*, a *golf-e.* (a designer of golf-courses), a *human-e.* (another variety of psychoanalyst), an *amusement-e.*, an *electric-signe-e.*, a *household-e.*, a *pageant-e.*, an *idea-e.*, a *ballistics-e.*, a *lace-e.* and a *sign-e.*[15] Perhaps the prize should go to the *dansant-e.* (an agent supplying dancers and musicians to nightclubs), or to the *hot-dog-e.*[16] The *exterminating-engineers* have a solemn national association and wear a distinguishing pin; whether or not they have tried to restrain non-member rat-catchers from calling themselves *engineers* I do not know. In 1923 the *Engineering News-Record* printed a final blast against all the pseudo-engineers then extant, and urged its engineer readers to boycott them. But this boycott apparently came to nothing, and soon thereafter it abated its indignation and resorted to laughter.[17] Next to *engineer, expert* seems to be the favorite talisman of Americans eager to augment their estate and dignity in this world. Very often it is hitched to an explanatory prefix, e.g., *housing-, planning-, hog-, erosion-, marketing-, boll-weevil-,* or *sheep-dip-,* but sometimes the simple adjective *trained-* suffices. When the Brain Trust came into power in Washington, the town began to swarm with such quacks, most of them recent graduates of the far-flung colleges of the land. One day a humorous member of Congress printed an immense list of them in the *Congressional Record*, with their salaries and academic dignities. He found at least one whose expertness was acquired in a seminary for chiropractors. During the John Purroy Mitchel "reform" administration in New York City (1914–18) so many bogus *experts* were put upon the pay-roll that special designations for them ran out, and in prodding through the Mitchel records later on Bird S. Coler discovered that a number had been carried on the books as *general experts.*

Euphemisms for things are almost as common in the United States as euphemisms for avocations. Dozens of forlorn little fresh-water colleges are called *universities,* and almost all *pawn-shops* are *loan-offices.* When *movie-cathedral* came in a few scoffers snickered, but by the generality of fans it was received gravely. *City,* in England, used to be confined to the seats of bishops, and even today it is applied only to considerable places, but in the United States it is commonly assumed by any town with paved streets, and in the statistical publications of the Federal government it is applied to all places of 8000 or more population. The American use of *store* for *shop,* like that of *help* for *servant,* is probably the product of an early effort at magnification. Before Prohibition saloons used to be *sample-rooms, buffets, exchanges, cafés* and *restaurants;* now they are *taverns, cocktail-rooms, taprooms, American-bars, stubes* and what not. Not long ago the *Furnished-Room Guide* undertook to substitute *hotelette* for *rooming-house,*[18] and in 1928 President E. L. Robins of the National *Fertilizer* Association proposed that the name of that organization be changed to the National Association of *Plant Food* Manufacturers or the American *Plant Food* Association.[19] In Pasadena the public garbage-wagons bear the legend: *Table-Waste Disposal Department.* The word *studio* is heavily overworked; there are *billiard-studios, tonsorial-studios, candy-studios,* and even *shoe-studios.*[20] Nor is this reaching out for sweet and disarming words confined to the lowly. Some time ago, in the *Survey,* the trade journal of the American uplifters, Dr. Thomas Dawes Eliot, associate professor of sociology in Northwestern University, printed a solemn argument in favor of abandoning all such harsh terms as *reformatory, house of refuge, reform school* and *jail.* "Each time a new phrase is developed," he said, "it seems to bring with it, or at least to be accompanied by, some measure of permanent gain, in standards or in viewpoint, even though much of the old may continue to masquerade as the new. The series, *alms, philanthropy, relief, rehabilitation, case work, family welfare,* shows such a progression from cruder to more refined levels of charity." Among the substitutions proposed by the learned professor were *habit-disease* for *vice, psycho-neurosis* for *sin, failure to compensate* for *disease, treatment* for *punishment, delinquent* for *criminal, unmarried mother* for *illegitimate mother, out of wedlock* for *bastard, behavior problem* for *prostitute, colony* for *penitentiary, school* for *reformatory, psychopathic hospital* for *insane asylum,* and *house of detention* for *jail.*[21] Many of these terms (or others like them) have been actually adopted. Practically all American insane asylums are now simple *hospitals,* many reformatories and houses of correction have been converted into *homes* or *schools,* all *almshouses* are now *infirmaries, county-farms* or *county-homes,* and most of the more advanced American penologists now speak of criminals as *psychopathic personalities.* By a law of New York it is provided that "in any local law, ordinance or resolution, or in any public or judicial proceeding, or in any process, notice, order, decree, judgment, record or other public document or paper, the term *bastard* or *illegitimate child* shall not be used, but the term *child born out of wedlock* shall be used in substitution therefor, and with the same force and effect." [22] Meanwhile, such harsh terms as *second-hand* and *ready-made* disappear from the American vocabulary. For the former the automobile dealers, who are ardent euphemists, have substituted *reconditioned, rebuilt, repossessed* and *used,* and for the latter department stores offer *ready-tailored, ready-to-wear* and *ready-to-put-on.* For *shop-worn* two of the current euphemisms are *store-used* and *slightly-second.*

The English euphemism-of-all-work used to be *lady.* Back in the Seventeenth Century the court-poet Edmund Waller thought it quite proper to speak of actresses, then a novelty on the English stage, as *lady-actors,* and even today the English newspapers frequently refer to *lady-secretaries, lady-doctors, lady-inspectors, lady-golfers* and *lady-champions.* *Women's wear,* in most English shops, is *ladies' wear.* But this excessive use of lady seems to be going out, and I note *women's singles* and *women's ice hockey* on the sports pages of the *London Daily Telegraph.*[23] The *Times* inclines the same way, but I observe that it still uses *Ladies' International* to designate a golf tournament, *ladies' round* and *ladies' championship* (golf and fencing).[24] In the United States *lady* is definitely out of favor. The *salesladies* of yesteryear are now all *saleswomen* or *salesgirls,* and the female superintendent of a hospital is not the *lady-superintendent,* but simply the *superintendent.* When women were first elected to Congress, the question as to how they should be referred to in debate engaged the leaders of the House of Representatives. For a while the phrase used was "the *lady* from So-and-so," but soon "the *gentlewoman*" was substituted, and this is now employed almost invariably. Its invention is commonly ascribed to the late Nicholas Longworth; if he actually proposed it, it was probably jocosely, for *gentlewoman* is clumsy, and in some cases, as clearly inaccurate as *lady.* The English get round the difficulty by using *the hon. member* in speaking of women M.P.'s, though sometimes the *hon. lady* is used.[25] A member who happens to be a military or naval officer is always, by the way, *the hon. and gallant member,* and a legal officer, say the Attorney-General or Solicitor-General, or a lawyer member in active practice, is *the hon. and learned member.* The English use *gentleman* much more carefully than we do, and much more carefully than they themselves use *lady. Gentleman-author* or *gentleman-clerk* would make them howl, but they commonly employ *gentleman-rider* and *gentleman-player* in place of our *amateur,* though *amateur* seems to be gaining favor. Here the man referred to is always actually a gentleman by their standards.

NOTES

1. Private communication, Sept. 28, 1935.

2. Realtor: Its Meaning and Use; Chicago (National Association of Real Estate Boards), 1925.

3. Letter to W. A. Frisbie, editor of the Minneapolis *Daily News*. This was in 1922. The letter was subscribed "Yours *realtorially*." A copy was sent to Mr. Lewis, who preserves it in his archives.

4. Private communication, Sept. 4, 1935.

5. Electragist, by Corneil Ridderhof, *American Speech*, Aug., 1927, p. 477. It means, according to Mr. Ridderhof, "a combined electrical dealer and contractor."

6. I am indebted here to Mr. W. M. Krieger, executive secretary of the organization, the headquarters of which are in Chicago.

7. *Casket* seems to have come in during the Civil War Period. In 1863 Nathaniel Hawthorne denounced it in Our Old Home as "a vile modern phrase, which compels a person . . . to shrink . . . from the idea of being buried at all." At the start it had a rival in *case*. The latter was used in the Richmond *Examiner's* report of the funeral of Gen. J. E. B. Stuart, May 13, 1864. But the *Examiner,* in the same report, used *corpse* and *hearse*.

8. Mortuary Nomenclature, *Hygeia*, Nov., 1925, p. 651.

9. The *Mortician*, by Elmer Davis, *American Mercury*, May, 1927.

10. *Editor and Publisher*, Jan. 30, 1932.

11. I proposed the use of bootician to designate a high-toned big-city bootlegger in the *American Mercury*, April, 1925, p. 450. The term met a crying need, and had considerable success. In March, 1927, the San José *Mercury-Herald* said: "Our bootleggers are now calling themselves *booticians*. It seems that *bootlegger* has some trace of odium about it, while *bootician* has none." (Reprinted in the Baltimore *Evening Sun*, April 4, 1927.) On July 23, 1931, according to the Associated Press, a man arrested in Chicago, on being asked his profession, answered proudly that he was a *bootician*.

12. In 1924 representatives of 3000 of them met in Chicago, and voted for *chirotonsor*. See the *Commonweal*, Nov. 26, 1924, p. 58.

13. There is a *Shoe Rebuilders'* Association in Baltimore. See the Baltimore *Evening Sun*, Oct. 17, 1935.

14. Hail, Columbia!; New York, 1921, pp. 92–3.

15. Many other varieties of engineers have been unearthed by other fanciers. On Oct. 19, 1935 *The New Yorker* announced the discovery of a *persuasion-e.—*

"a man sent somewhere by his company to try and sell somebody an idea that would be of advantage to the company." A few months before this the *Professional Engineer* found a *pajama-e.* in *The New Yorker's* advertising columns. For this last I am indebted to Mr. M. E. McIver, secretary of the American Association of Engineers. In *Popular Science,* Aug. 1935, a contributor called himself a *coffee-e.*

16. A curious anticipation of the American misuse of *engineer,* by an Englishman, is to be found in a memorandum submitted to Henry Dundas, first Viscount Melville, by Charles Stuart at the end of 1793. Dundas was Home Secretary from 1791 to 1794, and as such was in charge of the government's relations with the press. "I firmly believe, without any vanity," wrote Stuart, "that I know as much in the engineering of the press as any *press engineer* in Britain." See The History of the *Times;* London, 1925, p. 66. But Stuart's attempt to make the manipulation of the press a branch of engineering was not imitated, and there is no mention of pseudo-engineers in any of the English dictionaries.

17. See the issue for Jan. 15, 1925. Also, Some "Engineers" I Have Known, by a Civil Engineer, *Engineering News-Record,* April 19, 1923, p. 701. The engineers themselves have grossly misused the term designating them. In the Structure of the Engineering Profession, by Theodore J. Hoover, dean of the School of Engineering at Stanford University, *Journal of Engineering Education,* Jan., 1935, appears an exhaustive report upon what the 10,542 listed in "Who's Who in Engineering" call themselves. Mr. Hoover finds 2518 different titles, including such absurdities as *sales-e., sales-promotion-e., promotion-e., application-e., college-e., social-e., technical-publicity-e., bank-management-e.,* and *export-e.* He advocates a complete reform of professional nomenclature, but when I last heard from him he didn't seem to have much hope. On Feb. 21, 1935 the Associated Press reported that the National Society of Professional Engineers was trying to induce the American railroads to call their locomotive-engineers *enginemen.* The New York Central and the Pennsylvania, it was said, were already doing so.

18. See *The New Yorker,* Jan. 9, 1935, p. 74. *The New Yorker* expressed a waggish preference for *furnished-roomateria.*

19. United Press report, Nov. 13, 1928.

20. See *Studio,* by John T. Krumpelmann, *American Speech,* Dec., 1926, p. 158.

21. A Limbo for Cruel Words, *Survey,* June 15, 1922.

22. Laws of 1925, Ch. 515, in force April 9, 1925. I have to thank Mr. Sylvan Baruch of the New York Bar for calling my attention to this statute.

23. March 29, 1935.

24. April 12, 1935, p. 6.

25. I am indebted for the following to Mr. James Bone, London editor of the Manchester *Guardian:* "When a Minister answers a question in the House he

says *Yes, sir* or *No, sir,* whether the question is asked by a man or a woman M.P. The reason is that he is supposed to be addressing the Speaker. There was some laughter among young members when a Minister replied *Yes, sir* to a question by Lady Astor, but elderly members wrote to the papers at once, rebuking them and explaining the procedure." Some time ago I heard the trial of a case in one of the London Law Courts, with the Lord Chief Justice of England, Lord Hewart, on the bench. There were two women on the jury, but when they finished their labors he said "Thank you, *gentlemen.*"

MARGARET SCHLAUCH

Semantic Rejuvenation

Some of the most abstract terms in the language are really faded meta-phors. On examination it turns out that an earlier meaning, now forgotten, is often lively in the extreme. Hence an obvious means of invigorating our jejune vocabulary is to fall back on those lively older meanings. True enough, the average speaker does not know that they ever existed. He is not *reminded* that "express" once meant, literally and physically, "to press out." But he can learn it instantaneously from a context. It may be that only the archaic literal sense is intended, or it may be that both the physical and the metaphorical are to be grasped simultaneously. In any event, the impact of the divergent use on an attentive reader forces him to a new experience of the word, without sacrificing comprehension. An example of the use of "express" in this revivified fashion will be found in Emily Dickinson:

> Essential oils are wrung;
> The attar from the rose
> Is not expressed by suns alone,
> It is the gift of screws.

In the age of Shakespeare, intensive classical education had shaped a reading public (among the few, of course) who could sense the older meaning with less effort than many feel today. The plays offer repeated vivid uses of etymological rejuvenation of words. Horatio's "Season thy admiration for a while with an attent ear" makes use of the Latin sense of *admirari*, "to wonder at" something and of "attent" in the sense of "stretched." "Hast thou no *speculation* in those eyes?" recalls the literal meaning of *speculare*, "to gaze, look upon." "Occulted guilt" means guilt covered over, or hidden. When Troilus says "there's no maculation in thy heart" he reminds us of the concrete meaning of *macula*, namely "spot (of dirt)," and when he refers to his "sequent protestation" it is in the concrete sense of "my calling on witness, which now follows." Hamlet's injunction "Let it be tenable in your silence still" evokes the basic meaning of Latin *tenere*, "to hold"—not merely "to maintain a theoretical position." So when Laertes warns his sister that "nature, crescent, does not grow alone in thews and bulk," the adjective reminds us that *crescrere* meant "to grow," to mature in a physical sense. In *Troilus and Cressida* Ulysses can speak of "deracinating" a political state and thus call upon us to think of *racine*, a root, so that the meaning of "uproot" is conveyed in an unaccustomed startling manner. The usual word having lost emphasis, the learned one infuses new life by causing us to share in the original metaphoric synthesis.

Sophisticated writers still impose the etymological task upon their readers as part of the aesthetic experience. It may be said, in fact, that etymology is one of the devices by which readers are now called upon to share in the creative act. The enormous influence of English metaphysical poets of the seventeenth century on modern writers—notably the influence of Donne—has accentuated this etymological awareness. The reason for a return to metaphysical poets as a source of inspiration is not our subject here. But a consequence of it is certainly a recourse to similar linguistic devices.

James Joyce, for instance, has evinced etymological preoccupations throughout his entire work. When he says that one pugilist's fist is "proposed" under the chin of another, he intends the word as Latin *proponere*, "to place under"; and he is capable of using "supplant" as "to plant under" in describing the Gracehoper (i.e. Grasshopper) of *Finnegans Wake*: "he had a partner pair of findlestilts to *supplant* him." T. S. Eliot expects the same etymological collaboration from his readers in his simile from "The Love Song of J. Alfred Prufrock":

> Streets that follow like a tedious argument
> Of insidious intent
> To lead you to an overwhelming question. . . .

Like Shakespeare, he wishes you to remember that "intent" means a thing that is taut and stretched for action, and that "insidious" (Latin *insidiae*, "sitting or lurking within") means "ambushed" against an enemy. At the same time the literal metaphor of warfare is merged in the image of a verbal argument. In "Preludes" there is another figure of the many he evokes from the streets of a city:

> The conscience of a blackened street
> Impatient to assume the world.

Here it is necessary to remember that "assume" means "to take on" (*ad-sumere*) and hence "to play the part of." In his epithet "maculate giraffe" ("Sweeny among the Nightingales") he is doing exactly as Shakespeare did: reminding us that our faded theological term "immaculate conception" contains a sharp visual image of literal, physical spots.

So C. Day Lewis makes use of both the literal and figurative senses of "derelict mills" in "You that love England." He means lonely and abandoned mills, of course, but also mills that have simply and unmetaphorically been "left behind" (*de-linqui*) by those who formerly worked in them. And W. H. Auden, speaking in "Sir, No Man's Enemy" of "the distortions of ingrown virginity," surely intends us to feel the root meaning of "twist, physical bending from the norm" under the abstract "distortion." When he uses the expression "trains that *fume* in the station" he evokes the literal visual image "to smoke" as well as the later extended meaning "to be impatient."

Hart Crane's strange vigor is in part derived from the reminder of root meanings. Here are a few examples. In a description of an airplane flying over Mount Hatteras, the pilot is thus addressed:

> Remember, Falcon-Ace,
> Thou hast there in thy wrist a Sanskrit charge
> To conjugate infinity's dim marge—
> Anew. . . !

If the general sense is the quasi-magic power of dominating the horizons of infinity, the root meaning of "conjugate" is still felt as "to put a yoke on," rather than "to inflect a verb." In "Garden Abstract" the opening lines are

> The apple on its bough is her desire,—
> Shining suspension, mimic of the sun.

The abstract word "suspension" is to be interpreted as "the thing which is hung." In the haunting phrase "the silken skilled transmemberment of song" there is an enormous heightening of effect when the trite word "trans-formation" (passing of one form into another) is replaced by "trans-memberment" (passing of one member into another). This particular instance shows how readily an acquired skill in etymological rejuvenation will pass into creative independence in handling words.

SAMUEL JOHNSON

Preface to the Dictionary (1755)

It is the fate of those who toil at the lower employments of life, to be rather driven by the fear of evil, than attracted by the prospect of good; to be exposed to censure, without hope of praise; to be disgraced by miscarriage, or punished for neglect, where success would have been without applause, and diligence without reward.

Among these unhappy mortals is the writer of dictionaries; whom mankind have considered, not as the pupil, but the slave of science, the pioneer of literature, doomed only to remove rubbish and clear obstructions from the paths through which Learning and Genius press forward to conquest and glory, without bestowing a smile on the humble drudge that facilitates their progress. Every other author may aspire to praise; the lexicographer can only hope to escape reproach, and even this negative recompense has been yet granted to very few.

I have, notwithstanding this discouragement, attempted a Dictionary of the *English* language, which, while it was employed in the cultivation of every species of literature, has itself been hitherto neglected; suffered to spread, under the direction of chance, into wild exuberance; resigned to the tyranny of time and fashion; and exposed to the corruptions of ignorance, and caprices of innovation.

When I took the first survey of my undertaking, I found our speech copious without order, and energetick without rules: wherever I turned my view, there was perplexity to be disentangled, and confusion to be regulated; choice was to be made out of boundless variety, without any established principle of selection; adulterations were to be detected, without a settled test of purity; and modes of expression to be rejected or received, without the suffrages of any writers of classical reputation or acknowledged authority.

Having therefore no assistance but from general grammar, I applied myself to the perusal of our writers; and noting whatever might be of use to ascertain or illustrate any word or phrase, accumulated in time the materials of a dictionary, which, by degrees, I reduced to method, establishing to myself, in the progress of the work, such rules as experience and analogy suggested to me; experience, which practice and observation were continually increasing; and analogy, which, though in some words obscure, was evident in others.

In adjusting the ORTHOGRAPHY, which has been to this time unsettled and fortuitous, I found it necessary to distinguish those irregularities that are inherent in our tongue, and perhaps coeval with it, from others which the ignorance or negligence of later writers has produced. Every language has its anomalies, which, though inconvenient, and in themselves once unnecessary, must be tolerated among the imperfections of human things, and which require only to be registered, that they may not be increased, and ascertained, that they may not be confounded: but every language has likewise its improprieties and absurdities, which it is the duty of the lexicographer to correct or proscribe.

As language was at its beginning merely oral, all words of necessary or common use were spoken before they were written; and while they were unfixed by any visible signs, must have been spoken with great diversity, as we now observe those who cannot read to catch sounds imperfectly, and utter them negligently. When this wild and barbarous jargon was first reduced to an alphabet, every penman endeavoured to express, as he could, the sounds which he was accustomed to pronounce or to receive, and vitiated in writing such words as were already vitiated in speech. The powers of the letters, when they were applied to a new language, must have been vague and unsettled, and therefore different hands would exhibit the same sound by different combinations.

From this uncertain pronunciation arise in a great part the various dialects of the same country, which will always be observed to grow fewer, and less different, as books are multiplied; and from this arbitrary representation of sounds by letters, proceeds that diversity of spelling observable in the *Saxon* remains, and I suppose in the first books of every nation, which perplexes or destroys analogy, and produces anomalous formations, that, being once incorporated, can never be afterwards dismissed or reformed.

Of this kind are the derivatives *length* from *long*, *strength* from *strong*, *darling* from *dear*, *breadth* from *broad*, from *dry*, *drought*, and from *high*, *height*, which *Milton*, in zeal for analogy, writes *highth; Quid te exempta juvat spinis de pluribus una?* to change all would be too much, and to change one is nothing.

This uncertainty is most frequent in the vowels, which are so capriciously pronounced, and so differently modified, by accident or affectation, not only in every province, but in every mouth, that to them, as is well known to etymologists, little regard is to be shown in the deduction of one language from another.

Such defects are not errours in orthography, but spots of barbarity impressed so deep in the *English* language, that criticism can never wash them away: these, therefore, must be permitted to remain untouched; but many words have likewise been altered by accident, or depraved by ignorance, as the pronunciation of the vulgar has been weakly followed; and some still continue to be variously written, as authors differ in their care or skill: of these it was proper to inquire the true orthography, which I have always considered as depending on their derivation, and have therefore referred them to their original languages: thus I write *enchant, enchantment, enchanter,* after the *French,* and *incantation* after the *Latin;* thus *entire* is chosen rather than *intire,* because it passed to us not from the *Latin integer,* but from the *French entier.*

Of many words it is difficult to say whether they were immediately received from the *Latin* or the *French,* since at the time when we had dominions in *France,* we had *Latin* service in our churches. It is, however, my opinion, that the *French* generally supplied us; for we have few *Latin* words, among the terms of domestick use, which are not *French;* but many *French,* which are very remote from *Latin.*

Even in words of which the derivation is apparent, I have been often obliged to sacrifice uniformity to custom; thus I write, in compliance with a numberless majority, *convey* and *inveigh, deceit* and *receipt, fancy* and *phantom;* sometimes the derivative varies from the primitive, as *explain* and *explanation, repeat* and *repetition.*

Some combinations of letters having the same power, are used indifferently without any discoverable reason of choice, as in *choak, choke; soap, sope; fewel, fuel,* and many others; which I have sometimes inserted twice, that those who search for them under either form, may not search in vain.

In examining the orthography of any doubtful word, the mode of spelling by which it is inserted in the series of the dictionary, is to be considered as that to which I give, perhaps not often rashly, the preference. I have left, in the examples, to every author his own practice unmolested, that the reader may balance suffrages, and judge between us: but this question is not always to be determined by reputed or by real learning; some men, intent upon greater things, have thought little on sounds and derivations; some, knowing in the ancient tongues, have neglected those in which our words are commonly to be sought. Thus *Hammond* writes *fecibleness* for *feasibleness,* because I suppose he imagined it derived immediately from the *Latin;* and some words, such as *dependant, dependent; dependance, dependence,* vary their final syllable, as one or another language is present to the writer.

In this part of the work, where caprice has long wantoned without control, and vanity sought praise by petty reformation, I have endeavoured to proceed with a scholar's reverence for antiquity, and a grammarian's regard to the genius of our tongue. I have attempted few alterations, and among those few, perhaps the greater part is from the modern to the ancient practice; and I hope I may be allowed to recommend to those, whose thoughts have been perhaps employed too anxiously on verbal singularities, not to disturb, upon narrow views, or for minute propriety, the orthography of their fathers. It has been asserted, that for the law to be *known,* is of more importance than to be *right.* Change, says *Hooker,* is not made without inconvenience, even from worse to better. There is in constancy and stability a general and lasting advantage, which will always overbalance the slow improvements of gradual correction. Much less ought our written language to comply with the corruptions of oral utterance, or copy that which every variation of time or place makes different from itself, and imitate those changes, which will again be changed, while imitation is employed in observing them.

This recommendation of steadiness and uniformity does not proceed from an opinion, that particular combinations of letters have much influence on human happiness; or that truth may not be successfully taught by modes of spelling fanciful and erroneous: I am not yet so lost in lexicography, as to forget that *words are the daughters of earth, and that things are the sons of heaven.* Language is only the instrument of science, and words are but the signs of ideas: I wish, however, that the instrument might be less apt to decay, and that signs might be permanent, like the things which they denote.

In settling the orthography, I have not wholly neglected the pronunciation, which I have directed, by printing an accent upon the acute or elevated syllable. It will sometimes be found, that the accent is placed by the author quoted, on a different syllable from that marked in the alphabetical series; it is then to be understood, that custom has varied, or that the author has, in my opinion, pronounced wrong. Short directions are sometimes given where the sound of letters is irregular; and if they are sometimes omitted, defect in such minute observations will be more easily excused, than superfluity.

In the investigation both of the orthography and signification of words, their ETYMOLOGY was necessarily to be considered, and they were therefore to be divided into primitives and derivatives. A primitive word, is that which can be traced no further to any *English* root; thus *circumspect, circumvent, circumstance, delude, concave,* and *complicate,* though compounds in the *Latin,* are to us primitives. Derivatives, are all those that can be referred to any word in *English* of greater simplicity.

The derivatives I have referred to their primitives, with an accuracy sometimes needless; for who does not see that *remoteness* comes from *remote, lovely* from *love, concavity* from *concave,* and *demonstrative* from *demonstrate?* but this grammatical exuberance the scheme of my work did not allow me to repress. It is of great importance, in examining the general fabric of a language, to trace one word from another, by noting the usual modes of derivation and inflection; and uniformity must be preserved in systematical works, though sometimes at the expense of particular propriety.

Among other derivatives I have been careful to insert and elucidate the anomalous plurals of nouns and preterites of verbs, which in the *Teutonick* dialects are very frequent, and, though familiar to those who have always used them, interrupt and embarrass the learners of our language.

The two languages from which our primitives have been derived are the *Roman* and *Teutonick:* under the *Roman* I comprehend the *French* and provincial tongues; and under the *Teutonick* range the *Saxon, German,* and all their kindred dialects. Most of our polysyllables are *Roman,* and our words of one syllable are very often *Teutonick.*

In assigning the *Roman* original, it has perhaps sometimes happened that I have mentioned only the *Latin,* when the word was borrowed from the *French;* and considering myself as employed only in the illustration of my own language, I have not been very careful to observe whether the *Latin* word be pure or barbarous, or the *French* elegant or obsolete. . . .

Our knowledge of the northern literature is so scanty, that of words undoubtedly *Teutonick,* the original is not always to be found in any ancient language; and I have therefore inserted *Dutch* or *German* substitutes, which I consider not as radical, but parallel, not as the parents, but sisters of the *English.*

The words which are represented as thus related by descent or cognation, do not always agree in sense; for it is incident to words, as to their authors, to degenerate from their ancestors, and to change their manners when they change their country. It is sufficient, in etymological inquiries, if the senses of kindred words be found such as may easily pass into each other, or such as may both be referred to one general idea.

The etymology, so far as it is yet known, was easily found in the volumes where it is particularly and professedly delivered; and, by proper attention to the rules of derivation, the orthography was soon adjusted. But to COLLECT the WORDS of our language was a task of greater difficulty: the deficiency of dictionaries was immediately apparent; and when they were exhausted, what was yet wanting, must be sought by fortuitous and unguided excursions into books, and gleaned as industry should find, or chance should offer it, in the boundless chaos of a living speech. My search, however, has been either skilful or lucky; for I have much augmented the vocabulary. . . .

The words, thus selected and disposed, are grammatically considered; they are referred to the different parts of speech; traced, when they are irregularly inflected, through their various terminations; and illustrated by observations, not indeed of great or striking importance, separately considered, but necessary to the elucidation of our language, and hitherto neglected or forgotten by *English* grammarians.

That part of my work on which I expect malignity most frequently to fasten, is the *Explanation;* in which I cannot hope to satisfy those, who are perhaps not inclined to be pleased, since I have not always been able to satisfy myself. To interpret a language by itself is very difficult; many words cannot be explained by synonimes, because the idea signified by them has not more than one appellation; nor by paraphrase, because simple ideas cannot be described. When the nature of things is unknown, or the notion unsettled and indefinite, and various in various minds, the words by which such notions are conveyed, or such things denoted, will be ambiguous and perplexed. And such is the fate of hapless lexicography, that not only darkness, but light, impedes and distresses it; things may be not only too little, but too much known, to be happily illustrated. To explain, requires the use of terms less abstruse than that which is to be explained, and such terms cannot always be found; for as nothing can be proved but by supposing something intuitively known, and evident without proof, so nothing can be defined but by the use of words too plain to admit a definition. . . .

All the interpretations of words are not written with the same skill, or the same happiness: things equally easy in themselves, are not all equally easy to any single mind. Every writer of a long work commits errours, where there appears neither ambiguity to mislead, nor obscurity to confound him; and in a search like this, many felicities of expression will be casually overlooked, many convenient parallels will be forgotten, and many particulars will admit improvement from a mind utterly unequal to the whole performance.

But many seeming faults are to be imputed rather to the nature of the undertaking, than the negligence of the performer. Thus some explanations are unavoidably reciprocal or circular, as *hind, the female of the stag; stag, the male of the hind:* sometimes easier words are changed into harder, as *burial* into *sepulture* or *interment, drier* into *desiccative, dryness* into *siccity* or *aridity, fit* into *paroxysm;* for the easiest word, whatever it be, can never be translated into one more easy. But easiness and difficulty are merely relative, and if the present prevalence of our language should invite foreigners to this dictionary, many will be assisted by those words which now seem only to increase or produce obscurity. For this reason I have endeavoured frequently to join a *Teutonick* and *Roman* interpretation, as to CHEER, to *gladden,* or *exhilarate,* that every learner of *English* may be assisted by his own tongue.

The solution of all difficulties, and the supply of all defects, must be sought in the examples, subjoined to the various senses of each word, and ranged according to the time of their authors.

When I first collected these authorities, I was desirous that every quotation should be useful to some other end than the illustration of a word; I therefore extracted from philosophers principles of science; from historians remarkable facts; from chymists complete processes; from divines striking exhortations; and from poets beautiful descriptions. Such is design, while it is yet at a distance from execution. When the time called upon me to range this accumulation of elegance and wisdom into an alphabetical series, I soon discovered that the bulk of my volumes would fright away the student, and was forced to depart from my scheme of including all that was pleasing or useful in *English* literature, and reduce my transcripts very often to clusters of words, in which scarcely any meaning is retained; thus to the weariness of copying, I was condemned to add the vexation of expunging. Some passages I have yet spared, which may relieve the labour of verbal searches, and intersperse with verdure and flowers the dusty deserts of barren philology.

The examples, thus mutilated, are no longer to be considered as conveying the sentiments or doctrine of their authors; the word for the sake of which they are inserted, with all its appendant clauses, has been carefully preserved; but it may sometimes happen, by hasty detruncation, that the general tendency of the sentence may be changed: the divine may desert his tenets, or the philosopher his system.

Some of the examples have been taken from writers who were never mentioned as masters of elegance or models of style; but words must be sought where they are used; and in what pages, eminent for purity, can terms of manufacture or agriculture be found? Many quotations serve no other purpose, than that of proving the bare existence of words, and are therefore selected with less scrupulousness than those which are to teach their structures and relations.

My purpose was to admit no testimony of living authors, that I might not be misled by partiality, and that none of my cotemporaries might have reason to complain; nor have I departed from this resolution, but when some performance of uncommon excellence excited my veneration, when my memory supplied me, from late books, with an example that was wanting, or when my heart, in the tenderness of friendship, solicited admission for a favourite name.

So far have I been from any care to grace my pages with modern decorations, that I have studiously endeavoured to collect examples and authorities from the writers before the restoration, whose works I regard as *the wells of English undefiled,* as the pure sources of genuine diction. Our language, for almost a century, has, by the concurrence of many causes, been gradually departing from its original *Teutonick* character, and deviating towards a *Gallick* structure and phraseology, from which it ought to be our endeavour to recall it, by making our ancient volumes the ground-work of style, admitting among the additions of later times, only such as may supply real deficiencies, such as are readily adopted by the genius of our tongue, and incorporate easily with our native idioms.

But as every language has a time of rudeness antecedent to perfection, as well as of false refinement and declension, I have been cautious lest my zeal for antiquity might drive me into times too remote, and crowd my book with words now no longer understood. I have fixed *Sidney's* work for the boundary, beyond which I make few excursions. From the authors which rose in the time of *Elizabeth,* a speech might be formed adequate to all the purposes of use and elegance. If the language of theology were extracted from *Hooker* and the translation of the Bible; the terms of natural knowledge from *Bacon;* the phrases of policy, war, and navigation from *Raleigh;* the dialect of poetry and fiction from *Spenser* and *Sidney;* and the diction of common life from *Shakespeare,* few ideas would be lost to mankind, for want of *English* words, in which they might be expressed.

It is not sufficient that a word is found, unless it be so combined as that its meaning is apparently determined by the tract and tenour of the sentence; such passages I have therefore chosen, and when it happened that any author gave a definition of a term, or such an explanation as is equivalent to a definition, I have placed his authority as a supplement to my own, without regard to the chronological order, that is otherwise observed.

Some words, indeed, stand unsupported by any authority, but they are commonly derivative nouns, or adverbs, formed from their primitives by regular and constant analogy, or names of things seldom occurring in books, or words of which I have reason to doubt the existence.

There is more danger of censure from the multiplicity than paucity of examples; authorities will sometimes seem to have been accumulated without necessity or use, and perhaps some will be found, which might, without loss, have been omitted. But a work of this kind is not hastily to be charged with superfluities: those quotations, which to careless or unskilful perusers appear only to repeat the same sense, will often exhibit, to a more accurate examiner, diversities of signification, or, at least, afford different shades of the same meaning: one will show the word applied to persons, another to things; one will express an ill, another a good, and a third a neutral sense; one will prove the expression genuine from an ancient author; another will show it elegant from a modern: a doubtful authority is corroborated by another of more credit; an ambiguous sentence is ascertained by a passage clear and determinate; the word, how often soever repeated, appears with new associates and in different combinations, and every quotation contributes something to the stability or enlargement of the language.

When words are used equivocally, I receive them in either sense; when they are metaphorical, I adopt them in their primitive acceptation.

I have sometimes, though rarely, yielded to the temptation of exhibiting a genealogy of sentiments, by showing how one author copied the thoughts and diction of another: such quotations are indeed little more than repetitions, which might justly be censured, did they not gratify the mind, by affording a kind of intellectual history.

The various syntactical structures occurring in the examples have been carefully noted; the license or negligence with which many words have been hitherto used, has made our style capricious and indeterminate; when the different combinations of the same word are exhibited together, the preference is readily given to propriety, and I have often endeavoured to direct the choice.

Thus have I laboured by settling the orthography, displaying the analogy, regulating the structures, and ascertaining the signification of *English* words, to perform all the parts of a faithful lexicographer: but I have not always executed my own scheme, or satisfied my own expectations. The work, whatever proofs of diligence and attention it may exhibit, is yet capable of many improvements: the orthography which I recommend is still controvertible, the etymology which I adopt is uncertain, and perhaps frequently erroneous; the explanations are sometimes too much contracted, and sometimes too much diffused, the significations are distinguished rather with subtilty than skill, and the attention is harassed with unnecessary minuteness.

The examples are too often injudiciously truncated, and perhaps sometimes, I hope very rarely, alleged in a mistaken sense; for in making this collection I trusted more to memory, than, in a state of disquiet and embarrassment, memory can contain, and purposed to supply at the review what was left incomplete in the first transcription.

Many terms appropriated to particular occupations, though necessary and significant, are undoubtedly omitted; and of the words most studiously considered and exemplified, many senses have escaped observation.

Yet these failures, however frequent, may admit extenuation and apology. To have attempted much is always laudable, even when the enterprise is above the strength that undertakes it: To rest below his own aim is incident to every one whose fancy is active, and whose views are comprehensive; nor is any man satisfied with himself because he has done much, but because he can conceive little. When first I engaged in this work, I resolved to leave neither words nor things unexamined, and pleased myself with the prospect of the hours which I should revel away in feasts of literature, with the obscure recesses of northern learning which I should enter and ransack; the treasures with which I expected every search into those neglected mines to reward my labour, and the triumph with which I should display my acquisitions to mankind. When I had thus inquired into the original of words, I resolved to show likewise my attention to things; to pierce deep into every science, to inquire the nature of every substance of which I inserted the name, to limit every idea by a definition strictly logical, and exhibit every production of art or nature in an accurate description, that my book might be in place of all other dictionaries whether appellative or technical. But these were the dreams of a poet doomed at last to wake a lexicographer. I soon found that it is too late to look for instruments, when the work calls for execution, and that whatever abilities I had brought to my task, with those I must finally perform it. To deliberate whenever I doubted, to inquire whenever I was ignorant, would have protracted the undertaking without end, and, perhaps, without much improvement; for I did not find by my first experiments, that what I had not of my own was easily to be obtained: I saw that one inquiry only gave occasion to another, that book referred to book, that to search was not always to find, and to find was not always to be informed; and that thus to pursue perfection, was, like the first inhabitants of Arcadia, to chase the sun, which, when they had reached the hill where he seemed to rest, was still beheld at the same distance from them.

I then contracted my design, determining to confide in myself, and no longer to solicit auxiliaries, which produced more incumbrance than assistance: by this I obtained at least one advantage, that I set limits to my work, which would in time be ended, though not completed.

Despondency has never so far prevailed as to depress me to negligence; some faults will at last appear to be the effects of anxious diligence and persevering activity. The nice and subtle ramifications of meaning were not easily avoided by a mind intent upon accuracy, and convinced of the necessity of disentangling combinations, and separating similitudes. Many of the distinctions, which to common readers appear useless and idle, will be found real and important by men versed in the school philosophy, without which no dictionary can ever be accurately compiled, or skilfully examined.

Some senses however there are, which, though not the same, are yet so nearly allied, that they are often confounded. Most men think indistinctly, and therefore cannot speak with exactness; and consequently some examples might be indifferently put to either signification: this uncertainty is not to be imputed to me, who do not form, but register the language; who do not teach men how they should think, but relate how they have hitherto expressed their thoughts.

The imperfect sense of some examples I lamented, but could not remedy, and hope they will be compensated by innumerable passages selected with propriety, and preserved with exactness; some shining with sparks of imagination, and some replete with treasures of wisdom.

The orthography and etymology, though imperfect, are not imperfect for want of care, but because care will not always be successful, and recollection or information come too late for use.

That many terms of art and manufacture are omitted, must be frankly acknowledged; but for this defect I may boldly allege that it was unavoidable: I could not visit caverns to learn the miner's language, nor take a voyage to perfect my skill in the dialect of navigation, nor visit the warehouses of merchants, and shops of artificers, to gain the names of wares, tools and operations, of which no mention is found in books; what favourable accident, or easy inquiry brought within my reach, has not been neglected; but it had been a hopeless labour to glean up words, by courting living information, and contesting with the sullenness of one, and the roughness of another. . . .

Nor are all words which are not found in the vocabulary to be lamented as omissions. Of the laborious and mercantile part of the people, the diction is in a great measure casual and mutable; many of their terms are formed for some temporary or local convenience, and though current at certain times and places, are in others utterly unknown. This fugitive cant, which is always in a state of increase or decay, cannot be regarded as any part of the durable materials of a language, and therefore must be suffered to perish with other things unworthy of preservation.

Care will sometimes betray to the appearance of negligence. He that is catching opportunities which seldom occur, will suffer those to pass by unregarded, which he expects hourly to return; he that is searching for rare and remote things, will neglect those that are obvious and familiar: thus many of the most common and cursory words have been inserted with little illustration, because in gathering authorities, I forbore to copy those which I thought likely to occur whenever they were wanted. It is remarkable that, in reviewing my collection, I found the word SEA un-exemplified.

Thus it happens, that in things difficult there is danger from ignorance, and in things easy from confidence; the mind, afraid of greatness, and disdainful of littleness, hastily withdraws herself from painful searches, and passes with scornful rapidity over tasks not adequate to her powers, sometimes too secure for caution, and again too anxious for vigorous effort; sometimes idle in a plain path, and sometimes distracted in laby-rinths, and dissipated by different intentions.

A large work is difficult because it is large, even though all its parts might singly be performed with facility; where there are many things to be done, each must be allowed its share of time and labour, in the pro-portion only which it bears to the whole; nor can it be expected, that the stones which form the dome of a temple, should be squared and polished like the diamond of a ring.

Of the event of this work, for which, having laboured it with so much application, I cannot but have some degree of parental fondness, it is natural to form conjectures. Those who have been persuaded to think well of my design, will require that it should fix our language, and put a stop to those alterations which time and chance have hitherto been suffered to make in it without opposition. With this consequence I will confess that I flattered myself for a while; but now begin to fear that I have indulged expectation which neither reason nor experience can justify. When we see men grow old and die at a certain time one after another, from century to century, we laugh at the elixir that promises to prolong life to a thousand years; and with equal justice may the lexicographer be derided, who being able to produce no example of a nation that has preserved their words and phrases from mutability, shall imagine that his dictionary can embalm his language, and secure it from corruption and decay, that it is in his power to change sublunary nature, and clear the world at once from folly, vanity and affectation.

With this hope, however, academies have been instituted, to guard the avenues of their languages, to retain fugitives, and repulse intruders; but their vigilance and activity have hitherto been vain; sounds are too vola-tile and subtle for legal restraints; to enchain syllables, and to lash the wind, are equally the undertakings of pride, unwilling to measure its desires by its strength. The *French* language has visibly changed under the inspection of the academy; the style of *Amelot's* translation of father *Paul* is observed by *Le Courayer* to be *un peu passé;* and no *Italian* will maintain, that the diction of any modern writer is not perceptibly different from that of *Boccace, Machiavel,* or *Caro.*

Total and sudden transformation of a language seldom happen; conquests and migrations are now very rare: but there are other causes of change, which, though slow in their operation, and invisible in their progress, are perhaps as much superiour to human resistance, as the revolutions of the sky, or intumescence of the tide. Commerce, however necessary, however lucrative, as it depraves the manners, corrupts the language; they that have frequent intercourse with strangers, to whom they endeavour to accommodate themselves, must in time learn a mingled dialect, like the jargon which serves the traffickers on the *Mediterranean* and *Indian* coasts. This will not always be confined to the exchange, the warehouse, or the port, but will be communicated by degrees to other ranks of the people, and be at last incorporated with the current speech.

There are likewise internal causes equally forcible. The language most likely to continue long without alteration, would be that of a nation raised a little, and but a little, above barbarity, secluded from strangers, and totally employed in procuring the conveniences of life; either without books, or, like some of the *Mahometan* countries, with very few: men thus busied and unlearned, having only such words as common use requires, would perhaps long continue to express the same notions by the same signs. But no such constancy can be expected in a people polished by arts, and classed by subordination, where one part of the community is sustained and accommodated by the labour of the other. Those who have much leisure to think, will always be enlarging the stock of ideas; and every increase of knowledge, whether real or fancied, will produce new words, or combinations of words. When the mind is unchained from necessity, it will range after convenience; when it is left at large in the fields of speculation, it will shift opinions; as any custom is disused, the words that expressed it must perish with it; as any opinion grows popular, it will innovate speech in the same proportion as it alters practice.

As by the cultivation of various sciences a language is amplified, it will be more furnished with words deflected from their original sense; the geometrician will talk of a courtier's zenith, or the eccentrick virtue of a wild hero, and the physician of sanguine expectations and phlegmatick delays. Copiousness of speech will give opportunities to capricious choice, by which some words will be preferred, and others degraded; vicissitudes of fashion will enforce the use of new, or extend the signification of known terms. The tropes of poetry will make hourly encroachments, and the metaphorical will become the current sense: pronunciation will be varied by levity or ignorance, and the pen must at length comply with the tongue; illiterate writers will, at one time or other, by public infatuation, rise into renown, who, not knowing the original import of words, will use them with colloquial licentiousness, confound distinction, and forget propriety. As politeness increases, some expressions will be considered as too gross and vulgar for the delicate, others as too formal and ceremonious for the gay and airy; new phrases are therefore adopted, which must, for the same reasons, be in time dismissed. *Swift*, in his petty treatise on the *English* language, allows that new words must sometimes be introduced, but proposes that none should be suffered to become obsolete. But what makes a word obsolete, more than general agreement to forbear it? and how shall it be continued, when it conveys an offensive idea, or recalled again into the mouths of mankind, when it has once become unfamiliar by disuse, and unpleasing by unfamiliarity?

There is another cause of alteration more prevalent than any other, which yet in the present state of the world cannot be obviated. A mixture of two languages will produce a third distinct from both, and they will always be mixed, where the chief part of education, and the most conspicuous accomplishment, is skill in ancient or in foreign tongues. He that has long cultivated another language, will find its words and combinations crowd upon his memory; and haste and negligence, refinement and affectation, will obtrude borrowed terms and exotick expressions.

The great pest of speech is frequency of translation. No book was ever turned from one language into another, without imparting something of its native idiom; this is the most mischievous and comprehensive innovation; single words may enter by thousands, and the fabrick of the tongue continue the same; but new phraseology changes much at once; it alters not the single stones of the building, but the order of the columns. If an academy should be established for the cultivation of our style, which I, who can never wish to see dependence multiplied, hope the spirit of *English* liberty will hinder or destroy, let them, instead of compiling grammars and dictionaries, endeavour, with all their influence, to stop the license of translators, whose idleness and ignorance, if it be suffered to proceed, will reduce us to babble a dialect of *France*.

If the changes that we fear be thus irresistible, what remains but to acquiesce with silence, as in the other insurmountable distresses of humanity? It remains that we retard what we cannot repel, that we palliate what we cannot cure. Life may be lengthened by care, though death cannot be ultimately defeated: tongues, like governments, have a natural tendency to degeneration; we have long preserved our constitution, let us make some struggles for our language.

In hope of giving longevity to that which its own nature forbids to be immortal, I have devoted this book, the labour of years, to the honour of my country, that we may no longer yield the palm of philology, without a contest, to the nations of the continent. The chief glory of every people arises from its authors: whether I shall add any thing by my own writings to the reputation of *English* literature, must be left to time: much of my life has been lost under the pressures of disease; much has been trifled away; and much has always been spent in provision for the day that was passing over me; but I shall not think my employment useless or ignoble, if by my assistance foreign nations, and distant ages, gain access to the propagators of knowledge, and understand the teachers of truth; if my labours afford light to the repositories of science, and add celebrity to *Bacon,* to *Hooker,* to *Milton,* and to *Boyle.*

When I am animated by this wish, I look with pleasure on my book, however defective, and deliver it to the world with the spirit of a man that has endeavoured well. That it will immediately become popular I have not promised to myself: a few wild blunders, and risible absurdities, from which no work of such multiplicity was ever free, may for a time furnish folly with laughter, and harden ignorance in contempt; but useful diligence will at last prevail, and there never can be wanting some who distinguish desert; who will consider that no dictionary of a living tongue ever can be perfect, since while it is hastened to publication, some words are budding, and some falling away; that a whole life cannot be spent upon syntax and etymology, and that even a whole life would not be sufficient; that he, whose design includes whatever language can express, must often speak of what he does not understand; that a writer will some-times be hurried by eagerness to the end, and sometimes faint with weari-ness, under a task, which *Scaliger* compares to the labours of the anvil and the mine; that what is obvious is not always known, and what is known is not always present; that sudden fits of inadvertency will surprise vigilance, slight avocations will seduce attention, and casual eclipses of the mind will darken learning; and that the writer shall often in vain trace his memory at the moment of need, for that which yesterday he knew with intuitive readiness, and which will come uncalled into his thoughts tomorrow.

In this work, when it shall be found that much is omitted, let it not be forgotten that much likewise is performed; and though no book was ever spared out of tenderness to the author, and the world is little solicit-ous to know whence proceeded the faults of that which it condemns; yet it may gratify curiosity to inform it, that the *English Dictionary* was writ-ten with little assistance of the learned, and without any patronage of the great; not in the soft obscurities of retirement, or under the shelter of academick bowers, but amidst inconvenience and distraction, in sickness and in sorrow. It may repress the triumph of malignant criticism to ob-serve, that if our language is not here fully displayed, I have only failed in an attempt which no human powers have hitherto completed. If the lexicons of ancient tongues, now immutably fixed, and comprised in a few volumes, be yet, after the toil of successive ages, inadequate and delusive; if the aggregated knowledge, and co-operating diligence of the *Italian* academicians, did not secure them from the censure of *Beni;* if the embodied criticks of *France,* when fifty years had been spent upon their work, were obliged to change its economy, and give their second edition another form, I may surely be contented without the praise of perfection, which, if I could obtain, in this gloom of solitude, what would it avail me? I have protracted my work till most of those whom I wished to please have sunk into the grave, and success and miscarriage are empty sounds. I therefore dismiss it with frigid tranquility having little to fear or hope from censure or from praise.

DWIGHT MACDONALD

The String Untuned

The third edition of Webster's New International Dictionary (Unabridged), which was published last fall by the G. & C. Merriam Co., of Springfield, Massachusetts, tells us a good deal about the changes in our cultural climate since the second edition appeared, in 1934. The most important difference between Webster's Second (hereafter called 2) and Webster's Third (or 3) is that 3 has accepted as standard English a great many words and expressions to which 2 attached warning labels: *slang, colloquial, erroneous, incorrect, illiterate.* My impression is that most of the words so labelled in the 1934 edition are accepted in the 1961 edition as perfectly normal, honest, respectable citizens. Between these dates in this country a revolution has taken place in the study of English grammar and usage, a revolution that probably represents an advance in scientific method but that certainly has had an unfortunate effect on such nonscientific activities as the teaching of English and the making of dictionaries—at least on the making of this particular dictionary. This scientific revolution has meshed gears with a trend toward permissiveness, in the name of democracy, that is debasing our language by rendering it less precise and thus less effective as literature and less efficient as communication. It is felt that it is snobbish to insist on making discriminations —the very word has acquired a Jim Crow flavor—about usage. And it is assumed that true democracy means that the majority is right. This feeling seems to me sentimental and this assumption unfounded.

There have been other recent dictionaries calling themselves "unabridged," but they are to Webster's 3 as a welterweight is to a heavyweight. 3 is a massive folio volume (thirteen inches by nine and a half by four) that weighs thirteen and a half pounds, contains four hundred and fifty thousand entries—an "entry" is a word plus its definition—in

From *The New Yorker* magazine. © 1962 by The New Yorker Magazine, Inc. Reprinted by permission of the publisher.

2,662 pages, cost three and a half million dollars to produce, and sells for $47.50 up, according to binding. The least comparable dictionary now in print is the New Webster's Vest Pocket Dictionary, which bears on its title page the charmingly frank notation, "This dictionary is not published by the original publishers of Webster's Dictionary or by their successors." It measures five and a half inches by two and a half by a half, weighs two and a quarter ounces, has two hundred and thirty-nine pages, and costs thirty-nine cents. The only English dictionary now in print that *is* comparable to 3 is the great Oxford English Dictionary, a unique masterpiece of historical research that is as important in the study of the language as the King James Bible has been in the use of the language. The O.E.D. is much bigger than 3, containing sixteen thousand four hundred pages in thirteen folio volumes. It is bigger because its purpose is historical as well as definitive; it traces the evolution of each word through the centuries, illustrating the changes in meaning with dated quotations. The latest revision of the O.E.D. appeared in 1933, a year before Webster's 2 appeared. For the language as it has developed in the last quarter of a century, there is no dictionary comparable in scope to 3.

The editor of 2, Dr. William A. Neilson, president of Smith College, followed lexical practice that had obtained since Dr. Johnson's day and assumed there was such a thing as correct English and that it was his job to decide what it was. When he felt he had to include a sub-standard word because of its common use, he put it in, but with a warning label: *Slang, Dial.,* or even bluntly *Illit.* His approach was normative and his dictionary was an authority that pronounced on which words were standard English and which were not. Bets were decided by "looking it up in the dictionary." It would be hard to decide bets by appealing to 3, whose editor of fifteen years' standing, Dr. Philip Gove, while as dedicated a scholar as Dr. Neilson, has a quite different approach. A dictionary, he writes, "should have no traffic with . . . artificial notions of correctness or superiority. It must be descriptive and not prescriptive." Dr. Gove and the other makers of 3 are sympathetic to the school of language study that has become dominant since 1934. It is sometimes called Structural Linguistics and sometimes, rather magnificently, just Modern Linguistic Science. Dr. Gove gives its basic concepts as:

1. Language changes constantly.
2. Change is normal.
3. Spoken language is the language.
4. Correctness rests upon usage.
5. All usage is relative.

While one must sympathize with the counterattack the Structural Linguists have led against the tyranny of the schoolmarms and the purists, who have caused unnecessary suffering to generations of schoolchildren over such matters as *shall* v. *will* and the *who-whom* syndrome—someone has observed that the chief result of the long crusade against "It's me" is that most Americans now say "Between you and I"—it is remarkable what strange effects have been produced in 3 by following Dr. Gove's five little precepts, reasonable as each seems taken separately. Dr. Gove conceives of his dictionary as a recording instrument rather than as an authority; in fact, the whole idea of authority or correctness is repulsive to him as a lexical scientist. The question is, however, whether a purely scientific approach to dictionary-making may not result in greater evils than those it seeks to cure.

When one compares 2 and 3, the first difference that strikes one is that 2 is a work of traditional scholarship and hence oriented toward the past, while 3—though in many ways more scholarly, or at least more academic, than 2—exhales the breezy air of the present. This is hardly surprising, since the new school of linguistics is non-historical, if not anti-historical. Henry Luce's *Time* rather than Joseph Addison's *Spectator* was the hunting ground for 3's illustrative quotations. There is a four-and-a-half-page list of consultants. Its sheer bulk is impressive—until one begins to investigate. One can see why James W. Perry had to be consulted on Non-numerical Computer Applications and Margaret Fulford on Mosses and Liverworts, but it seems overdoing it to have *two* consultants on both Hardware and Salvation Army, and some people might even question the one apiece on Soft Drinks, Boy Scouts, Camp Fire Girls, and Girl Guiding, as well as the enrolling of Mr. Arthur B. LaFar, formerly president of the Angostura-Wuppermann bitters company, as consultant on Cocktails. Such padding is all the more odd, considering that the editors of 3 have forgotten to appoint anybody in Philosophy, Political Theory, or Theatre. The old-fashioned 2 had six consultants on Catholic Church and Protestant Churches. 3 has only one, on Catholic Church. But it also has one on Christian Science, a more up-to-date religion.

The G. & C. Merriam Co. has been publishing Webster's dictionaries since 1847, four years after Noah Webster died. Work on 3 began the day 2 went to press, but it gathered real momentum only fifteen years ago, when Dr. Gove began building up his staff of lexicographers. The first step was to sort out the words of 2 into a hundred and nine categories, so that specialized-definition writers could deal with them. It took five women two and a half years to do this. ("'If seven maids with seven mops swept it for half a year, Do you suppose,' the Walrus said, 'That they could get it clear?'"—*Lewis Carroll*.) After that, all that had to be done was to write new definitions for most of the three hundred and fifty thousand entries that were taken over from 2, to select and write a hundred thousand new entries, to collect four and a half million quotations illustrating word usage, and to distribute them among the definition writers. The scope of the operation may be suggested by the fact that in chemistry alone the lexicographers gathered two hundred and fifty thousand quotations and took six and a half years to write the definitions. After that, it was up to the Lakeside Press, of Chicago, to set type from a manuscript that was as bristling with revisions and interlineations, mostly in longhand, as a Proust manuscript. At first they gave the printers clean, retyped copy, but they soon found that the extra step produced an extra crop of errors. The printing was done by the Riverside Press, of Cambridge, Massachusetts, a long-established firm, like Merriam, whose dictionaries it has been printing for almost a century. But antiquity is relative. There is no one at Riverside like the compositor at Oxford's Clarendon Press who began setting type for the O.E.D. in 1884 and was still at it when the last volume came off the presses in 1928.

In seeking out and including all the commonly used words, especially slang ones, the compilers of 3 have been admirably diligent. Their definitions, in the case of meanings that have arisen since 1900 or so, are usually superior (though, because of the tiny amount of a dictionary it is possible to read before vertigo sets in, all generalizations must be understood to be strictly impressionistic). They have also provided many more quotations (this is connected with the linguistic revolution), perhaps, indeed, too many more. It is quite true, as the promotional material for 3 claims, that this edition goes far beyond what is generally understood by the term "revision" and may honestly be termed a new dictionary. But I should advise the possessors of the 1934 edition to think carefully before they turn it in for the new model. Although the publishers have not yet destroyed the plates of 2, they do not plan to keep it in print, which is a pity. There are reasons, which will presently appear, that buyers should be given a choice between 2 and 3, and that, in the case of libraries and schools, 3 should be regarded as an up-to-date supplement to 2 rather than a replacement of it.

Quantitative comparison between 2 and 3 must be approached cautiously. On the surface, it is considerably in 2's favor: 3,194 pages v. 2,662. But although 2 has six hundred thousand entries to 3's four hundred and fifty thousand, its entries are shorter; and because 3's typography is more compact and its type page larger, it gets in almost as much text as 2. The actual number of entries dropped since 2 is not a hundred and fifty thousand but two hundred and fifty thousand, since a hundred thousand new ones have been added. This incredible massacre—almost half the words in the English language seem to have disappeared between 1934 and 1961—is in fact incredible. For the most part, the dropped entries fall into very special categories that have less to do with the language than with methods of lexicography. They are: variants; "nonce words," like *Shakespearolatry* ("excessive reverence or devotion to Shakespeare"), which seemed a good idea at the time, or for the nonce, but haven't caught on; a vast number of proper names, including nearly every one in both the King James and the Douay Bibles; foreign terms; and obsolete or archaic words. This last category is a large one, since 2 includes "all the literary and most of the technical and scientific words and meanings in the period of Modern English beginning with the year 1500," plus all the words in Chaucer, while 3, in line with its modernization program, has advanced the cut-off date to 1755. A great many, perhaps most, of the entries dropped from 2 were in a section of small type at the foot of each page, a sort of linguistic ghetto, in which the editors simply listed "fringe words"—the definitions being limited to a synonym or often merely a symbol—which they thought not important enough to put into the main text. 3 has either promoted them to the text or, more frequently, junked them.

Some examples of the kinds of word that are in 2 but not in 3 are: *arrousement, aswowe* (in a swoon), *dethronize, devoration* (act of devouring), *disagreeance, mummianize* (mummify), *noyous* (annoying), *punquetto* (strumpet), *ridiculize,* and *subsign* (subscribe). Two foreign words that one might expect to find in 3 were left out because of insufficient "backing"; i.e., the compilers didn't find enough usages to justify inclusion. They were *Achtung* and *niet;* the researchers must have skipped spy movies and Molotovian diplomacy. *Pot holder* was left out, after considerable tergiversating, because (a) for some reason the compilers found little backing for it, and (b) it was held to be self-explanatory (though considering some of the words they put in . . .). If it had been considered to be a single word, it would have been admitted, since one rule they followed was: No word written solid is self-explanatory.

The hundred thousand new entries in 3 are partly scientific or technical terms, partly words that have come into general use since 1934. The sheer quantity of the latter is impressive. English is clearly a living, growing language, and in this portion of their task the compilers of 3 have done an excellent job. Merriam-Webster has compiled some interesting lists of words in 3 that are not in 2.

Some of the political ones are:

character assassination	loyalty oath
desegregation	McCarthyism
freedom of speech	segregated

globalize   red-baiting
hatemonger   shoo-in
integrationist   sit-in
welfare capitalism   subsistence economy

Among the new entries in the cocktail-party area are:

club soda   name-dropping
elbow bending   pub crawler
gate-crasher   quick one
glad-hander   rumpot
good-time Charlie   silent treatment
Irish coffee   table-hop
jungle juice   yakety-yak

The most important new aspect of 3, the rock on which it has been erected, is the hundred thousand illustrative quotations—known professionally as "citations" or "cites"—drawn from fourteen thousand writers and publications. (Another hundred thousand "usage examples" were made up by the compilers.) Most of the cites are from living writers or speakers, ranging from Winston Churchill, Edith Sitwell, Jacques Maritain, J. Robert Oppenheimer, and Albert Schweitzer to Billy Rose, Ethel Merman, James Cagney, Burl Ives, and Ted Williams. Many are from publications, extending from the Dictionary of American Biography down to college catalogues, fashion magazines, and the annual report of the J. C. Penney Company. The hundred thousand cites were chosen from a collection of over six million, of which a million and a half were already in the Merriam-Webster files; four and a half million were garnered by Dr. Gove and his staff. (The O.E.D. had about the same number of cites in its files—drawn mostly from English literary classics—but used a much larger proportion of them, almost two million, which is why it is five or six times as long as 3.) For years everybody in the office did up to three hours of reading a day—the most, it was found, that was possible without attention lag. Dr. Gove presently discovered a curious defect in this method: the readers tended to overlook the main meanings of a word and concentrate on the peripheral ones; thus a hundred and fifty cite slips were turned in for *bump* as in burlesque stripping but not one for *bump* as in a road. To compensate for this, he created a humbler task force, whose job it was to go through the gutted carcasses of books and magazines after the first group had finished with them and arbitrarily enter on a slip one word—plus its context—in the first sentence in the fourth line from the top of each surviving page. The percentage of useful slips culled by this method approximated the percentage of useful slips made out by the readers who had used their brains. Unsettling.

The cites in 2 are almost all from standard authors. Its cite on *jocund* is from Shakespeare; 3's is from Elinor Wylie. Under *ghastly* 2 has cites from Gray (two), Milton (three), Poe, Wordsworth, Shakespeare, Shelley, Hawthorne, and—as a slight concession to modernity—Maurice Hewlett. 3 illustrates *ghastly* with cites from Louis Bromfield, Macaulay, Thackeray, Thomas Herbert, Aldous Huxley, H. J. Laski, D. B. Chidsey, and J. C. Powys. For *debonair*, 2 has Milton's "buxom, blithe and debonair," while 3 has H. M. Reynolds' "gay, brisk and debonair." One may think, as I do, that 3 has dropped far too many of the old writers, that it has overemphasized its duty of recording the current state of the language and skimped its duty of recording the past that is still alive (Mr. Reynolds would hardly have arrived at his threesome had not Mr. Milton been there before). A decent compromise would have been to include both, but the editors of 3 don't go in for compromises. They seem imperfectly aware of the fact that the past of a language is part of its present, that tradition is as much a fact as the violation of tradition.

The editors of 3 have labored heroically on pronunciation, since one of the basic principles of the new linguistic doctrine is that Language is Speech. Too heroically, indeed. For here, as in other aspects of their labors, the editors have displayed more valor than discretion. Sometimes they appear to be lacking in common sense. The editors of 2 found it necessary to give only two pronunciations for *beserk* and two for *lingerie*, but 3 seems to give twenty-five for the first and twenty-six for the second. (This is a rough estimate; the system of notation is very complex. Dr. Gove's pronunciation editor thinks there are approximately that number but says that he is unable to take the time to be entirely certain.) Granted that 2 may have shirked its duty, one may still find something compulsive in the amplitude with which 3 has fulfilled its obligations. Does anybody except a Structural Linguist need to know that much? And what use is such plethora to a reader who wants to know how to pronounce a word? The new list of pronunciation symbols in 3 is slightly shorter than the one in 2 but also—perhaps for that reason—harder to understand. 2 uses only those nice old familiar letters of the alphabet, with signs over them to indicate long and short and so on. (It also repeats its pronunciation guide at the foot of each page, which is handy; 3 does not, to save space and dollars, so one has to flop over as much as thirteen and a half pounds of printed matter to refer back to the one place the guide appears.) 3 also uses the alphabet, but there is one catastrophic exception. This is an upside-down "e," known in the trade as a "schwa," which stands for a faint, indistinct sound, like the "e" in *quiet*, that is unnervingly common and that can be either "a," "e," "i," "o," or "u," according to circumstance.

Things get quite lively when you trip over a schwa. *Bird* is given straight
as *bûrd* in 2, but in 3 it is *bərd, bə̄d,* and *bəid.* This last may be *boid,*
but I'm not sure. Schwa trouble. ("Double, double schwa and trouble."—
Shakespeare.)

Almost all 3's pictures are new or have been redrawn in a style that is
superior to 2's—clearer and more diagrammatic. The new cut of "goose,"
with no less than twenty-four parts clearly marked, is a special triumph.
The other animal illustrations, from *aardvark* to *zebu,* are less picturesque
but more informative than those in 2. The illustrations are—rightly—
chosen for utility rather than ornament. On facing pages we have pictures
of *coracles, corbel,* and *corbiesteps,* all definitely needed, though, on
another, *pail* might have been left to the imagination. One of the few
illustrations repeated from 2 is *digestive organs,* and a fine bit of un-
compromising realism it is, too.

I notice no important omissions in 3. *Namby-pamby* is in. However, it
was coined—to describe the eighteenth-century Ambrose Philips' insipid
verses—not "by some satirists of his time" but by just one of them, Henry
Carey, whose celebrated parody of Philips is entitled "Namby-Pamby."
Bromide is in ("a conventional and commonplace or tiresome person"),
but not the fact that Gelett Burgess invented it. Still, he gets credit for
blurb and *goop. Abstract expressionism* is in, but *Tachism* and *action
painting* are not. The entries on Marxist and Freudian terms are skimpy.
Id is in, but without citations and with too brief a definition. *Ego* is
defined as Fichte, Kant, and Hume used it but not as Freud did. The
distinction between *unconscious* and *subconscious* is muffed; the first is
adequately defined and the reader is referred to the latter; looking that
up, he finds "The mental activities just below the threshold of consciousness; *also:* the aspect of the mind concerned with such activities that is
an entity or a part of the mental apparatus overlapping, equivalent to,
or distinct from the unconscious." I can't grasp the nature of something
that is overlapping, equivalent to, *or* distinct from something else. While
dialectical materialism and *charisma* (which 2 treats only as a theological
term, although Max Weber had made the word common sociological
currency long before 1934) are in, there is no *mass culture,* and the full
entry for the noun *masses* is "pl. of mass." There is no reference to Marx
or even to Hegel under *reify,* and under *alienation* the closest 3 comes
to this important concept of Marxist theory is "the state of being alienated
or diverted from normal function," which is illustrated by "alienation of
muscle." Marx is not mentioned in the very brief definition of *class
struggle.*

The definitions seem admirably objective. I detected only one major lapse:

> McCarthyism—a political attitude of the mid-twentieth century closely allied to know-nothingism and characterized chiefly by opposition to elements held to be subversive and by the use of tactics involving personal attacks on individuals by means of widely publicized indiscriminate allegations esp. on the basis of unsubstantiated charges.

I fancy the formulator of this permitted himself a small, dry smile as he leaned back from his typewriter before trudging on to *McClellan saddle* and *McCoy* (the real). I'm not complaining, but I can't help remembering that the eponymous hero of *McCarthyism* wrote a little book with that title in which he gave a rather different definition. The tendentious treatment of *McCarthyism* contrasts with the objectivity of the definition of *Stalinism,* which some of us consider an even more reprehensible *ism:* "The political, economic and social principles and policies associated with Stalin; *esp:* the theory and practice of communism developed by Stalin from Marxism-Leninism." The first part seems to me inadequate and the second absurd, since Stalin never had a theory in his life. The definitions of *democratic* and *republican* seem fair: "policies of broad social reform and internationalism in foreign affairs" v. "usu. associated with business, financial, and some agricultural interests and with favoring a restricted governmental role in social and economic life." Though I wonder what the Republican National Committee thinks.

One of the most painful decisions unabridgers face is what to do about those obscene words that used to be wholly confined to informal discourse but that of late, after a series of favorable court decisions, have been cropping up in respectable print. The editors of 2, being gentlemen and scholars, simply omitted them. The editors of 3, being scientists, were more conscientious. All the chief four- and five-letter words are here, with the exception of perhaps the most important one. They defend this omission not on lexical grounds but on the practical and, I think, reasonable ground that its inclusion would have stimulated denunciations and boycotts. There are, after all, almost half a millon other words in their dictionary—not to mention an investment of three and a half million dollars—and they reluctantly decided not to imperil the whole enterprise by insisting on that word.

Two useful features of 2 were omitted from 3: the gazetteer of place names and the biographical dictionary. They were left out partly to save money—they took up a hundred and seventy-six pages, and the biographical dictionary had to be brought up to date with each new printing—

and partly because Dr. Gove and his colleagues, more severe than the easygoing editors of 2, considered such items "encyclopedic material" and so not pertinent to a dictionary. The force of this second excuse is weakened because although they did omit such encyclopedic features of 2 as the two pages on *grasses*, they put in a page-and-a-half table of currencies under *money* and three and a half pages of *dyes*. It is also worth noting that Merriam-Webster added a new item to its line in 1943—the Webster's Biographical Dictionary. While I quite understand the publishers' reluctance to give away what their customers would otherwise have to buy separately, I do think the biographical dictionary should have been included—from the consumer's point of view, at any rate.

However, the editors have sneaked in many proper names by the back door; that is, by entering their adjectival forms. *Walpolian* means "1: of, relating to, or having the characteristics of Horace Walpole or his writings," and "2: of, relating to, or having the characteristics of Robert Walpole or his political policies," and we get the death dates of both men (but not the birth dates), plus the information that Horace was "Eng. man of letters" and Robert "Eng. statesman" (though it is not noted that Horace was Robert's son). This method of introducing proper names produces odd results. Raphael is in (*Raphaelesque, Raphaelism, Raphaelite*), as are Veronese (*Veronese green*) and Giotto and Giorgione and Michelangelo, but not Tintoretto and Piero della Francesca, because they had the wrong kind of names. Caravaggio had the right kind, but the editors missed him, though *Caravaggesque* is as frequently used in art criticism as *Giottesque*. All the great modern painters, from Cézanne on, are omitted, since none have appropriate adjectives. Yeats is in (*Yeatsian*) but not Eliot, Pound, or Frost (why not *Frosty?*). Sometimes one senses a certain desperation, as when *Smithian* is used to wedge in Adam Smith. *Menckenian* and *Menckenese* get an inch each, but there is no *Hawthornean*, no *Melvillesque*, no *Twainite*. All the twentieth-century presidents are in—Eisenhower by the skin of *Eisenhower jacket*—except Taft and Truman and Kennedy. Hoover has the most entries, all dispiriting: *Hoover apron* and *Hooverize*, because he was food administrator in the First World War; *Hooverville*, for the depression shanty towns; *Hoovercrat*, for a Southern Democrat who voted for him in 1928; and *Hooverism*.

This brings up the matter of capitalization. 2 capitalized proper names; 3 does not, with one exception. There may have been some esoteric reason of typographical consistency. Whatever their reasons, the result is that they must cumbersomely and forever add *usu. cap.* (Why *usu.* when it is *alw?*) The exception is *God*, which even these cautious linguisticians couldn't quite bring themselves to label *usu. cap. Jesus* is out because of adjectival deficiency, except for *Jesus bug*, a splendid slang term, new to me, for the waterbug ("fr. the allusion to his walking on water," the "his" being firmly lower case). He does get in via His second name, which, luckily, has given us a rather important adjective, *usu. cap.*

At first glance, 3's typography is cleaner and more harmonious. Dr. Gove estimates that the editors eliminated two million commas and periods (as after adj., n., and v.), or eighty pages' worth. A second glance shows a major and, from a utilitarian point of view, very nearly a fatal defect. Words that have more than one meaning—and many have dozens —are much easier to follow in 2, which gives a new paragraph to each meaning, than in 3, which runs the whole entry as one superparagraph. ("What! Will the line stretch out to the crack of doom?"—*Shakespeare.*) Thus 2 not only starts each new meaning of *cut* with a paragraph but also puts in an italicized heading: *Games & Sports, Bookbinding, Card Playing, Motion Pictures.* In 3 one has to look through a solid paragraph of nine inches, and there are no headings. The most extreme example I found was 3's entry on the transitive verb *take*, which runs on for a single paragraph two feet eight inches long, in which the twenty-one main meanings are divided only by boldfaced numerals; there follow, still in the same paragraph, four inches of the intransitive *take*, the only sign of this gear-shifting being a tiny printer's squiggle. *Take* is, admittedly, quite a verb. The Oxford English Dictionary gives sixty-three meanings in nine feet, but they are spaced out in separate paragraphs, as is the mere foot and a half that 2 devotes to *take*.

A second glance also suggests second thoughts about the richness of citations in 3. Often it seems *plethoric*, even *otiose* ("lacking use or effect"). The chief reason 3's entries on multiple-meaning words are so much longer than 2's is that it has so many more citations. Many are justified and do indeed enrich our sense of words, but a good thing can be overdone. The promotional material for 3 mentions the treatment of *freeze* as an improvement, but does anybody really need such illustrative richness as:

> 6a: to make (as the face) expressionless [with instructions to recognize no one; and in fact he did *freeze* his face up when an old acquaintance hailed him—Fletcher Pratt] [a look of incredulity *froze* his face . . . and his eyes went blank with surprise—Hamilton Basso] b. to preserve rigidly a particular expression on [he still sat, his face *frozen* in shame and misery—Agnes S. Turnbull]

The question is rhetorical.

One of the problems of an unabridger is where completeness ends and madness begins. The compilers of 2 had a weakness for such fabrications

as *philomuse, philomythia* ("devotion to legends . . . sometimes, loqua-
ciousness"), *philonoist* ("a seeker of knowledge"), *philophilosophos*
("partial to philosophers"), *philopolemic, philopornist* ("a lover of
harlots"), and *philosopheress* (which means not only a woman philosopher, like Hannah Arendt, but a philosopher's wife, like Xantippe).
These are omitted by the compilers of 3, though they could not resist
philosophastering ("philosophizing in a shallow or pretentious manner").
But why do we need *nooky* ("full of nooks") or *namecaller* ("one that
habitually engages in name-calling") or all those "night" words, from
night clothes—"garments worn in bed," with a citation from Jane Welsh
Carlyle, of all people—through *nightdress, nightgear, nightgown, night-
robe, nightshirt,* and *nightwear?* What need of *sea boat* ("a boat adapted
to the open sea") or *sea captain* or *swimming pool* ("a pool suitable for
swimming," lest we imagine it is a pool that swims) or *sunbath* ("exposure
to sunlight"—"or to a sun lamp," they add cautiously) or *sunbather* ("one
that takes sunbaths")? Why *kittenless* ("having no kitten")? Why need
we be told that *white-faced* is "having the face white in whole or in part"?
Or that *whitehanded* is "having white hands"? (They missed *whitelipped.*)

Then there are those terrible negative prefixes, which the unwary unabridger gets started on and slides down with sickening momentum. 3
has left out many of 2's absurdities: *nonborrower, nonnervous, non-Mo-
hammedan, non-Welsh, non-walking.* But it adds some of its own: *non-
scientist, nonphilatelic, non-inbred, nondrying* (why no *nonwetting?*)
nonbank ("not being or done by a bank"), and many other non-useful and
nonsensical entries. It has thirty-four pages of words beginning with *un-,*
and while it may seem carping to object to this abundance, since the O.E.D.
has three hundred and eighty such pages, I think, given the difference in
purpose, that many may be challenged. A reasonably bright child of
ten will not have to run to Daddy's Unabridged to find the meaning of
unreelable ("incapable of being wound on a reel"), *unlustrous* ("lacking
luster"), or *unpowdered* ("not powdered"). And if it's for unreasonably
dumb children, why omit *unspinnable, unshining,* and *unsanded?*

For a minor example of gnostimania, or scholar's knee, see the treatment of numbers. Every number from *one* to *ninety-nine* is entered and
defined, also every numerical adjective. Thus when the reader hits *sixty*
he goes into a skid fifteen inches long. *Sixty* ("being one more than 59
in number") is followed by the pronoun ("60 countable persons or things
not specified but under consideration and being enumerated") and the
noun ("six tens: twice 30: 12 fives," etc.). Then comes *sixty-eight*
("being one more than 67 in number") and *sixty-eighth* ("being number
68 in a countable series"), followed by *sixty-fifth, sixty-first,* and so on.
The compilers of 2 dealt with the *sixty* problem in a mere two entries

totalling an inch and a half. But the art of lexicography has mutated into a "science" since then. ("*Quotation mark* . . . sometimes used to enclose . . . words . . . in an . . . ironical . . . sense . . . or words for which a writer offers a slight apology.") In reading 3 one sometimes feels like a subscriber who gets two hundred and thirty-eight copies of the May issue because the addressing machine got stuck, and it doesn't make it any better to know that the operators jammed it on purpose.

My complaint is not that 3 is all-inclusive—that is, unabridged—but that *pedantry* is not a synonym of *scholarship*. I have no objection to the inclusion of such pomposities, mostly direct translations from the Latin, as *viridity* (greenness), *presbyopic* (farsighted because of old age), *vellication* (twitching), *pudency* (modesty), and *vulnerary* (wound-healing). These are necessary if only so that one can read James Gould Cozzens' "By Love Possessed," in which they all occur, along with many siblings. And in my rambles through these 2,662 pages I have come across many a splendid word that has not enjoyed the popularity it deserves. I think my favorites are *pilpul*, from the Hebrew *to search*, which means "critical analysis and hairsplitting; casuistic argumentation"; *dysphemism*, which is the antonym of *euphemism* (as, *axle grease* for *butter* or *old man* for *father*), *subfusc*, from the Latin *subfuscus*, meaning brownish, which is illustrated with a beautiful citation from Osbert Sitwell ("the moment when the word Austerity was to take to itself a new subfusc and squalid twist of meaning")—cf. the more familiar *subacid*, also well illustrated with "a little subacid kind of . . . impatience," from Laurence Sterne; *nanism*, which is the antonym of *gigantism*; *mesocracy*, which is the form of government we increasingly have in this country; and *lib-lab*, which means a Liberal who sympathizes with Labor—I wish the lexicographers had not restored the hyphen I deleted when I imported it from England twenty years ago. One might say, and in fact I will say, that H. L. Mencken, whose prose was dysphemistic but never subfusc, eschewed pilpul in expressing his nanitic esteem for lib-lab mesocracy. Unfortunately, 3 omits 2's *thob* ("to think according to one's wishes"), which someone made up from *think-opinion-believe*, or else I could also have noted Mencken's distaste for thobbery.

Dr. Gove met the problem of *ain't* head on in the best traditions of Structural Linguistics, labelling it—reluctantly, one imagines—*substandard* for *have not* and *has not*, but giving it, unlabelled, as a contraction of *am not*, *are not*, and *is not*, adding "though disapproved by many and more common in less educated speech, used orally in most parts of the U.S. by many cultivated speakers esp. in the phrase *ain't I*." This was courageous indeed; when Dr. C. C. Fries, the dean of Structural Linguists today, said, at a meeting of the Modern Language Association several years ago, that *ain't* was not wholly disreputable, a teapot tempest boiled up in the press. When Dr. Gove included a reference to the entry on *ain't* in the press announcement of 3, the newspapers seethed again, from the Houston *Press* ("IT AIN'T UNCOUTH TO SAY AIN'T NOW") to the San Francisco *Examiner* ("AIN'T BAD AT ALL—IN NEWEST REVISED DICTIONARY") and the *World-Telegram* ("IT JUST AIN'T TRUE THAT AIN'T AIN'T IN THE DICTIONARY"). But moral courage is not the only quality a good lexicographer needs. Once the matter of education and culture is raised, we are right back at the nonscientific business of deciding what is correct—*standard* is the modern euphemism—and this is more a matter of a feeling for language (what the trade calls *Sprachgefühl*) than of the statistics on which Dr. Gove and his colleagues seem to have chiefly relied. For what Geiger counter will decide who is in fact educated or cultivated? And what adding machine will discriminate between *ain't* used because the speaker thinks it is standard English and *ain't* used because he wants to get a special effect? "Survival must have quality, or it ain't worth a bean," Thornton Wilder recently observed. It doesn't take much *Sprachgefühl* to recognize that Mr. Wilder is here being a mite folksy and that his effect would be lost if *ain't* were indeed "used orally in most parts of the U.S. by many cultivated speakers." Though I regret that the nineteenth-century schoolteachers without justification deprived us of *ain't* for *am not*, the deed was done, and I think the *Dial. or Illit.* with which 2 labels all uses of the word comes closer to linguistic fact today.

The pejorative labels in 2 are forthright: *colloquial, erroneous, incorrect, illiterate.* 3 replaces these self-explanatory terms with two that are both fuzzier and more scientific-sounding: *substandard and nonstandard.* The first "indicates status conforming to a pattern of linguistic usage that exists throughout the American language community but differs in choice of word or form from that of the prestige group in that community," which is academese for "Not used by educated people." *Hisself* and *drownded* are labelled *substand.*, which sounds better than *erron.*—more democratic. *Nonstandard* "is used for a very small number of words that can hardly stand without some status label but are too widely current in reputable context to be labelled *substand.*" *Irregardless* is given as an example, which for me again raises doubts about the compilers' notion of a reputable context. I think 2's label for the word, *erron. or humorous,* more accurate.

The argument has now shifted from whether a dictionary should be an authority as against a reporter (in Dr. Gove's terms, prescriptive v. descriptive) to the validity of the prescriptive guidance that 3 does in fact give. For Dr. Gove and his colleagues have not ventured to omit all qualitative discriminations; they have cut them down drastically from 2, but they have felt obliged to include many. Perhaps by 1988, if the Structural Linguists remain dominant, there will be a fourth edition, which will simply record, without labels or warnings, all words and non-words that are used widely in "the American language community," including such favorites of a former President as *nucular* (warfare), *individuous*, and *mischievious*. But it is still 1962, and 3 often does discriminate. The trouble is that its willingness to do so has been weakened by its scientific conscience, so that it palters and equivocates; this is often more misleading than would be the omission of all discriminations.

One drawback to the permissive approach of the Structural Linguists is that it impoverishes the language by not objecting to errors if they are common enough. ("And how should I presume?"—*T. S. Eliot.*) There is a natural tendency among human beings, who are *by def.* fallible, to confuse similar-sounding words. "One look at him would turn you nauseous," Phil Silvers said on television one night, as better stylists have written before. Up to now, dictionaries have distinguished *nauseous* (causing nausea) from *nauseated* (experiencing nausea); 2 labels *nauseous* in the sense of experiencing nausea *obs.*, but it is no longer *obs.* It is simply *erron.*, a fact you will not learn from 3, which gives as its first definition, without label, "affected with or inclining to nausea." So the language is *balled up* and *nauseous* is telescoped into *nauseated* and nobody knows who means which exactly. The magisterial Fowler—magisterial, that is, until the Structural Linguists got to work—has an entry on Pairs & Snares that makes sad reading now. He calls *deprecate* and *depreciate* "one of the altogether false pairs," but 3 gives the latter as a synonym of the first. It similarly blurs the distinction between Fowler's *forcible* ("effected by force") and *forceful* ("full of force"), *unexceptional* ("constituting no exception to the general rule") and *unexceptionable* ("not open or liable to objection," which is quite a different thing). A Pair & Snare Fowler doesn't give is *disinterested* (impartial) and *uninterested* (not interested); 2 lists the *uninterested* sense of *disinterested* but adds, "*now rare*"; even such permissive lexicographers as Bergen and Cornelia Evans, in their "Dictionary of Contemporary American Usage," state firmly, "Though *disinterested* was formerly a synonym for *uninterested,* it is not now so used." But 3 gives *disinterested* as a synonym of *uninterested.*

Each such confusion makes the language less efficient, and it is a dictionary's job to *define* words, which means, literally, to set limits to them. 3 still distinguishes *capital* from *capitol* and *principle* from *principal,* but how many more language-community members must join the present sizable band that habitually confuses these words before they go down the drain with the others? Perhaps nothing much is lost if almost everybody calls Frankenstein the monster rather than the man who made the monster, even though Mrs. Shelley wrote it the other way, but how is one to deal with the *bimonthly* problem? 2 defines it as "once in two months," which is correct. 3 gives this as the first meaning and then adds, gritting its teeth, "*sometimes:* twice a month." (It defines *biweekly* as "every two weeks" and adds "2: twice a week.") It does seem a little awkward to have a word that can mean every two weeks *or* every eight weeks, and it would have been convenient if 3 had compromised with scientific integrity enough to replace its perfectly accurate *sometimes* with a firm *erroneous*. But this would have implied authority, and authority is the last thing 3's modest recorders want. ("Let this cup pass from me."—*New Testament*.)

The objection is not to recording the facts of actual usage. It is to failing to give the information that would enable the reader to decide which usage he wants to adopt. If he prefers to use *deprecate* and *depreciate* interchangeably, no dictionary can prevent him, but at least he should be warned. Thus 3 has under *transpire*—"4: to come to pass; happen, occur." 2 has the same entry, but it is followed by a monitory pointing hand: "*transpire* in this sense has been disapproved by most authorities on usage, although the meaning occurs in the writings of many authors of good standing." Fair enough. I also prefer 2's handling of the common misuse of *infer* to mean *imply*—"5: loosely and erroneously, to imply." 3 sounds no warning, and twice under *infer* it advises "compare imply." Similarly, 2 labels the conjunctive *like* "illiterate" and "incorrect," which it is, adding that "in the works of careful writers [it] is replaced by *as*." 3 accepts it as standard, giving such unprepossessing citations as "impromptu programs where they ask questions much like I do on the air—Art Linkletter" and "wore his clothes like he was . . . afraid of getting dirt on them—*St. Petersburg (Fla.) Independent*." *Enthuse* is labelled *colloq.* in 2 but not in 3. It still sounds *colloq.* if not *godawf.* to me, nor am I impressed by 3's citations, from writers named L. G. Pine and Lawrence Constable and from a trade paper called *Fashion Accessories*. Or consider the common misuse of *too* when *very* is meant, as "I was not too interested in the lecture." 2 gives this use but labels it *colloq.* 3 gives it straight and cites Irving Kolodin: "an episodic work without too consistent a texture"; Mr. Kolodin probably means "without a very consistent texture," but how does one know he doesn't mean "without an excessively consistent [or monotonous] texture"? In music criticism such ambiguities are not too helpful.

In dealing with words that might be considered slang, 2 uses the label wherever there is doubt, while 3 leans the other way. The first procedure seems to me more sensible, since no great harm is done if a word is left waiting in the antechamber until its pretensions to being standard have been thoroughly tested (as long as it is admitted into the dictionary), while damage may be done if it is prematurely admitted. Thus both 2 and 3 list such women's-magazine locutions as *galore, scads, scrumptious,* and *too-too,* but only 2 labels them slang. (Fowler's note on *galore* applies to them all: "Chiefly resorted to by those who are reduced to relieving the dullness of matter by oddity of expression.") Thus *rummy, spang* (in the middle of), and *nobby* are in both, but only 2 calls them slang.

Admittedly, the question is most difficult. Many words begin as slang and then rise in the world. Dean Swift, a great purist, objected to *mob* (from the Latin *mobile vulgus*), *banter, bully,* and *sham;* he also objected to *hyp,* which has disappeared as slang for *hypochondriac,* and *rep,* which persists for *reputation* but is still labelled slang even in 3. Some slang words have survived for centuries without bettering themselves, like the Jukes and the Kallikaks. *Dukes* (fists) and *duds* (clothes) are still slang, although they go back to the eighteenth and the sixteenth century, respectively.

The definition of *slang* in 3 is "characterized primarily by connotations of extreme informality . . . coinages or arbitrarily changed words, clipped or shortened forms, extravagant, forced, or facetious figures of speech or verbal novelties usu. experiencing quick popularity and relatively rapid decline into disuse." A good definition (Dr. Gove has added that slang is "linguistically self-conscious"), but it seems to have been forgotten in making up 3, most of whose discriminations about slang strike me as arbitrary. According to 3, *scram* is not slang, but *vamoose* is. "*Goof* 1" ("to make a mistake or blunder") is not slang, but "*goof* 2" ("to spend time idly or foolishly") is, and the confusion is compounded when one finds that Ethel Merman is cited for the non-slang *goof* and James T. Farrell for the slang *goof.* "*Floozy* 1" ("an attractive young woman of loose morals") is standard, but "*floozy* 2" ("a dissolute and sometimes slovenly woman") is slang. Can even a Structural Linguist make such fine distinctions about such a word? The many synonyms for *drunk* raise the same question. Why are *oiled, pickled,* and *boiled* labelled slang if *soused* and *spiflicated* are not? Perhaps cooking terms for *drunk* are automatically slang, but why?

I don't mean to *imply* (see *infer*) that the compilers of 3 didn't give much thought to the problem. When they came to a doubtful word, they took a staff poll, asking everybody to check it, after reviewing the accumulated cites, as either slang or standard. This resulted in *cornball's* being entered as slang and *corny's* being entered as standard. Such scientific, or quantitative, efforts to separate the goats from the sheep produced the absurdities noted above. Professor Austin C. Dobbins raised this point in *College English* for October, 1956:

> But what of such words as *boondoggle, corny, frisk, liquidate, pinched, bonehead, carpetbagger, pleb, slush fund,* and *snide?* Which of these words ordinarily would be considered appropriate in themes written by cultivated people? According to the editors of the ACD [the American College Dictionary, the 1953 edition, published by Random House] the first five of these words are slang; the second five are established usage. To the editors of WNCD [Webster's New Collegiate Dictionary, published by Merriam-Webster in the same year] the first five of these words represent established usage; the second five are slang. Which authority is the student to follow?

Mr. Dobbins is by no means hostile to Structural Linguistics, and his essay appears in a recent anthology edited by Dr. Harold B. Allen, of the University of Minnesota, an energetic proponent of the new school. "Perhaps the answer," Mr. Dobbins concludes, "is to advise students to study only one handbook, consult one dictionary, listen to one instructor. An alternate suggestion, of course, is for our textbooks more accurately to base their labels upon studies of usage." Assuming the first alternative is ironical, I would say the second is impractical unless the resources of a dozen Ford Foundations are devoted to trying to decide the matter scientifically—that is, statistically.

Short of this Land of Cockaigne, where partridges appear in the fields ready-roasted, I see only two logical alternatives: to label all doubtful words slang, as 2 does, or to drop the label entirely, as I suspect Dr. Gove would have liked to do. Using the label sparingly, if it is not to produce bizarre effects, takes a lot more *Sprachgefühl* than the editors of 3 seem to have possessed. Thus *horse* as a verb ("to engage in horseplay") they accept as standard. The citations are from Norman Mailer ("I never horse around much with the women") and J. D. Salinger ("I horse around quite a lot, just to keep from getting bored"). I doubt whether either Mr. Mailer or Mr. Salinger would use *horse* straight; in these cites, I venture, it is either put in the mouth of a first-person narrator or used deliberately to get a colloquial effect. Slang is concise and vivid—*jalopy* has advantages over *dilapidated automobile*—and a few slang terms salted in a formal paragraph bring out the flavor. But the user must know he *is* using slang, he must be aware of having introduced a slight discord into his harmonics, or else he coarsens and blurs his expression. This information he will not, for the most part, get from 3. I hate to think what monstrosities of prose foreigners and high-school students will produce if they take 3 seriously as a guide to what is and what is not standard English.

Whenever the compilers of 3 come up against a locution that some (me, or I) might consider simply wrong, they do their best, as Modern Linguists and democrats, to be good fellows. The softening-up process begins with substituting the euphemistic *substandard* for 2's blunt *erroneous* and *illiterate*. From there it expands into several forms. *Complected* (for *complexioned*) is *dialect* in 2, *not often in formal use* in 3. *Learn* (for teach) is *now a vulgarism* in 2, *now chiefly substand.* in 3. (*Chiefly* is the thin end of the wedge, implying that users of standard English on occasion exclaim, "I'll learn you to use bad English!") *Knowed* is listed as the past of *know*, though *broke* is labelled substandard for *broken*—another of those odd discriminations. Doubtless they counted noses, or citation slips, and concluded that "Had I but knowed!" is standard while "My heart is broke" is substandard.

(To be entirely fair, perhaps compulsively so: If one reads carefully the five closely printed pages of Explanatory Notes in 3, and especially paragraphs 16.0 through 16.6 (twelve inches of impenetrable lexical jargon), one finds that light-face small capitals mean a cross-reference, and if one looks up KNOW—which is given after *knowed* in light-face small capitals—one does find that *knowed* is dialect. This is not a very practical or sensible dictionary, one concludes after such scholarly labors, and one wonders why Dr. Gove and his editors did not think of labelling *knowed* as substandard right where it occurs, and one suspects that they wanted to slightly conceal the fact or at any rate to put off its exposure as long as decently possible.)

The systematic softening or omitting of pejorative labels in 3 could mean: (1) we have come to use English more loosely, to say the least, than we did in 1934; or (2) usage hasn't changed, but 3 has simply recorded The Facts more accurately; or (3) the notion of what is a relevant Fact has changed between 2 and 3. I suspect it is mostly (3), but in any case I cannot see *complected* as anything but *dialected*.

In 1947 the G. & C. Merriam Co. published a little book entitled "Noah's Ark"—in reference to Noah Webster, who began it all—celebrating its first hundred years as the publisher of Webster dictionaries. Toward the end, the author, Robert Keith Leavitt, rises to heights of eloquence which have a tinny sound now that "Webster" means not 2 but 3:

> This responsibility to the user is no light matter. It has, indeed, grown heavier with every year of increasing acceptance of Webster. Courts, from the United States Supreme Court down, rely on the *New International's* definitions as a sort of common law: many a costly suit

has hinged on a Webster definition, and many a citizen has gone behind prison bars or walked out onto the streets a free man, according to the light Webster put upon his doings. The statute law itself is not infrequently phrased by legislators in terms straight out of Webster. Most daily newspapers and magazines, and nearly all the books that come off the press, are edited and printed in accordance with Websterian usage. Colleges and schools make the *New International* their standard, and, for nearly half a century, students have dug their way through pedantic obscurity with the aid of the *Collegiate*. In business offices the secretary corrects her boss out of Webster and the boss holds customers and contractors alike in line by citing how Webster says it shall be done. In thousands upon thousands of homes, youngsters lying sprawled under the table happily absorb from Webster information which teachers have striven in vain to teach them from textbooks. Clear through, indeed, to the everyday American's most trivial and jocose of doings, Webster is the unquestioned authority.

While this picture is a bit idyllic—Clarence Barnhart's American College Dictionary, put out by Random House, is considered by many to be at least as good as the Webster Collegiate—it had some reality up to 1961. But as of today, courts that Look It Up In Webster will often find themselves little the wiser, since 3 claims no authority and merely records, mostly deadpan, what in fact every Tom, Dick, and Harry is now doing —in all innocence—to the language. That freedom or imprisonment should depend on 3 is an alarming idea. The secretary correcting her boss, if he is a magazine publisher, will collide with the unresolved *bimonthly* and *biweekly* problem, and the youngsters sprawled under the table will happily absorb from 3 the information that *jerk* is standard for "a stupid, foolish, naïve, or unconventional person." One imagines the themes: "Dr. Johnson admired Goldsmith's literary talent although he considered him a jerk." The editors of the New Webster's Vest Pocket Dictionary, thirty-nine cents at any cigar store, label *jerk* as *coll.* But then they aren't Structural Linguists.

The reviews of 3 in the lay press have not been enthusiastic. *Life* and the *Times* have both attacked it editorially as a "say-as-you-go" dictionary that reflects "the permissive school" in language study. The usually solemn editorialists of the *Times* were goaded to unprecedented wit:

> A passel of double-domes at the G. & C. Merriam Company joint in Springfield, Mass. [the editorial began], have been confabbing and yakking for twenty-seven years—which is not intended to infer that they have not been doing plenty work—and now they have finalized Webster's Third New International Dictionary, Unabridged, a new edition of that swell and esteemed word book.

Those who regard the foregoing paragraph as acceptable English prose will find that the new Webster's is just the dictionary for them.

But the lay press doesn't always prevail. The irreverent may call 3 "Gove's Goof," but Dr. Gove and his editors are part of the dominant movement in the professional study of language—one that has in the last few years established strong beachheads in the National Council of Teachers of English and the College English Association. One may grant that for the scientific study of language the Structural Linguistic approach is superior to that of the old grammarians, who overestimated the importance of logic and Latin, but one may still object to its transfer directly to the teaching of English and the making of dictionaries. As a scientific discipline, Structural Linguistics can have no truck with values or standards. Its job is to deal only with The Facts. But in matters of usage, the evaluation of The Facts is important, too, and this requires a certain amount of general culture, not to mention common sense—commodities that many scientists have done brilliantly without but that teachers and lexicographers need in their work.

The kind of thinking responsible for 3 is illustrated by Dr. Gove's riposte, last week, to the many unfavorable reviews of his dictionary: "The criticisms involve less than one per cent of the words in the dictionary." This quantitative approach might be useful to novelists who get bad reviews. It is foolproof here; a reviewer who tried to meet Dr. Gove's criterion and deal with a sizable proportion of 3's words—say, ten per cent—would need forty-five thousand words just to list them, and if his own comments averaged ten words apiece he would have to publish his five-hundred-thousand-word review in two large volumes. Some odd thinking gets done up at the old Merriam-Webster place in Springfield.

Dr. Gove's letter to the *Times* objecting to its editorial was also interesting. "The editors of *Webster's Third New International Dictionary* are not amused by the ingenuity of the first paragraph of your editorial," it began loftily, and continued, "Your paragraph obscures, or attempts to obscure, the fact that there are so many different degrees of standard usage that dictionary definitions cannot hope to distinguish one from another by status labelling." (But the *Times'* point was precisely that the editors did make such distinctions by status labelling, only they were the wrong distinctions; i.e., by omitting pejorative labels they accepted as standard words that, in the opinion of the *Times,* are not standard.) There followed several pages of citations in which Dr. Gove showed that the *Times* itself had often used the very words it objected to 3's including as standard language. "If we are ever inclined to the linguistic pedantry that easily fails to distinguish moribund traditions from genuine living usage [the adjectives here are perhaps more revealing than Dr. Gove intended] we have only to turn to the columns of the *Times*," Dr. Gove concluded. The *Times* is the best newspaper in the world in the gathering and printing of news, but it has never been noted for stylistic distinction. And even if it were, the exigencies of printing a small book every day might be expected to drive the writers and editors of a news-paper into usages as convenient as they are sloppy—usages that people with more time on their hands, such as the editors of an unabridged dictionary, might distinguish from standard English.

There are several reasons that it is important to maintain standards in the use of a language. English, like other languages, is beautiful when properly used, and beauty can be achieved only by attention to form, which means setting limits, or de-fining, or dis-criminating. Language expresses the special, dis-tinctive quality of a people, and a people, like an individual, is to a large extent defined by its past—its traditions—whether it is conscious of this or not. If the language is allowed to shift too rapidly, without challenge from teachers and lexicographers, then the special character of the American people is blurred, since it tends to lose its past. In the same way a city loses its character if too much of it is torn down and rebuilt too quickly. "Languages are the pedigrees of nations," said Dr. Johnson.

The effect on the individual is also unfortunate. The kind of permissive-ness that permeates 3 (the kind that a decade or two ago was more common in progressive schools than it is now) results, oddly, in less rather than more individuality, since the only way an individual can "express himself" is in relation to a social norm—in the case of language, to standard usage. James Joyce's creative distortions of words were pos-sible only because he had a perfect ear for orthodox English. But if the very idea of form, or standards, is lacking, then how can one violate it? It's no fun to use *knowed* for *known* if everybody thinks you're just trying to be standard.

Counting cite slips is simply not the way to go about the delicate business of deciding these matters. If nine-tenths of the citizens of the United States, including a recent President, were to use *inviduous*, the one-tenth who clung to *invidious* would still be right, and they would be doing a favor to the majority if they continued to maintain the point. It is perhaps not democratic, according to some recent users, or abusers, of the word, to insist on this, and the question comes up of who is to decide at what point change—for language does indeed change, as the Structural Linguists insist—has evolved from *slang, dial., erron.,* or *sub-stand.* to *standard.* The decision, I think, must be left to the teachers, the professional writers, and the lexicographers, and they might look up Ulysses' famous defense of conservatism in Shakespeare's "Troilus and Cressida":

> The heavens themselves, the planets and this centre
> Observe degree, priority and place,
> Insisture, course, proportion, season, form,
> Office and custom in all line of order. . . .
> Take but degree away, untune that string,
> And, hark, what discord follows! Each thing meets
> In mere oppugnancy. The bounded waters
> Should lift their bosoms higher than the shores
> And make a sop of all this solid globe.
> Strength should be lord of imbecility
> And the rude son should strike his father dead.
> Force should be right, or rather right and wrong
> (Between whose endless jar justice resides)
> Should lose their names, and so should justice too.
> Then every thing includes itself in power,
> Power into will, will into appetite
> And appetite, a universal wolf,
> So doubly seconded with will and power,
> Must make perforce a universal prey
> And, last, eat up himself. . . .

Dr. Johnson, a dictionary-maker of the old school, defined *lexicographer* as "a harmless drudge." Things have changed. Lexicographers may still be drudges, but they are certainly not harmless. They have untuned the string, made a sop of the solid structure of English, and encouraged the language to eat up himself.

JAMES SLEDD

The Lexicographer's Uneasy Chair

". . . this latest dictionary to bear the Merriam-Webster label is an intellectual achievement of the very highest order." SUMNER IVES IN *Word Study*

". . . the anxiously awaited work that was to have crowned cisatlantic linguistic scholarship with a particular glory turns out to be a scandal and a disaster." WILSON FOLLETT IN THE *Atlantic*

"Somebody had goofed."

ETHEL MERMAN IN *Webster's Third New International Dictionary*

But who? Is the goof trademarked, a Merriam-Webster, or is scholarship in Springfield trans-*Atlantic?* The experts will have to answer that question, and thoughtful laymen after using the new dictionary for a long time. This review has more modest aims. Mainly it examines a few issues which less inhibited critics have already raised, suggests some possible limitations of their criticisms, and urges that the serious work of serious scholars must be seriously judged.

Everyone knows that the *Third International* is an entirely new dictionary for use today. In this eighth member of a series which began in 1828, the Merriam Company has invested over $3,500,000, almost three times the cost of the 1934 *New International,* so that the statements in *Webster's Third* are backed by over a century of experience, by the evidence of more than 10,000,000 citations, and by the knowledge and skill of a large permanent staff and more than 200 special consultants. To a reviewer, those facts should be rather sobering.

Some editors, however, and some reviewers have not been restrained from prompt attacks. They have criticized the *Third International* for its failure to include expected encyclopedic matter, for its technique of definition, and especially for its treatment of what is called usage; and they have charged Dr. Gove and his associates with unwise innovations motivated by the desire to destroy all standards of better and worse in the use of English. While insisting upon the responsibility of lexicographers, some of the attackers have not been equally alert to the responsibility of critics.

The question of motives can be dismissed at once. The lexicographers at the Merriam Company, it may safely be assumed, have just one motive:

From *College English,* 23 (May 1962). Reprinted by the permission of the National Council of Teachers of English and James Sledd.

to make the best possible dictionaries. They may have failed, in one respect or another; but such innovations as they actually have made have not been made without the most serious and responsible consideration.

The charge of unwise innovation has two parts: first, that an innovation has been made; and second, that it is unwise. Some of the critics have assumed that the editors of the *Third International* have departed from established lexicographical custom by assuming the role of historians, not lawgivers. One reviewer, indeed, to prove his accusation that the lexicographers had abandoned authority for permissiveness, quoted a part of their statement that "the standard of English pronunciation . . . is the usage that now prevails among the educated and cultured people to whom the language is vernacular." He had not bothered to read precisely the same statement in the 1934 *New International*.

More generally, too many of the unfavorable critics have ignored the whole history of English lexicography since Samuel Johnson: they have hurried to denounce an innovation as unwise before establishing the fact of innovation. Already in the eighteenth century, the ideal of the standard and standardizing dictionary had been sharply questioned. The encyclopedist Ephraim Chambers declared his view that "the Dictionary-Writer is not supposed to have any hand in the things he relates; he is no more concerned to make the improvements, or establish the significations, than the historian" to fight the battles he describes. Even Johnson said of himself that he did not "form, but register the language," that he did not "teach men how they should think, but relate how they have hitherto expressed their thoughts"; and when Englishmen a century later set out to make the great *Oxford Dictionary*, they assumed from the beginning that the lexicographer is "an historian" of the language, "not a critic." It may be that professional lexicographers have been on the wrong track for two centuries and that in two hours an amateur can set them straight; but in that event the amateur and not the lexicographer would be the innovator. He would do well, before attempting to put his lawgiving theory into practice, to face Johnson's doubts in that magnificent "Preface" and to ask himself the unanswerable question how rational choice among the resources of a language is possible for the man who does not know what those resources are.

The relation between a dictionary and an encyclopedia is another problem whose history should have been better known to some reviewers. Few lexicographers are likely to solve it either to their own full satisfaction or to the satisfaction of all their readers. From the *Third International*, the objectors miss the gazetteer and the biographical dictionary of the 1934 volume, and they dislike the new decision to restrict the word-list "to generic words . . . as distinguished from proper names that are not generic." Other readers might just as well make opposite complaints. The hairy-nosed wombat and the hickory shuckworm do not greatly interest the average American, who has equally little need to know the incubation period of the ostrich or the gestation period of the elephant, to contemplate the drawing of a milestone marked "Boston 20 miles," or to examine a colorplate of fishes which is a slander to the catfish and the brook trout; and the occasional philologist might hope for a dictionary which explains words and leaves to the encyclopedia, as Murray said, the description of things. But who can say that he knows infallibly how such decisions should be made? Murray did not claim infallibility but admitted inconsistency in his omission of *African* and inclusion of *American*. Since man and the universe cannot be put between two covers, some things must be omitted; "selection is guided by usefulness"; and usefulness can be guessed at but not measured. Readers who can get the use of a Webster's unabridged will have access to an encyclopedia. They should consult it when they need to know about people and places. Meanwhile they may be grateful that the *Third International* has made space for as many quotations as it now includes. A dictionary without quotations is like a table of contents without a book.

There remain, of the critics' favorite subjects, the technique of definition and the matter of usage. The technique of definition is briefly explained in the editor's preface:

> The primary objective of precise, sharp defining has been met through development of a new dictionary style based upon completely analytical one-phrase definitions throughout the book. Since the headword in the definition is intended to be modified only by structural elements restrictive in some degree and essential to each other, the use of commas either to separate or to group has been severely limited, chiefly to units in apposition or in series. The new defining pattern does not provide for a predication which conveys further expository comment. . . . Defining by synonym is carefully avoided by putting all unqualified or undifferentiated terms in small capital letters. Such a term in small capitals should not be considered a definition but a cross-reference to a definition of equivalent meaning that can be substituted for the small capitals.
>
> A large number of verbal illustrations mostly from the mid-twentieth century has been woven into the defining pattern with a view to contributing considerably to the user's interest and understanding by showing a word used in context.

If it is not naively optimistic to expect most critics of a dictionary to agree on anything, general approval may be expected for careful synonymies and for the distinction between a synonym and a definition; and the value of illustrative quotations has been demonstrated by centuries of English lexicography. The objection that not many mid-century authors deserve quotation has already been answered, for it is only another form of the notion that the lexicographer should be a lawgiver and not a historian. It would, moreover, be rash to suggest either that many of the quotations are not particularly informative or that identification by the mere names of the authors makes it impossible to check the quotations or to examine them in their contexts: with 10,000,000 quotations to choose from, the editors must know the possibilities of choice more fully than any critic, and precise references would take up much valuable space.

The definitions themselves are another matter. Without advancing any claim to special competence, an ordinary reader may fairly report that he finds some of the definitions extraordinarily clumsy and hard to follow and that as an English teacher he would not encourage his students to follow the new Merriam-Webster model. The one-phrase definitions of nouns in particular may become confusing because in English it is hard to keep track of the relations among a long series of prepositional phrases, participial phrases, and relative clauses; the reader may simply forget what goes with what, if indeed he ever can find out. A less serious criticism is that the new typeface and the long entries unbroken by indentation are bad for middle-aged eyes. Real mistakes, of course, are extremely rare, but a fisherman may be pardoned an objection to the fourth numbered definition of the noun *keeper* as "a fish large enough to be legally caught." The crime is not catching but keeping an undersized or oversized fish.

Perhaps such a quibble is itself no keeper, and some criticism of the dictionary's treatment of usage has been equally frivolous. An excellent bad example appeared in *Life*, whose editors compressed a remarkable amount of confusion into a single sentence when they attacked "Editor Gove" for "saying that if a word is misused often enough, it becomes acceptable." Though one can argue how much use and by what speakers is enough, consistency would force *Life's* editors into silence. Their sacred kye are scrawnier than Pharaoh's seven kine, and it is shocking that the influence of such a magazine should force learning to debate with ignorance.

Yet so loud a stridulation of critics cannot simply be ignored. There is a real question whether the *Third International*, though justly called "the most comprehensive guide to usage currently available," has recorded usage as precisely as it might have done. Were the editors right to abandon "the status label *colloquial*"? Have they adequately reported not only what people say and write but also those opinions concerning speech and writing which properly enter into their own definitions of *standard* and of *Standard English?* Those are legitimate questions to ask of a dictionary "prepared with a constant regard for the needs of the high school and college student" and of the general reader. However diffidently and respectfully, a reviewer must give the best answers that he can.

Several reasons have been offered, by various authorities, for the abandonment of the label *colloquial.* Those reasons are not all alike. It is one thing to say that we cannot know "whether a word out of context is colloquial or not" (Gove), that lexicographers cannot distinguish the "many different degrees of standard usage" by status labels but can only suggest them by quotations (Gove), or that "the bases for discrimination are often too subtle for exact and understandable verbal statement" (Ives); it is quite another thing to argue against marking words *colloquial* because many readers have wrongly concluded that a word so marked is somehow bad (Ives). In a matter to which the editors must have given their best thought, the variety itself of these justifications and the failure to order them in any coherent and inclusive statement is somewhat puzzling; and the impertinent might be tempted to inquire how 200,000 quotations will enable the inexpert reader to do what 10,000,000 quotations did not make possible for the expert lexicographer or how a dictionary can be made at all if nothing can go into it which the ignorant might misinterpret. One reason for the widespread misinterpretation of the policy adopted is surely that the underlying theory has not been clearly explained.

And that is not all. The very defenses of the new policy appear sometimes to refute the contention that finer discriminations are not possible than those in *Webster's Third.* When the newspapers attack the dictionary for listing words like *double-dome* and *finalize* as standard, defenders reply by citing other slangy or colloquial or much reprobated terms from the columns of those same newspapers. What is the force of the attack or the defense unless the intelligent layman can draw precisely that distinction between "the formal and informal speech and writing of the educated" which the *Third International* refuses to draw for him? If he lacked that ability, both attackers and defenders would be wasting their citations.

Much can be said, of course, about the confusion of styles in modern writing. Perhaps distinctions among styles are now indeed less clear and stable than they were in a less troubled age; perhaps the clumsier writers do ignore the existing distinctions while the sophisticated use them to play sophisticated tunes; perhaps the scrupulously objective lexicographer cannot establish those distinctions from his quotation slips alone. For all that, distinctions do exist. They exist in good writing, and they exist in the linguistic consciousness of the educated. Dr. Gove's definers prove they exist when they give *egghead* as a synonym for *double-dome* but then define *egghead* in impeccably formal terms as "one with intellectual interests or pretensions" or as "a highly educated person." Such opposition between theory and practice strikes even a timid and generally admiring reviewer as rather odd, as though some notion of scientific objectivity should require the scientist to deny that he knows what he knows because he may not know how he knows it.

In the absence, then, of convincing argument to the contrary, a simple reader is left with the uneasy feeling that the abandonment of "*Colloq.*" was a mistake which the introduction of more quotations does not quite rectify and that as a teacher he must now provide foreigners and inexperienced students both with some general principles of linguistic choice and with specific instruction in instances where the new dictionary does not discriminate finely enough among stylistic variants. The dictionary leaves unlabeled many expressions which this teacher would not allow a beginning writer to use in serious exposition or argument except for clearly intended and rather special effects: (*to be caught*) *with one's pants down, dollarwise, stylewise* (*s.v. -wise*), (*to give one*) *the bird, dog* "something inferior of its kind," *to enthuse, to level* "deal frankly," *schmaltz, chintzy, the catbird seat, to roll* "rob," *to send* "delight," *shindig, shook-up, square* "an unsophisticated person," *squirrelly, to goof,* and the like. Enforcing such modest niceties will now be more difficult; for classroom lawyers and irate parents will be able to cite the dictionary which the teacher has taught Johnny how to read but which has collapsed the distinction between formal and informal Standard English. Similar difficulties could occur with various mild obscenities, such as *pissed off* and *pisspoor,* which should be marked not only as slang but with some one of the warning labels that the dictionary attaches to the almost quite adequately recorded four-letter words; and the label *slang* itself might well be more freely used with the various synonyms for *drunk—stewed, stinko, stoned, tight, tanked, sozzled, potted, pie-eyed, feeling no pain, blind, looped, squiffed, boiled, fried, high,* etc. Odzooks!

The convenience of a classroom teacher, however, is a rather petty criterion by which to judge a great dictionary, and the tiny handful of evidence here alleged must not be taken as justifying the shrill lament that *Webster's Third* is "a scandal and a disaster." The wake has been distinctly premature. Both the dictionary and the language it records are likely to survive the keening critics, whose exaggerations are something of a stumbling block themselves. The mere extent of the information in a dictionary unabridged should fix in a reviewer's mind the salutary knowledge that as no one man can make such a book, so no one man can judge it; but the popular reviews of the *Third International* have merely skimmed its surface and have said little of its technical features or substantial accomplishments. The present discussion will conclude with a few slight remarks on some such matters and with the renewed insistence that longer use and more expert study will be necessary before the dictionary can be definitively judged.

Teachers of elementary composition may be especially interested in the dictionary's three well-filled pages on English punctuation. As several recent grammarians have done, the editors attempt to establish definite relations between pointing and intonation, and they pursue that end with some care and vigor: the theory that punctuation may in part be taught by relating it to pitch-contours and to pauses here receives a better-than-average statement.

Yet the composition teacher may still be sceptical. For one thing, no account of English intonation has deserved or won universal acceptance. The editors themselves thus seem to postulate more than the three "pauses" allowed in the Trager-Smith phonology, which their description directly or indirectly follows. What is worse is the failure of the proposed relationships between speech and pointing as one moves from dialect to dialect: rules that may hold in one region do not hold in another. For much Southern American speech and for much Southern British, it is simply not the case that "the rising pause . . . is usually indicated in writing by a comma"; for many speakers and writers in many areas, an exclamation point may correspond to a *low*-pitched "terminal stress" as well as to a high one; and a colon may be used in writing not just for "a fading or sustained pause in speech" but for a "rising pause" or for no pause at all. The editors have weakened their case by stating it too simply and too strongly.

For the linguistically inclined, Mr. Edwin Artin's extensive "Guide to Pronunciation" will have a particular attraction. The "Guide" is just that—a guide; "not a treatise on phonetics" or a structural dialectologist's systematic account of American pronunciation, but an explanation of the way the editors have used their new alphabet in their transcriptions. Though the forgetful will regret that the key is no longer before them at each opening, and though a stern phonemicist might call the whole system sloppy, the new alphabet is an arguable solution to an extremely complex theoretical and practical problem and a definite improvement over the more complicated yet less accurate and more misleading diacritical key in the *Webster's* of 1934. The objective in devising the alphabet "was a set of symbols which would represent each speech sound which distinguishes one word from another and each difference in sound which is associated with some large region of the country" (Ives), so that the editors might record both the formal and the informal pronunciations actually heard in cultivated conversation from speakers of the standard dialects in the various regions. The *Third International* can thus do fuller justice than its predecessor did to regional variation and to modes of speech less artificial than the "formal platform speech" of the earlier work.

Like every competent writer on American pronunciation, Mr. Artin will be criticized as well as praised. He writes, indeed, at a particularly difficult time, when phonological theory is so unsettled that rival groups among the linguists can scarcely communicate with one another. Since pleasing one group of theorists means displeasing its opponents, since it is easily possible to please neither or none, and since Mr. Artin does not include in his "Guide" the sort of general and historical information which could be found in the corresponding section of the 1934 dictionary, perhaps he will not have so large an audience as Kenyon reached. His readers will be the kind who will argue the results of equating the medial consonants of *tidal* and *title* because in some dialects they are phonetically identical or of distinguishing them because the preceding diphthongs may be of different lengths and because the consonants of *tide* and *titular* clearly differ. Other readers, if they find the "Guide" hard going, will not risk too much confusion by limiting their study to the table of symbols and to the short section on pronunciation in the "Explanatory Notes."

Within the dictionary proper, the word-list first invites examination. Like the addenda to the later editions of the *Second*, the vexing miscellaneous entries at the bottoms of the pages are now gone from *Webster's Third*, either dropped or worked into the main alphabet; numerous obsolete words have disappeared, since the cut-off date has been advanced from 1500 to 1755; and further space for additions has been found by rejecting many no longer useful terms from the rapidly changing and never generally current technical vocabulary with which both the *Second* and the *Third International* are stuffed. This plethora of scientific and technical terms, carefully gathered in an elaborate reading program, is of course no plethora at all but only a comfortable supply for the scientist and technologist, who seem pleased with the dictionary's coverage of their fields; and a general dictionary must make room as well for some regionalisms, for a certain amount of recent slang, and for the new words in general use which so eloquently damn our culture. When all this has been done, it would be unfair to complain that perhaps not enough attention has been paid to the distinctive vocabularies of English-speaking nations other than Britain and the United States.

Beyond the word-list, neither space nor the reviewer's competence will allow him to go. He has few complaints about spelling, the only loud one being against *alright;* as far as a layman's knowledge goes, the etymologies are accurate, and beyond that point they remain clear and comprehensible; the discrimination and the arrangement of senses impose silence on the reader who has not studied them with the same care that went into their making; and the synonymies have already proved their practical value. A sweeping conclusion will not be expected of a review whose thesis is that the prematurity of sweeping conclusions has already been sufficiently exemplified, but a moderately serious examination has made a few things perfectly plain about the *Third International.* As a completely new, independent, responsibly edited, unabridged dictionary, no other work can rival it on precisely its own ground. Its merits are infinitely greater than those of the reviews which have lightly questioned them. Time and the experts will ultimately decide its just rank in the world of English lexicography, whether above, below, or alongside its predecessor; but meanwhile it can usefully fill a place in the libraries of a generation.

BERGEN EVANS

But What's a Dictionary For?

The storm of abuse in the popular press that greeted the appearance of
Webster's Third New International Dictionary is a curious phenomenon.
Never has a scholarly work of this stature been attacked with such un-
bridled fury and contempt. An article in the *Atlantic* viewed it as a
"disappointment," a "shock," a "calamity," "a scandal and a disaster."
The New York *Times*, in a special editorial, felt that the work would
"accelerate the deterioration" of the language and sternly accused the
editors of betraying a public trust. The *Journal* of the American Bar
Association saw the publication as "deplorable," "a flagrant example of
lexicographic irresponsibility," "a serious blow to the cause of good
English." *Life* called it "a non-word deluge," "monstrous," "abominable,"
and "a cause for dismay." They doubted that "Lincoln could have
modelled his Gettysburg Address" on it—a concept of how things get
written that throws very little light on Lincoln but a great deal on *Life*.

What underlies all this sound and fury? Is the claim of the G. & C.
Merriam Company, probably the world's greatest dictionary maker, that
the preparation of the work cost $3.5 million, that it required the efforts
of three hundred scholars over a period of twenty-seven years, working
on the largest collection of citations ever assembled in any language—is
all this a fraud, a hoax?

So monstrous a discrepancy in evaluation requires us to examine basic
principles. Just what's a dictionary for? What does it propose to do?
What does the common reader go to a dictionary to find? What has the
purchaser of a dictionary a right to expect for his money?

Before we look at basic principles, it is necessary to interpose two
brief statements. The first of these is that a dictionary is concerned with

From *The Atlantic Monthly*, May 1962. © 1962 by The Atlantic Monthly Company,
Boston 16, Mass. Reprinted by permission of the author.

words. Some dictionaries give various kinds of other useful information. Some have tables of weights and measures on the flyleaves. Some list historical events, and some, home remedies. And there's nothing wrong with their so doing. But the great increase in our vocabulary in the past three decades compels all dictionaries to make more efficient use of their space. And if something must be eliminated, it is sensible to throw out these extraneous things and stick to words.

Yet wild wails arose. The *Saturday Review* lamented that one can no longer find the goddess Astarte under a separate heading—though they point out that a genus of mollusks named after the goddess is included! They seemed to feel that out of sheer perversity the editors of the dictionary stooped to mollusks while ignoring goddesses and that, in some way, this typifies modern lexicography. Mr. Wilson Follett, folletizing (his mental processes demand some special designation) in the *Atlantic,* cried out in horror that one is not even able to learn from the Third International "that the Virgin was Mary the mother of Jesus"!

The second brief statement is that there has been even more progress in the making of dictionaries in the past thirty years than there has been in the making of automobiles. The difference, for example, between the much-touted Second International (1934) and the much-clouted Third International (1961) is not like the difference between yearly models but like the difference between the horse and buggy and the automobile. Between the appearance of these two editions a whole new science related to the making of dictionaries, the science of descriptive linguistics, has come into being.

Modern linguistics gets its charter from Leonard Bloomfield's *Language* (1933). Bloomfield, for thirteen years professor of Germanic philology at the University of Chicago and for nine years professor of linguistics at Yale, was one of those inseminating scholars who can't be relegated to any department and don't dream of accepting established categories and procedures just because they're established. He was as much an anthropologist as a linguist, and his concepts of language were shaped not by Strunk's *Elements of Style* but by his knowledge of Cree Indian dialects.

The broad general findings of the new science are:

1. All languages are systems of human conventions, not systems of natural laws. The first—and essential—step in the study of any language is observing and setting down precisely what happens when native speakers speak it.

2. Each language is unique in its pronunciation, grammar, and vocabulary. It cannot be described in terms of logic or of some theoretical, ideal language. It cannot be described in terms of any other language, or even in terms of its own past.

3. All languages are dynamic rather than static, and hence a "rule" in any language can only be a statement of contemporary practice. Change is constant—and normal.

4. "Correctness" can rest only upon usage, for the simple reason that there is nothing else for it to rest on. And all usage is relative.

From these propositions it follows that a dictionary is good only insofar as it is a comprehensive and accurate description of current usage. And to be comprehensive it must include some indication of social and regional associations.

New dictionaries are needed because English has changed more in the past two generations than at any other time in its history. It has had to adapt to extraordinary cultural and technological changes, two world wars, unparalleled changes in transportation and communication, and unprecedented movements of populations.

More subtly, but pervasively, it has changed under the influence of mass education and the growth of democracy. As written English is used by increasing millions and for more reasons than ever before, the language has become more utilitarian and more informal. Every publication in America today includes pages that would appear, to the purist of forty years ago, unbuttoned gibberish. Not that they are; they simply show that you can't hold the language of one generation up as a model for the next.

It's not that you mustn't. You *can't*. For example, in the issue in which *Life* stated editorially that it would follow the Second International, there were over forty words, constructions, and meanings which are in the Third International but not in the Second. The issue of the New York *Times* which hailed the Second International as the authority to which it would adhere and the Third International as a scandal and a betrayal which it would reject used one hundred and fifty-three separate words, phrases, and constructions which are listed in the Third International but not in the Second and nineteen others which are condemned in the Second. Many of them are used many times, more than three hundred such uses in all. The Washington *Post*, in an editorial captioned "Keep Your Old Webster's," says, in the first sentence, "don't throw it away," and in the second, "hang on to it." But the old Webster's labels *don't* "colloquial" and doesn't include "hang on to," in this sense, at all.

In short, all of these publications are written in the language that the Third International describes, even the very editorials which scorn it. And this is no coincidence, because the Third International isn't setting up any new standards at all; it is simply describing what *Life*, the Washington *Post*, and the New York *Times* are doing. Much of the dictionary's material comes from these very publications, the *Times*, in particular, furnishing more of its illustrative quotations than any other newspaper.

And the papers have no choice. No journal or periodical could sell a single issue today if it restricted itself to the American language of twenty-eight years ago. It couldn't discuss half the things we are interested in, and its style would seem stiff and cumbrous. If the editorials were serious, the public—and the stockholders—have reason to be grateful that the writers on these publications are more literate than the editors.

And so back to our questions: what's a dictionary for, and how, in 1962, can it best do what it ought to do? The demands are simple. The common reader turns to a dictionary for information about the spelling, pronunciation, meaning, and proper use of words. He wants to know what is current and respectable. But he wants—and has a right to—the truth, the full truth. And the full truth about any language, and especially about American English today, is that there are many areas in which certainty is impossible and simplification is misleading.

Even in so settled a matter as spelling, a dictionary cannot always be absolute. *Theater* is correct, but so is *theatre*. And so are *traveled* and *travelled, plow* and *plough, catalog* and *catalogue,* and scores of other variants. The reader may want a single certainty. He may have taken an unyielding position in an argument, he may have wagered in support of his conviction and may demand that the dictionary "settle" the matter. But neither his vanity nor his purse is any concern of the dictionary's; it must record the facts. And the fact here is that there are many words in our language which may be spelled, with equal correctness, in either of two ways.

So with pronunciation. A citizen listening to his radio might notice that James B. Conant, Bernard Baruch, and Dwight D. Eisenhower pronounce *economics* as ECKuhnomiks, while A. Whitney Griswold, Adlai Stevenson, and Herbert Hoover pronounce it EEKuhnomiks. He turns to the dictionary to see which of the two pronunciations is "right" and finds that they are both acceptable.

Has he been betrayed? Has the dictionary abdicated its responsibility? Should it say that one *must* speak like the president of Harvard or like the president of Yale, like the thirty-first President of the United States or like the thirty-fourth? Surely it's none of its business to make a choice. Not because of the distinction of these particular speakers; lexicography, like God, is no respecter of persons. But because so widespread and conspicuous a use of two pronunciations among people of this elevation shows that there *are* two pronunciations. Their speaking establishes the fact which the dictionary must record.

Among the "enormities" with which *Life* taxes the Third International it its listing of "the common mispronunciation" *heighth*. That it is labeled a "dialectal variant" seems, somehow, to compound the felony. But one hears the word so pronounced, and if one professes to give a full account of American English in the 1960s, one has to take some cognizance of it. All people do not possess *Life's* intuitive perception that the word is so "monstrous" that even to list it as a dialect variation is to merit scorn. Among these, by the way, was John Milton, who, in one of the greatest passages in all literature, besought the Holy Spirit to raise him to the "highth" of his great argument. And even the *Oxford English Dictionary* is so benighted as to list it, in full boldface, right alongside of *Height* as a variant that has been in the language since at least 1290.

Now there are still, apparently, millions of Americans who retain, in this as in much else, some of the speech of Milton. This particular pronunciation seems to be receding, but the *American Dialect Dictionary* still records instances of it from almost every state on the Eastern seaboard and notes that it is heard from older people and "occasionally in educated speech," "common with good speakers," "general," "widespread."

Under these circumstances, what is a dictionary to do? Since millions speak the word this way, the pronunciation can't be ignored. Since it has been in use as long as we have any record of English and since it has been used by the greatest writers, it can't be described as substandard or slang. But it is heard now only in certain localities. That makes it a dialectal pronunciation, and an honest dictionary will list it as such. What else can it do? Should it do?

The average purchaser of a dictionary uses it most often, probably, to find out what a word "means." As a reader, he wants to know what an author intended to convey. As a speaker or writer, he wants to know what a word will convey to his auditors. And this, too, is complex, subtle, and forever changing.

An illustration is furnished by an editorial in the Washington *Post* (January 17, 1962). After a ringing appeal to those who "love truth and accuracy" and the usual bombinations about "abdication of authority" and "barbarism," the editorial charges the Third International with "pretentious and obscure verbosity" and specifically instances its definition of "so simple an object as a door."

The definition reads:

> a movable piece of firm material or a structure supported usu. along one side and swinging on pivots or hinges, sliding along a groove, rolling up and down, revolving as one of four leaves, or folding like an

accordion by means of which an opening may be closed or kept open for passage into or out of a building, room, or other covered enclosure or a car, airplane, elevator, or other vehicle.

Then follows a series of special meanings, each particularly defined and, where necessary, illustrated by a quotation.

Since, aside from roaring and admonishing the "gentlemen from Springfield" that "accuracy and brevity are virtues," the *Post's* editorial fails to explain what is wrong with the definition, we can only infer from "so simple" a thing that the writer takes the plain, downright, man-in-the-street attitude that a door is a door and any damn fool knows that.

But if so, he has walked into one of lexicography's biggest booby traps: the belief that the obvious is easy to define. Whereas the opposite is true. Anyone can give a fair description of the strange, the new, or the unique. It's the commonplace, the habitual, that challenges definition, for its very commonness compels us to define it in uncommon terms. Dr. Johnson was ridiculed on just this score when his dictionary appeared in 1755. For two hundred years his definition of a network as "any thing reticulated or decussated, at equal distances, with interstices between the intersections" has been good for a laugh. But in the merriment one thing is always overlooked: no one has yet come up with a better definition! Subsequent dictionaries defined it as a mesh and then defined a mesh as a network. That's simple, all right.

Anyone who attempts sincerely to state what the word *door* means in the United States of America today can't take refuge in a log cabin. There has been an enormous proliferation of closing and demarking devices and structures in the past twenty years, and anyone who tries to thread his way through the many meanings now included under *door* may have to sacrifice brevity to accuracy and even have to employ words that a limited vocabulary may find obscure.

Is the entrance to a tent a door, for instance? And what of the thing that seals the exit of an airplane? Is this a door? Or what of those sheets and jets of air that are now being used, in place of old-fashioned oak and hinges, to screen entrances and exits. Are they doors? And what of those accordion-like things that set off various sections of many modern apartments? The fine print in the lease takes it for granted that they are doors and that spaces demarked by them are rooms—and the rent is computed on the number of rooms.

Was I gypped by the landlord when he called the folding contraption that shuts off my kitchen a door? I go to the Second International, which the editor of the *Post* urges me to use in preference to the Third International. Here I find that a door is

The movable frame or barrier of boards, or other material, usually turning on hinges or pivots or sliding, by which an entranceway into a house or apartment is closed and opened; also, a similar part of a piece of furniture, as in a cabinet or bookcase.

This is only forty-six words, but though it includes the cellar door, it excludes the barn door and the accordion-like thing.

So I go on to the Third International. I see at once that the new definition is longer. But I'm looking for accuracy, and if I must sacrifice brevity to get it, then I must. And, sure enough, in the definition which raised the *Post's* blood pressure, I find the words "folding like an accordion." The thing *is* a door, and my landlord is using the word in one of its currently accepted meanings.

We don't turn to a work of reference merely for confirmation. We all have words in our vocabularies which we have misunderstood, and to come on the true meaning of one of these words is quite a shock. All our complacency and self-esteem rise to oppose the discovery. But eventually we must accept the humiliation and laugh it off as best we can.

Some, often those who have set themselves up as authorities, stick to their error and charge the dictionary with being in a conspiracy against them. They are sure that their meaning is the only "right" one. And when the dictionary doesn't bear them out they complain about "permissive" attitudes instead of correcting their mistake.

The New York *Times* and the *Saturday Review* both regarded as contemptibly "permissive" the fact that one meaning of one word was illustrated by a quotation from Polly Adler. But a rudimentary knowledge of the development of any language would have told them that the underworld has been a far more active force in shaping and enriching speech than all the synods that have ever convened. Their attitude is like that of the patriot who canceled his subscription to the *Dictionary of American Biography* when he discovered that the very first volume included Benedict Arnold!

The ultimate of "permissiveness," singled out by almost every critic for special scorn, was the inclusion in the Third International of *finalize*. It was this, more than any other one thing, that was given as the reason for sticking to the good old Second International—that "peerless authority on American English," as the *Times* called it. But if it was such an authority, why didn't they look into it? They would have found *finalize* if they had.

And why shouldn't it be there? It exists. It's been recorded for two generations. Millions employ it every day. Two Presidents of the United States—men of widely differing cultural backgrounds—have used it in formal statements. And so has the Secretary-General of the United Nations, a man of unusual linguistic attainments. It isn't permitting the word but omitting it that would break faith with the reader. Because it is exactly the sort of word we want information about.

To list it as substandard would be to imply that it is used solely by the ignorant and the illiterate. But this would be a misrepresentation: President Kennedy and U Thant are highly educated men, and both are articulate and literate. It isn't even a freak form. On the contrary, it is a classic example of a regular process of development in English, a process which has given us such thoroughly accepted words as *generalize, minimize, formalize,* and *verbalize.* Nor can it be dismissed on logical grounds or on the ground that it is a mere duplication of *complete.* It says something that *complete* doesn't say and says it in a way that is significant in the modern bureaucratic world: one usually *completes* something which he has initiated but *finalizes* the work of others.

One is free to dislike the word. I don't like it. But the editor of a dictionary has to examine the evidence for a word's existence and seek it in context to get, as clearly and closely as he can, the exact meaning that it conveys to those who use it. And if it is widely used by well-educated, literate, reputable people, he must list it as a standard word. He is not compiling a volume of his own prejudices.

An individual's use of his native tongue is the surest index to his position within his community. And those who turn to a dictionary expect from it some statement of the current status of a word or a grammatical construction. And it is with the failure to assume this function that modern lexicography has been most fiercely charged. The charge is based on a naïve assumption that simple labels can be attached in all instances. But they can't. Some words are standard in some constructions and not in others. There may be as many shades of status as of meaning, and modern lexicography instead of abdicating this function has fulfilled it to a degree utterly unknown to earlier dictionaries.

Consider the word *fetch,* meaning to "go get and bring to." Until recently a standard word of full dignity ("Fetch me, I pray thee, a little water in a vessel"—I Kings 17:10), it has become slightly tainted. Perhaps the command latent in it is resented as undemocratic. Or maybe its use in training dogs to retrieve has made some people feel that it is an undignified word to apply to human beings. But, whatever the reason, there is a growing uncertainty about its status, and hence it is the sort of word that conscientious people look up in a dictionary.

Will they find it labeled "good" or "bad"? Neither, of course, because either applied indiscriminately would be untrue. The Third International lists nineteen different meanings of the verb *to fetch*. Of these some are labeled "dialectal," some "chiefly dialectal," some "obsolete," one "chiefly Scottish," and two "not in formal use." The primary meaning—"to go after and bring back"—is not labeled and hence can be accepted as standard, accepted with the more assurance because the many shades of labeling show us that the word's status has been carefully considered.

On grammatical questions the Third International tries to be equally exact and thorough. Sometimes a construction is listed without comment, meaning that in the opinion of the editors it is unquestionably respectable. Sometimes a construction carries the comment "used by speakers and writers on all educational levels though disapproved by some grammarians." Or the comment may be "used in substandard speech and formerly also by reputable writers." Or "less often in standard than in substandard speech." Or simply "dial."

And this very accurate reporting is based on evidence which is presented for our examination. One may feel that the evidence is inadequate or that the evaluation of it is erroneous. But surely, in the face of classification so much more elaborate and careful than any known heretofore, one cannot fly into a rage and insist that the dictionary is "out to destroy . . . every vestige of linguistic punctilio . . . every criterion for distinguishing between better usages and worse."

Words, as we have said, are continually shifting their meanings and connotations and hence their status. A word which has dignity, say, in the vocabulary of an older person may go down in other people's estimation. Like *fetch*. The older speaker is not likely to be aware of this and will probably be inclined to ascribe the snickers of the young at his speech to that degeneration of manners which every generation has deplored in its juniors. But a word which is coming up in the scale—like *jazz*, say, or, more recently, *crap*—will strike his ear at once. We are much more aware of offenses given us than of those we give. And if he turns to a dictionary and finds the offending word listed as standard—or even listed, apparently —his response is likely to be an outburst of indignation.

But the dictionary can neither snicker nor fulminate. It records. It will offend many, no doubt, to find the expression *wise up*, meaning to inform or to become informed, listed in the Third International with no restricting label. To my aging ears it still sounds like slang. But the evidence— quotations from the *Kiplinger Washington Letter* and the *Wall Street Journal*—convinces me that it is I who am out of step, lagging behind. If such publications have taken to using *wise up* in serious contexts, with no punctuational indication of irregularity, then it is obviously respectable. And finding it so listed and supported, I can only say that it's nice to be informed and sigh to realize that I am becoming an old fogy. But, of course, I don't have to use it (and I'll be damned if I will! "Let them smile, as I do now, At the old forsaken bough Where I cling").

In part, the trouble is due to the fact that there is no standard for standard. Ideas of what is proper to use in serious, dignified speech and writing are changing—and with breathtaking rapidity. This is one of the major facts of contemporary American English. But it is no more the dictionary's business to oppose this process than to speed it up.

Even in our standard speech some words are more dignified and some more informal than others, and dictionaries have tried to guide us through these uncertainties by marking certain words and constructions as "colloquial," meaning "inappropriate in a formal situation." But this distinction, in the opinion of most scholars, has done more harm than good. It has created the notion that these particular words are inferior, when actually they might be the best possible words in an informal statement. And so—to the rage of many reviewers—the Third International has dropped this label. Not all labels, as angrily charged, but only this one out of a score. And the doing so may have been an error, but it certainly didn't constitute "betrayal" or "abandoning of all distinctions." It was intended to end a certain confusion.

In all the finer shades of meaning, of which the status of a word is only one, the user is on his own, whether he likes it or not. Despite *Life's* artless assumption about the Gettysburg Address, nothing worth writing is written *from* a dictionary. The dictionary, rather, comes along afterwards and describes what *has been* written.

Words in themselves are not dignified, or silly, or wise, or malicious. But they can be used in dignified, silly, wise, or malicious ways by dignified, silly, wise, or malicious people. *Egghead,* for example, is a perfectly legitimate word, as legitimate as *highbrow* or *long-haired.* But there is something very wrong and very undignified, by civilized standards, in a belligerent dislike for intelligence and education. *Yak* is an amusing word for persistent chatter. Anyone could say, "We were just yakking over a cup of coffee," with no harm to his dignity. But to call a Supreme Court decision *yakking* is to be vulgarly insulting and so, undignified. Again, there's nothing wrong with *confab* when it's appropriate. But when the work of a great research project, employing hundreds of distinguished scholars over several decades and involving the honor of one of the greatest publishing houses in the world, is described as *confabbing* (as the New York *Times* editorially described the preparation of the Third International), the use of this particular word asserts that the lexicographers had merely sat around and talked idly. And the statement becomes undignified—if not, indeed, slanderous.

The lack of dignity in such statements is not in the words, nor in the dictionaries that list them, but in the hostility that deliberately seeks this tone of expression. And in expressing itself the hostility frequently shows that those who are expressing it don't know how to use a dictionary. Most of the reviewers seem unable to read the Third International and unwilling to read the Second.

The *American Bar Association Journal,* for instance, in a typical outburst ("a deplorable abdication of responsibility"), picked out for special scorn the inclusion in the Third International of the word *irregardless.* "As far as the new Webster's is concerned," said the *Journal,* "this meaningless verbal bastard is just as legitimate as any other word in the dictionary." Thirty seconds spent in examining the book they were so roundly condemning would have shown them that in it *irregardless* is labeled "nonstand"—which means "nonstandard," which means "not conforming to the usage generally characteristic of educated native speakers of the language." Is that "just as legitimate as any other word in the dictionary"?

The most disturbing fact of all is that the editors of a dozen of the most influential publications in America today are under the impression that *authoritative* must mean *authoritarian.* Even the "permissive" Third International doesn't recognize this identification—editors' attitudes being not yet, fortunately, those of the American people. But the Fourth International may have to.

The new dictionary may have many faults. Nothing that tries to meet an ever-changing situation over a terrain as vast as contemporary English can hope to be free of them. And much in it is open to honest, and informed, disagreement. There can be linguistic objection to the eradication of proper names. The removal of guides to pronunciation from the foot of every page may not have been worth the valuable space it saved. The new method of defining words of many meanings has disadvantages as well as advantages. And of the half million or more definitions, hundreds, possibly thousands, may seem inadequate or imprecise. To some (of whom I am one) the omission of the label "colloquial" will seem meritorious; to others it will seem a loss.

But one thing is certain: anyone who solemnly announces in the year 1962 that he will be guided in matters of English usage by a dictionary published in 1934 is talking ignorant and pretentious nonsense.

PART TWO

The History of English

Why study the history of our language? Why not ignore the past and simply study today's language, the one we actually use and wish to use more effectively? The essays in this section say, in effect, that if we know how our language got to be the way it is, we are likely to use it with increased confidence and judgment. Strictly speaking, we are all from the provinces, but we need not be provincial.

In the first essay, Margaret Schlauch takes us across Europe so that we can hear similarities in words and sentences from one country to another which imply descent from a few ancient language families. From one of those families, the Germanic, modern English developed. The stages of that development are outlined by the late E. G. Mathews and Professor J. N. Hook of the University of Illinois. A closer view of one stage is offered by Professor Albert C. Baugh of the University of Pennsylvania, who describes how the vocabulary of English was greatly enlarged during the Renaissance by borrowings from classical and foreign languages. The reactions of Elizabethans to this process provide an instructive historical background to modern reactions to the rapid growth and change in our word-stock in recent years. In the concluding essay in this section, Professor Albert H. Marckwardt of the University of Michigan describes the language which Elizabethans brought to America in early colonial times.

MARGARET SCHLAUCH

Family Relationships Among Languages

In happier times, it was possible to cross the length and breadth of
Europe by train in so few days that the journey could still be conveniently
measured by hours. Paris to Berlin, fifteen hours; Berlin to Moscow, forty
hours; Berlin to Milan, twenty hours. In certain parts of that complex
and explosive continent, it was necessary to change one's official language
three or four times in the course of a pilgrimage which in the United
States would appear to be, in length, a mere uneventful hop. You could
cross the English Channel and find yourself greeted within a couple of
hours by the slow even courtesy of a Dutch immigration officer; a few
more hours and a Belgian would appear at the door of your compartment
and, in French idiom sounding somehow un-French, make the same
routine demands with a courtesy of a different tang. Then eastwards, you
could encounter the clipped precision of German officialdom, followed
by softer accents emanating from the speakers of a series of Western
Slavonic national languages. And to the south there lay, also easily accessible, the varied music of Mediterranean Romance languages, maintaining
a certain insidious charm even as spoken by the stampers of passports and
openers of trunks. The landscape might not change perceptibly at the
political borders, but there would be a stir in your compartment, a coming and going of people, new phrases to be caught on the wing as
travelers passed by in the corridor; and as you sat in your corner eagerly
experiencing the linguistic kaleidoscope of the continent, you would strain
to catch the first sounds of the new idiom as fresh companions settled
themselves about you. The Dutch commercial travelers condoling or con-
gratulating with one another in measured tones on the current market
would give place to a group of French *permissionaires* exchanging rapid
chaff on the exploits of their leave, in an esoteric professional jargon of

considerable gayety; their still-warm places might be occupied by a do-
mestic group on the German border, *Vati* and *Mutti* complete with
Bruderlein and *Schwesterlein* who were sure to be the silent, well-be-
haved recipients of a series of solicitous imperatives. Cries from the
station platforms might echo in your mind in rich polyglot confusion at
the end of such a long journey eastwards: *"Cigarren! Cigaretten!"—"Paris-
Soir! Figaro!"—"Abfahrt!"—"Het is al tien uur."—"A la aduana . . ." "Agua
mineral, chocolade . . ." "Priidjote, pozhaluista!"*

Certainly these differences in tongue would be bewildering in the extreme to any traveler, until instruction and experience could bring order
out of the chaos of aural impressions. But an enthusiast who set out to
acquire some smattering of the languages in a series of countries to be so
traversed would soon begin to observe some curious parallelisms in the
words learnt to designate the same object. For two or even more languages he would find repeated similarities, remote but still perceptible,
not only in individual words but in the manner in which these words were
put together in sentences. Naïve observers explain these similarities by
talking of a vague "mixture" or "corruption." When they come across a
sentence in Dutch like *"Ik heb het gekoopt voor mijnen zoon"* they are
pleased and surprised to observe how much it resembles English "I have
bought it for my son" or German *"Ich habe es fur meinen Sohn gekauft."*
And so they inform you gleefully, with all the assurance of a non-linguist:
"Dutch is a funny language; it's a mixture of English and corrupt German."

A Hollander would of course protest vehemently that Dutch is no more
corrupt, funny, or mixed than any other national speech in Europe, and he
would be quite right. There is another way of explaining its gratifying
resemblance to things we already know.

Let us take a single sentence and follow its land-changes, its mutations,
over a fairly wide territory—as territories are reckoned in Europe.

Suppose you begin a trip in Sweden, and you find yourself seated with
a mother who is anxiously supervising the box lunch of several small
children. She turns solicitously to one of them and says, "Did you get any
cookies (or apples, or candies)?" And the child replies: "Yes, Mother, I
have three." In Swedish that would be, *"Ja, moder, jag har tre."* In Norway, to the west, or Denmark, to the south, it would be almost the same:
"Já, mor, jeg har tre."

The slight differences in vowel sound and in sentence melody do not
disguise the fact that we are listening to the same words. A moment's
reflection will suggest the right explanation. We are not confronted by a
borrowing or "mixture" in any case. The three Scandinavian languages
mentioned are equally ancient. At one time they were identical, for all

practical purposes. A traveler in olden times (let us say the ninth century) could traverse the whole length of Norway or Sweden and pass to the southern extremity of Denmark without any change in his speech. Everywhere he would hear children say: "*Ja, móðir, ek hefi þrjá.*" (The last word was pronounced [θrja:].) The changes and differences developed during centuries, rather rapidly in Denmark, more slowly in Sweden. As a result, we now have diversity where once there was unity. Three national languages, equally venerable, have replaced Old Scandinavian. They are extremely close relatives, but none could claim parental precedence over the others. If any branch of Scandinavian could exact respect on the grounds of conservatism (that is, fidelity to the parent, the Old Scandinavian) it would be modern Icelandic, spoken in the distant island which Norwegians settled in the ninth century. Here children still say: "*Já, móðir, ek hefi þrjá.*" The values of the vowels have changed slightly; that is all.

When the train crosses from Denmark into Germany, a greater change becomes apparent. Here the maternal inquiry elicits the answer, "*Ja, Mutter, ich habe drei.*" In Holland or the Flemish-speaking parts of Belgium, tow-headed lads murmur, "*Ja, moeder* (or *moer*) *ik heb drie.*" The cleavage is greater, but the separate words still look distinctly familiar. We can even group the versions of our little sentence to show where two or more languages show particular likeness:

ICELANDIC:	*Já, móðir, ek hefi þrjá.*
SWEDISH:	*Ja, moder, jag har tre.*
DANISH:	*Ja, mor, jeg har tre.*
NORWEGIAN:	*Ja, mor, jeg har tre.*
GERMAN:	*Ja, Mutter, ich habe drei.*
DUTCH:	*Ja, Moeder, ik heb drie.*
FLEMISH:	*Ja, Moeder, ik heb drie.*
ENGLISH:	Yes, Mother, I have three.

German stands somewhat apart because its consonants show certain peculiarities: it alone has a [t] between vowels (that is, intervocalic) in the word for mother. Still, it is clear that we are still dealing with variations on the same theme.

Just as the Scandinavian examples revealed close kinship among themselves, so all of those in the extended list show some degree of relationship with one another. Sentences betraying the close linguistic ties within this same group could be multiplied indefinitely. Such being the case, we are justified in speaking of a "family" of languages, borrowing a metaphor from the realm of human relations.

PARENT GERMANIC

Detailed comparisons of this sort indicate that all the members of this Germanic group go back to a single parent language, now lost, spoken as a unity somewhere between the first century B.C. and the first A.D. We call this lost parent language Primitive Germanic. Its modern descendants are grouped into what is known as the Germanic family of European languages. English is one of them. The precise geographical location of Primitive Germanic is not known. We can surmise the nature of its sounds (*phonology*) and inflections (*morphology*) with what is probably fair accuracy, however, because of some early literature and inscriptions dating back to a time when the separate descendants had as yet separated very little from one another. The runic inscription on the Gallebus horn belongs to this early period. It was Old Scandinavian, but it might almost have been composed in an early form of any of the others mentioned.

By comparative study it has been established which sounds in the quoted words are most faithful to the original language. We know that English has preserved the initial consonant of the word "three" [θ] as spoken in Primitive Germanic; but that Icelandic, Flemish, and Dutch have kept the consonant at the end of the first person pronoun singular (*ik*), which has been lost in English and transformed in the others. Back of the multiplicity of extant forms we can feel our way to the existence of the single speech called parent Germanic.

ROMANCE LANGUAGES

But now let us continue the journey south. In Belgium our anxious Flemish mother may be replaced by a fellow-country-woman who speaks French. Her child will say something strikingly different from anything heard so far. "*Oui, mère* (or *maman*), *j'en ai trois.*" As the train goes southwards towards that fertile cradle of cultures, the Mediterranean basin, it may be routed towards the Pyrenees, or across the Alps into Italy. If it should cross the Iberian peninsula you would hear in Spain: "*Si madre,* (*yo*) *tengo tres;* and in Portugal: "*Sim, mãe, tenho tres.*" But if it should take you across the barrier which Hannibal—even Hannibal— found all but impassable, down the steep slopes to the smiling Lombard plains, you would hear: "*Si, madre, ce n'ho tre.*" And even across the Adriatic, on the far side of the Balkan peninsula, hardy descendants of the Roman army and Roman colonists will be saying in Rumanian: "*Da, mama mea, eu am trei.*"

The similarities are apparent:

FRENCH:	*Oui, mère, j'en ai trois.*
SPANISH:	*Si, madre, (yo) tengo tres.*
PORTUGUESE:	*Sim, mãe, tenho tres.*
ITALIAN:	*Si, madre, ce n'ho tre.*
RUMANIAN:	*Da, mama mea, eu am trei.*

The situation is comparable to the one which diverted and possibly mystified you in Germanic territory. You have been traversing lands where the people communicate with one another in tongues clearly descended from a single parent. This time the parent language was a form of Latin: not the solemn speech, stilted and formal, which was reserved for polite literature and speeches in the forum, but the popular or "vulgar" Latin spoken by common people throughout the length and breadth of the Roman territory. Plain soldiers, tavern keepers, itinerant merchants, freedmen, small traders, naturalized citizens of all the polyglot Roman provinces, must have used this form of discourse as an international *lingua franca*. In this idiom they bought and sold, exchanged jokes, flirted, lamented, and consoled with one another. We know from late written documents and inscriptions (especially those on the humbler tombstones of poor folk) just how ungrammatical, rapid, informal, and even slangy this Latin was, compared with the intricate and highly mannered periods of a Cicero. People had become impatient with the many case endings required in classical Latin, and were reducing them to two or three. Even these were treated with playful carelessness. The verb was handled in a different way—a more vivid one—to show changes in tense; and the word order was simplified. Moreover, slang words triumphed completely over traditional ones in some provinces. Ordinary people in Gaul (perhaps emulating the jargon of the army) stopped referring to the human head as *caput,* and substituted *testa* or "pot," from which comes modern French *tête*. It is as if all persons speaking English should have fallen into the way of saying "my bean" for the same object, so that it became the accepted word, while "head" was lost entirely.

The popular Roman speech differed from one province to another because popular locutions do tend always to be regional, and because the Romans came in contact with widely differing types of native speech. Thus the pronunciation and even the grammar were affected by the underlying populations. In one place the Latin word *habere* continued to be used for "to have"; in the Spanish peninsula, however, it so happened that *tenere,* meaning "to hold," came to be used in its place in the more general sense of "to have." That is why our imaginary Spanish child says *tengo* instead of any form of the classical *habere*. The number "three," on the other hand, varies only slightly in the series of Romance sentences quoted. The numbers have remained fairly stable in the various daughter languages perpetuated from vulgar Latin. One of the factors tending to preserve a similarity in them throughout the ages has been their similar experience in developing a strong stress accent during the transition to the Middle Ages. This new accentuation caused similar losses in unaccented syllables in a given word in all Mediterranean areas. There were differences, of course, in the forms that emerged; but certainly not enough to make the results unrecognizably alien to one another.

The neo-Latin languages (if the expression may be permitted) give us another example, therefore, of a family which bears its signs of consanguinity very legibly on the external aspect of each of its members. In Roman times, Latin itself could claim cousins (in the ancient *Italic* group) which have since been lost.

THE SLAVIC FAMILY

And here is one further example of language relationship which may metaphorically be called close consanguinity. In eastern Europe a sharp-eared traveler on an international train will also have an opportunity to detect fundamental similarity behind the changing visages of national speech. A farflung territory is occupied by people speaking *Slavic* languages and dialects. It would be possible to pursue the transformation of our key sentence addressed to an imaginary Slavic mother to the east as follows:

CZECHISH:	*Ano, matko, mam tři.*
POLISH:	*Tak, matko, man trzy.*
RUSSIAN:	*Da, matj, u menjá tri.*

When our international train crosses into the Soviet Union, it will pass through various sections of Russia showing distinct dialect colorings. Ukrainian, for instance, shows enough differentiation to be dignified as a national language, with an official spelling of its own. Even an untutored eye, however, can see how close it is to the official language of Great Russia, the classical medium of literature known to the world as "Russian." In the Balkan states, South Slavic languages show these perceptible nuances of our chosen theme. For instance, the Bulgarian version of it would be: "*Da, maika, imom tri.*"

Once again, we are justified in assuming that centuries ago there was a single language from which these cousins descended. About the seventh century it was probably still fairly unified. In the ninth century a southern dialect of this early Slavic (Old Bulgarian) was written down in a translation of the Bible made by Saints Cyril and Methodius. The text helps us to get quite a clear picture of parent Slavic, just as runic inscriptions bring us close to Primitive Germanic, and unofficial documents of the Roman Empire tell us much about Vulgar Latin.

INDO-EUROPEAN, PARENT OF PARENTS

Slavic, Romance, and Germanic represent three families of languages spoken in Europe today. But surely it must be clear that similarities link these families to one another besides linking the smaller subdivisions within each given family. In *all* the national languages surveyed so far, it will be noticed, the word for "mother" began with the labial nasal [m]; in a considerable number a dental [t], [ð], or [d] appeared in the middle of the word after the first vowel. Likewise in *all* of the languages listed, "three" began with a dental [t], [d], or [θ], followed by an [r]. Why is this?

Clearly, at a still earlier period than the days of early (prehistoric) Germanic and Slavonic, and of Vulgar Latin, there must have been a more ancient and inclusive unity which embraced all three.

The same procedure, if pursued farther, would have revealed to us other major families belonging to the same larger embracing unity in Europe and parts of Asia. These are:

Celtic, including Irish, Highland Scottish, Welsh, and Breton. (In modern Irish, "mother" is *mathair* and "three" is *tri*.)

Baltic, including Lettish, Lithuanian, and an extinct dialect once spoken in the territory of modern Prussia (Old Prussian). The word for "mother" is *motina*, not closely related to the cognates already cited. *Tris* for "three" is, on the other hand, an obvious cognate.

Hellenic, including modern Greek dialects, some of which go back to very ancient times. (An ancient Greek dialect, Attic, spoken in the city of Athens, produced a body of literature of enduring splendor. Its word for "mother" was *matèr* and for "three," *treîs*. This is the classical language studied in school.)

Albanian, the national language of Albania, with no close relatives outside its own borders. Here "three" is *tre*; but the word for "mother" is not related to the forms in the above languages. A new form, *nona*, has replaced the Indo-European term preserved elsewhere.

Armenian, spoken in Armenia (between Europe and Asia Minor), is, like Albanian, a language with many diverse elements borrowed from outside, but it has an independent history traceable back to the fifth or sixth century A.D. Its word for "mother," *mair*, is easily recognizable as a cognate of the others given; not so, however, is *erek* for "three."

Even in Asia there are languages with venerable histories and rich literary heritage which can be recognized as members of the same linguistic clan:

Indian, including Hindustani, Bengali, Marathi, and Hindi. These dialects are descended from Old Indian, preserved to us in a classical literary form (Sanskrit) which dates back to the fifteen century B.C. or even several hundred years earlier. Sanskrit, despite its great antiquity, still shows close generic resemblance to its modern European cousins. Its word for "mother" was *mātr* and for "three," *tri.*

Iranian, very closely related to Sanskrit, was spoken in the Persian highlands while Indian was spreading over the interior of India. It produced an early literature in the form of Zoroastrian hymns. Since those ancient times Persian has been subjected to large foreign infiltration, notably Arabic, but its structure still reveals its kinship with the other groups listed.

Hittite, a language spoken by people frequently mentioned in the Bible, is now extinct. Cuneiform inscriptions give us enough material to reveal its fundamental character. Some sort of relationship it surely must have had with the members of the broad family of families now being surveyed, but the precise nature of that relationship is still under discussion.

Tocharian, now extinct, is represented by some fragmentary texts (probably antedating the tenth century), which were discovered in eastern Turkestan in a Buddhist monastery. The material is too scanty to permit of definitive analysis, but it shows relationship to the above subsidiary groups.

Our railroad trip beginning with Germanic territory has taken us far afield, even to the shores of the Indus River in Asia. Even so, and despite the most baffling diversities, skilled comparison of key words has been able to establish that the miniature families surveyed do undoubtedly belong to the same large, inclusive family already postulated to account for likenesses observed among Germanic, Slavonic, and Romance (from Old Italic).

Back of the smaller families lay a single family; attached to this single family it is almost certain there must have been a single language. We call the whole family by the name "Indo-European," a term generally preferred today to "Indo-Germanic" or "Aryan," both of which could easily be misunderstood. That is to say, every language mentioned so far is an Indo-European language, no matter what smaller group it may belong to.

J. N. HOOK AND E. G. MATHEWS

Changes in the English Language

EXAMPLES OF OLD ENGLISH

At first glance a selection from Old English appears to be in a foreign tongue. More careful scrutiny reveals that some of the words are almost the same as ours, that others have undergone considerable change, and that still others have vanished. Modern English has lost some of the grammatical constructions that formerly existed.

Here is the Lord's Prayer in the Old English (West Saxon) version of approximately a thousand years ago:

> Fæder ūre þū þe eart on heofonum sī þīn nama gehālgod. Tō becume þīn rīce. Gewurþe ðīn willa on eorðan swā swā on heofonum. Ūrne gedæghwāmlīcan hlāf syle ūs tō dæg. And forgyf ūs ūre gyltas swā swā wē forgyfað ūrum gyltendum. And ne gelæd þū ūs on costnunge ac ālȳs ūs of yfele. Sōþlīce.

Detailed comment on these few lines would fill many pages; here we shall look at only a few words and constructions. Word order was much less fixed in Old English than it is today: notice the Old English forms of *Father our* and *be thy name hallowed* as examples. Case endings are used with nouns, as in *heofonum* (heaven), *eorðan* (earth), *gyltas* (debts), and *gyltendum* (debtors). Adjectives had to agree in case, number, and gender with their nouns: *ūre, ūrne,* and *ūrum* are today simply *our.* The word *rīce* is now translated as *kingdom,* but it is actually a cognate of *Reich* which survives in German. The symbols þ (thorn) and ð (eth) were both used for *th.* Since Old English times some words have been reduced in the number of syllables: *gehālgod* (hallowed), *gedæghwāmlīcan* (daily), *forgyfað* (forgive). Spelling was much more phonetic than that of today; in general, there were no silent letters. In pronunciation, vowel

From *Modern American Grammar and Usage.* © 1956 The Ronald Press Company. Reprinted by permission of the publisher.

sounds were more similar to those found in modern continental languages than to those in Modern English; and consonant sounds were not much different from those of Modern English. Punctuation marks other than periods were rare, and even periods were not used very systematically by the scribes.

As a second example consider the following lines from the epic poem *Beowulf*. The manuscript is generally believed to be in the hand of a scribe of the late tenth century. This passage tells of King Hrothgar's sorrow over the killing of his friend and follower by a hideous demon:

Hrothgar spoke	defender of the Scyldings
Hrōðgār maþelode	helm Scyldinga:
Not ask thou about happiness.	Sorrow is renewed
Ne frīn þū æfter sǣlum	Sorh is genīwod
of the Danes for the people	Dead is Aeschere
Denigea lēodum.	Dēad is Æschere
Irmenlaf's	elder brother
Yrmenlāfes	yldra brōþor
my confidant	and my counselor
mīn rūnwita	ond mīn rǣdbora
shoulder-companion	when we in battle
eaxlgestealla	ðonne wē on orlege
head protected	when clashed together troops
hafelan weredon	þonne hniton fēþan
boar-helmets struck	Such should hero be
eoferas cnysedan	Swylc scolde eorl wesan
nobleman good from old times	as Aeschere was.
æþeling ǣrgōd	swylc Æschere wæs.

Even the literal translation of this passage does not seem very clear today. A more free translation might go like this: "Hrothgar, the defender of the Scyldings, spoke: 'Do not ask about happiness, because sorrow has come again to the Danish people. Aeschere is dead. He was Irmenlaf's older brother and my confidant and counselor. He stood at my shoulder when in battle we protected our heads and hewed the boar-helmets as troops clashed. Every hero should be as Aeschere was, a nobleman good to recall from old times.'"

Notice, in comparing these translations, how word order has changed. Observe also how large a proportion of the Old English words have dropped out of the language. Some of them remain, however, in recognizable form: *helm* is a cousin of our *helmets*, *æfter* is *after*, *dēad* has changed only its pronunciation, *yldra brōþor* is still recognizable, *þonne* has become *then*, *wē* and *is* are unchanged in spelling, *scolde*, is similar to *should*, *eorl* has altered its meaning and become *earl*, *ǣrgōd* contains the ancestors of *ere* and *good*, and *wæs* is obviously *was*.

Inflectional endings are much more important in Old English than in Modern; for example, *Scyldinga* (genitive plural) requires here a three-word translation, *of the Scyldings;* and *lēodum* also requires either a three-word translation, *for* (or *to*) *the people,* or a revised word order. The endings of such words as *rūnwita, fēþan,* and *eoferas* help, along with the context, to show whether the word is to be regarded as a subject or an object. In Modern English we depend more upon word order and upon "function words" such as prepositions than we do upon inflections.

Old English grammar may be made a subject for special study. Here you have seen illustrated only a few of its most obvious characteristics.

EXAMPLE OF MIDDLE ENGLISH

When we move forward about four hundred years, from the late tenth to the late fourteenth century, we see that the language has changed rather drastically. Here are lines from the Prologue of Chaucer's *Canterbury Tales,* describing the squire, son of the knight:

With him ther was his sone a yong Squyer

(lover)   (aspirant to knighthood)
A lovyere and a lusty bacheler

(curly) (as if)
With lokkes crulle as they were leyd in presse.

Of twenty yeer of age he was I gesse.

.   .   .   .

(Embroidered)   (meadow)
Embrouded was he, as it were a mede

(flowers)
Al ful of fresshe floures whyte and rede.

(playing the flute)
Singinge he was or floyting al the day.

He was as fresh as is the month of May.

Short was his goune with sleves long and wyde.

(excellently)
Wel coude he sitte on hors and faire ryde.

(compose the words)
He coude songes make and wel endyte

(Joust)   (also)   (draw)
Juste and eek daunce and wel purtreye and wryte.

(hotly)   (in the night-time)
So hote he lovede that by nightertale

He sleep namore than dooth a nightingale.

This passage is closer to Modern English in word order than most Old English was. Only in two or three places, such as "He coude songes make," does the order seem very strange to us. Inflectional endings of Middle English were considerably reduced from Old English. In a noun an -s or -es usually signified either a genitive singular or any case of the plural. (The battle between an -s and an -en plural was almost decided by Chaucer's time, although in a few words such as oxen the -en plural never surrendered.) Adjectival forms had in general been reduced to two, one for the "strong" singular, and a second for the strong plural and the "weak" singular and plural. Verbs were somewhat simplified also; in the past tense no distinction was retained between singular and plural or between first, second, and third person, and the past tense and past participle were often identical, as they are in most verbs today.

Of all the things that have happened to English, the reduction of inflectional endings and the increased inflexibility of word order have been most important in giving the language its modern characteristics. Although these changes were not completed in Middle English and will never be completed while the language lives, they were far advanced by the year 1500, a date chosen rather arbitrarily as the beginning of Modern English.

SOME OF THE DEVELOPMENTS IN MODERN ENGLISH

Since 1500 English word order has become still more fixed, and living inflections have been reduced to seven: an -s or -es plural for nearly all nouns, an -s ending for most third person singular verbs in the present tense, an -ed ending for most verbs in the past tense, an -ing form for verbs, a special past participle for some verbs, an -er ending for the comparative degree of many adjectives and some adverbs, and an -est ending for the superlative degree of the same words.

In other ways grammar has changed only slightly. Representative of the many comparatively small changes are the use of do in questions (Does he consent? rather than Elizabethan Consents he?) and the growth in frequency of the progressive tenses (He was speaking, for instance, often replacing He spoke). Steadily increasing reliance upon prepositional phrases, greater employment of subordinate clauses, the increase in verb-adverb (or verb-preposition) combinations ("I ran into an old friend"), and a tendency to use almost any word as more than one part of speech—these are but a few of the Modern English developments that later will be treated in more detail.

In the eighteenth century some grammarians, failing to recognize the inevitability of linguistic change, strove to stop or at least retard it. They believed that change in a language is undesirable; since Latin was the most highly regarded language, and since Latin had not changed much in fifteen hundred years or so, change must be bad. (Those who held this theory failed to realize that Latin would probably have changed a great deal if it had not become a dead language, and that in monks' Latin it actually did change considerably.) They believed also that the loss of inflections should be stopped to prevent further "deterioration."

The results of the efforts of these few grammarians may be illustrated by referring to a couple of pronouns and a few verbs. The distinction between *who* and *whom*, which is not essential for clarity, was erratically observed during the eighteenth century. But under pressure from prescriptive grammarians, teachers and editors began to insist upon strict maintenance of *whom* as an object. Several verbs, including *blow, know*, and *throw*, were moving toward a "weak" or "regular" past tense and past participle: *blow, blowed, blowed*, and so on. They were thus following other verbs that had made the shift without hurting the language: as examples, *help* once had *healp* as one past form and *holpen* as the past participle; *climb* had *clamb* and *clumben*; *chew* had *ceaw* and *cowen*. Certainly *blowed* would be no worse than *climbed* or *chewed*, but the prescribers wanted no more "deterioration." As a result of their efforts and those of their intellectual descendants the use of *blowed, knowed*, and *throwed* may even today keep an able person from being employed for a white collar position.

Similarly, in the eighteenth century, a tendency toward identical forms for past tense and past participle was noticeable. The verb *sing* was tending toward *sing, sung, sung; write* toward *write, wrote, wrote*. The original title of Thomas Gray's most famous poem was "Elegy Wrote in a Country Churchyard." But once more the reactionaries went to work, and the schools ever since have insisted upon different forms for the past tense and past participle of *drink, give, ride, shrink, sing, sink, write*, and other verbs. How many million child-hours have been spent on mastering these forms is beyond calculation. Totally false conceptions of "correctness" have resulted from this wasted effort.

Perhaps the most noticeable change that has occurred since 1500 is not in grammar but in vocabulary. Through borrowings from dead Latin, dead Greek, and most of the important living languages of the world, English has multiplied its store of words manyfold. Since no one can precisely define what a word is, no one can say how many words are now in the language. One clue to the number is that unabridged dictionaries have about 600,000 entries. But since no lexicographer would claim that his dictionary lists every existing word in the language, the total may be much larger.

WHY THE LANGUAGE HAS CHANGED

A language changes because things happen to people. If we could imagine the impossible—a society in which nothing happened—there would be no changes in language. But except possibly in a cemetery, things are constantly happening to people: they eat, drink, sleep, talk, make love, meet strangers, struggle against natural perils, and fight against one another. They slowly adapt their language to meet the changing conditions of their lives. Although the changes made in one generation may be small, those made in a dozen generations may enormously affect the language. The big and little phases of history—fashions, fads, inventions, the influence of a leader, a war or two, an invasion or two, travel to a foreign land, the demands of business intercourse—may alter a language so much that a Rip Van Winkle who slept two or three hundred years might have trouble in making himself understood when he awoke. Even in a relatively quiet society, linguistic change proceeds inexorably.

Think, if you will, of the English language as a river. Its headwaters are the closely interrelated Teutonic languages of the Angles, Saxons, and Jutes, who lived mainly in the northern part of what is now Germany. They provided the basic grammatical structure of the language that we call English; they provided most of its linguistic heritage; they provided its basic words, the common everyday words that still are the most important in our simple communications. But to the basic elements brought in by these Teutonic peoples many additions have been made.

When the Teutons began invading and settling in the British Isles in 449 A.D., they found in possession the Celts, who previously had been pushed about by Roman soldiers for several centuries. The Teutons pushed the Celts about some more, finally tending to localize them in what we now call Ireland, Wales, and parts of Scotland. But the Teutonic language was influenced somewhat by the Celtic and indirectly by the Latin which the Celts had fragmentarily learned. So in English we have words of Celtic ancestry such as *brat, cairn,* and *crag,* and the place names *Aberdeen* (*Aber* = river mouth), *Avon* (river), *Caerleon, Cardiff, Carlyle* (*caer* or *car* = fortress), *Dundee, Dunbarton, Dunbar* (*dun* = hill), *Inchcape* (*inch* = island), *Kildare, Kilpatrick* (*kill* = church). And as a result of the early and indirect Latin tributary (which existed on the Continent even before the invasions of Britain) we have *wall* and *street* and *port,* words that give promise of enduring even longer than the Roman constructions that they name; and we have place names: Roman *Londinium* (originally Celtic) is now *London, Eboracum* (also once Celtic) has undergone considerable transformation to appear as *York,* and Latin *castra,* a military camp, appears both in England and the United States in *Lancaster, Worcester, Leicester, Gloucester, Chester, Dorchester, Rochester.* Thus Latin and Celtic are early tributaries of English.

By the end of the sixth century Latin was to renew its influence upon English. In 597 Roman missionaries began coming to the British Isles in an attempt to Christianize the inhabitants. They introduced such church words as *altar, creed, mass,* and *nun* and some homely words such as *beet, pine, cheese,* and *cup.* Some of the words that the priests brought over had been borrowed by Latin from Greek: *bishop, deacon, martyr, church, devil, priest, monk, pope, psalm, dish,* and *plum.* So once more a double tributary entered the river of the English language.

In the seventh and most of the eighth centuries the Anglo-Saxon inhabitants of the British Isles lived a relatively peaceful existence—simple by modern standards, but maybe happier than a more complex society can be. But starting in about 790, "Northmen" or Danes began to invade the islands. They were rough and vigorous; in 793, "the heathen men miserably destroyed God's church at Lindisfarne with rapine and slaughter," a contemporary account says. The forays grew into expeditions; the Danes began to colonize; Alfred the Great for a while paid them tribute but then organized military forces and compelled the invaders to sign a peace treaty. One of the terms of the treaty was that the Danes accept Christianity. Since the chief difference between the Danes and the Anglo-Saxons had been in religion, this concession meant that the two groups, already speaking kindred and often mutually intelligible languages, would merge. However, attacks by new groups of Danes, not covered by the treaty, continued, and early in the eleventh century a Danish king, Cnut, ruled in England.

It is often difficult to separate the linguistic contributions of the Danes from the closely related Anglo-Saxon, but apparently we owe to Danish such words as *fellow, husband, law, wrong,* and a number of words with an *sk* sound, as *skill, scale, scare, skirt* (*shirt,* a cognate form, is from Anglo-Saxon), *skin, sky, score,* and *bask.* Numerous English place names are Danish in origin. Danish *thwaite* (piece of ground) appears in many names such as *Stonethwaite, Hallthwaite; thorp* (village) is in names like *Lowthorpe* and *Northorpe; by* (town) is in *Derby, Kirkby, Selby, Whitby,* etc.; *toft* (a clearing) is in *Lowestoft.*

The next big tributary came from north via east. Northmen, later called Normans, had begun moving into France at about the time that the Danes invaded England. They were flexible people who adopted French as their language, changing it somewhat in the process. They made of Normandy one of the most vigorous and ambitious states of Europe. In 1066, after the death of England's Edward the Confessor, the Duke of

Normandy decided that he would attempt to gain the crown of his late cousin, and at Hastings he earned the more glorious title of William the Conqueror. His people moved into the British Isles, relegated natives to the rank of second-class citizens, and eventually concentrated their grip upon England as they lost their continental footholds.

Now began the period of greatest linguistic turmoil that English has known. England was a country of two languages: the Norman French of the ruling classes and the English of the conquered. The Bishop of Worcester was deposed in 1095 because he was "an idiot who did not know French." French was used in the churches, in the courts, in important business transactions, and in the schools. But inevitably the two groups had to meet. A French landowner had to give instructions to his tenants; an English farmer or smith had to try to sell his goods or his skills; intermarriage became frequent. Each group picked up words from the other. However, just as American occupation troops learned only the rudiments of German, Italian, and Japanese after World War II, the Normans did not learn the intricacies of English nor did the English learn the intricacies of Norman French. Each group learned only the fundamentals.

Before the Norman conquest there had been signs that grammatical inflections were being reduced—the dative and accusative cases, for instance, were blending their forms. But the coming of the Normans seems to have expedited such change. At any rate, after the Normans had been in England for about three centuries, English inflections were not nearly so numerous.

The two groups gradually blended. So did their vocabularies, and to a much smaller extent their grammar, although the impact of Norman French upon English was less than one might think. But partly as a result of that impact, and more largely as a result of other, less tangible causes, grammatical gender was replaced by natural gender, word order became less free as inflections were reduced, pronunciations changed, and many words from Norman French, French, and Latin entered the language.

Chaucer's contemporary, John Gower, in the fourteenth century wrote three major works—one in English, one in French, and one in Latin. He chose three languages because he was not sure which language would become standard in England, and he wanted one of his works to be in the language that endured. Had he lived fifty years later, he would have had no difficulty in seeing that English was going to be the winner.

During the Renaissance two more large tributaries entered English. These, of course, were in the form of additional Latin and Greek contributions. Thousands of words came into the English vocabulary during this period, including huge numbers of relatively useless terms that lived briefly and were then buried in soon-to-be-forgotten graves. English spellings were also influenced by the new interest in the Classical languages. Learned men perhaps foolishly proclaimed that the orthography of English words should reveal their Latin backgrounds. They therefore recommended the spellings *debt* and *doubt,* even though the *b*'s in these words were not pronounced, and even though the French, from whom the English had borrowed both words, had already dropped the *b*'s that existed in Latin. A number of words with *tio,* like *nation,* had also been taken from the French, which often used a phonetically accurate *c* instead of *t;* in English the sound in question was pronounced as *s* or *sh,* but Renaissance scholars insisted that the Latin *t* be retained. Many other of our present illogical spellings may be attributed to the scholars of the Renaissance.

During the Renaissance period and later, the feeling grew that English grammar should be described in the terminology of Latin grammar. Sometimes that procedure was not objectionable, for many elements of the two languages were similar. But when the grammarians insisted upon finding in English everything that existed in Latin, when they made of Latin a procrustean bed into which English must be in some way fitted, and when they ignored the fact that English was basically a Teutonic and not an Italic language, they did irreparable harm to many generations of persons who wanted to acquire a clear understanding of the structure and peculiarities of the language.

Since the Renaissance, many small tributaries have enlarged the stream of English. These cannot be listed in chronological order. Latin has kept appearing, as have French and Greek. Italian has contributed many of the technical terms of music. Dutch has given sailing terms like *ahoy, boom, deck, hoist, skipper, sloop,* and *yacht.* Spanish has given, directly or indirectly, miscellaneous words like *matador, vanilla, armada, alligator,* and *mosquito.* North American Indian has contributed such words as *hominy, Mississippi* (an Algonquin word meaning "big river," not "Father of Waters"), *moccasin, moose, opossum, papoose, pemmican, raccoon, skunk, squaw, toboggan, tomahawk, wampum,* and *wigwam.* Among other contributing languages, with one or two representative words from each, have been Bengali, (*bungalow*); Persian (*azure*); Slavic (*polka, vampire, mammoth*); Hebrew (*amen, hallelujah, behemoth*); Hungarian (*goulash*); Tartar (*khan*); Malay (*amuck, gong, cockatoo*); Indian (*rajah, nabob, khaki, yogi*); Australian (*boomerang, kangaroo*); South American Indian (*alpaca, condor, jaguar, quinine*); Polynesian (*taboo, tattoo*); African (*gumbo, mumbo jumbo, okra*). Even Chinese has given us some words (*tea, typhoon, chop suey,* and *chow mein*); Chinese Pidgin English has contributed the familiar *chopstick;* Japanese has given us *tycoon, kimono, judo,* and *ju-jitsu.*

The borrowing has of course gone the other way, also, although the details need not concern us here. English and American gastronomic and athletic terms, for instance, have been incorporated in many European languages. An American can use the terms *cocktail* and *beefsteak* with satisfactory results in almost any European restaurant.

Why did English change? Simply because many things happened to many people in many countries. Had the Angles, Saxons, and Jutes moved southeast instead of southwest, the language of the British Isles might never have been Teutonic. Had Harold defeated William the Conqueror at Hastings in 1066, the language of today might have been considerably different, perhaps more complicated in morphology, more simple in syntax. Had the English been stay-at-homes, their language might have lacked some of the versatility, the expressiveness, and the color that we believe it now has.

ALBERT C. BAUGH

The Enrichment of the Language
During the Renaissance

THE PROBLEM OF ENRICHMENT. In 1531 Sir Thomas Elyot, statesman as well as scholar, published what has been described as the first book on education printed in English. He called it *The Governour* since it had to do with the training of those who in the future would be occupied at court. The dedication to Henry the Eighth is couched in the following terms:

> I late consideringe (moste excellent prince and myne onely re-doughted soveraigne lorde) my duetie that I owe to my naturall contray with my faythe also of aliegeaunce and othe . . . I am (as God juge me) violently stered to *devulgate* or sette fourth some part of my studie, trustynge therby tacquite me of my dueties to God, your hyghnesse, and this my contray. Wherfore takinge comfort and boldenesse, partly of your graces moste benevolent inclination towarde the universall weale of your subjectes, partly inflamed with zele, I have now enterprised to *describe* in our vulgare tunge the fourme of a juste publike weale: . . . Whiche *attemptate* is nat of presumption to teache any persone, I my selfe havinge moste nede of teachinge: but onely to the intent that men which wil be studious about the weale publike may fynde the thinge therto expedient compendiously writen. And for as moch as this present boke treateth of the *education* of them that hereafter may be demed worthy to be governours of the publike weale under your hyghnesse . . . I *dedicate* it unto your hyghnesse as the fyrste frutes of my studye, verely trustynge that your moste excellent wysedome wyll therein *esteme* my loyall harte and diligent endevour . . . Protestinge unto your excellent majestie that where I commende herin any one vertue or *dispraise* any one vice I meane the generall description of thone and thother without any other particuler

meanynge to the reproche of any one persone. To the whiche protestation I am nowe dryven throughe the malignite of this present tyme all
disposed to malicious detraction . . .

In this passage we have an early example of the attempt to improve the
English language. The words printed in italics were all new in Elyot's
day; two of them (*education, dedicate*) are first found in the English
language as he uses them in this dedication. Two others (*esteem* and
devulgate) are found in the sense here employed only one year earlier.
Several others could be instanced which, although recorded slightly
earlier, were not yet in general use.[1] In so short a passage these new words
are fairly numerous, but not more numerous than in the rest of his book,
and, what is more important, they are not the innovations of a pedant
or an extremist. Other writers who could be cited were less restrained
in their enthusiasm for words drawn from Latin and Greek and French.
Nor are these new words in Elyot the result of chance. They are part of
a conscious effort to enrich the English vocabulary.

We have already indicated that enlarging the vocabulary was one of
the three major problems confronting the modern languages in the eyes
of men in the sixteenth century. And it is not difficult to see why this
was so. The Renaissance was a period of increased activity in almost every
field. It would have been strange if the spirit of inquiry and experiment
that led to the discovery of America, the reform of the church, the Coper-
nican theory, and the revolution of thought in many fields should have
left only language untouched. The rediscovery of Latin and Greek literature led to new activity in the modern languages and directed attention
to them as the medium of literary expression. The result was a healthy
desire for improvement. The intellectual aspect of the Revival of Learning had a similar effect. The scholarly monopoly of Latin throughout the
Middle Ages had left the vernaculars undeveloped along certain lines.
Now that this monopoly was being broken, the deficiencies of English
were at the same time revealed. English was undoubtedly inadequate,
as compared with the classical languages, to express the thought which
those languages embodied and which in England was now becoming part
of a rapidly expanding civilization. The translations that appeared in
such numbers convinced men of the truth of this fact. The very act of
translation brings home to the translator the limitations of his medium and
tempts him to borrow from other languages the terms whose lack he feels
in his own. For men to whom Latin was almost a second mother tongue
the temptation to transfer and naturalize in English important Latin
radicals was particularly great. It was so, too, with French and Italian.
In this way many foreign words were introduced into English. One may

say that the same impulse that led men to furnish the English mind with the great works of classical and other literatures led them to enrich the English language with words drawn from the same source. New words were particularly needed in various technical fields, where English was notably weak. The author of a *Discourse of Warre* justifies his introduction of numerous military terms by an argument that was unanswerable: "I knowe no other names than are given by strangers, because there are fewe or none at all in our language."

It is not always easy, however, to draw the line between a word that is needed, because no equivalent term exists, and one which merely expresses more fully an idea that could be conveyed in some fashion with existing words. We can appreciate the feeling of a scholar for whom a familiar Latin word had a wealth of associations and a rich connotation; we must admit the reasonableness of his desire to carry such a word over into his English writing. The transfer is all the more excusable when one is convinced that English would be better for having it and that it is a patriotic duty to employ one's knowledge in so worthy a cause as that of improving the national speech. This motive actuated many men who were both earnest and sincere in their desire to relieve English of the charge of inadequacy and inelegance. Thus Elyot apologizes for introducing the word *maturity:* "Wherfor I am constrained to usurpe a latine worde . . . , which worde, though it be strange and darke [obscure], yet . . . ones brought in custome, shall be facile to understande as other wordes late commen out of Italy and Fraunce . . . Therfore that worde *maturitie* is translated to the actis of man, . . . reservyng the wordes *ripe* and *redy* to frute and other thinges seperate from affaires, as we have nowe in usage. *And this do I nowe remembre for the necessary augmentation of our langage.*" In another place he says, "I intended to augment our Englyshe tongue, wherby men shulde as well expresse more abundantly the thynge that they conceyved in theyr hartis, . . . havyng wordes apte for the pourpose: as also interprete out of greke, latyn or any other tonge into Englysshe as sufficiently as out of any one of the said tongues into an other." In any case, whether "of pure necessitie in new matters, or of mere braverie to garnish it self withall"—to quote a phrase of Mulcaster's—English acquired in the sixteenth and early seventeenth century thousands of new and strange words.

The greater number of these new words were borrowed from Latin. But they were not exclusively drawn from that source. Some were taken from Greek, a great many from French, and not a few from Italian and Spanish. Even the older periods of English and occasionally the local dialects were drawn upon to embellish the language, in this case chiefly the language of poetry. We shall see more particularly in a moment the character of the additions made at this time, but before doing so we must consider the conflicting views that different people held concerning their desirability.

THE OPPOSITION TO INKHORN TERMS. The wholesale borrowing of words from other languages did not meet with universal favor. The strangeness of the new words was an objection to some people. As Edward Phillips said in his *New World of Words,* "some people if they spy but a hard word are as much amazed as if they had met with a Hobgoblin." Even Elyot's prestige did not save him from criticism on this score. In a book published two years after *The Governour* he alludes to "divers men . . . [who] doo shewe them selfes offended (as they say) with my strange termes," and he attempts to justify his practice. Other men were purists by nature and took their stand on general principles. Such a man was Sir John Cheke. His attitude is interesting because he was himself a fine classical scholar and might have been expected to show sympathy for classical borrowings. In a letter to Sir Thomas Hoby, prefaced to Hoby's translation of *The Courtier* (1561), he wrote:

> I am of this opinion that our own tung shold be written cleane and pure, unmixt and unmangeled with borowing of other tunges, wherin if we take not heed by tijm, ever borowing and never payeng, she shall be fain to keep her house as bankrupt. For then doth our tung naturallie and praisablie utter her meaning, when she bouroweth no counterfeitness of other tunges to attire her self withall, but useth plainlie her own, with such shift, as nature, craft, experiens and folowing of other excellent doth lead her unto, and if she want at ani tijm (as being unperfight she must) yet let her borow with suche bashfulnes, that it mai appeer, that if either the mould of our own tung could serve us to fascion a woord of our own, or if the old denisoned wordes could content and ease this neede, we wold not boldly venture of unknowen wordes.

Ascham's admiration for Cheke led him to a similar attitude. Some considered the use of learned words mere pedantry and tried to drive them out by ridicule, calling them "inkhorn" terms. Sir Thomas Chaloner, who translated Erasmus' *Praise of Folly* in 1549, is an example:

> Such men therfore, that in deede are archdoltes, and woulde be taken yet for sages and philosophers, maie I not aptelie calle theim foolelosophers? For as in this behalfe I have thought good to borowe a littell of the Rethoriciens of these daies, who plainely thynke theim selfes demygods, if lyke horsleches thei can shew two tongues, I meane to mingle their writings with words sought out of strange langages, as if it were alonely thyng for theim to poudre theyr bokes with ynkehorne

termes, although perchaunce as unaptly applied as a gold rynge in a sowes nose. That and if they want suche farre fetched vocables, than serche they out of some rotten Pamphlet foure or fyve disused woords of antiquitee, therewith to darken the sence unto the reader, to the ende that who so understandeth theim maie repute hym selfe for more cunnyng and litterate: and who so dooeth not, shall so muche the rather yet esteeme it to be some high mattier, because it passeth his learnyng.

The strongest objection, however, to the new words was on the score of their obscurity. The great exponent of this view was Thomas Wilson, whose *Arte of Rhetorique* (1553) was several times reprinted in the course of the century and was used by Shakespeare. In a classic passage on "Plainnesse, what it is" he makes a savage attack on inkhorn terms and illustrates the fault by a burlesque letter overloaded with them:

Among all other lessons this should first be learned, that wee never affect any straunge ynkehorne termes, but to speake as is commonly received: neither seeking to be over fine, nor yet living over-carelesse, using our speeche as most men doe, and ordering our wittes as the fewest have done. Some seeke so far for outlandish English, that they forget altogether their mothers language. And I dare sweare this, if some of their mothers were alive, thei were not able to tell what they say: and yet these fine English clerkes will say, they speake in their mother tongue, if a man should charge them for counterfeiting the Kings English. Some farre journeyed gentlemen at their returne home, like as they love to goe in forraine apparell, so thei wil pouder their talke with oversea language. He that commeth lately out of Fraunce will talke French English and never blush at the matter. An other chops in with English Italienated, and applieth the Italian phrase to our English speaking, the which is, as if an Oratour that professeth to utter his mind in plaine Latine, would needes speake Poetrie, and farre fetched colours of straunge antiquitie. . . . The unlearned or foolish phantasticall, that smelles but of learning (such fellowes as have seen learned men in their daies) wil so Latin their tongues, that the simple can not but wonder at their talke, and thinke surely they speake by some revelation. I know them that thinke *Rhetorique* to stande wholie upon darke wordes, and hee that can catche an ynke horne terme by the taile, him they coumpt to be a fine Englisheman, and a good *Rhetorician*. And the rather to set out this foly, I will adde suche a letter as William Sommer himselfe, could not make a better for that purpose. Some will thinke and sweare it too, that there was never any such thing written: well, I will not force any man to beleeve it, but I will say thus much, and abide by it too, the like have been made heretofore, and praised above the Moone.

A letter devised by a Lincolnshire man, for a voyde benefice, to a gentleman that then waited upon the Lorde Chauncellour, for the time being.

Pondering, *expending*,[1] and *revoluting* with my selfe, your *ingent* [2] *affabilitie*, and *ingenious capacity* for *mundaine* affaires: I cannot but *celebrate*, & *extol* your *magnifical dexteritie* above all other. For how could you have *adepted* [3] such *illustrate* prerogative, and *dominicall superioritie*, if the fecunditie of your *ingenie* [4] had not been so *fertile* and wonderfull pregnant. Now therefore being *accersited* [5] to such *splendente* renoume and dignitie *splendidious*: I doubt not but you will *adjuvate* [6] such poore *adnichilate* [7] orphanes, as whilome ware *condisciples* [8] with you, and of *antique* familiaritie in Lincolneshire. Among whom I being a *scholasticall panion*,[9] *obtestate* [10] your *sublimitie*, to *extoll* mine infirmitie. There is a Sacerdotall dignitie in my *native* Countrey, *contiguate* to me, where I now *contemplate*: which your worshipfull benignitie could sone *impetrate* [11] for mee, if it would like you to extend your sedules, and *collaude* [12] me in them to the right honourable lord Chaunceller, or rather *Archgrammacian* of Englande. You know my literature, you knowe the *pastorall* promotion. I *obtestate* your *clemencie*, to *invigilate* [13] thus much for me, according to my *confidence*, and as you knowe my condigne merites for such a *compendious* living. But now I *relinquish* to *fatigate* your intelligence, with any more *frivolous verbositie*, and therfore he that rules the climates, be evermore your beautreux, your fortresse, and your bulwarke. *Amen*.

Dated at my *Dome*,[14] or rather Masion place in Lincolneshire, the *penulte* of the moneth Sextile. *Anno Millimo, quillimo, trillimo*.
                                   Per me Johannes Octo.

What wiseman reading this Letter, will not take him for a very Caulf that made it in good earnest, and thought by his ynke pot termes to get a good Parsonage?

[1] weighing mentally (L. *expendere*)   [2] huge (L. *ingens*)
[3] attained (L. *adeptus*)   [4] mind, intellect (L. *ingenium*)
[5] brought (L. *accersitus*)   [6] aid (L. *adjuvare*)
[7] reduced to nothing (L. *ad nihil*)   [8] fellow-students
[9] companion   [10] call upon (L. *obtestari*, to call upon as a witness)
[11] procure (L. *impetrare*)   [12] recommend
[13] be watchful   [14] house (L. *domus*)

In the letter included in the above passage the italicized words were new in Wilson's day and therefore somewhat strange and obscure—dark, as he says—to the ordinary reader. Of the forty-five, thirty are not found before the sixteenth century, and the remaining fifteen are of such infrequent occurrence as to be considered by him inkhorn terms. It is interesting to note in passing that many of them are in common use today.

THE DEFENSE OF BORROWING. The attitude revealed in these utterances was apparently not the prevailing one. There were many more
who in precept or practice approved of judicious importations. As Dryden
wrote somewhat later, "I trade both with the living and the dead, for
the enrichment of our native tongue. We have enough in England to
supply our necessity, but if we will have things of magnificence and
splendour, we must get them by commerce." [2] The innovators had precedent on their side. Not only had English borrowed much in the past,
but, as they frequently pointed out, all other languages, including Latin
and Greek, had enriched themselves in this way.[3] The strangeness of the
new words, they argued, would soon wear off. As Mulcaster observed,
we must first become acquainted with any new thing "and make the thing
familiar if it seme to be strange. For all strange things seme great novelties, and hard of entertainment at their first arrivall, till theie be acquainted: but after acquaintance theie be verie familiar, and easie to
entreat . . . Familiaritie and acquaintance will cause facilitie, both in
matter and in words." The charge of obscurity was also met. Elyot maintained that throughout *The Governour* "there was no terme new made by
me of a latine or frenche worde, but it is there declared so playnly
by one mene or other to a diligent reder that no sentence is therby made
derke or harde to be understande." Not all men could say as much, but
in theory this was their aim. The position of the defender was in general
summed up by George Pettie, the translator of Guazzo's *Civile Conversation:*

> For the barbarousnesse [1] of our tongue, I must lykewyse say that
> it is much the worse for them [the objectors], and some such curious
> fellowes as they are: who if one chaunce to derive any woord from
> the Latine, which is insolent to their eares (as perchaunce they wyll
> take that phrase to be) they foorthwith make a jest at it, and terme it
> an Inkehorne terme. And though for my part I use those woords as
> litle as any, yet I know no reason why I should not use them, and I
> finde it a fault in my selfe that I do not use them: for it is in deed the
> ready way to inrich our tongue, and make it copious, and it is the way
> which all tongues have taken to inrich them selves. . . . Wherefore
> I marveile how our English tongue hath crackt it credite,[2] that it may
> not borrow of the Latine as well as other tongues: and if it have broken,
> it is but of late, for it is not unknowen to all men how many woordes
> we have fetcht from thence within these fewe yeeres, which if they
> should be all counted inkepot termes, I know not how we should
> speake any thing without blacking our mouthes with ink: for what
> woord can be more plaine then this word *plaine,* and yet what can
> come more neere to the Latine? What more manifest then *manifest?*
> and yet in a maner Latine: What more commune then *rare,* or lesse

rare then *commune,* and yet both of them comming of the Latine? But you wyll say, long use hath made these woords curraunt: and why may not use doo as much for these woords which we shall now derive? Why should not we doo as much for the posteritie as we have received of the antiquitie? [3]

[1] Corruption by foreign elements.
[2] An allusion to Cheke's statement quoted on p. 136.
[3] Edited by Sir Edward Sullivan (2v., London, 1925), Pettie's Preface.

A little later some sanction for the borrowings was derived from authority. Bullokar says (1616) "it is familiar among best writers to usurpe strange words."

COMPROMISE. The opposition to inkhorn terms was at its height in the middle of the sixteenth century. At the end of Elizabeth's reign it had largely spent its force. By this time borrowing had gone so far that the attack was rather directed at the abuse of the procedure than at the procedure itself. The use of unfamiliar words could easily be overdone. It was the enthusiast and the pedant who brought down the criticism of rea-sonable men upon the practice and caused them to condemn it in more sweeping terms than they knew at heart were justified or were consistent with their own usage. Puttenham, for example, although issuing a warning against inkhorn terms, admits having to use some of them himself, and seeks to justify them in particular instances. He defends the words *scien-tific, major domo, politien* (politician), *conduct* (verb), and others. The word *significative,* he says, "doth so well serve the turne, as it could not now be spared: and many more like usurped Latine and French words: as, *Methode, methodicall, placation, function, assubtiling, refining, compendi-ous, prolixe, figurative, inveigle,* a term borrowed of our common lawyers, *impression,* also a new terme, but well expressing the matter, and more than our English word . . . Also ye finde these wordes, *penetrate, pen-etrable, indignitie,* which I cannot see how we may spare them, whatso-ever fault wee finde with Ink-horne termes: for our speach wanteth wordes to such sence so well to be used." Even Wilson, after exercising his wit in the lively bit of burlesque quoted above, proceeds at once to qualify his disapproval: "Now whereas wordes be received, as well Greke as Latine, to set furthe our meanyng in thenglishe tongue, either for lacke of store, or els because wee would enriche the language: it is well doen to use them, and no man therin can be charged for any affectation when all other are agreed to folowe the same waie," and he cites some that meet with his approval. Each man who used a new word doubtless felt the justification of it, and in a matter about which only time could bring agreement, ran the risk of having his innovations disliked by others.

As Ben Jonson remarked in his *Discoveries*, "A man coins not a new word without some peril and less fruit; for if it happen to be received, the praise is but moderate; if refused, the scorn is assured." Some of the words which Puttenham defends have not stood the test of time, and some of those he objects to, such as *audacious, egregious, compatible*, have won a permanent place in the language. One who used any considerable number of new words was in a way on the defensive. Chapman in presenting his translation of Homer says: "For my varietie of new wordes, I have none Inckepot I am sure you know, but such as I give pasport with such authoritie, so significant and not ill sounding, that if my countrey language were an usurer, or a man of this age speaking it, hee would thanke mee for enriching him." Obscurity is always a valid object of criticism, and if the word 'inkhorn' could be hurled at an opponent, it was sure to strike him in a vulnerable spot. It was thus that Nash attacked Harvey,[4] who, it must be confessed, lent himself to such an attack. He replied in kind [5] and was able to convict Nash of *interfuseth, finicallitie, sillogistrie, disputative, hermaphrodite, declamatorie, censoriall moralizers, unlineall usurpers of judgement, infringement to destitute the inditement*, and a dozen similar expressions. Not the least interesting feature about the whole question of learned borrowings is the way it aroused popular interest. It even got in the playhouses. In the stage quarrel known as the "War of the Theatres" Ben Jonson delivered a purge to Marston in the *Poetaster* (1601), relieving him of *retrograde, reciprocal, incubus, lubrical, defunct, magnificate, spurious, inflate, turgidous, ventosity, strenuous, obstupefact*, and a number of similar words. The attitude of most men seems to have been one of compromise. No Elizabethan could avoid wholly the use of the new words. Men differed chiefly in the extent to which they allied themselves with the movement or resisted the tendency. As is so often the case, the safest course was a middle one, to borrow, but "without too manifest insolence and too wanton affectation."

PERMANENT ADDITIONS. From the exaggeration of a man like Wilson one might get the impression that much of the effort to introduce new words into the language was pedantic and ill-advised. Some of the words Wilson ridicules seem forced and in individual cases were certainly unnecessary. But it would be a mistake to conclude that all or even a large part of the additions were of this sort. Indeed the surprising thing about the movement here described is the number of words that we owe to this period and that seem now to be indispensable. Many of them are in such common use today that it is hard for us to realize that to the Elizabethan they were so strange and difficult as to be a subject of controversy. When Elyot wished to describe a democracy he said, "This maner of governaunce was called in Greke *democratia,* in Latine *popularis potentia,* in Englisshe the rule of the comminaltie." If he were not to have to refer to "the rule of the commonalty" by this roundabout phrase, he could hardly do better than to try to naturalize the Greek word. Again he felt the need of a single word for "all maner of lerning, which of some is called the world of science, of other the circle of doctrine, which is in one word of Greke, *encyclopedia.*" Though purists might object, the word *encyclopedia* filled a need in English and it has lived on. The words that were introduced at this time were often basic words—nouns, adjectives, verbs. Among nouns we may note as examples *anachronism, allurement, allusion, atmosphere, autograph, capsule, denunciation, dexterity, disability, disrespect, emanation, excrescence, excursion, expectation, halo, inclemency, jurisprudence.* The examples are chosen at random. Among adjectives we find *abject* (in our sense of 'down in spirit'), *agile, appropriate, conspicuous, dexterous, expensive, external, habitual, hereditary, impersonal, insane, jocular, malignant.* Few of these we could dispense with. But it is among the verbs, perhaps, that we find our most important acquisitions, words like *adapt, alienate, assassinate, benefit* (first used by Cheke, who thought "our language should be writ pure"!), *consolidate, disregard* (introduced by Milton), *emancipate, eradicate, erupt, excavate, exert, exist, exhilarate, extinguish, harass, meditate* (which Sidney apparently introduced). It is hard to exaggerate the importance of a movement which enriched the language with words such as these.

Most of the words in this list are Latin. But some of them were earlier acquired by Latin from Greek. Examples are *anachronism, atmosphere, autograph.* Others might be added, such as *antipathy, antithesis, caustic, chaos, chronology, climax, crisis, critic, dogma, emphasis, enthusiasm, epitome, parasite, parenthesis, pathetic, pneumonia, scheme, skeleton, system, tactics.* Indeed most of the Greek words in English until lately have come to us either through Latin or French. But in the Renaissance the renewed study of Greek led to the introduction of some Greek words at first hand. Such, for example, are *acme, anonymous, catastrophe, criterion, ephemeral, heterodox, idiosyncrasy, lexicon, misanthrope, ostracize, polemic, tantalize, thermometer,* and *tonic.*

ADAPTATION. In entering the language some words retained their original form, others underwent change. Words like *climax, appendix, epitome, exterior, delirium, axis* still have their Latin form. The adaptation of others to English was effected by the simple process of cutting off the Latin ending. *Conjectural* (L. *conjectural–is*), *consult* (L. *consult–are*), *exclusion* (L. *exclusion–em*), and *exotic* (L. *exotic–us*) show how easily in many cases this could be done. But more often a further change was necessary to bring the word into accord with the usual English forms. Thus the Latin ending *–us* in adjectives was changed to *–ous* (*conspicu–s > conspicuous*) or was replaced by *–al* as in *external* (L. *externus*). Latin nouns ending in *–tas* were changed in English to *–ty* (*celerity < celeritas*) because English had so many words of this kind borrowed from French where the Latin *–tatem* regularly became *–té*. For the same reason nouns ending in *–antia, –entia* appear in English with the ending *–ance, –ence* or *–ancy, –ency*, while adjectives ending in *–bilis* take the usual English (or French) ending *–ble*. Examples are *consonance, concurrence, constancy, frequency, considerable, susceptible*. Many English verbs borrowed from Latin at this time end in *–ate* (*create, consolidate, eradicate*). These verbs were formed on the basis of the Latin past participle (e.g., *exterminatus,* whereas the French *exterminer* represents the Latin infinitive *exterminare*). The English practice arose from the fact that the Latin past participle was often equivalent to an adjective and it was a common thing in English to make verbs out of adjectives (*busy, dry, darken*).

REINTRODUCTIONS AND NEW MEANINGS. Sometimes the same word has been borrowed more than once in the course of time. The Latin words *episcopus* and *discus* appear in Old English as *bishop* and *dish* and were again borrowed later to make our words *episcopal* and *disc* (also *dais, desk,* and *discus*). In the same way *chaos* and *malignity* were apparently reintroduced in the sixteenth century. The word *intelligence* is used once in Gower and occasionally in the fifteenth century, but in *The Governour* Elyot remarks that "*intelligence* is nowe used for an elegant worde where there is mutuall treaties or appoyntementes, eyther by letters or message." A word when introduced a second time often carries a different meaning, and in estimating the importance of the Latin and other loan-words of the Renaissance it is just as essential to consider new meanings as new words. Indeed, the fact that a word had been borrowed once before and used in a different sense is of less significance than its reintroduction in a sense that has continued or been productive of new ones. Thus the word *fastidious* is found once in 1440 with the significance "proud, scornful," but this is of less importance than the fact that both More and Elyot use it a century later in its more usual Latin sense of "distasteful, disgusting." From this it was possible for the modern meaning to develop, aided no doubt by the frequent use of the word in Latin with the force of "easily disgusted, hard to please, over nice." Chaucer uses the words *artificial, declination, hemisphere* in astronomical senses, but their present use is due to the sixteenth century; and the word *abject,* although found earlier in the sense of "cast off, rejected," was reintroduced in its present meaning in the Renaissance.

REJECTED WORDS. There are some things about language that we cannot explain. One of them is why certain words survive while others, apparently just as good, do not. Among the many new words that were introduced into English at this time there was a goodly number that we have not permanently retained. Some are found used a few times and then forgotten. Others enjoyed a rather longer life without becoming in any sense popular. A few were in sufficiently common use for a while to seem assured of a permanent place, but later, for some reason, lost favor and dropped out of use. *Uncounsellable,* for example, was very common in the seventeenth century, but after that practically disappeared. Some of the new words were apparently too learned and smelled too much of the lamp. *Anacephalize,* a Greek word meaning "to sum up," was of this sort and the more unnecessary since we had already adopted the Latin *recapitulate. Deruncinate* (to weed) was another although it was no worse than *eradicate* for which we had the English expression *to root out.* Elyot's *adminiculation* (aid), *illecebrous* (delicate, alluring), and *obfuscate* (hidden) are of the same sort. Some words might logically have survived but did not. *Expede* (to accomplish, expedite) would have been parallel to *impede. Cohibit* (to restrain) is like *inhibit* and *prohibit. Demit* (to send away) was common in the sixteenth and seventeenth centuries and would have been as natural as *commit* or *transmit,* but *dismiss* gradually replaced it. It is in fact not uncommon to find words discarded in favor of somewhat similar formations. Examples are *exsiccate* (to dry) alongside of *desiccate, emacerate* (emaciate), *discongruity* (incongruity), *appendance* (appendage). In some cases we have preferred a word in a shorter form: *cautionate* (caution), *consolate* (console), *attemptate* (attempt), *denunciate* (denounce). Often there seems to be no explanation but chance or caprice to account for a word's failure to survive. *Eximious* (excellent, distinguished) is frequently found in seventeenth century literature and was used by Browning, but is now unknown or at least very rare. *Mansuetude* (mildness) likewise has a history that extends from Chaucer to Browning but is no longer used. We have given up *disaccustom, disacquaint, disadorn,* etc., but we say *disabuse, disaffect, disagree.* Shakespeare used *disquantity* as a verb meaning to lessen in quantity or diminish. Sometimes we have kept one part of speech and discarded another. We say *exorbitant* but not *exorbitate* (to stray from the ordinary course), *approbation* but not *approbate, consternation* but not *consternate.* The most convincing reason for the failure of a new word to take hold is that it was not needed. *Aspectable* (visible), *assate* (to roast) and the noun *assation, exolete* (faded), *suppeditate* (furnish, supply), and many other rejected words were unnecessary, and there was certainly no need for *temulent* when we had *drunk, intoxicated,* and a score of other expressions of various degrees of respectability to express the idea. We must look upon the borrowings of this period as often experimental. New words were being freely introduced at the judgment or caprice of the individual. They were being tried out, sometimes in various forms. In Shakespeare's day no one could have told whether we should say *effectual, effectuous, effectful, effectuating,* or *effective.* Two of these five options have survived. It was necessary for time to do the sifting.

REINFORCEMENT THROUGH FRENCH. It is not always possible to say whether a word borrowed at this time was taken over directly from Latin or indirectly through French, for the same wholesale enrichment was going on in French simultaneously and the same words were being introduced in both languages. Often the two streams of influence must have merged. But that English borrowed many words from Latin at first hand is indicated in a number of ways. The word *fact* represents the Latin *factum* and not the French *fait,* which was taken into English earlier as *feat.* The many verbs like *confiscate, congratulate, exonerate* are formed from the Latin participle (*confiscat–us,* etc.) and not from the French *confisquer, congratuler, exonerer,* which are derived from the infinitives *confiscare,* etc. Caxton has the form *confisk,* which is from French, but the word did not survive in this shape. The form *prejudicate* is from Latin while *prejudge* represents the French *prejuger.* In the same way *instruct* and *subtract* show their Latin ancestry (*instructus, subtractus*) since the French *instruire* and *subtraire* would have become in English *instroy* (like *destroy*) and *subtray* (which is found in the fifteenth century). Our word *conjugation* is probably a direct importation from Latin (*conjugation–em*) since the more usual form in French was *conjugaison.* Sometimes the occurrence of a word in English earlier than in French (e.g., *obtuse*) points to the direct adoption from Latin, as does the use of some words like *confidence, confident* in senses which the same words in French do not have, but which are expressed in French by the forms *confiance, confiant.*

There still remain, however, a good many words which might equally well have come into English from Latin or French. Verbs like *consist* and *explore* could come either from the Latin *consistere* and *explorare* or the French *consister* and *explorer. Conformation, conflagration,* and many other similar nouns may represent either Latin *conformation–em, conflagration–em,* or French *conformation, conflagration.* It is so with words like *fidelity, ingenuity, proclivity,* where the Latin *fidelitat–em* developed into French *fidélité,* but English possessed so many words of this kind from French that it could easily have formed others on the same pattern. So adjectives like *affable, audible, jovial* may represent the Latin *affabilis* or the French *affable,* etc., and others like *consequent, modest, sublime* can have come equally well from the Latin or the French forms. It is really not important which language was the direct source of the English words since in either case they are ultimately of Latin origin. In many cases French may have offered a precedent for introducing the Latin words into English and have assisted in their general adoption.

WORDS FROM THE ROMANCE LANGUAGES. Sixteenth-century purists objected to three classes of strange words, which they characterized as *inkhorn terms, oversea language,* and *Chaucerisms.* For the foreign borrowings in this period were by no means confined to learned words taken from Latin and Greek. The English vocabulary at this time shows words adopted from more than fifty languages,[6] the most important of which (besides Latin and Greek) were French, Italian, and Spanish. English travel in France and consumption of French books is reflected in such words as *alloy, ambuscade, baluster, bigot, bizarre, bombast, chocolate, comrade, detail, duel, entrance, equip, equipage, essay, explore, genteel, mustache, naturalize, probability, progress, retrenchment, shock, surpass, talisman, ticket, tomato, vogue,* and *volunteer.* But the English also traveled frequently in Italy, observed Italian architecture and brought back not only Italian manners and styles of dress but Italian words. Protests against the Italianate Englishman are frequent in Elizabethan literature, and the objection is not only that the Englishmen came back corrupted in morals and affecting outlandish fashions, but that they "powdered their talk with oversea language."[7] Nevertheless, Italian words like Italian fashions were frequently adopted in England. Words like *algebra, argosy, balcony, cameo, capricio* (the common form of *caprice* until after the Restoration), *cupola, design, granite, grotto, piazza, portico, stanza, stucco, trill, violin, volcano* began to be heard on the lips of Englishmen or to be found in English books. Many other Italian words were introduced through French or adapted to French forms, words like *battalion, bankrupt, bastion, brusque, brigade, carat, cavalcade, charlatan, frigate, gala, gazette, grotesque, infantry, parakeet,* and *rebuff.* Many of these preserved for a time their Italian form. From Spanish and Portuguese English adopted *alligator* (*el lagarto* the lizard), *anchovy, apricot, armada, armadillo, banana, bastiment, bastinado, bilbo, bravado, brocade* (often employed in the form *brocado*), *barricade* (often *barricado,* as in Shakespeare), *cannibal, canoe, cedilla, cocoa, corral, desperado, embargo, hammock, hurricane, maize, mosquito, mulatto, negro, peccadillo, potato, renegado* (the original form of *renegade*), *rusk, sarsaparilla, sombrero, tobacco,* and *yam.* Many of these words reflect the Spanish enterprise on the sea and colonization of the American continent. As in the case of Italian words, Spanish words sometimes entered English through French or took a French form. *Grenade, palisade, escalade,* and *cavalier* are examples, although commonly found in the sixteenth and seventeenth centuries in the form *grenado, palisado, escalado, cavaliero,* even when the correct Spanish form would have been *granada, palisada,* and *escalada.* Sometimes the influence of all these languages combined to give us our English word, as in the case of *galleon, gallery, pistol, cochineal.*[8] Thus the cosmopolitan tendency, the spirit of exploration and adventure, and the interest in the New World which was being opened up show themselves in an interesting way in the growth of our vocabulary, and contributed along with the more intellectual forms of activity to the enrichment of the English language.

THE METHOD OF INTRODUCING THE NEW WORDS. The Latin words which form so important an element in the English vocabulary have generally entered the language through the medium of writing. Unlike the Scandinavian influence and to a large extent the French influence after the Norman Conquest, the various Latin influences, except the earliest, have been the work of churchmen and scholars. If the words themselves have not always been learned words, they have needed the help of learned men to become known. This was particularly true in the Renaissance. Even the words borrowed from the Romance languages in this period came in often through books, and the revivals and new formations from native material were due to the efforts of individual writers and their associates. It is impossible, of course, to say who was responsible for the introduction of each particular word, but in certain cases we can see an individual man at work—like Sir Thomas Elyot—conscious of his innovations and sometimes pausing to remark upon them. Another writer who introduced a large number of new words was Elyot's older contemporary, Sir Thomas More. To More we owe the words *absurdity, acceptance, anticipate, combustible, compatible* (in our sense), *comprehensible, concomitance, congratulatory, contradictory, damnability, denunciation, detector, dissipate, endurable, eruditely, exact, exaggerate, exasperate, explain, extenuate, fact, frivolous, impenitent, implacable, incorporeal, indifference, insinuate, inveigh, inviolable, irrefragable, monopoly, monosyllable, necessitate, obstruction, paradox, pretext,* and others. Elyot, besides using some of these, gives us *accommodate, adumbrate, adumbration, analogy, animate, applicate* (as an alternative to the older *apply*), *beneficence, encyclopedia, excerpt, excogitate, excogitation, excrement, exhaust, exordium, experience* (verb), *exterminate, frugality, implacability, infrequent, inimitable, irritate, modesty, placability,* etc.[9] The lists have been made long, at the risk of being wearisome, in order that they might be the more impressive. So far as we now know, these words had not been used in English previously. In addition both writers employ many words which are recorded from only a few years before. And so they either introduced or helped to establish many new words in the language. What More and Elyot were doing was being done by numerous others, and it is necessary to recognize the importance of individuals as "makers of English" in the sixteenth and early seventeenth century.

ENRICHMENT FROM NATIVE SOURCES. By far the greater part of the additions to the English vocabulary in the period of the Renaissance was drawn from sources outside of English. The popular favor shown to all kinds of foreign words seems to have implied a disparagement of English resources that was resented in some quarters. Gabriel Harvey remarked that "in Inglande . . . nothinge is reputid so contemptible, and so baselye and vilelye accountid of, as whatsoever is taken for Inglishe, whether it be handsum fasshions in apparrell, or seemely and honorable in behaviour, or choise wordes and phrases in speache, or anye notable thinge else . . . that savorith of our owne cuntrye and is not ether merely or mixtely outlandishe." [10] But, as we have seen, there were purists like Cheke, and there were also others who believed that English could very well develop new words from old roots or revive expressions that had gone out of use. Cheke was so strongly opposed to the borrowing of Latin and Greek words that he sought wherever possible for English equivalents. Thus, in his translation of the Gospel of St. Matthew, where the Authorized Version reads *lunatic* he wrote *mooned,* and in the same way he said *toller* for *publican, hundreder* for *centurion, foresayer* for *prophet, byword* for *parable, freshman* for *proselyte, crossed* for *crucified, gainrising* for *resurrection.* The poets, of course, were rather more given to the revival of old words, especially words that were familiar to them in Chaucer. For this reason their revivals and new formations that suggested an older period of English were sometimes referred to as Chaucerisms. Among poets who consciously made use of old words to enlarge the poetical vocabulary the most important was Spenser, although there were also others, such as Thomas Drant, the translator of Horace, whose influence on Spenser has not been fully appreciated, and to a lesser degree Milton.

These poetical innovations were of several kinds. Some were old words revived, like *astound, blameful, displeasance, enroot, doom, forby* (hard by, past), *empight* (fixed, implanted), *natheless, nathemore, mickle, whilere* (a while before). Others were new, such as *askew, filch, flout, freak.* The origin of these is often uncertain; they may have been of dialectal provenience. Some were definitely coinages, such as Spenser's *bellibone* (a fair maid, possibly from *belle et bonne*), *blatant, braggadocio, chirrup, cosset* (lamb), *delve* (pit, den), *dit* (song), *scruze* (apparently a telescope word combining *screw* and *squeeze*), *squall* (to cry), and *wrizzled* (wrinkled, shriveled). Finally, many were simply adaptations and derivatives of old words, such as *baneful, briny, changeful, drear* (from *dreary*), *hapless, oaten, sunshiny,* or *wolfish.* Some of the innovations had a look much more rustic and strange than these, and, as in the case of inkhorn terms and oversea words, opinion varied as to their desirability. Sidney criticized Spenser for the "framing of his stile to an old rustick language," and Ben Jonson went so far as to say that "Spenser in affecting the ancients writ no language." But the poet also had his defenders. His friend "E.K." wrote, ". . . in my opinion it is one special prayse of many whych are dew to this poete, that he hath laboured to restore as to their rightfull heritage such good and naturall English words . as have ben long time out of use and almost cleane disherited." The defenders, moreover, could have pointed to the fact that the same method of enriching the language was being urged in France. The words which English acquired in this way are not nearly so numerous as those obtained from outside, but when all is said the fact remains that to Spenser and others who shared his views we owe a great many useful words. *Belt, bevy, craggy, dapper, forthright, glen, glee, glance, surly, blandishment, birthright, changeling, elfin, endear, disrobe, don, enshrine, drizzling, fleecy, grovel, gaudy, gloomy, merriment, rancorous, shady, verdant, wakeful, wary,* and *witless* by no means exhaust the list. Many of these have passed from the language of poetry into common use, and, what is equally important, a vital principle of English word-formation was being kept alive.

NOTES

1. Benevolent, enterprise, studious, endeavor, protest, reproach, malignity. The statements in the text are based upon the dated citations in the *NED.* An earlier occurrence of any word is always possible. For example, in a translation by Skelton (c. 1485) of the *History of the World* by Diodorus Siculus over 800 Latin innovations occur, many earlier than the first instance recorded in the *NED.* But the work exists in a unique Ms. and has never been published. While its influence on the English language was probably negligible, it shows that the attitude of the sixteenth-century innovators was not without precedent. See F. M. Salter, *John Skelton's Contribution to the English Language* (Ottawa, 1945; *Trans. Royal Soc. of Canada*). The purpose of this and the following paragraphs, of course, is to record the efforts of Elyot and others to enrich the English language by the conscious importation of words which they believed were needed.

2. Dedication to his translation of the *Aeneid* (1697).

3. In France the same argument was being employed: "To wish to take away

from a learned man who desires to enrich his language the freedom sometimes to adopt uncommon words would be to restrain our language, not yet rich enough, under a more rigorous law than that which the Greeks and Romans gave themselves." (DuBellay, *Deffence et Illustration,* Chap. VI.)

4. In *Strange Newes,* or *Four Letters Confuted* (1592).

5. *Pierce's Supererogation* (1593).

6. See Murray's preface to volume VII of the *NED.*

7. Carew, in *The Excellency of the English Tongue,* says: "Soe have our Italyan travilers brought us acquainted with their sweet relished phrases which (soe their condicions crept not in withall) weere the better tollerable." (*Eliz. Critical Essays,* II. 290.)

8. galleon   = F. *galion,* Sp. *galeon,* Ital. *galeone.*
   gallery   = F. *galerie,* Sp., Port., and Ital. *galeria.*
   pistol   = F. *pistole,* Sp. and Ital. *pistola.*
   cochineal = F. *cochenille,* Sp. *cochinilla,* Ital. *cocciniglia.*

That the Italian and Spanish words borrowed by English at this time reflect the general commerce of ideas is clear from the fact that the same words were generally being adopted by French. Cf. B. H. Wind, *Les mots italiens introduits en français au XVIe siècle* (Deventer, 1928) and Richard Ruppert, *Die spanischen Lehn- und Fremdwörter in der französischen Schriftsprache* (Munich, 1915).

9. A number of the words here listed antedate the earliest quotation in the *New English Dictionary.* The More list is based (with additions) upon J. Delcourt, *Essai sur la langue de Sir Thomas More d'après ses œuvres anglaises* (Paris, 1914). Both lists, but especially Elyot's, could be largely extended by words which have not survived, such as *adminiculation* (aid), *allect* (allure), *allective, circumscription* (description or account), *comprobate* (sanction), *concinnity* (harmony, congruity), *condisciple* (schoolfellow), etc. It may be noted that More was equally given to new formations from native material (see pp. 148–9).

10. *Eliz. Critical Essays,* I. 124.

ALBERT H. MARCKWARDT

The Language of the Colonists

In considering the history and development of American English we must remember that the courageous bands who ventured westward into the unknown with Captain John Smith or on board the *Mayflower*, as well as those who followed them later in the seventeenth century, were speaking and writing the English language as it was currently employed in England. Consequently, whatever linguistic processes operated to produce the differences between American and British English which exist today must either have taken place in American English after the colonists settled on this continent or have occurred in British English after the emigrants left their homeland. Or, as a third possibility, there may have been changes in both divisions of the language after the period of settlement. We cannot, however, escape the conclusion of original identity and subsequent change.

Our first concern, therefore, is with the kind of English spoken by Smith's Virginians, Calvert's Marylanders, the Plymouth Fathers, the Bostonians of the Massachusetts Bay Colony, Roger Williams' Rhode Islanders, and Penn's Quakers. What was the state of the language at the time they left the shores of their native England?

The answer to this entails making a comparison between the memorable dates of our early colonial history with those pertinent to the English literary scene throughout the seventeenth century. It shows, for example, that Jonson was at the height of his career and that Shakespeare was still writing when Jamestown was settled. Plymouth Colony was founded before the publication of Shakespeare's First Folio and less than a decade after the completion of the Authorized Version of the Bible.

Dryden, who is often called the father of modern prose, was not born until after the settlement of the second colony in New England. His

Essay of Dramatic Poesy was not written until the capture of New York by the English, nor were the essays of Cowley, equally modern in style and temper. The publication date of *Paradise Lost* is somewhat later, and that of *Pilgrim's Progress* actually follows King Philip's War in point of time. I mention these in particular because we often think of these last two works as indicative of the same kind of dissent against the Anglican Church as that which is reflected in the colonial settlement, particularly in the north. Yet Massachusetts, Connecticut, and Rhode Island were all established and flourishing by the time these books appeared. Even such late prose representative of Elizabethan exuberance, complication, involution, and to some extent lack of discipline as Burton's *Anatomy of Melancholy* and Browne's *Religio Medici* postdate the establishment of the early New England settlements.

The émigrés who accompanied Smith and Bradford had learned their native language long before the years 1607 and 1620 respectively. Many of them were mature; some were old. Even a man of forty on the Jamestown expedition would presumably have learned to speak English about 1570; John Rolfe, the future husband of Pocahontas, acquired his native tongue probably in 1587. A young man of twenty-one, John Alden for example, in the Mayflower company must have learned English at the height of Shakespeare's career; Miles Standish, when Shakespeare was beginning to write. In short, the earliest English colonists in the New World were speaking Elizabethan English, the language of Shakespeare, Lyly, Marlowe, Lodge, and Green, when they came to America—not the measurably different English of Dryden, Defoe, and Bunyan. This is important and necessary for our understanding of some of the distinctive features which American English was to develop later on.

Next, what was the general state of Elizabethan English? How many people spoke it? The population of England, excluding Ireland and Scotland, in Shakespeare's time has been estimated at 4,460,000. This is a little more than the present population of Massachusetts, somewhat less than that of Michigan. Of these, probably 200,000 lived in London in 1600; the population in 1605 is given as 224,275. This is approximately the population of Syracuse, New York, or of Oklahoma City. These people and possibly 25,000 more in the immediate vicinity spoke London English, the regional variety which was in the process of becoming a standard for the English-speaking world as a whole.

Naturally the language sounded somewhat different from its twentieth-century counterpart. Certain though not all of these differences provide us with a partial explanation of the current variations in pronunciation between British and American English. For one thing, many words which are now pronounced with the vowel of *meat* had, at the time of the earliest settlements in America, the quality of present-day English *mate*. In fact, Londoners were accustomed to hear both the *ee* and the *ay* sounds in such words as *meat, teach, sea, tea, lean,* and *beard.* The conservative *ay* pronunciation continued in the language as late as the time of Pope. On occasion Shakespeare was capable of rhyming *please* with *knees* and at other times with *grace.* Without this double pronunciation a speech such as that by Dromio, "Marry sir, she's the Kitchin wench, & al *grease* (*grace*)" would have lost its punning effect.

It is quite possible that words which today have the vowel of *mate* were also pronounced at times with the vowel of *sand.* In addition to the play on the words *grease* and *grace* cited in the foregoing paragraph, there is in *All's Well* another punning passage involving a common or highly similar pronunciation of *grace* and *grass:*

> CLOWN. Indeed sir she was the sweete margerom of the sallet or rather the hearbe of grace.
>
> LAFEW. They are not hearbes you knave, they are nose-hearbes.
>
> CLOWN. I am no great Nevuchadnezar sir, I have not much skill in grace.

A rhyme such as the following from *Venus and Adonis* suggests the same conclusion:

> Even so poor birds, deceived with painted grapes . . .
> Even so she languisheth in her mishaps.

There was undoubtedly quite as much fluctuation in words which are generally spelled with *oo;* those of the *food, good,* and *flood* classes respectively. It is only recently that the pronunciation of many of these words has become standardized. All three of these words constitute one of Shakespeare's rhymes, and a half-century later Dryden rhymed *flood* with *mood* and *good.* Even today certain words of this class (*roof, room, root, hoof, coop, soot,* etc.) are pronounced variously in different parts of the United States.

At the time of which we are writing, the vowel of *cut* had but recently developed in London speech and was not yet a feature of all the English dialects. Combinations of *ir, er,* and *ur* in words like *bird, learn,* and *turn* had not long before coalesced into a vowel which was more like the sound to be heard over most of the United States today than that which is characteristic of southern British English. Contemporary pronunciation was far from settled in words like *clerk,* which seemed to be classed part of the time with the sound of *dark* and at other times with the vowel of *jerk.* Moreover, this variation affected many more words than it does now. Shakespeare rhymed *convert* with *art, serve* with *carve, heard* with *regard.*

In addition, the language at that time had no sound like the stressed vowel of present-day *father* or *calm*. The diphthongs characteristic of such words as *house* and *loud* had, instead of the *ah* first element commonly employed today, a sound something like the final vowel of *Cuba*. The whole diphthong was pronounced in a manner quite similar to that which may be heard at the present time in tidewater Virginia or in the Toronto area. The diphthong in words like *bite* and *bide* began with this same neutral element. The so-called short *o* sound of *cot* and *fog* was always pronounced with the lips somewhat rounded, as in Modern English *fall*.

Nor were the stress patterns of Shakespeare's English absolutely identical with those of the modern period. A line such as "The light will show, character'd in my brow," indicates clearly that in such a trisyllabic word as *character'd*, the stress had not yet shifted to the first syllable. A good many two-syllable words which now stress the first, at that time had the accent on the second. Note, "And there I'll rest, as after much *turmoil*." Many derivatives in -*able* had a distinct stress, at least secondary in value, on the suffix. A line such as "What *acceptable* audit canst thou leave?" can scarcely be read in any other fashion.

Many words show a double stress pattern: *sincere* with stress at times on the first and at times on the second syllable; *confiscate* on occasion has initial stress, and elsewhere on the second syllable. It is probably fair to say that just as with vowel quality, the language during the Elizabethan period permitted somewhat more latitude than it does today.

It must be kept in mind, moreover, that the pronunciations which have just been discussed reflect only the language practices of the inhabitants of London and its environs, constituting approximately 5 per cent of the five million who spoke English at that time. The remaining 95 per cent spoke the regional or provincial dialects. Those who live in the United States find it hard to conceive of the extent to which regional dialects may differ even today within an area no larger than one of our moderate-size states.

At the present time, to select just a single instance, a word such as *about* will be pronounced with the stressed vowel of *bite* in Devon, with the vowel of *boot* along the Scottish border, with the vowel of *father* and a final consonant more like *d* than *t* in London Cockney, and with a pronunciation something like *abaeut* in Norfolk.

To anyone who has grown up in a tradition of relative linguistic uniformity over a territory virtually three million square miles in area, such differences in speech present in a country only one-sixtieth as large are startling, to say the least. But in the England of today, regional dialects are confined to a relatively small portion of the population as compared with three centuries ago. There can be little question about the wide prevalence of dialect and the general lack of uniformity of speech among the vast majority of the settlers of the seventeenth century.

Seventeenth-century English differed from its modern counterpart in other aspects of speech as well. Although the language had in general developed most of the inflections which are used in present-day English— the noun plurals, the object form *them* in the plural pronoun, the past tense and past participle forms of the weak verb—a few interesting earlier features still remained. Among these were the double forms of the pronoun of address: *thou* and *ye* or *you*. Because the distribution of these was governed partly by considerations of social rank and in part on the basis of emotional overtones, their very presence in the language made for a subtlety which today must be achieved through quite different means. Note, for example, in the following well-known passage from the first part of *Henry IV*, how the choice of pronouns reflects Hotspur's shift of mood from jesting concealment to stern warning, concluding with a gentler and more intimate tone:

> Come, wilt *thou* see me ride?
> And when I am o'horseback, I will swear
> I love *thee* infinitely. But hark *you*, Kate;
> I must not have *you* henceforth question me
> Whither I go, nor reason whereabout.
> Whither I must, I must; and, to conclude,
> This evening must I leave *you*, gentle Kate.
> I know *you* wise; but yet no farther wise
> Than Harry Percy's wife. Constant *you* are,
> But yet a woman; and for secrecy,
> No lady closer; for I well believe
> *Thou* wilt not utter what *thou* dost not know;
> And so far will I trust *thee*, gentle Kate.

And again in Kate's preceding speech but one, her change from exaggeration to gentle entreaty is indicated in precisely the same manner.

> Come, come, *you* paraquito, answer me
> Directly unto this question that I ask.
> In faith, I'll break *thy* little finger, Harry,
> And if *thou* wilt not tell me all things true.

Actually, at one point slightly later than Shakespeare's time, this matter of the second personal pronoun became a politico-religious issue. The Quakers, committed to a belief in the innate equality of all men, interpreted the duality of the pronoun of address as a negation of that equality and argued, quite intemperately at times, for a return to an older state of the language where the two forms were differentiated solely on the basis of number. In the following passage, George Fox, the founder and leader of the sect, set forth his views in no uncertain terms.

> Do not they speak false English, false Latine, false Greek . . . and false to the other Tongues, . . . that doth not speak *thou* to *one*, what ever he be, Father, Mother, King, or Judge; is he not a Novice and Unmannerly, and an Ideot and a Fool, that speaks *You* to *one*, which is not to be spoken to a *singular*, but to many? O Vulgar Professors and Teachers, that speaks Plural when they should Singular . . . Come you Priests and Professors, have you not learnt your Accidence?

It is worth noting that the English language did eventually go along with Fox's democratic notions by giving up the pronoun differentiation based upon social status, but in so doing, ironically selected the form which he considered inappropriate for the task.

This double supply of pronouns also carried with it an accompanying difference in verb structure, for *thou* as subject regularly demanded a verb ending in *-est. Ye* or *you* as subjects were accompanied merely by the simple or root form of the verb. Thus we would have had at this time *thou teachest* but *ye* or *you teach, thou knowest* but *you know.* After the *thou* forms fell into disfavor, so too did the verb inflections in *-est,* leaving the second person singular of the verb identical with the first person and with all forms of the plural.

In addition Elizabethan English represents a period of change from an earlier *-eth* inflection for the third person singular of the verb to the *-s* forms characteristic of the language today. There is an interesting difference here between the practice of Shakespeare and that of the contemporary King James Version of the Bible. The latter regularly uses *-eth:* "He maketh me to lie down in green pastures." In his ordinary dramatic prose, Shakespeare employs *-s* regularly for all verbs except *have* and *do,* which retain the archaic *hath* and *doth* (the latter only occasionally) presumably because these were learned as individual forms early in life by the average speaker instead of as part of an over-all pattern.

Even here, however, one must exercise due caution in interpreting the *-eth* spellings. In the middle of the seventeenth century one Richard Hodges wrote *A Special Help to Orthographie,* which consisted chiefly in listing words "alike in sound but unlike both in their signification and writing." Among the homophonic pairs which appear in this treatise are *roweth* and *rose, wrights,* and *righteth, Mr. Knox* and *knocketh.* He goes on to say in explanation:

> Therefore, whensoever *eth* cometh in the end of any word, wee may pronounce it sometimes as *s,* and sometimes like *z,* as in these words,

namely, in *bolteth it,* and *boldeth it,* which are commonly pronounc't, as if they were writen thus, *bolts* it, and *bolds* it: save onely in such words, where either *c, s, sh, ch, g,* or *x* went before it: as in *graceth, pleaseth, washeth, matcheth, rageth, taxeth:* for these must still remaine as two syllables. Howbeit, if men did take notice, how they use to speak, in their ordinary speech to one another, they might plainly perceive, that in stead of *graceth,* they say *graces,* and so they pronounce al other words of this kinde, accordingly.

Unquestionably the best way to acquire a feeling for many of the differences between the language of today and that of the age of Elizabeth is to observe with some care a selection of one of the earliest examples of what might be called American English. The following selection from William Bradford's *History of Plimoth Plantation* will serve the purpose:

> In these hard and difficulte beginnings they found some discontents and murmurings arise amongst some, and mutinous speeches and carriages in other; but they were soone quelled and overcome by the wisdome, patience, and just and equall carrage of things by the Gov[erno]r and better part, which clave faithfully togeather in the maine. But that which was most sadd and lamentable was, that in 2 or 3 moneths time halfe of their company dyed, espetialy in Jan: and February, being the depth of winter, and wanting houses and other comforts; being infected with the scurvie and other diseases, which this long voiage and their inacomodate condition had brought upon them; so as ther dyed some times 2 or 3 of a day, in the aforesaid time; that of 100 and odd persons, scarce 50 remained. And of these in the time of most distres, ther was but 6 or 7 sound persons, who, to their great comendations be it spoken, spared no pains, night nor day, but with abundance of toil and hazard of their owne health, fetched them woode, made them fires, drest them meat, made their beads, washed their lothsome cloaths, cloathed and uncloathed them; in a word, did all the homly and necessarye offices for them which dainty and quesie stomacks cannot endure to hear named; and all this willingly and cherfully, without any grudging in the least, shewing herin their true love unto their freinds and bretheren. A rare example and worthy to be remembered. Tow of these 7 were Mr. William Brewster, ther reverend Elder, and Myles Standish, ther Captein and Military comander, unto whom my selfe, and many others, were much beholden in our low and sicke condition. And yet the Lord so upheld these persons, as in this generall calamity they were not at all infected either with sickness, or lamnes. And what I have said of these, I may say of many others who dyed in this generall visitation, and others yet living, that whilst they had health, yea, or any strength continuing, they were not wanting to

any that had need of them. And I doute not but their recompence is with the Lord.

But I may not hear pass by an other remarkable passage not to be forgotten. As this calamitie fell among the passengers that were to be left here to plant, and were hasted a shore and made to drinke water, that the sea-men might have the more bear, and one in his sickness desiring but a small can of beere, it was answered, that if he were their owne father he should have none; the disease begane to fall amongst them also, so as allmost halfe of their company dyed before they went away, and many of their officers and lustyest men, as the boatson, gunner, 3 quarter-maisters, the cooke, and others. At which the m[aste]r was something strucken and sent to the sick a shore and tould the Gov[erno]r he should send for beer for them that had need of it, though he drunke water homward bound.

Most noticeable, perhaps, in the passage just quoted are a number of words no longer current in the language. Among them are *inacomodate* and *hasted*. *Yea, unto,* and *beholden* are rarely employed except in certain set phrases and at times in religious connections. Other words have come to be used in contexts quite unlike those in which they appear in this passage. For instance, *carriages* no longer signifies behavior in the abstract sense; *clothed,* here meaning the specific act of dressing, has become more general in its use. *Offices* is used here in the sense of services; *lustiest* to mean healthiest. Though by no means inclusive, these examples suggest the changes which have taken place in the English vocabulary during the last three centuries, both with respect to the words it comprises and the meanings of these words.

Likewise, certain changes in the forms of words have taken place. Almost at the beginning of the passage, *other* was used as a plural pronoun, although the modern form *others* appears later on. *Scarce,* in an adverbial use, indicates that the fetish of the *-ly* ending was somewhat less strong at that time than it is at present. As might be expected, the most pronounced differences are in the verb forms, where *clave* and *drunke* appear as past tenses and *strucken* as a past participle.

Differences in syntax are even more numerous. The plural form of the abstractions *discontents* and *murmurings* would be unlikely to appear in present-day usage, as would *commendations*. Closely connected with this same problem of number is the lack of agreement between subject and verb in, "There was but 6 or 7 sound persons." The word *as* in constructions like, "so as ther dyed," and "as in this generall calamity," would today be replaced by *that*. At the same time, certain pronominal uses of *that* in this selection would unquestionably call for *who* in the language of today.

Even more striking than any of these features is the sentence structure. In general the sentences lack unity and are replete with dangling phrases and clauses. The first sentence in the selection contains fifty-three words, the second eighty-three, and the third attains a total of one hundred and six. These are all long according to modern standards. Ironically enough, the third sentence is followed by an eight word fragment that does not fit the modern pattern of the conventional sentence at all. In the second sentence the parallelism of the phrases introduced by *being* and *wanting* is faulty. The majority of the sentences are without coherence and direction in the present sense of these terms.

The proper conclusion, however, is not that Bradford was a bad writer —in fact he was not—but that there were differences between seventeenth-century prose and our own. Some of these differences are purely a matter of historical development. The roots of our modern forms and practices were already in the language. It is even more important to recognize this as a period prior to a certain codification, settlement, one might almost say a jelling, of English written prose. A man's spelling was still his own concern, as is clearly evident, and so too, to some extent, were his sentences. If this codification or jelling took place after the two speech areas, England and America, were already separated, it is more than possible that the settling processes might not work out in the same way in both places.

Consequently, since the earliest American settlers employed Elizabethan English, it is the highly variable and complex character of that medium that provides us with an explanation of the beginning of the divergence in the two great streams of our language. It remains to be seen how, and through what means, this divergence developed throughout the course of the intervening centuries.

PART THREE

The Structure of English

To acquire confidence and judgment in the use of our language, we need to know not only how English developed but also what it actually sounds and looks like today. The description of a spoken language is the linguist's first step toward objective mastery of its structure. It is hard to look accurately and dispassionately at anything as much a part of us as our own language. The technique of observation is easier to manage when it is applied to someone else's language. Something of that technique is explained in the first essay in this section by Professor H. A. Gleason, Jr., who prepares missionaries to deal with languages for which there are no interpreters, dictionaries, or grammars. One of the necessary tools in the objective description of a language is a system of symbols for reporting spoken sounds, and such a system adapted to English is illustrated here in an essay by Professor Paul Roberts of Cornell University. These sounds or segmental phonemes, which strike a foreigner as disorganized noise, are in fact further patterned by stress, pitch, and pauses or junctures (sly twitch or slight witch)—terms which Professor Roberts explains in the third selection. How precise linguistic description can be, and how much we are unconsciously influenced in our thinking as well as in our speaking by such deep-seated linguistic patterns as the structure of one-syllable words, are points explained by Benjamin Lee Whorf. Walter Winchell may coin "thrub" but he will never coin "srub." There are arguments against Whorf's "linguistic relativity principle," but his discussion of the study of language as an exact science makes clear some attitudes which all linguists believe are necessary to the profitable examination of linguistic phenomena. One method whereby the grammar as well as the sounds of a living language may be discovered and described objectively is illustrated by Charles C. Fries in an essay taken from his influential *American English Grammar*. An introductory outline of a grammar based on such an objective description of our language is presented in the essay by Dudley Bailey, professor of English at the University of Nebraska, and Dona W. Brown and Wallace C. Brown, professors of English at the University of Kansas City. This outline illustrates only one of the current methods of grammatical analysis which show promise, but its assumptions and its descriptions are a good example of the kind of radical skepticism the linguistic analyst must have.

Other essays in this section deal with the relations between spoken and written English. Punctuation, as Harold Whitehall shows, is largely one of the often crude devices by which we try to translate the meaningful tones of the speaking voice into writing and print. (Was he mad? Was he mad!) A far cruder device is spelling. How our spelling got that way is explained by the late distinguished Danish linguist, Otto Jespersen, who gives "if not rational at any rate historical reasons" for the differences between our sounds and our spellings. Our surprising anxiety about spelling and its effect on our attitude toward language in general are problems critically examined in the essay by Professor Robert A. Hall, Jr., of Cornell University. The notion that one should simply write as one speaks is discussed by Harold Whitehall, who reminds us that "to speak with a local accent is not disadvantageous; to write serious prose with a local accent definitely is." Written English, Whitehall adds, "must be more carefully organized than speech in order to overcome its communicative deficiencies as compared with speech."

H. A. GLEASON, JR.

Language

As you listen to an unfamiliar language you get the impression of a torrent of disorganized noises carrying no sense whatever. To the native speaker it is quite otherwise. He pays little attention to the sounds, but concerns himself instead with some situation which lies behind the act of speech and is, for him, somehow reflected in it. Both you and he have failed to grasp the nature of the phenomenon. Neither the casual observer nor the usual native speaker can give any real information about a language. To be sure, some people, Americans perhaps more than most others, have decided notions about language. But the ideas held and discussed come far short of giving a complete picture of the language and sometimes have very little relationship to the facts. Even people with considerable education are often wholly unable to answer certain quite simple questions about their language. For most people language is primarily a tool to be used, rather than a subject for close and critical attention.

It is probably well that it is so. Yet there are important human problems into which language enters intimately and on which it exerts such a profound influence that an understanding of its mechanism would contribute materially to their solutions. Moreover, every phase of human activity is worthy of study. Thus, for practical reasons, as well as to satisfy man's innate curiosity, language deserves careful and intelligent study.

Language has so many interrelationships with various aspects of human life that it can be studied from numerous points of view. All are valid and useful, as well as interesting in themselves. Linguistics is the science which attempts to understand language from the point of view of its internal structure. It is not, of course, isolated and wholly autonomous, but it does have a clearly and sharply delimited field of inquiry, and has developed its own highly effective and quite characteristic method. It must draw upon such sciences as physical acoustics, communications theory, human physiology, psychology, and anthropology for certain basic concepts and necessary data. In return, linguistics makes its own essential contributions to these disciplines. But however closely it may be related to other sciences, it is clearly separate by reason of its own primary concern with the structure of language.

What then is this structure? Language operates with two kinds of material. One of these is sound. Almost any sort of noise that the human vocal apparatus can produce is used in some way in some language. The other is ideas, social situations, meanings—English lacks any really acceptable term to cover the whole range—the facts or fantasies about man's existence, the things man reacts to and tries to convey to his fellows. These two, insofar as they concern linguists, may conveniently be labeled *expression* and *content*.

The foreigner who hears merely a jumble of sounds has not really heard the language, not even the part of it which we have called *expression*. All that he has heard is sounds, the material which language uses to carry its message. This is not the domain of the linguist, but that of the physicist. The latter can analyze the stream of speech as sound and learn many things about it. His findings have both theoretical and practical importance; the designs of telephones, radios, and much other electronic equipment depends in an essential way upon such findings. They also contribute basic data to linguistics, and to numerous other sciences, including psychology and physiology, as well as to physics itself.

The linguist is concerned with sound as the medium by which information is conveyed. To serve in this way, speech must be something quite different from the jumble of sound apparent to the foreigner. It is, in fact, an organized system or structure, and it is this structure that lies within the subject field of linguistics. The linguist analyzes speech as an orderly sequence of specific kinds of sounds and of sequences of sounds. It is orderly in terms of a very complex set of patterns which repeatedly recur and which are at least partially predictable. These patterns form the structure of *expression*, one major component of language in the sense that the linguist uses the term.

The native speaker has his attention focused on something else, the subject of the discourse. This may be a situation which is being described, some ideas which are being presented, or some social formula which is being repeated. None of these things are language, any more than are the sounds which convey speech. The subject of the discourse stands on the opposite side and in much the same relationship to speech as do the sounds. The speaker comprehends what he is talking about in terms of an organizing structure. This structure causes him to select certain features for description and determines the ways in which he will interrelate them. It also cuts the situation up into portions in a characteristic way. These selected features, like the sounds mentioned above, also form patterns which recur, and which are at least partially predictable. These recurrent patterns are the structure of *content*, a second major component of language as the linguist treats it.

Finally, these two structures are intimately related and interacting. Parts of the structure of expression are associated in definite ways with parts of the structure of content. The relations between these two complex structures are themselves quite complex. In every language they are different from what is found in every other language. The differences may be profound and extensive, or they may be relatively slight. But in every instance, the two structures are intricate and their relationships quite characteristic.

The native speaker uses this complex apparatus easily and without conscious thought of the process. It seems to him simple and natural. But to a speaker of another of the world's three thousand languages it may present quite a different picture. It may give an impression of being cumbersome, illogical, or even ridiculous. Actually, of course, the strange language is merely different. A true picture of language can only be had by seeing languages more objectively. Such a view will emphasize the immense complexity, the arbitrariness, and the high degree of adequacy for their purposes—features which are shared by all languages in spite of their divergencies.

The dual structure of language can best be made clear by an example. . . .

Consider a rainbow or a spectrum from a prism. There is a continuous gradation of color from one end to the other. That is, at any point there is only a small difference in the colors immediately adjacent at either side. Yet an American describing it will list the hues as *red, orange, yellow, green, blue, purple,* or something of the kind. The continuous gradation of color which exists in nature is represented in language by a series of discrete categories. This is an instance of structuring of content. There is nothing inherent either in the spectrum or the human perception of it which would compel its division in this way. The specific method of division is part of the structure of English.

By contrast, speakers of other languages classify colors in much different ways. In the accompanying diagram, a rough indication is given of the way in which the spectral colors are divided by speakers of English, Shona (a language of Rhodesia), and Bassa (a language of Liberia).

English:

purple	blue	green	yel-low	orange	red

Shona:

cips^{w}uka	citema	cicena	cips^{w}uka

Bassa:

hui	zīza

The Shona speaker divides the spectrum into three major portions. *Cips^{w}uka* occurs twice, but only because the red and purple ends, which he classifies as similar, are separated in the diagram. Interestingly enough, *citema* also includes black, and *cicena* white. In addition to these three terms there are, of course, a large number of terms for more specific colors. These terms are comparable to English *crimson, scarlet, vermilion,* which are all varieties of *red.* The convention of dividing the spectrum into three parts instead of into six does not indicate any difference in visual ability to perceive colors, but only a difference in the way they are classified or structured by the language.

The Bassa speaker divides the spectrum in a radically different way: into only two major categories. In Bassa there are numerous terms for specific colors, but only these two for general classes of colors. It is easy for an American to conclude that the English division into six major colors is superior. For some purposes it probably is. But for others it may present real difficulties. Botanists have discovered that it does not allow sufficient generalization for discussion of flower colors. Yellows, oranges, and many reds are found to constitute one series. Blues, purples, and purplish reds constitute another. These two exhibit fundamental differences that must be treated as basic to any botanical description. In order to state the facts succinctly it has been necessary to coin two new and more general color terms, *xanthic* and *cyanic,* for these two groups. A Bassa-speaking botanist would be under no such necessity. He would find *zīza* and *hui* quite adequate for the purpose, since they happen to divide the spectrum in approximately the way necessary for this purpose.

Now for a simple statement of structure in the expression part of language: The sounds used by English are grouped into consonants and vowels (and some other categories). These are organized into syllables in a quite definite and systematic way. Each syllable must have one and only one vowel sound. It may have one or more consonants before the vowel, and one or more after the vowel. There are quite intricate restrictions on the sequences that may occur. Of all the mathematically possible combinations of English sounds, only a small portion are admitted as complying with the patterns of English structure. Not all of these are actually used, though the unused ones stand ready in case they should ever be needed. Perhaps some day a word like *ving* may appear in response to a new need. *Shmoo* was drawn out of this stock of unused possibilities only a few years ago. But *ngvi* would be most unlikely: it simply is not available as a potential English word, though it contains only English sounds.

Six of these permissible sequences of sounds are somehow associated with the six portions into which English language-habits structure the spectrum. These are the familiar *red, orange, yellow, green, blue, purple.* This association of expression and content is merely conventional. There is no reason why six others could not be used, or why these six could not be associated with different parts of the spectrum. No reason, that is, except that this is the English-language way of doing it, and these are conventions to which we must adhere reasonably closely if we are to be understood. Sometime in the past history of the language, these conventions became established and have persisted with only gradual changes since. In their ultimate origins, all such conventions are the results of more or less accidental choices. It is largely fortuitous that the spectrum came to be so divided, that the specific words were attached to the colors so distinguished, or, indeed, that the sounds from which they were formed were so organized that these words were possible. These irrational facts, with many others like them, constitute the English language. Each language is a similarly arbitrary system.

The three major components of language, as far as language lies within the scope of linguistics, are the structure of expression, the structure of content, and vocabulary. The latter comprises all the specific relations between expression and content—in the familiar terminology, words and their meanings.

Vocabulary comes and goes. It is the least stable and even the least characteristic of the three components of language. That portion of the vocabulary which changes most freely is sometimes referred to as "slang." But even staid and dignified words are constantly being created and continually passing out of active use, to be preserved only in literature which is dated by their very presence. While certain types of words are more transient than others, none are absolutely immortal. Even the most familiar and commonly used words, which might be expected to be most stable, have a mortality rate of about twenty percent in a thousand years.

Moreover, in the life history of an individual speaker the birth and death of words is very much more frequent than in the language community as a whole. Every normal person probably learns at least three words every day, over a thousand a year, and forgets old ones at an appreciable but lower rate. This figure must be a minimum, because most people have total vocabularies which could only be reached through even more rapid acquisition of vocabulary during at least part of their life.

We have no comparable method by which the rate of change of content structure can be estimated. The learning of new vocabulary, particularly technical terms associated with the learning of new concepts, does of course imply certain minor changes. But it is quite evident that change rarely touches the most basic features in any given language. With regard to the structure of expression the facts are clearer. Few, unless they learn a second language, will add, substract, or change any of their basic sound patterns after they reach adolescence. Grammatical constructions may increase, but at a rate much slower than the increase of vocabulary. Vocabulary is indeed the transient feature of language.

In learning a second language, you will find that vocabulary is comparatively easy, in spite of the fact that it is vocabulary that students fear most. The harder part is mastering new structures in both content and expression. You may have to free yourself from the bondage of thinking of everything as either singular or plural. Perhaps the new language will organize content into singular, dual, and plural (here meaning "three or more"). Or perhaps the new language will not give routine consideration to the matter. English speakers can never make a statement without saying something about the number of every object mentioned. This is compulsory, whether it is relevant or not. In Chinese, objects are noted as singular or plural only when the speaker judges the information to be relevant. The Chinese experience suggests that it actually seldom is, for that language operates with only occasional references to number.

You will have to make similar changes in habits of thought and of description of situations in many other instances. You may, for example, have to learn to think of every action as either completed or incomplete, and to disregard the time of the action unless it has special relevance. The reorganization of thinking and perception may extend much deeper than such changes. In some languages, situations are not analyzed, as they are in English, in terms of an actor and an action. Instead the fundamental cleavage runs in a different direction and cannot be easily stated in English. Some of these divergencies between languages have been described by Benjamin L. Whorf. His formulation has been widely debated and perhaps is not at present susceptible to rigorous testing. Yet the papers are very suggestive and can be read with profit by every student of linguistics or languages.

You will also have to reorganize your habits of making and hearing sounds. You will have to discriminate between sounds that you have learned to consider the same. You will find that others, in clear contrast in English, function as one, and you will have to learn to respond to them as to one sound. Patterns which seem impossible will have to become facile, and you will have to learn to avoid some English patterns that seem to be second nature.

The most difficult thing of all, however, is that these profound changes will have to become completely automatic. You will have to learn to use them without effort or conscious attention. In this learning process constant disciplined practice is essential. Special ability may be helpful, but probably much less so than is popularly supposed. An understanding of the basic principles of language structure—that is, the results of modern linguistic research—while not indispensable, can contribute in many ways.

As we listen to a person speaking our native language we hear not only what is said, but also certain things about the speaker. If he is an acquaintance, we recognize him. If not, we identify him as male or female and perhaps obtain some idea of his age, his education, and his social background. A person's voice serves at least two functions in communication. One is linguistic, in that it serves as the vehicle of the expression system of language. The other is non-linguistic, in that it carries information of a quite different sort about the speaker.

This distinction is made, at least roughly, even by the unsophisticated. If we are told to REPEAT exactly what another says, we will duplicate (provided our memory serves us adequately) every feature which is included in the language expression system. We can do that, if it is our own language, even without understanding the content. In repeating we will make no effort to reproduce anything beyond the linguistically pertinent features. If, however, we are asked to MIMIC another, we attempt to reproduce not only the linguistic features, but every discernible characteristic. Few can mimic with any degree of success, whereas every normal native speaker can, perhaps with a little practice, repeat exactly up to the limit imposed by his memory span.

The most basic elements in the expression system are the *phonemes*. These are the sound features which are common to all speakers of a given speech form and which are exactly reproduced in repetition. In any language, there is a definite and usually small number of phonemes. In English there are forty-six. Out of this limited inventory of units, the whole expression system is built up. In many respects the phonemes are analogous to the elements of chemistry, ninety-odd in number, out of which all substances are constructed.

The phoneme is one of those basic concepts, such as may be found in all sciences, which defy exact definition. Yet some sort of working characterization is necessary before we go on. The following is hardly adequate beyond a first introduction to the subject, but will make it possible to proceed with the analysis and enumeration of the phonemes of English. . . .

With this in mind, we may define a *phoneme* as a minimum feature of the expression system of a spoken language by which one thing that may be said is distinguished from any other thing which might have been said. Thus, if two utterances are different in such a way that they suggest to the hearer different contents, it must be because there are differences in the expressions. The difference may be small or extensive. The smallest difference which can differentiate utterances with different contents is a difference of a single phoneme. This description is best illustrated by a full-scale application in the presentation of the phonemic system of a language. . . .

There are two things about phonemes that must be explicitly pointed out in anticipation of any such presentation:

Phonemes are part of the system of one specific language. The phonemes of different languages are different, frequently incommensurable. It is for this reason that a foreigner hears only a jumble which he cannot repeat. The sounds of the unfamiliar language do not fit into his phonemic system, and so he can comprehend no order in a simple utterance. If anything which is said about the phonemes of one language happens to apply to those of another, we must regard it as fortuitous.

Phonemes are features of the spoken language. Written language has its own basic unit, the grapheme. Something will be said about this later. If, of necessity, written words are cited as illustrations, it must be constantly borne in mind that the written form is not, and cannot be, an illustration of a phoneme. Instead, it is the spoken form which the written form is expected to elicit which illustrates the phoneme under discussion. This inevitably introduces a major difficulty into the presentation. The illustrative words have been selected with the intention that they should be as generally as possible pronounced by all Americans in the same way. Undoubtedly this principle of selection fails in some instances because of dialect and individual peculiarities of the writer and the reader. Such instances will not vitiate the argument. For some Americans other examples might be needed, but examples can be found which will lead to the same results.

The thinking that most Americans do about language is almost exclusively concerned with written English. A written language is, of course, a valid and important object of linguistic investigation. It can, however, easily mislead the unwary. Most of the misunderstandings which Americans have about language arise from a failure to keep clearly in mind the nature and limitations of a written language.

A written language is typically a reflection, independent in only limited ways, of spoken language. As a picture of actual speech, it is inevitably imperfect and incomplete. To understand the structure of a written language one must constantly resort either to comparison with the spoken language or to conjecture. Unfortunately, recourse has been too largely to the latter. Moreover, conjecture has been based not so much upon an intimate knowledge of the ways of languages in general (the results of descriptive linguistics) as to a priori considerations of supposed logic, to metaphysics, and to simple prejudice. While logic and metaphysics are important disciplines and can make significant contributions to an understanding of language, the customary manner of applying them has redounded neither to their credit nor to the elucidation of language structure. Linguistics must start with thorough investigation of spoken language before it proceeds to study written language. This is true of languages with long histories of written literature, such as English, no less than those of isolated tribes which have never known of the possibility of writing.

The second basic unit in the expression system is the *morpheme*. This again cannot be exactly defined . . . For the present, however, let us characterize a *morpheme* as follows: It is the unit on the expression side of language which enters into relationship with the content side. A morpheme is typically composed of one to several phonemes. The morpheme differs fundamentally from the phoneme, which has no such relationship with content. That is, phonemes have no meanings; morphemes have meanings.

The simpler words of English are morphemes. Other words consist of two or more morphemes. Like the phonemes, the morphemes enter into combinations in accordance with definite and intricate patterns. The expression structure is merely the sum of the patterns of arrangement of these two basic units.

Using the phoneme and the morpheme as their basic units, linguists have been able to build a comprehensive theory of the expression side of language, and to make detailed and comprehensive statements about the expression systems of specific languages. This is what is ordinarily called *descriptive linguistics*. It is the basic branch of linguistic science. Others are *historical linguistics*, dealing with the changes of languages in time, and *comparative linguistics,* dealing with the relationships between languages of common origin. Descriptive linguistics is conventionally divided into two parts. *Phonology* deals with the phonemes and sequences of phonemes. *Grammar* deals with the morphemes and their combinations.

In some respects linguistics has developed more precise and rigorous methods and attained more definitive results than any other science dealing with human behavior. Linguists have been favored with the most obviously structured material with which to work, so this attainment is by no means due to any scientific superiority of linguists over other social scientists. It is also the direct result of the discovery of the phoneme, a discovery which allows the data to be described in terms of a small set of discrete units. Within a given language, a given sound is either a certain phoneme or it is not; there can be no intergradation. This fact eliminates from linguistics a large measure of the vagueness and lack of precision characteristic of most studies of human behavior. It would be presumptuous to claim that this advantage has been thoroughly exploited by linguists, but it is certainly fair to say that in some places, linguistics has achieved an appreciable measure of scientific rigor and has the foundations for further development in this regard.

The chief evidence for the high order of development of linguistics as a science lies in the reproducibility of its results. If two linguists work independently on the same language, they will come out with very similar statements. There may be differences. Some of these differences will be predictable. Very seldom will any of the differences be deep-seated. Usually it will be quite possible to harmonize the two statements and show that by simple restatements one result can be converted into the other. That is, the two results will have differed largely in inconsequential ways, often only in external form.

The content side of linguistics has developed much less rapidly and to a very much less impressive extent than the study of expression. Indeed, it cannot as yet justifiably be called a science. Undoubtedly this has been a source of frustration in linguistics as a whole. One of the greatest shortcomings of descriptive work with the expression aspect of language has been a lack of understanding of the relationships between expression and content, and the inability to use the analysis of content in attacking related problems in expression. Here is the great frontier in linguistic knowledge on which we may look for progress in the next decades.

There have been three reasons for this neglect of the content side. First, linguists have been late in comprehending the real significance of the two-sided nature of language. Their attention has been diverted from this basic problem by the great advances being made within the analysis of expression.

Second, there has been no way to gain access to the content structure except through the expression structure. This requires an inferential method which has not appealed to linguists busy with building a highly rigorous method for the handling of more directly observed data. Content has therefore had an inferior status in the eyes of linguists.

Third, the content, apart from its structure, has not been amenable to any unified study. The substance of content is, of course, the whole of human experience. Thousands of scientists have labored, each in some one of numerous disciplines, in elucidating this mass of material. But there is no one approach which can comprehend the whole and so serve as a starting point for comparison of the different structures which can be imposed upon it. Only isolated portions of the content system can as yet be studied as structure imposed on a measurable continuum of experience. The examples of structuring of color concepts discussed above suggest the possibilities and make the lack of further opportunities for comparison the more tantalizing.

In contrast, the expression plane starts with much simpler materials. The sounds producible by the human voice can be studied comprehensively by several approaches. Two of these have reached the degree of precision which makes them useful to linguistics: *articulatory phonetics,* a branch of human physiology, and *acoustic phonetics,* a branch of physics. . . . It is hard to imagine the scientific study of the expression aspect of speech attaining anywhere near the present degree of development without the aid of phonetics. The structure can be systematically described only because the underlying sounds can be accurately described and measured.

PAUL ROBERTS

Phonemes

DEFINITION OF A PHONEME

English has a total of forty-five sound units called *phonemes*. A phoneme is not exactly a single sound. It is rather a collection of similar
sounds which are likely to sound identical to the speaker of the language.
For example, English has a phoneme /p/, which occurs in the words
pin, nip, spin, appear, upper. All these "p" sounds are different. /p/ is
not the same at the beginning of a word as at the end, not the same
before a stressed syllable as after one, and so on. Yet these differences
are not significant for English, and we who speak English have learned
to ignore them.

In some languages these differences *are* significant. A speaker of Hindi
or Korean, for example, would feel that the "p" in *pin* and the "p" in *spin*
are not the same sound at all, for in these languages these sounds belong
to separate phonemes. Such a person learning English would have to
train himself to overlook this difference. On the other hand, we, if we
were to learn Hindi or Korean, would have to train ourselves to recognize
the difference and to react to it.

Languages differ widely in the number of phonemes they have. English, as we have said, has forty-five. Other languages have as few as
eighteen or twenty or as many as seventy or eighty.

VOWELS AND CONSONANTS

Of our forty-five English phonemes, twelve are intonation phonemes—
units of stress, pitch, and juncture. . . . The other thirty-three are vowels
and consonants—twenty-four consonants and nine vowels. This is for the
language as a whole. Many individual speakers, however, have only seven
or eight vowels.

From *English Sentences* by Paul Roberts. © 1962 by Harcourt, Brace & World, Inc.
Reprinted by permission of the publisher.

We shall not try here to describe the mechanism by which the sounds are produced but shall instead focus our attention on the result. The key given below relates principally to the author's California speech. This key will serve well enough to indicate the consonants occurring the country over; in the vowels there is more variation, and some readers will probably use quite different vowels in some of the words given.

Here, then, is the key. Note that when we write phonemes, we put them in diagonal lines to distinguish them from letters of the ordinary alphabet.

/p/   The first sound in *pin*, second in *spin*, last in *nip*.
/t/   The first sound in *tick*, second in *stick*, last in *kit*.
/k/   The first sound in *cat*, second in *scat*, last (ck) in *tack*.
/b/   The first sound in *ban*, last in *nab*.
/d/   The first and last sounds in *dad*.
/g/   The first and last sounds in *gag*.
/c/   The first sound (ch) in *chin*, last (tch) in *watch*.
/j/   The first sound in *Jim* or *gin*, last (dge) in *fudge*.
/f/   The first sound in *fall*, last (gh) in *laugh*.
/θ/   The first sound (th) in *thick*, last (th) in *breath*.
/s/   The first sound in *sin*, last in *hiss*.
/š/   The first sound (sh) in *shake*, last (sh) in *smash*.
/v/   The first sound in *vine*, last (ve) in *give*.
/ð/   The first sound (th) in *then*, last (the) in *breathe*.
/z/   The first sound in *zeal*, last in *his*.
/ž/   The last sound (ge) in *rouge*, as most people say it; the middle consonant in *vision* or *measure*.
/m/   The first and last sounds in *mum*.
/n/   The first and last sounds in *Nan*.
/ŋ/   The last sound (ng) in *sing, hang, tongue*.
/l/   The first sound in *law*, last (ll) in *fall*.
/r/   The first and last sounds in *roar*. (But many speakers do not pronounce a final /r/ in *roar*.)
/y/   The first sound in *you*.
/w/   The first sound in *woo*.
/h/   The first sound in *his, hike, who*.
/i/   The vowel sound in *pit, bin, ship, tick, knit, fill, sing, pish, his, hiss*.
/e/   The vowel sound in *hep, beck, dead, beg, breath, flesh, strength*.
/æ/   The vowel sound in *nap, sack, bag, last, razz, rang, pal*.
/ɨ/   For many speakers the first vowel in *sugar* or *children*. Some speakers do not have this vowel except in syllables with weak stress, where it is very common, or before /r/, as in *sir, girl, fur*.
/e/   The vowel sound in *but, dug, flood, tough, tongue*.

/a/   For the author, the vowel sound in *hot, cot, bomb, balm, rob, shock.*
       Many speakers have /ɔ/ in some of these words.
/u/   The vowel sound in *put, could, foot, pull, rook, stood.*
/o/   This does not occur except as part of a diphthong in most American
       speech. Some New Englanders have it in *home* or *whole.*
/ɔ/   For the author, the vowel sound in *law, wash, fought, caught, hog.*
       Some speakers have /a/ in some of these words.

DIPHTHONGS

In addition to these simple sounds, English has a variety of diphthongs,
consisting of one of the simple vowels plus a gliding sound. We represent
the glide with /y/ or /w/, depending on what sort of glide it is. Here are
some common diphthongs:

/iy/   The vowel sound in *he, heat, field, beam, beat, sneak, queen,
       clean.*
/ey/   The vowel sound in *way, rain, Spain, plain, blame, stay, scale,
       steak, snare.*
/ay/   The vowel sound in *my, sky, write, kind, style, mice.*
/ɔy/   The vowel sound in *boy, boil, coin, Troy, point.*
/aw/   The vowel sound in *out, bout, round, mouse, cow.*
/ow/   The vowel sound in *go, snow, rode, moan, drove.*
/uw/   The vowel sound in *who, moo, rude, tomb, cool, few.*

Many other diphthongs occur in the various dialects of English. You may
have others in addition to or in place of these.

Now here are examples of words written in phonemic transcription.
Some people might pronounce some of them differently. The pronuncia-
tions given are common, though not universal, in the Central and Western
United States.

pick	/pik/	train	/treyn/	rough	/rəf/
rib	/rib/	laugh	/læf/	cuff	/kəf/
drive	/drayv/	dream	/driym/	bent	/bent/
hung	/həη/	pink	/piηk/	scream	/skriym/
out	/awt/	toes	/towz/	boil	/bɔyl/
food	/fuwd/	sir	/sir/	quick	/kwik/
should	/šud/	suds	/sədz/	talked	/tɔkt/
gross	/grows/	full	/ful/	sticks	/stiks/
grows	/growz/	zone	/zown/	bags	/bægz/
maimed	/meymd/	veiled	/veyld/	hopes	/howps/
rouge	/ruwž/	judged	/jəjd/	chips	/cips/

nudge	/nəj/	youth	/yuwθ/	these	/ðiyz/
vines	/vaynz/	thick	/θik/	then	/ðen/
wants	/wants/	thin	/θin/	crashed	/kræšt/

In words of more than one syllable, syllables with weak stress are likely to have the vowel /ɨ/. The vowel /ə/ often occurs under weak stress at the beginning and end of words. Other possibilities are:

father	/fáðɨr/	chicken	/cíkɨn/	measure	/méžɨr/
woman	/wúmɨn/	about	/əbáwt/	ended	/éndɨd/
women	/wímɨn/	event	/əvént/	whether	/hwéðɨr/
vision	/vížɨn/	sugar	/šúgɨr/	pretty	/prítiy/
meager	/míygɨr/	shambles	/šǽmbɨlz/	drowning	/dráwniŋ/
singing	/síŋiŋ/	reproach	/rɨprówc/	sofa	/sówfə/

PAUL ROBERTS

Intonation

THE PUNCTUATION OF SPEECH

In recent years it has become increasingly clear that any discussion of English punctuation that takes no account of the intonation in speech patterns is, if not meaningless, at least highly artificial. Intonation is to punctuation what vowels and consonants are to letters of the alphabet. There is, to be sure, no exact relationship in either case. We do not spell words just as we pronounce them, and our punctuation marks do not come near showing all the intonation that occurs in our sentences. But ultimately we get our letters from the vowels and consonants of speech, and so do we ultimately get our commas and periods and semicolons from the intonation of speech. Therefore, before we go on to examine the punctuation habits of American writers, we need to get a rough idea of the intonation of American speech.

The idea will necessarily be rough because intonation is not an easy thing to study. It is in one sense obvious and plain and in another obscure and difficult. We all of us react accurately to the intonation signals of the language. If we didn't, we would constantly misunderstand and be misunderstood. Gross differences are easy to see. Anyone can perceive a difference between "Was he mad?" and "Was he mad!" and can perceive further that the difference subsists not in vowels and consonants but in something we call "tone of voice." But to understand just what this "tone of voice" consists of, what physical features make one sentence different from the other, is another matter.

The difficulty of studying intonation can be seen in the fact that, although mankind has been studying language for thousands of years, it is only in the last decade or so that linguists have achieved a useful grasp of the features of intonation. Indeed, much still remains obscure, and many details are still being debated. But enough has been done that we can now see the main structure of intonation, or at least of English intonation.

Intonation consists of three features, which are called *stress, pitch,* and *juncture.* Stress is simply the loudness or softness with which sounds are uttered. Pitch is the frequency with which voiced sounds vibrate as they issue from the glottis. If they vibrate relatively fast, we have what we call high pitch; if they vibrate relatively slowly, we have low pitch. Juncture, which is closely related to both pitch and stress, is a way of marking division points in speech by lengthening out the sounds adjacent to the break.

Presumably all languages have intonation. One cannot speak without speaking softly or loudly or without vibration of voiced sounds, and presumably in all languages there is some variation, the discourse being not all on one level of loudness or at one vibration frequency. But languages differ markedly in the use they make of vibration features. Some languages use intonation lexically, to distinguish between different words, much as speakers of English use vowels and consonants. The best known of such languages is Chinese. In Chinese the sounds [ma], for instance, produce any of four different words, depending on the pitch pattern with which they are uttered.

English, like many other languages, uses intonation chiefly for syntactical purposes or for discriminating between different emotional states. We have had the examples "Was he mad?" and "Was he mad!" where one intonation pattern signals a question and the other an exclamation. Consider also the many different attitudes or emotions that can be signaled by the intonation used on the word "well" or on the word "oh."

We shall have various other examples as we examine the three intonation features one by one.

STRESS

Stress has been defined as the loudness or softness with which sounds are uttered. We can see it working in many pairs of words in which one member is a noun and the other a verb; the noun in such pairs has a loud stress on the first syllable and the verb the loud stress on the root syllable. For instance, if I say, "What's your object?" I pronounce *ob* more loudly than *ject.* But if I say, "I object" the *ject* is louder than the *ob.* If one were to reverse the stresses in these sentences, the sentences would sound un-English.

Other such pairs are *súbject* and *subjéct, cóntrast* and *contrást, próduce and prodúce, réwrite* (*a rewrite man*) and *rewríte, invíte* and the dialectal *ínvite*. Stress is thus a signal distinguishing between members of different form classes, though sometimes it is only one of the signals. For instance *refúse* and *refúse* are distinguished by stress and also by contrasting final consonants. *Anticipate* and *anticipation* are distinguished by stress and also by the suffix on the noun.

But there are more than two contrasting stresses in English speech as can be seen by contrasting the pronunciations of *separate* in "I'll separate them" and "They are separate." In both sentences *separate* has the heaviest stress on the first syllable. In the adjective, the second and third syllables have about equal stress. But in the verb the third syllable has a weaker stress than the first but a heavier stress than the second.

Using such and more complicated methods of comparison, linguists have arrived at the conclusion that English speech has four contrasting levels of stress. Since the contrasts are used to distinguish between different meanings, they are phonemic, and the four stress levels are four different phonemes, just as vowels and consonants are phonemes.

The four stress phonemes are named and symbolized as follows:

PRIMARY STRESS (the loudest): / ´ /
SECONDARY STRESS (next to loudest): / ^ /
TERTIARY STRESS (next to softest): / ` /
WEAK STRESS (the softest): / ˇ /

These stress levels are relative, not absolute. That means that primary stresses, for instance, do not all have the same volume. I may generally speak more loudly than you do, so that my typical tertiary stresses are louder than your typical primary stresses. Nevertheless we would each have the four contrasting stress levels in our respective sentences.

Or I may speak more loudly at some times than at others. I can say the sentence "I'll separate them" twice, once very loudly and once very softly. But both times there would be clear stress contrasts between *sep* and *ar* and *ate*.

The four stress contrasts do not appear in every utterance we make. If we speak a two-word sentence, like "Shut up," obviously only two stresses can appear. It is only when we examine longer stretches of speech that the four-stress pattern of English emerges.

The four can be seen in the following sentences. All might be spoken in other ways, but they would frequently be uttered as marked:

John's on the sofa.

Where's the streetcar?

He's a foolish wiseman.

FUNCTIONS OF STRESS IN ENGLISH

It is not our purpose to analyze accurately the intonation of English sentences. This is a task for the expert. We can content ourselves with noting some of the obvious contrasts that distinguish meanings.

For instance, if the sentence "He is my brother" is pronounced with the primary stress on the first syllable of *brother*, we have a simple statement of fact. You wanted to know who he was, and I told you. But if we shift the primary stress, we get different meanings:

> He is my brother. (not the other fellow)
>
> He is my brother. (Why do you deny it?)
>
> He is my brother. (not Sam's)

Or consider these:

> That's a nice mess.
>
> That's a nice mess.
>
> That's a nice mess.

Stress is used extensively to signal different kinds of modification. We had the sentence "This is an orderly room," which we called ambiguous. But it is ambiguous in writing only, not in speech:

> This is an orderly room. (a room for orderlies)
>
> This is an orderly room. (in good order)

Or

> He's a fine clerk. (a good one)
>
> He's a fine clerk. (collects fines)

Thus we see that, in general, when an adjective modifies a noun, we have primary stress on the noun and secondary on the adjective:

> a handsome man
>
> a strange story
>
> an old streetcar

But when a noun modifies another noun, we generally have primary stress on the modifier and tertiary stress on the head-word:

> a city man
>
> a bottle plant
>
> a used-car dealer

Stress also distinguishes the two kinds of V-ing * words that modify nouns. V-ing modifiers like the one in "reading room" take the primary stress on the modifier with tertiary on the headword:

> a reading room
>
> a dancing school
>
> a waiting list

But V-ing modifiers like that in "burning room" have secondary stress on the modifier and primary on the noun:

> a burning room
>
> a laughing girl
>
> a soaring plane

Consequently, constructions like "a smoking room" can be ambiguous only in writing, never in speech:

> a smoking room (a room on fire)
>
> a smoking room (a room for smoking)

Native speakers of English manage these pitch structures so automatically that they seldom think of them. It is only when someone, accidentally or intentionally, does violence to the patterns that the patterns become obvious. It is nothing special to see "a dancing school," but "a dancing school" would be quite a sight. So would "a reading room" or "a laughing girl" (girl who makes her living laughing, like "a dancing girl"?). On the other hand, "calling cards" are fairly common; they're just visiting humorists. And "French teachers" are nearly as plentiful as "French teachers."

* Verb in the -ing form.

PITCH

Pitch we have defined as the frequency of vibration of voiced sounds coming from the glottis. The glottis, you may remember, is the opening in the larynx through which the breath passes on its way to the mouth. If the glottis is wide open, there is no vibration, and we get unvoiced sounds, like /s/. If the glottis is partly closed, a tension resulting in vibration is set up, and we get voiced sounds, like /z/. All the vowels and more than half the consonants in English are voiced.

Pitch is of course important to music. In music variation in pitch produces what we call melody. (Notice that you can "sing" the sound z-z-z- but that you can't sing s-s-s-.) But it is important also in ordinary language. We use it in English not only to convey various states of emotion but also as an integral part of our syntax.

English has four pitch phonemes, as it has four stress phonemes. These are usually given numbers, rather than names. The number 4 indicates the highest pitch and 1 the lowest, thus:

> HIGH PITCH: /4/
> NEXT TO HIGH: /3/
> NEXT TO LOW: /2/
> LOWEST PITCH: /1/

Like the stress phonemes, these four pitches are relative, not absolute. They cannot be defined as so many vibrations per second. They are simply points of contrast set up in the speech of individuals as they speak particular sentences. In general, children have higher pitch than adults, and women have higher pitch than men. Thus a child's low pitch may be higher than an adult's high pitch. But the child will have the four pitch contrasts within his register, and the adult will have them in his.

In scientific work, pitch is usually written with the numbers only, thus:

$$\overset{2}{\text{Where are you}} \overset{3}{\text{go}}\overset{1}{\text{ing?}}$$

This would indicate that the sentence begins on the second pitch level, rises to the third on the first syllable of *going*, and falls to the first on the second syllable of *going*.

For general purposes, however, it is a little easier to show pitch with lines rather than numbers. A line just under the letters indicates pitch 2; a line well under indicates pitch 1; a line just above the letters indicates pitch 3; and a line well above indicates pitch 4. Thus:

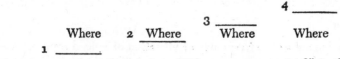

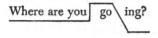

Then we can show the pitch in "Where are you going?" in this way:

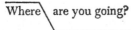

FUNCTIONS OF PITCH

Let us see, then, some of the uses made of pitch in English. The example already given shows a very common pitch pattern for ordinary statements and for questions introduced by interrogatives. It is a 2–3–1 pattern. We begin on the second pitch, rise to the third on the stressed syllable, and fall to the first at the end. In American English (not so commonly in British) the third pitch level frequently coincides with the primary stress.

But many variations are possible. We can put a bit of panic into the question by rising to the highest (fourth) pitch on the primary stress:

Where are you | go \ ing?

Thus a mother might address a child tottering toward the brink of a precipice.

We put in exasperation by rising twice to the third level:

Where | are \ you | go \ ing?

This suggests that we've had trouble with you before and are getting tired of it.

If we want to insist on the *where*, we get the third level at the beginning:

Where \ are you going?

Don't tell me you're going; I know that; now I want to know *where*.

A double rise will often come after persistent questioning:

Where \ are you | go \ ing?

I've asked you several times without getting an answer; now I want one.

Thus considerable meaning of one kind and another can be added to the simple question by variation in the pitch.

There is a widely spread notion that we regularly signal questions by a rise in pitch. The voice rises, it is said, at the end of a question, and falls at the end of a statement. This is only partially true. To be sure, most statements in American English end in a fall to the lowest pitch:

He's my ⌐bro⌐⸜ ther.

I'm very fond of ba ⌐na⸜ nas.

But, as we have seen, questions may have the same pitch pattern. Indeed, this is the regular pattern for questions beginning with an interrogative—*who, where, whose, what, why,* etc.:

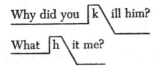

Why did you ⌐k⸜ ill him?

What ⌐h⸜ it me?

However, we have another type of question which does not usually end with a fall in pitch. This is the *yes/no* question—i.e., a question that can be answered by *yes* or *no.* Such questions are signaled not by interrogatives but by a reversal of subject and verb or of subject and auxiliary, as well as by the different pitch pattern:

Did you ⌐kill him?

Are you fond of ba ⌐nanas?

Is he ⌐going somewhere?

These sentences can also be uttered with the 2–3–1 pattern, but this will add a note of insistence. Compare these:

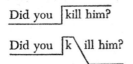

Did you ⌐kill him?

Did you ⌐k⸜ ill him?

In the first I am simply making a polite inquiry. In the second, I am attempting to brush aside your evasions and get at the essential fact.

Thus a rising pitch at the end could scarcely be described as *the* question signal in English. A great many questions end in falling pitch, and in the others there are usually more obvious question signals present. Sometimes, however, pitch contrast will be the only signal of a question. Compare these:

He's a good ⌐sal\esman, ⌐isn't he

He's a good ⌐sal\esman, ⌐i\sn't he

The first is a question; it calls for an answer—yes or no. But the second isn't really a question. The person spoken to is not expected to answer but to agree.

We also use rising pitch when we repeat a question, either because we haven't understood it or because we are surprised at its being asked. Thus:

FIRST SPEAKER: Where are you ⌐go\ing?

SECOND SPEAKER: Where am I ⌐going?

This indicates that the second speaker didn't quite catch the question and wants it repeated.

Or consider this colloquy:

Charlie's going to play third ⌐b\ase.

Charlie's going to play third ⌐base?

The repetition of the question without the fall indicates the second speaker's surprise at the assignment. He could show that he is simply stunned by it by saying it this way:

Charlie's going to play third ⌐base?

Such words as *who, when, where, how* can signal two entirely different kinds of questions, depending on the pitch:

We need to appoint a secretary.

Okay. W͞\ho?

Let's appoint Ed secretary.

W/͟ho?

The first *who* is an ordinary question. The second *who* indicates either that the speaker didn't catch the name or is surprised at it. And similarly:

I'm going to Europe next summer.

H \ ow?

I'm going to Europe in a canoe.

H / ow?

Thus the variations in English pitch are manifold. But they all carry clear meaning to which we react effortlessly.

The third feature of English intonation is juncture. This is at once the hardest to understand and, for us, the most important, since it is the part of intonation most directly related to punctuation.

Juncture may be very roughly described as various kinds of breaks or division points in the flow of speech. As there are four stress phonemes and four pitch phonemes, so there are four juncture phonemes, though one of these is quite different from the other three. The juncture phonemes are generally named after the symbols used to indicate them, thus:

PLUS JUNCTURE:	/+/
SINGLE-BAR JUNCTURE:	/|/
DOUBLE-BAR JUNCTURE:	/||/
DOUBLE-CROSS JUNCTURE:	/#/

PLUS JUNCTURE

Plus juncture, so called because linguists indicate it with a plus sign when they transcribe speech, is the difference between "gray train" and "great rain." These expressions are uttered with exactly the same vowel and consonant phonemes: /greytreyn/. They are pronounced with the same pitch and stress. There is no pause, in the usual sense, in either. Yet, if one were to read the utterances say fifty times, in mixed up order, to a native speaker of English, he would be able to tell which was which most if not all of the time. The only inference is that he must hear a distinguishing difference. What is it?

What he hears is a different variety in the phonemes. . . A phoneme is not a single sound but a bundle of similar sounds called allophones. We have one allophone of /t/ occurring in the final position, as in /set/; another allophone occurs when /t/ is followed by /r/ as in /trip/. Similarly one allophone of /r/ occurs when the sound is initial, as in /rip/; quite a different allophone occurs when /r/ follows /t/, as in /trip/. In "gray train" the hearer hears the allophone of /t/ that precedes /r/ and the allophone of /r/ that follows /t/; in "great rain" he hears the allophone of /t/ that occurs at the end of words and the allophone of /r/ that occurs at the beginning of words. This is indicated in phonemic transcription by writing the sign of plus juncture at one place or the other: /grey+treyn/ or /greyt+reyn/.

Other examples of the operation of plus juncture can be noted in the pronunciation differences between "seem able" and "see Mable," "another directed person" and "an other-directed person," "fly trap" and "flight wrap," "dough pad" and "dope ad." Often, of course, such similar structures are distinguished by other signals in addition to plus juncture. Thus "neat owl" and "knee towel" would have different allophones of the /t/ phoneme but also a different position for the primary stress.

SINGLE-BAR JUNCTURE

Plus juncture is for us of mostly academic interest. Obvious writing problems are not closely bound to the occurrence or non-occurrence of plus juncture. The other three junctures, however, connect in one way or another with the punctuation marks of writing.

Single-bar juncture is linked to the occurrence of primary stresses in an utterance. Let us take this sentence:

The men of the family milked the goats.

A sentence of this sort is most commonly spoken with just one primary stress; the primary stress falls toward the end of the sentence:

The men of the family milked the goats.

But it could also be uttered with two primary stresses.

The men of the family milked the goats.

Now if we say it this way there is a kind of break between *family* and *milked.* This is not so much a pause as a lengthening out of the final syllable of *family.* The pitch stays the same. That is, we go into the word *milked* at about the same pitch that we left off on the last syllable of *family,* like this:

The men of the ⌐fa＼mily milked the ⌐g＼oats.

Now this break or division in the utterance is called single-bar juncture. It can occur only between primary stresses, and it consists of a lengthening out of the phonemes before the break with a sustention of the pitch level across the break.

The sentence could have three primary stresses. In that case, there would be two single-bar junctures:

The ⌐m\en of the ⌐fa\mily milked the ⌐g\oats.

Or we could write it thus, showing just the junctures:

The men | of the family | milked the goats.

This would be a very slow and emphatic way of speaking the sentence.

A hundred years or so ago it was conventional to mark most single-bar junctures with commas. In recent times, however, the tendency has been toward less punctuation, and modern writers are less likely to use commas where these junctures occur. Learners, who overpunctuate as often as they under-punctuate, often do put commas in such positions. They may write, for example, "The men of the family, milked the goats." If they are challenged by a teacher, they will very likely say, "I put a comma there because there would be a pause there if the sentence were spoken." Presumably what they mean by "pause" is single-bar juncture. As we have seen, there could be such a juncture in this position, a primary stress on family, followed by a lengthening out of the last syllable of the word with the sentence continuing on the same pitch level. But whether there is or not, the experienced writer would not use a comma. Single-bar junctures in such constructions are not ordinarily shown by punctuation.

DOUBLE-BAR JUNCTURE

Double-bar juncture, however, is usually indicated by punctuation, and it will be useful to understand the difference. Let us compare these two sentences:

> The people who were sick didn't go.
> My friend Al who was sick didn't go.

The first sentence could be spoken with no internal juncture or with one or two single-bar junctures:

> The people who were sick didn't go.
> The people who were sick | didn't go.
> The people | who were sick | didn't go.

These vary principally in emphasis and speed of delivery. None would normally have any punctuation.

But the second sentence is quite different. In the first place, it would normally have three primary stresses, not just one or two:

My friend Aĺ who was sićk didn't gó.

Secondly, the pitch would go something like this:

My friend ⌐A\1⌐,   who was ⌐s\ick⌐,   didn't ⌐g\o.

Note the upturn in the pitch after *Al* and after *sick*. This is double-bar juncture. As in single-bar juncture, there is a lengthening out of the phonemes before the break. But the pitch, instead of continuing level across the break, rises toward, but not to, the next higher pitch.

Many American speakers would use single-bar junctures in this sentence in place of double-bar. But all speakers would use junctures, two of them, in the places indicated. In this sentence type we do not sometimes use the junctures and sometimes not, as in the type, "the people who were sick didn't go."

Double-bar juncture is frequently marked in writing by a comma, though sometimes dashes or other marks are used. Our sentences would of course be punctuated this way:

> The people who were sick didn't go.
> My friend Al, who was sick, didn't go.

This contrast in junctures reflects a contrast in the structure of the sentences. In the first sentence, *who were sick* is part of the noun cluster *the people who were sick*. The S-group modifies the headword *people*. But in the second sentence *who was sick* is not part of a cluster. There is no unit *my friend Al who was sick* in this sentence. *Who was sick* is here really a sentence modifier, another idea applying against the main idea of the sentence. One idea is that Al didn't go, another that Al was sick. But we would not say that the first sentence is separable in this way. In the first sentence *who were sick* is an integral part of the noun cluster. The meaning is not that people were sick and people didn't go but that those particular people who were sick didn't go.

The marking off of sentence modifiers from the sentences they modify is an important function of double-bar juncture. Here are some further examples. If you say them aloud, you may be able to hear the slight upturn of the pitch. Many speakers will normally employ the sustained pitch of single-bar instead. Commas, of course, would replace the juncture signs in conventional writing:

Ordinarily || we stayed home.
(Cf. "We ordinarily stayed home" in which *ordinarily* is part of the verb cluster and there is no juncture.)
When he fell on his face || we laughed heartily.
(Cf. "We laughed heartily when he fell on his face.")
Charlie || having a guilty conscience || consulted the chaplain.
(Cf. "Anyone having a guilty conscience should consult the chaplain.")
We knew || nevertheless || that there would be trouble.
(Cf. "We nevertheless expected trouble.")
The teacher shook my hand || smiling at me warmly.
(Cf. "The teacher frowned at the girl who was smiling at me warmly.")

Sometimes double-bar juncture will be the only signal distinguishing meanings. Compare these:

Mr. Simkin hired me because I had an honest face.
Mr. Simkin hired me || because I had an honest face.

The first sentence would be a response to the question "Why did Mr. Simkin hire you?" The second would be a response to the question "What did Mr. Simkin do?" In the first sentence, the S-group is a verb modifier. In the second it is a sentence modifier.

Double-bar juncture also occurs between units in a series. If we count aloud—*one, two, three, four*—we have double-bar juncture after each unit but the last one: one || two || three || four. After *one, two,* and *three* there will be a prolongation of the sound accompanied by an upturn in the pitch. If we put a double-bar juncture after *four* in this series, it will signal that we are not done counting, and the hearer will wait for us to say "five."

The same juncture occurs in series of units other than numbers:

We bagged a lion || an antelope || and a giraffe.
He worked all day || danced all night || and died young.
He made his way through the woods || across the stream || and up the mountain.
He was young || courageous || and optimistic.

Commas would indicate these junctures in most American writing.

Double-bar juncture occurs also at the end of certain questions, particularly those of the *yes/no* variety. If we speak the sentence "Is he ready" we will probably rise to the third pitch level on the syllable with primary stress:

Is he ⌐ready

But the sentence will end not on a level third pitch but with the upturn of double-bar juncture, something like this:

Is he |ready

This is normal in questions or other sentences ending on the third pitch.

DOUBLE-CROSS JUNCTURE

The last of the junctures—double-cross juncture—is a falling off into silence, usually from the low pitch. We have seen that the pitch pattern 2–3–1 is most common for statements and some questions in American English:

He's |re \ady.

But the pitch doesn't end with level pitch but falls at the very end:

He's |re \ady.

This fall is double-cross juncture, so called because linguists use a double cross (#) to mark it in transcribing speech. Double-cross juncture is the most important of the features dividing our speech into sentences. It is presumably the feature which gave early writers the idea of using periods. . . .

BENJAMIN LEE WHORF

Linguistics as an Exact Science

The revolutionary changes that have occurred since 1890 in the world of science—especially in physics but also in chemistry, biology, and the sciences of man—have been due not so much to new facts as to new ways of thinking about facts. The new facts themselves of course have been many and weighty; but more important still, the realms of research where they appear—relativity, quantum theory, electronics, catalysis, colloid chemistry, theory of the gene, Gestalt psychology, psychoanalysis, unbiased cultural anthropology, and so on—have been marked to an unprecedented degree by radically new concepts, by a failture to fit the world view that passed unchallenged in the great classical period of science, and by a groping for explanations, reconciliations, and restatements.

I say new ways of *thinking* about facts, but a more nearly accurate statement would say new ways of *talking* about facts. It is this *use of language upon data* that is central to scientific progress. Of course, we have to free ourselves from that vague innuendo of inferiority which clings about the word "talk," as in the phrase "just talk"; that false opposition which the English-speaking world likes to fancy between talk and action. There is no need to apologize for speech, the most human of all actions. The beasts may think, but they do not talk. "Talk" *ought to be* a more noble and dignified word than "think." Also we must face the fact that science begins and ends in talk; this is the reverse of anything ignoble. Such words as "analyze," "compare," "deduce," "reason," "infer," "postulate," "theorize," "test," and "demonstrate," mean that whenever a scientist does something, he talks about this thing that he does. As Leonard Bloomfield has shown, scientific research begins with a set of sentences which point the way to certain observations and experiments, the results

From *Language, Thought, and Reality: Selected Writings of Benjamin Lee Whorf*, ed. John B. Carroll, 1956. Reprinted by permission of The Massachusetts Institute of Technology Press.

of which do not become fully scientific until they have been turned back into language, yielding again a set of sentences which then become the basis of further exploration into the unknown. This scientific use of language is subject to the principles or the laws of the science that studies all speech—linguistics.

As I was concerned to point out in a previous article, "Science and Linguistics," we all hold an illusion about talking, an illusion that talking is quite untrammeled and spontaneous and merely "expresses" whatever we wish to have it express. This illusory appearance results from the fact that the obligatory phenomena within the apparently free flow of talk are so completely autocratic that speaker and listener are bound unconsciously as though in the grip of a law of nature. The phenomena of language are background phenomena, of which the talkers are unaware or, at the most, very dimly aware—as they are of the motes of dust in the air of a room, though the linguistic phenomena govern the talkers more as gravitation than as dust would. These automatic, involuntary patterns of language are not the same for all men but are specific for each language and constitute the formalized side of the language, or its "grammar"—a term that includes much more than the grammar we learned in the textbooks of our school days.

From this fact proceeds what I have called the "linguistic relativity principle," which means, in informal terms, that users of markedly different grammars are pointed by their grammars toward different types of observations and different evaluations of externally similar acts of observation, and hence are not equivalent as observers but must arrive at somewhat different views of the world. From each such unformulated and naïve world view, an explicit scientific world view may arise by a higher specialization of the same basic grammatical patterns that fathered the naïve and implicit view. Thus the world view of modern science arises by higher specialization of the basic grammar of the western Indo-European languages. Science of course was not *caused* by this grammar; it was simply colored by it. It appeared in this group of languages because of a train of historical events that stimulated commerce, measurement, manufacture, and technical invention in a quarter of the world where these languages were dominant.

The participants in a given world view are not aware of the idiomatic nature of the channels in which their talking and thinking run, and are perfectly satisfied with them, regarding them as logical inevitables. But take an outsider, a person accustomed to widely different language and culture, or even a scientist of a later era using somewhat different language of the same basic type, and not all that seems logical and inevitable to the participants in the given world view seems so to him. The reasons that officially pass current may strike him as consisting chiefly of highly idiomatic *façons de parler*. Consider the answers that were at one time given even by learned men to questions about nature: Why does water rise in a pump? Because nature abhors a vacuum. Why does water quench fire? Because water is wet or because the fiery principle and the watery principle are antithetical. Why do flames rise? Because of the lightness of the element fire. Why can one lift a stone with a leather sucker? Because the suction draws the stone up. Why does a moth fly toward a light? Because the moth is curious or because light attracts it. If once these sentences seemed satisfying logic but today seem idiosyncrasies of a peculiar jargon, the change is not because science has discovered new facts. Science has adopted new linguistic formulations of the old facts, and now that we have become at home in the new dialect, certain traits of the old one are no longer binding upon us.

We moderns are not yet in a position to poke fun at the wiseacres of old who explained various properties of water by its wetness. The terminology which we apply to language and cultural phenomena is often of a piece with the wetness of water and nature's abhorrence of a vacuum. The researches of linguists into the ways of languages many and diverse are needed if we are to think straight and escape the errors which unconscious acceptance of our language background otherwise engenders. An increasing contribution from linguistics to the general philosophy of science is demanded by the new ways of thinking implied by those new realms of science cited at the beginning of this essay. It is needed for science's next great march into the unknown.

The situation is not likely to be aided by the philosophical and mathematical analyst who may try to exploit the field of higher linguistic symbolism with little knowledge of linguistics itself. Unfortunately the essays of most modern writers in this field suffer from this lack of apprenticeship training. To strive at higher mathematical formulas for linguistic meaning while knowing nothing correctly of the shirt-sleeve rudiments of language is to court disaster. Physics does not begin with atomic structures and cosmic rays, but with motions of ordinary gross physical objects and symbolic (mathematical) expressions for these movements. Linguistics likewise does not begin with meaning nor with the structure of logical propositions, but with the obligatory patterns made by the gross audible sounds of a given language and with certain symbolic expressions of its own for these patterns. Out of these relatively simple terms dealing with gross sound patterning are evolved the higher analytical procedures of the science, just as out of the simple experiments and mathematics concerning falling and sliding blocks of wood is evolved all the higher mathematics of physics up into quantum theory. Even the facts of sound patterning are none too simple, but they illustrate the unconscious, obligatory, background phenomena of talking as nothing else can.

For instance, the structural formula for words of one syllable in the English language (Fig. 1) looks rather complicated; yet for a linguistic

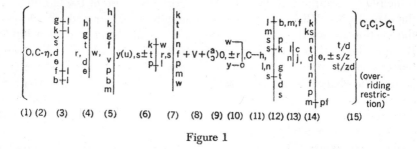

(1) (2) (3)   (4)   (5)   (6)   (7)   (8) (9) (10) (11) (12) (13) (14)   (15)

Figure 1

pattern it is rather simple. In the English-speaking world, every child between the ages of two and five is engaged in learning the pattern expressed by this formula, among many other formulas. By the time the child is six, the formula has become ingrained and automatic; even the little nonsense words the child makes up conform to it, exploring its possibilities but venturing not a jot beyond them. At an early age the formula becomes for the child what it is for the adult; no sequence of sounds that deviates from it can even be articulated without the greatest difficulty. New words like "blurb," nonsense words like Lewis Carroll's "mome raths," combinations intended to suggest languages of savages or animal cries, like "glub" and "squonk"—all come out of the mold of this formula. When the youth begins to learn a foreign language, he unconsciously tries to construct the syllables according to his formula. Of course it won't work; the foreign words are built to a formula of their own. Usually the student has a terrible time. Not even knowing that a formula is back of all the trouble, he thinks his difficulty is his own fault. The frustrations and inhibitions thus set up at the start constantly block his attempts to use foreign tongues. Or else he even *hears* by the formula, so that the English combinations that he makes sound to him like real French, for instance. Then he suffers less inhibition and may become what is called a "fluent" speaker of French—bad French!

If, however, he is so fortunate as to have his elementary French taught by a theoretic linguist, he first has the patterns of the English formula explained in such a way that they become semi-conscious, with the result that they lose the binding power over him which custom has given them, though they remain automatic as far as English is concerned. Then he acquires the French patterns without inner opposition, and the time for attaining command of the language is cut to a fraction. To be sure, probably no elementary French is ever taught in this way—at least not in public institutions. Years of time and millions of dollars' worth of wasted educational effort could be saved by the adoption of such methods, but men with the grounding in theoretic linguistics are as yet far too few and are chiefly in the higher institutions.

Let us examine the formula for the English monosyllabic word. It looks mathematical, but it isn't. It is an expression of pattern symbolics, an analytical method that grows out of linguistics and bears to linguistics a relation not unlike that of higher mathematics to physics. With such pattern formulas various operations can be performed, just as mathematical expressions can be added, multiplied, and otherwise operated with; only the operations here are not addition, multiplication, and so on, but are meanings that apply to linguistic contexts. From these operations conclusions can be drawn and experimental attacks directed intelligently at the really crucial points in the welter of data presented by the language under investigation. Usually the linguist does not need to manipulate the formulas on paper but simply performs the symbolic operations in his mind and then says: "The paradigm of Class A verbs can't have been reported right by the previous investigator"; or "Well, well, this language must have alternating stresses, though I couldn't hear them at first"; or "Funny, but *d* and *l* must be variants of the same sound in this language," and so on. Then he investigates by experimenting on a native informant and finds that the conclusion is justified. Pattern-symbolic expressions are exact, as mathematics is, but are not quantitative. They do not refer ultimately to number and dimension, as mathematics does, but to pattern and structure. Nor are they to be confused with theory of groups or with symbolic logic, though they may be in some ways akin.

Returning to the formula, the simplest part of it is the eighth term (the terms are numbered underneath), consisting of a V between plus signs. This means that every English word contains a vowel (not true of all languages). As the V is unqualified by other symbols, any one of the English vowels can occur in the monosyllabic word (not true of all syllables of the polysyllabic English word). Next we turn to the first term, which is a zero and which means that the vowel may be preceded by nothing; the word may begin with a vowel—a structure impossible in many languages. The commas between the terms mean "or." The second term is *C* minus a long-tailed η. This means that a word can begin with any single English consonant except one—the one linguists designate by a long-tailed η, which is the sound we commonly write *ng*, as in "hang." This *ng* sound is common at the ends of English words but never occurs at the beginnings. In many languages, such as Hopi, Eskimo, or Samoan, it is a common beginning for a word. Our patterns set up a terrific re-sistance to articulation of these foreign words beginning with *ng*, but as soon as the mechanism of producing *ng* has been explained and we learn that our inability has been due to a habitual pattern, we can place the *ng* wherever we will and can pronounce these words with the greatest of ease. The letters in the formula thus are not always equivalent to the letters by which we express our words in ordinary spelling but are un-equivocal symbols such as a linguist would assign to the sounds in a regular and scientific system of spelling.

According to the third term, which consists of two columns, the word can begin with any consonant of the first column followed by *r*, or with *g, k, f,* or *b* followed by *l*. The *s* with a wedge over it means *sh*. Thus we have "shred," but not "shled." The formula represents the fact that "shled" is un-English, that it will suggest a Chinese's pronunciation of "shred" or a German's of "sled" (*sl* is permitted by term 7). The Greek theta means *th;* so we have "thread" but not "thled," which latter suggests either a Chinese saying "thread" or a child lisping "sled." But why aren't *tr, pr,* and *pl* in this third term? Because they can be preceded by *s* and so belong in term 6. The fourth term similarly means that the word can begin with a consonant of the first column followed by *w. Hw* does not occur in all dialects of English; in ordinary spelling it is written backward, *wh.* If the dialect does not have *hw,* it pronounces the spelled *wh* simply as *w. Thw* occurs in a few words, like "thwack" and "thwart," and *gw,* oddly enough, only in proper names, like Gwen or Gwynn. *Kw,* ordinarily spelled *qu,* can have *s* before it and therefore belongs in term 6.

The fifth term indicates that the word may begin with one of the first-column consonants followed by *y,* but only when the vowel of the word is *u;* thus we have words like "hue" (*hyuw*), "cue," "few," "muse." Some dialects have also *tyu, dyu,* and *nyu* (e.g., in "tune, "due," and "new"), but I have set up the formula for the typical dialects of the northern United States which have simple *tu, du, nu* in these words. The sixth term indicates pairs that can commence a word either alone or preceded by *s,* that is, *k, t,* or *p* followed by *r,* also *kw* and *pl* (think of "train," "strain"; "crew," "screw"; "quash," "squash"; "play," "splay"). The seventh term, which means the word can begin with *s* followed by any one of the consonants of the second column, completes the part of the word that can precede its vowel.

The terms beyond the eighth show what comes after the vowel. This portion is rather more complex than the beginning of the word, and it would take too long to explain everything in detail. The general principles of the symbolism will be clear from the preceding explanations. The ninth term, with its zero, denotes that a vowel can end the word if the vowel is *a*—which means (1) the vowel of the article "a" and the exclamation "huh?" and (2) the vowel of "pa," "ma," and the exclamations "ah!" and "bah!"—or the vowel can end the word if it is the *aw* sound, as in "paw," "thaw." In some dialects (eastern New England, southern United States, South British) the vowel ending occurs in words which are *spelled* with *ar*, like "car," "star" (*ka, sta*, in these dialects), but in most of the United States' dialects and in those of Ireland and Scotland these words end in an actual *r*. In eastern New England and South British dialects, but not in southern United States, these words cause a linking *r* to appear before a vowel beginning a following word. Thus for "far off" your Southerner says *fa of;* your Bostonian and your Britisher say *fa rof*, with a liquid initial *r;* but most of the United States says *far of*, with a rolled-back *r*. For some dialects, term 9 would be different, showing another possible final vowel, namely, the peculiar sound which the Middle Westerner may notice in the Bostonian's pronunciation of "fur," "cur," (*fe, ke*) and no doubt may find very queer. This funny sound is common in Welsh, Gaelic, Turkish, Ute, and Hopi, but I am sure Boston did not get it from any of these sources.

Can one-syllable words end in *e, i, o,* or *u?* No, not in English. The words so spelled end in a consonant sound, *y* or *w*. Thus "I," when expressed in formula pattern, is *ay*, "we" is *wiy*, "you" is *yuw*, "how" is *haw*, and so on. A comparison of the Spanish *no* with the English "No!" shows that whereas the Spanish word actually ends with its *o* sound trailing in the air, the English equivalent closes upon a *w* sound. The patterns to which we are habituated compel us to close upon a consonant after most vowels. Hence when we learn Spanish, instead of saying *como no*, we are apt to say *kowmow now;* instead of *si*, we say our own word "see" (*siy*). In French, instead of *si beau*, we are apt to say "see bow."

Term 10 means that *r, w,* or *y* may be interpolated at this point except when the interpolation would result in joining *w* and *y* with each other. Term 11 means that the word may end in any single English consonant except *h;* this exception is most unlike some languages, e.g., Sanskrit, Arabic, Navaho, and Maya, in which many words end in *h*. The reader can figure out terms 12, 13, and 14 if he has stuck so far. A small *c* means *ch* as in "child"; *j* is as in "joy." Term 13, which contains these letters, expresses the possibility of words like "gulch," "bulge," "lunch," and "lounge." Term 14 represents the pattern of words like "health," "width," "eighth," (*eytθ*), "sixth," "xth" (*eksθ*). Although we can say "nth" power or "fth" power, it takes effort to say the unpermitted "sth" power or "hth" power. "Hth" would be symbolized *eycθ, the star meaning that the form does not occur. Term 14, however, allows both *mθ* and *mpf*, the latter in words like "humph" or the recent "oomph" (*umpf*). The elements of term 15 may be added after anything—the *t* and *s* forms after voiceless sounds, the *d* and *z* after voiced sounds. Thus "towns" is *tawnz*, with *wnz* attained by term 10 plus 11 plus 15; whereas "bounce" is *bawns*, with *wns* by 10 plus 12. Some of the combinations resulting in this way are common; others are very rare but still are possible English forms. If Charlie McCarthy should pipe up in his coy way, "Thou oomphst, dost thou not?" or a Shakespearean actor should thunder out, "Thou triumphst!" the reason would be that the formula yields that weird sputter *mpfst* by term 14 plus term 15. Neither Mr. Bergen nor Mr. Shakespeare has any power to vary the formula.

The overriding factor applicable to the whole expression is a prohibition of doubling. Notwithstanding whatever the formula says, the same two consonants cannot be juxtaposed. While by term 15 we can add *t* to "flip" and get "flipt" ("flipped"), we can't add *t* to "hit" and get "hitt." Instead, at the point in the patterns where "hitt" might be expected we find simply "hit" (I hit it yesterday, I flipt it yesterday). Some languages, such as Arabic, have words like "hitt," "fadd," and so on, with both paired consonants distinct. The Creek Indian language permits three, e.g., nnn.

The way the patterns summarized in this formula control the forms of English words is really extraordinary. A new monosyllable turned out, say, by Walter Winchell or by a plugging ad man concocting a name for a new breakfast mush, is struck from this mold as surely as if I pulled the lever and the stamp came down on his brain. Thus linguistics, like the physical sciences, confers the power of prediction. I can predict, within limits, what Winchell will or won't do. He may coin a word "thrub," but he will not coin a word "srub," for the formula cannot produce an *sr*. A different formula indicates that if Winchell invents any word beginning with *th*, like "thell," or "therg," the *th* will have the sound it has in "thin," not the sound it has in "this" or "there." Winchell will not invent a word beginning with this latter sound.

We can wheeze forth the harshest successions of consonants if they are only according to the patterns producing the formula. We easily say "thirds" and "sixths," though "sixth" has the very rough sequence of four consonants, *ksθs*. But the simpler "sisths" is against the patterns and so is harder to say. "Glimpst" ("glimpsed") has *gl* by term 3, *i* by 8, *mpst* by 12 plus 15. But "dlinpfk" is eliminated on several counts: Term 3 allows for no *dl*, and by no possible combination of terms can one get *npfk*. Yet the linguist can say "dlinpfk" as easily as he can say "glimpsed." The formula allows for no final *mb*; so we do not say "lamb" as it is spelled, but as *lam*. "Land," quite parallel but allowed by the formula, trips off our tongues as spelled. It is not hard to see why the "explanation," still found in some serious textbooks, that a language does this or that "for the sake of euphony" is on a par with nature's reputed abhorrence of a vacuum.

The exactness of this formula, typical of hundreds of others, shows that while linguistic formulations are not those of mathematics, they are nevertheless precise. We might bear in mind that this formula, compared with the formulation of some of the English (or other) grammatical patterns that deal with meaning, would appear like a simple sum in addition compared with a page of calculus. It is usually more convenient to treat very complex patterns by successive paragraphs of precise sentences and simpler formulas so arranged that each additional paragraph presupposes the previous ones, than to try to embrace all in one very complex formula.

Linguistics is also an experimental science. Its data result from long series of observations under controlled conditions, which, as they are systematically altered, call out definite, different responses. The experiments are directed by the theoretic body of knowledge, just as with physics or chemistry. They usually do not require mechanical apparatus. In place of apparatus, linguistics uses and develops *techniques.* Experimental need not mean quantitative. Measuring, weighing, and pointer-reading devices are seldom needed in linguistics, for quantity and number play little part in the realm of pattern, where there are no variables but, instead, abrupt alternations from one configuration to another. The mathematical sciences require exact measurement, but what linguistics require is, rather exact "patternment"—an exactness of relation irrespective of dimensions. Quantity, dimension, magnitude, are metaphors since they do not properly belong in this spaceless, relational world. I might use this simile: Exact measurement of lines and angles will be needed to draw exact squares or other regular polygons, but measurement, however precise, will not help us to draw an exact circle. Yet it is necessary only to discover the principle of the compass to reach by a leap the ability to draw perfect circles. Similarly, linguistics has developed techniques which, like compasses, enable it without any true measurement at all to specify *exactly* the patterns with which it is concerned. Or I might perhaps liken the case to the state of affairs within the atom, where also entities appear to alternate from configuration to configuration rather than to move in terms of measurable positions. As alternants, quantum phenomena must be treated by a method of analysis that substitutes a point in a pattern under a set of conditions for a point in a pattern under another set of conditions—a method similar to that used in analysis of linguistic phenomena.

Physics and chemistry, dealing with inanimate matter, require chiefly inanimate apparatus and substances for their experiments. As conducted today upon a large scale, they require highly wrought physical equipment at every step, immense investments in physical plant. Their experiments are costly to conduct, both absolutely and relatively to the number of scientists. Experimental biology uses much inanimate apparatus, too, but its fundamental apparatus is its experimental animals and plants and their food, housing, and growth facilities. These also are expensive in the quantities needed. No one grudges the expense, either here or in the physical sciences, so long as an increase in human knowledge and welfare is promised.

The apparatus of linguistics is much less expensive than that of these sciences, but it, too, costs money. The experimental linguist, like the biologist, uses and must have experimental animals. Only, his "animals" are human. They are his informants and must be paid for working with him. Sometimes he must make trips to Indian reservations or African villages where his informants live; at other times it is more economical to transport them to him. They provide the field for experimental investigation. They are apparatus, not teachers. It is as important to study in this way languages of Indians, Africans, and other aborigines as it is to study the English dialects of Brooklyn, Boston, Richmond, or London.

While informants are the basic apparatus, the linguist can improve and speed up his work with the aid of mechanical tools, just as the biologist studies his animals and plants with the aid of microscopes, x-ray machines, and other costly instruments. The linguist is aided by judicious use of good phonographic reproducing devices. Much could also be done with the help of business machines.

Although linguistics is a very old science, its modern experimental phase, which stresses the analysis of unwritten speech, could be called one of the newest. So far as our knowledge goes, the science of linguistics was founded, or put on its present basis, by one Panini in India several centuries before Christ. Its earliest form anticipated its most recent one. Panini was highly algebraic, i.e., pattern symbolic, in his treatment; he used formulas in a very modern way for expressing the obligatory patterns of Sanskrit. It was the Greeks who debased the science. They showed how infinitely inferior they were to the Hindus as scientific thinkers, and the effect of their muddling lasted two thousand years. Modern scientific linguistics dates from the rediscovery of Panini by the Western world in the early Nineteenth Century.

Yet linguistics is still in its infancy so far as concerns wherewithal for its needed equipment, its supply of informants, and the minimum of tools, books, and the like. Money for mechanical aids, such as I referred to above, is at present only a happy dream. Perhaps this condition results from lack of the publicity the other sciences receive and, after all, fairly earn. We all know now that the forces studied by physics, chemistry, and biology are powerful and important. People generally do not yet know that the forces studied by linguistics are powerful and important, that its principles control every sort of agreement and understanding among human beings, and that sooner or later it will have to sit as judge while the other sciences bring their results to its court to inquire into what they mean. When this time comes, there will be great and well-equipped laboratories of linguistics as there are of other exact sciences.

CHARLES C. FRIES

A Classification of Grammatical Phenomena

In the attempt to gather, analyze, and record the significant facts from
any such mass of material as the specimens here examined, one cannot
depend upon general impressions and note only the special forms that
attract attention. If he does, the unusual forms and constructions or those
that differ from his own practice will inevitably impress him as bulking
much larger in the total than they really are. Those forms and constructions that are in harmony with the great mass of English usage will escape
his notice. This seems to me to be a fundamental difficulty with the
earlier editions of Mencken's *The American Language* and accounts in
part for the difference between his representations of "The Common
Speech" and the results given here. Mencken, for example, prints in the
1924 edition of his book the "Declaration of Independence in American,"
as one of his "Specimens of the American Vulgate" or, as he says, "translated into the language they use every day." [1]

> When things get so balled up that the people of a country have to
> cut loose from some other country, and go it on their own hook, with-
> out asking no permission from nobody, excepting maybe God Almighty,
> then they ought to let everybody know why they done it, so that every-
> body can see they are on the level, and not trying to put nothing over
> on nobody.
>   All we got to say on this proposition is this: first, you and me is as
> good as anybody else, and maybe a damn sight better; second, nobody
> ain't got no right to take away none of our rights; every man has got a
> right to live, to come and go as he pleases, and to have a good time
> however he likes, so long as he don't interfere with nobody else. That
> any government that don't give a man these rights ain't worth a damn;

also, people ought to choose the kind of government they want themselves, and nobody else ought to have no say in the matter.

In the 176 words here quoted there are, for example, five uses of the
multiple negative. Every negative statement except one has two or three
negative particles. This excessive use of the multiple negative construction cannot be found in any actual specimens of Vulgar English. Even in
Old English, where the use of the double negative was normal, less than
35 per cent of the total negative statements occur with multiple negative
particles. Such a complete use of the multiple negative construction as
Mencken displays will only be heard from those who consciously attempt
to caricature Vulgar English. Most of the comic writers produce their language effects in similar fashion by seizing upon a few such especially
noticeable or spectacular forms and expressions of Vulgar English and
then working them excessively. Such representations of Vulgar English
become grossly inaccurate both because the amount of deviation from
the standard forms is greatly exaggerated and also because many of the
forms characteristic of Vulgar English that are not sufficiently picturesque
to be funny are completely ignored.[2]

In order to avoid errors of this kind we have in the study of this material tried first to record *all* the facts in each category examined. For
example, every preterit and past participle form was copied on a separate
slip of paper in order that we might determine not only the kind of variety
that existed in actual usage but also something of the relative amounts of
that variation. In similar fashion all instances with forms expressing number in verbs and in demonstratives used attributively as well as in sub-
stantives were gathered to form the basis of the summaries we offer
concerning concord in number. We do not assume that the absolute frequency of occurrence of particular forms in the limited material here
examined is in itself significant; we have simply tried to make sure of the
relative frequency of the language usages appearing here in order to give
proportion to our picture of actual practice and to prevent a false emphasis upon unusual or picturesquely interesting items.

This approach to the gathering and analysis of the language facts to
be observed in our material made necessary some system of classification
by which those facts of essentially similar nature should be inevitably
brought together. We were seeking to record as completely as possible
the methods used by the English language to express grammatical ideas
and to discover the precise differences in these methods as employed by
the various social dialects. The outlines of our grouping quite naturally
settled themselves. The facts gathered in an early preliminary study of our
material all fitted into a classification made up of three general types of
devices to express grammatical ideas.

First of all there were the *forms* of words. The way in which the word *tables* differs from the word *table* indicates one grammatical idea; the way in which *roasted* differs from *roast*, or *grew* from *grow* expresses another; and the way in which *harder* differs from *hard* shows another. These examples illustrate the expression of grammatical ideas by the *forms* of words. Other ideas, however, are also shown by word forms as *truth* differing from *true*, or *kindness* from *kind*, or *rapidly* from *rapid*, or *stigmatize* from *stigma*, or *national* from *nation*, or *writer* from *write*. These latter derivational forms will not be included here although it is difficult to draw an exact line between them and the grammatical forms with which we are especially concerned. It is enough for our purpose to point out that most of these derivational forms are, in Present-day English, chiefly vocabulary or word-formation matters rather than inflectional matters and that we have limited our study to grammatical structure and have excluded vocabulary. But these "forms of words" as we shall use them are interpreted broadly to include even entirely different words as *we* or *me* or *us* in relation to *I*, *went* in relation to *go*, and *worse* in relation to *bad*.[3]

Second, there were the uses of *function* words. These words frequently have very little meaning apart from the grammatical relationship they express. Examples are *of* in "A house *of* stone," or *with* in "He struck the animal *with* a rod," or *more* in "A *more* important battle," or *have* in "They *have* had their reward," or *going* in "He is *going* to go to New York." Many of the grammatical ideas formerly expressed by the *forms* of words are now expressed by such function words.

Third, there were the uses of *word order*. Word order is often an important item of the idiom of a language, but it is not always a grammatical device as it is in English. In Latin, for example, the periodic structure with the verb at the end occurs very frequently, but the word order in such a sentence as "Nero hominem interfecit" has nothing whatever to do with indicating the so-called "subject" and "object." The basic meaning of the Latin sentence remains unchanged with every possible order of these three words. In English, however, "Nero killed the man" and "The man killed Nero" express very different ideas and that difference comes to us solely through the order in which the words are placed. Some of the grammatical ideas formerly expressed in English by the forms of words are now expressed by *word order*.

All the language facts gathered from the letters here examined were classified in one of these three groups—the uses of the forms of words, the uses of function words, or the uses of word order—and there studied. In respect to each group the description will first set forth the practice of Group I or "standard" English and then indicate the deviations from that practice, characteristic of Group III, or of Group II and Group III combined. Some of the significance of these language facts will, however, be best revealed by showing them in relation to similar situations as they appeared in older stages of the English language, for even complete statistics of the relative frequency of two alternative forms in any single period of language history can never give us a guide as to the relative importance of those forms or the direction of change. For such purposes the statistics must be viewed in relation to the situation in a previous or in a later period. For example, if we were living at the close of the first quarter of the fifteenth century, the bare fact that the alternative pronoun forms *them* and *hem* were used with a relative frequency of approximately 20 per cent of *them* to 80 per cent of *hem* would tell us little without the knowledge that *hem* was the form that was being superseded and that the tendency to use *them* in its place had already progressed one fifth of the way along which the forms *they* and *their* had already gone much farther. In the effort therefore to make clear the significance of the records of contemporary English which formed the basis of this study it will frequently be necessary to picture the present usage against the background of the practice in older stages of the language. We shall try always to deal with the patterns of the language to which particular forms belong and to show the path along which these patterns have developed.

It will be clearly evident as we proceed that the three general types of grammatical processes in accord with which our language material has been classified and are not now and have not been in the history of the English language thoroughly coordinate or of equal value. As a matter of fact any one of the three could have served quite adequately all necessary grammatical needs. Instead, they overlap in the expression of grammatical ideas and in some respects may be said to compete for the expression of the same ideas. The function-word method and the word-order method of expressing dative and accusative relationships have, for example, almost entirely displaced the inflectional method. In the early stages of the language there is no doubt that the use of the forms of words as a grammatical process was much more important than the grammatical uses of either word order or of function words. Some of the problems of usage in Present-day English arise where there is such a so-called conflict between two types of grammatical processes for the expression of a single grammatical idea. While, therefore, we shall classify and describe our language details in accord with the demands of each of the three types of grammatical processes indicated above, it will be necessary to discuss them in relation to the historical patterns with which they are connected and sometimes to refer to the use of a competing type of grammatical process for the expression of the same idea. . . .

NOTES

1. H. L. Mencken, *The American Language* (New York, Alfred A. Knopf, 3rd ed., 1924), p. 398. See, however, the following quotation from the 4th edition, 1936, Preface, p. vii: "I have also omitted a few illustrative oddities appearing in that edition [the 3rd edition]—for example, specimens of vulgar American by Ring W. Lardner and John V. A. Weaver and my own translations of the Declaration of Independence and Lincoln's Gettysburg Address. The latter two, I am sorry to say, were mistaken by a number of outraged English critics for examples of Standard American, or of what I proposed that Standard American should be. Omitting them will get rid of that misapprehension. . . ."

2. See also Professor Robert J. Menner's comments in his article "The Verbs of the Vulgate," *American Speech*, January, 1926, pp. 230–231. Concerning *The American Language* he says, "but Mencken seems to have gathered his forms from all kinds of sources, oral and written; it is impossible to distinguish those he has observed personally from those he has found in contemporary writers of comic stories. Furthermore, he gives the impression of preferring to record as characteristic of the common speech whatever is furthest removed from the language of literature. . . ."

Part of Professor Menner's remarks concerning the accuracy of the writers of comic stories follows: "Ring Lardner . . . employs only forms of the verb which are familiar, or at least conceivable, in colloquial speech. But he besprinkles the conversation of his characters with barbarisms much more plentifully and consistently than they occur in actual life. This is the inevitable exaggeration of comic art. 'He win 10 bucks,' is funnier than 'He won 10 bucks,' and Mr. Lardner now uses the preterite *win* almost consistently, though, according to my observation of oral practice, it is used, even in class D, only once out of ten times."

3. For a thorough analysis of the problem involved here see Leonard Bloomfield, *Language* (New York, Henry Holt and Co., 1933), pp. 207–246. On pages 222 and 223 occur the following statements: ". . . The structure of a complex word reveals first, as to the more immediate constituents, an outer layer of *inflectional* constructions, and then an inner layer of constructions of *word-formation*. In our last example [the word *actresses*], the outer, inflectional layer is represented by the construction of actress with [-ez], and the inner word formational layer by the remaining constructions, of *actor* with -*ess* and of *act* with [-r]. . . . Another peculiarity of inflection, in contrast with word-formation, is the rigid parallelism of underlying and resultant forms. Thus, nearly all English singular nouns underlie a derived plural noun, and, vice versa, nearly all English plural nouns are derived from a singular noun. Accordingly, English nouns occur, for the most part in parallel *sets of two*; a singular noun (*hat*) and a plural noun derived from the former (*hats*). Each such set of forms is

called a *paradigmatic* set or *paradigm,* and each form in the set is called an *inflected form* or *inflection* . . . It is this parallelism also, which leads us to view entirely different phonetic forms, like *go: went,* as morphologically related (by suppletion): *go* as an infinitive (parallel, say, with *show*) and *went* as a past-tense form (parallel, then, with *showed*)."

DONA WORRALL BROWN,
WALLACE C. BROWN, AND DUDLEY BAILEY

Grammar in a New Key

Probably the most important single fact about ordinary language is that it also has two kinds of symbols, both of which work together to express the total meaning of any utterance. This fact is not widely known; yet, if the basic distinction between these two ways of expressing meaning is not fully understood, it is impossible to understand the nature of grammar. These two kinds of symbols we shall call the "vocabulary" elements and the "grammatical" elements. The vocabulary elements include the thousands and thousands of words or parts of words that can be found, not in sentences, but in random lists, dictionaries, spelling-books, and the glossary sections of foreign-language textbooks. Following is a brief list of this kind:

table	happy	soon
walk	throw	mis-
street	apple	un-

This part of the language is often called our vocabulary. The first kind of language that a child learns is in this area—such words as: *mamma, bottle, baby,* and *dolly.* As children grow up and expand this knowledge, they are said to have increased their vocabulary. And when we do not understand the meaning of one of these symbols, we usually look it up in a dictionary. There we find "definitions" of what the symbol stands for in the non-language world. The study of the relationship between these kinds of symbols and their meanings is sometimes called "semantics."

The second kind of symbol—the grammatical symbol—differs basically from the vocabulary symbol, and in describing this difference we shall find the analogy with mathematics most useful. Like the "signs" in mathe-

From *Form in Modern English.* © 1958 by Oxford University Press, Inc. Reprinted by permission of the publisher.

matics, all grammatical symbols have one thing in common: they do not represent directly the ideas that they stand for. Rather, they operate like a system of shorthand, or like a code, for which the study of grammar provides a cipher or key. For example, when we want to use a grammatical symbol to add the idea of "past time" to a word, such as *walk* in the list above, we do not say or write "walk in the past." Instead, we use the shorthand-like symbol -*ed*, which stands for "earlier than," just as the mathematical symbol $>$ stands for "greater than." Again, we might take the vocabulary symbol *chair*. If we wished to add to this word the idea of "more than one," it is almost certain that we would say *chairs*. When this form of the word is used, the idea of more-than-oneness has not been expressed by vocabulary means (we have not said "more than one"): we have used instead a grammatical symbol, the simple letter -*s*, which is a kind of shorthand for the idea of "more than one."

To illustrate this point in a more complex way, following is a list of vocabulary elements which might appear in a simple sentence:

1. Henry   3. build
2. house   4. old

And let us suppose that we want to express these additional ideas:

5. that *old* qualifies our idea of the man Henry,
6. that *build* expresses an assertion,
7. that the building is continuing at the present time,
8. that Henry is the builder,
9. that the result of the building is the house,
10. that there is a only one house,
11. and that a completed statement is intended.

The resulting sentence would be:

Old Henry is building a house.

What makes it possible to condense all of these complex ideas into six words? The answer, of course, is grammar: in the sentence above the ideas numbered 5–11 have been translated into the code of grammatical "signs." By using a different set of such signs with the four words which convey the vocabulary meaning—*Henry, house, build,* and *old*—it would be possible to express some very different ideas, such as:

An old building housed Henry.

The nature of the grammatical symbols can be revealed most dramatically when the vocabulary elements in a sentence are blanked out and only the grammatical symbols are expressed. Following are a few sentences of this kind:

A—al—will be—en about our—into—s.
Do—ed—s—ly—at the—ion?
This—of—'s—s that—are—ing to the—s.

These sentences would probably be "Greek" to most people. Actually, they are full of meaning, but it is a kind of meaning which is mysterious to the uninitiated precisely because of the fact that the grammatical elements are a type of code symbol. Now the question arises: How does one find the key to the meanings in this kind of sentence? As a rule, we do not consult a dictionary, although a few of these symbols are explained there. The only way fully to understand them is, of course, through the study of grammar. This brings us back to the question posed at the beginning of this chapter: What is grammar? After what has been said, the answer must be: GRAMMAR IS THE STUDY OF A SYSTEM OF LANGUAGE CODE SYMBOLS AND THE MEANINGS THAT THESE SYMBOLS EXPRESS. This grammatical apparatus is called the "structure" of the language, and the kind of grammar that describes it is called "structural grammar."

There are three types of grammatical symbols, which both the spoken and written language have in common. These are called the "major grammatical devices." The first, and least well known, is the device of WORD ORDER, which involves the fixed position of the words in a sentence; second, and best known, is the device of INFLECTION, which involves changes in the spelling and pronunciation of a word; the third is the FUNCTION WORD, a kind of grammatical word, which differs basically from the vocabulary words described above.[1] Punctuation, which of course is used only in the written language, may also be considered a grammatical device, but it is a minor one, because the uses of the various marks of punctuation are not completely standardized in modern English, and therefore cannot always be depended on to convey grammatical meaning with complete exactness.

The meanings expressed by these grammatical devices, in contrast to those expressed by any one of the vocabulary symbols, are the most frequently used ideas. A person probably would not mention the vocabulary symbols *chair, house, build,* or *old* more than once or twice a day under ordinary circumstances, and *Henry* would probably get into the conversation even less often unless a gentleman of that name were a close friend or relative. But the ideas of "performer of an action," "time of an action," "result of an action," "qualification," "how many?" and other ideas usually expressed in our language by grammatical symbols are used by everyone hundreds of times a day. Because these symbols are in such frequent use, it is very convenient that they can be expressed by the shorthand-like method of the grammatical devices instead of the more cumbersome longhand of the vocabulary elements. If we did not have grammar, our plight would be almost as ridiculous as that of the Laputians in *Gulliver's Travels*, who, disdaining language altogether, insisted on carrying around with them all the things they expected to talk about during the day!

In other respects, however, these two areas of meaning do not differ significantly. One cannot take a list of ideas and sort them into two distinct columns, one marked "vocabulary" and the other marked "grammatical." Distinctions between them can be made only according to the means by which they are expressed in a given sentence—whether by a vocabulary symbol or a grammatical symbol. This point is borne out by the fact that in any language there is a borderline area in which certain ideas may be expressed by either type of symbol. In English, for example, the idea of something happening in the future may be, and usually is, expressed by a grammatical symbol. When we say, "She will go," we use a special grammatical word (*will*) to express this idea. But futurity may also be expressed by vocabulary means: we may say, "She goes tomorrow." Here we have expressed the idea by using the word *tomorrow*, an idea which the grammatical form of the verb (*goes*) does not express at all. Again, more-than-oneness is usually expressed grammatically in English: in "We have miles to go," the -s added to *mile* is the grammatical sign of more-than-oneness. On the other hand, in the phrase "many a mile" the idea of plurality is expressed not by a grammatical device but by the vocabulary element *many*.

Furthermore, languages vary among themselves as to what meanings should be expressed by grammatical symbols. The Alaskan Eskimo language, for example, has separate grammatical forms to express tense in nouns, as have a number of American Indian languages. One African language is said to have a grammatical method for expressing the idea of "squareness"! And in its earliest period, our own English language (Old English) had a separate grammatical form for expressing the idea of "twoness" (duality) in pronouns as distinct from "oneness" and "more than twoness" (plurality). Modern English, of course, has no way of expressing any of these ideas by means of grammatical devices.

A surprisingly large number of people raise the question: Why should one study grammar at all? The whole problem of the nature of grammar and the desirability of teaching it was informally and excellently discussed by Mr. E. B. White in a 1957 issue of *The New Yorker* magazine. After remarking that English usage has become "hot news," Mr. White continues:

> Through the turmoil and the whirling waters [of usage] we have reached a couple of opinions of our own about the language. One is that a schoolchild should be taught grammar—for the same reason that

a medical student should study anatomy. Having learned about the exciting mysteries of an English sentence, the child can then go forth and speak and write any damn way he pleases. We knew a countryman once who spoke with wonderful vigor and charm, but ungrammatically. In him the absence of grammar made little difference, because his speech was full of juice. But when a dullard speaks in a slovenly way, his speech suffers not merely from dullness but from ignorance, and his whole life, in a sense, suffers—though he may not feel pain.

The living language is like a cowpath: it is the creation of the cows themselves, who, having created it, follow it or depart from it according to their whims or their needs. From daily use, the path undergoes change. A cow is under no obligation to stay in the narrow path she helped make, following the contour of the land, but she often profits by staying with it and she would be handicapped if she didn't know where it was and where it led to. Children obviously do not depend for communication on a knowledge of grammar; they rely on their ear, mostly, which is sharp and quick. But we have yet to see the child who hasn't profited from coming face to face with a relative pronoun at an early age, and from reading books, which follow the paths of centuries.[2]

Actually, everyone agrees that all civilized people have standards of speech and writing and that the teaching of these standards is an important part of education. In the basic college composition course, for example, all students are expected to know and use the acceptable grammatical forms, and anyone would probably feel cheated if he were not helped in these matters. He is also expected to learn a great deal about the intricate business of putting words, phrases, clauses, and marks of punctuation in their proper places in order to form effective and unambiguous structures of communication. And these are all matters of grammar. For the past two hundred years many "rules" have been passed down from generation to generation, which are supposed to solve these problems. Most of these rules are familiar to students even before they come to college. They have been told, for example, that "the form of the verb must agree with its subject in person and number," that "a pronoun must be in the objective case form if it is the object of a verb or preposition," and that "adjective phrases must not dangle." Rules of this kind are important, of course; but it is often not realized that they cannot even be understood unless or until a great deal is first known about "the exciting mysteries of an English sentence" to which the *New Yorker* article refers.

One of the most serious obstacles to good writing is the tendency to compose confusing sentences, especially sentences that have double meanings (ambiguities). Most people know about such problems, but few people realize that they are problems in grammar—that bad sentences of this kind are caused by a misunderstanding of the modern English system of grammar. The following sentences are simple examples of this kind of grammatical confusion:

> He gave her dog biscuits.
> The visitors were drinking in the open air.
> He loved racing horses.
> Ask Mr. Smith who is sitting by the window.
> Clara Schumann was too busy to compose herself.

Unless they are being intentionally humorous, people write sentences like these because they are not aware that they have allowed another meaning, beyond the one they intended, to intrude. And it takes a considerable insight into the subject of grammar to see why this has happened.

In general, these difficulties are caused by a lack of awareness of the fact that the written language, in contrast to the spoken language, has grammatical deficiencies which make written communication difficult and invite ambiguities and confusions. What most people do not realize is that the spoken language has a large battery of very effective grammatical symbols that are lacking in the written language. They include, first, the various kinds of vocal intonations, such as stress and pitch. For example, we usually indicate a declarative sentence by a drop in the voice pitch, whereas at the end of a question the voice usually rises. Running words together without a pause and making an extra long pause are also important grammatical devices. Even gestures and facial expressions may clarify the meaning of a spoken utterance. These devices are usually in a writer's mind as he composes sentences, but he too often forgets that the reader, unlike the listener, cannot hear or see them, and he therefore does not make his meaning clear. The first sentence above—"He gave her dog biscuits"—is a good illustration of this kind of failure on the part of a writer. This sentence would not be ambiguous at all when spoken, for the devices of pitch and stress would make the meaning clear, but in the written language it has two meanings: (1) he gave biscuits to her dog, and (2) he gave dog biscuits to her. The writer of this sentence undoubtedly "heard" a distinct stress and pitch pattern which expressed the meaning he intended—but, alas, his reader could not.

The process of learning to write with clarity and emphasis involves (among other things, of course) knowing how to use the relatively limited number of written devices that must take the place of the missing spoken ones. In the sentence about the dog biscuits, for example, a careful writer could have found several ways to clarify the meaning. For one thing, the words *the* or *some* (both very powerful grammatical symbols) used in the right sentence position, would have eliminated the ambiguity:

> He gave her dog *the* (or *some*) biscuits.
> He gave her *the* (or *some*) dog biscuits.

NOTES

1. For this threefold division of the major grammatical devices, we are indebted to Charles Carpenter Fries, *American English Grammar* (New York, 1940).

2. From an article by E. B. White, © 1957, The New Yorker, Inc.

DONA WORRALL BROWN,
WALLACE C. BROWN, AND DUDLEY BAILEY

Grammatical Distribution

. . . In modern English sentences the words tend to fall into recognizable patterns. We tend to use certain words in certain places and never in others; we tend to change the forms of some words in one way and of others in another; and we tend to use some words with other words and never with still others. Thus the student of language soon learns to anticipate some combinations of words and to doubt that he will find others. In this respect he is like the geologist on a prospecting trip, who knows that certain metals always appear together in the earth. Along with uranium, he would expect to find lead and a group of rare and newly discovered metals. He knows that he will likely find gold and silver together, copper with arsenic and zinc, bromine with chlorine, sodium with potassium, and magnesium with calcium. On the other hand, he would be greatly surprised to find silver or copper with uranium, or platinum with sulphur.

In short, all analysts observe a principle of distribution in their fields: some of the elements they deal with may be expected only in certain places and with certain accompaniments; others will be found in others. When we come to words in sentences, we find that they have their own kind of distribution. We find that some words are found only in certain places with a limited group of other words; and still other words are found only in very different contexts. Certain words are capable of a set of inflectional changes which other words cannot undergo. Some words are limited to a single place or context; others are able to function in various places and to assume various forms.

Some examples make this clear. Let us consider the two italicized words in the following sentences:

>They *manage* a movie theater.
>The firm changed *management.*

If these words are considered only from the point of view of their vocabulary meaning, it would be natural to group them together, since both have to do with the idea of "managing." But if they are considered from another point of view, it is clear that they are very different and cannot be grouped together at all. First, it is obvious that they have different spellings: the word *management* has a *-ment* suffix, which *manage* does not. Second, their respective positions in the two sentences cannot be interchanged. Third, a *-d* inflection could be added to *manage* in order to change the time of the action, but this could not be done to *management.* On the other hand, an *-s* could be added to *management* to change the number of the word, which could not be done to *manage* to express this same idea. Fourth, *management* may be preceded by the word *the,* but *manage* cannot. By substituting other words for *manage* in this sentence, such as *own, operate, pass,* or *want,* it can be demonstrated that there are many other words which may use the same set of devices as *manage,* so we may assume that all these words belong to the same kind of group. There is also a large number of words that could be substituted for *management,* such as *foreman, director,* or *location.* These, clearly, belong to a second kind of group. These differences and similarities indicate a distinctive way of "distributing" words, and the categories formed by this kind of distribution are called the "parts of speech."

From the examples above, it is clear that words are distributed as one part of speech or another, according to the grammatical devices used with them. In other words, each part of speech has a unique combination, or grouping, of grammatical devices that distinguishes it from other parts of speech. The words "combination" and "grouping" should be emphasized, since each part of speech has a rather large number of grammatical devices which may be associated with it. It is too bad that this is true, for grammar would surely be an easier subject if each part of speech were marked by one special device, such as a circle written over the word, or an *x* written below it. Instead, one part of speech may have as many as a dozen grammatical signs, some of which may be connected with it in one context or another. For example, it is possible for one part of speech to appear in six different positions in the sentence, to have four different inflected forms, and three types of function words. In most instances, it is only by using a combination of these devices that the word may be established as a specific part of speech.

In a given sentence, of course, a word will not be accompanied by all the possible devices that mark it as a certain part of speech, but by a selection from them. Usually two or three will be sufficient. For example, in the sentence

The trumpets will play the finale

trumpets is established as a noun by three devices: one word-order device, one inflection, and one function word; *play* is established as a verb by two devices: one word order and one function word. Sometimes, however, only one device is expressed. This is true of the word *manage* (in the example on page 218), which is established as a verb by word order alone. Since it is possible for a part of speech to be indicated by this one device, some words that belong to different parts-of-speech groups often look confusingly alike. This is true of the word *yellow* in the following sentences:

Yellow is my favorite color. (noun)
Newspapers *yellow* with age. (verb)
I like my *yellow* dress. (adjective)

It is often regarded as a grammatical curiosity that there are a few apparently identical words that may appear in sentences as five different parts of speech. *Round* is one of these:

The last *round* was the best of all.
The *round* package was for George.
We *round* the corner on two wheels.
The carousel went *round* and *round*.
The bandit fled *round* the corner.

All these *rounds* are spelled and pronounced alike; they all derive from the same word, the Latin *rotundus,* meaning "wheel-shaped." But from the point of view of grammar, these *rounds* are not alike at all. The first one is a noun, the second an adjective, the third a verb, the fourth an adverb, and the last a preposition. These words appear to be alike only because the device of inflection has not been used with them in these sentences. Other types of devices, however, are clearly expressed and it is these devices that establish such words as different parts of speech.

When a word is changed from one part of speech to another by means of a change in one or more of the three major grammatical devices, and by this means alone, this operation is called FUNCTIONAL SHIFT. Modern English uses this method very frequently. Words such as *garden, fear, paper, salt, price, smoke, dawn, wash, contact,* and *base,* to mention only a few, are shifted about freely in ordinary usage from noun to verb to adjective and vice versa, merely by changing the grammatical devices. The three "gardens" in the following sentence illustrate this kind of shift:

> We shall *garden* with *garden* tools in the *garden*.

This means that, contrary to what many people think, there is seldom anything in the vocabulary meaning of the word that limits it to one part of speech. Words that have been "defined" for us as "nouns" often turn out to be verbs, and similarly, "verbs" often are really nouns: we read that a man has *authored* a book or *chairmaned* a committee, that his hand has the *trembles*, or that he has been to a *steak fry*, or that he has been given an *assist*. In a sense the vocabulary part of a word is like an all-purpose tool, which has many different uses, depending on the attachments (the grammatical devices) used with it at any special time.

For this reason, there is little use in learning "definitions" of the parts of speech that are based on meaning. Since words shift about from one part of speech to another in such Protean fashion, no definition of this kind can be devised that is not full of holes. For example, the usual definition of a noun is that it "is the name of a person, place, or thing." But *red* is the name of a color, *north* the name of a direction, and *cement* the name of a material; yet an examination of the grammatical devices connected with these words in the following sentences will reveal that none of them are nouns:

> The *red* balloon burst, and my face turned *red*.
> We drove *north* into the *north* end of the city.
> This system of *cement* highways will *cement* friendly relations between the two countries.

Similarly, the definition of a verb—that it expresses action—might lead one to think that the word *walk* in the sentence *We went for a walk*, is a verb; but the grammatical symbols show that this word is not a verb but a noun.

While functional shift is probably the most common method used in modern English for converting a word from one part of speech to another, there is another more traditional method that is also used. This involves the use of a special kind of prefix or suffix. We could, for example, have made *round* into an adjective by using, in addition to one or more of the three major grammatical devices, the suffix *-ish*: "The *roundish* package is for mother." Or we could have used the prefix *a-* to convey the idea that *round* is either an adverb or a preposition.

> The carousel went *around* and *around*.
> The bandit fled *around* the corner.

Similarly, in our sentences on page 218 the suffix-*ment* was used to help convert the verb *manage* into a noun. Also *-er* could have been used for the same purpose. There are literally hundreds of these prefixes and suffixes, but two or three more examples will be enough to show how they operate. Some nouns and adjectives may be changed into verbs by adding the suffixes *-ize* or *-en*: *standard* to *standardize, rational* to *rationalize, strength* to *strengthen, weak* to *weaken,* etc. A noun may be made into an adjective by using the suffixes *-y* or *-al*: *dirt* to *dirty, condition* to *conditional*. And most adjectives may be changed into adverbs by adding *-ly*: *perfect—perfectly, smooth—smoothly, proud—proudly*, etc. More than one suffix is often used at once. The word *nationalization* contains three of these: *-al, -iza*, and *-tion*.

At first sight, these prefixes and suffixes seem to be very much like the forms which we called inflections earlier; and in one way they are, for, like inflections, they express variations in grammatical ideas by changes in the spelling of words. But there is one very important difference: unlike true inflections, these prefixes and suffixes are not removable. Once added, they become a permanent part of the vocabulary meaning of the word. For this reason we shall call them "permanent" forms. The word *standardize*, a verb form, illustrates this point. This word retains the *-ize* ending under all circumstances, whether it is in the present tense form (*standardizes*), for example, or the past tense form (*standardized*). The regular inflections used in this example are, by contrast, removable elements (the *-s* may be put on or taken off or it may be changed to *-ed*), which are added to the permanent forms, just as they may be added to any other word used as a verb. In a sense, the endings that are used to create the permanent forms are like the plaster that helps to characterize an enclosure as a room; the plaster is a permanent part of the room. The inflections are more like the furnishings which may be added or taken away, depending on whether we want to create the effect of a formal living room, a recreation room, or a study.

As we shall see later, these permanent forms are not an absolute sign that a word is a given part of speech, any more than plaster is an absolute sign that an enclosure is a room. In most instances where prefixes or suffixes are used, at least one of the three major grammatical devices is needed in addition to the permanent ending to establish the function of the word. Furthermore, this method of forming parts of speech is used less frequently today than it was in earlier periods of the language. We are more inclined today to let the major grammatical devices do the work for us. Also the major devices are always more important in establishing grammatical meaning; for, whenever the idea conveyed by them is in conflict with the idea indicated by the permanent form, it is the devices that determine the grammatical meaning of the word. For example, the word *desperation* in the expression *desperation measure* has the permanent form of the noun, but its position before a noun is one of the major grammatical devices that indicates that a word is an adjective, and it is this latter device that determines the part of speech.

All of these things will become much clearer as we progress. . . . It is enough for us to know at this point that there are two ways of marking a given word as a part of speech: first, by the use of the three major grammatical devices; second, by the use of the permanent forms.

About nine hundred years ago an English monk divided the parts of speech into eight groups. These are as follows:

> The verb (from the Latin *verbum,* meaning "the word," which suggests that this part of speech is very important).
> The noun (from the Latin *nomen,* meaning "a name" for something).
> The pronoun (from the Latin *pronomen,* meaning "for a name," that is, a word used in place of a noun).
> The preposition (from the Latin *praepositio,* meaning "place before").
> The adjective (from the Latin *adjectivus,* meaning "added to").
> The adverb (from the Latin *adverbium,* meaning "next to the verb").
> The conjunction (from the Latin *conjunctus,* meaning "joined with").
> The interjection (from the Latin *interjectus,* meaning "thrown between").

This is not the only way words have been divided to indicate differences in their grammatical form and meaning. During the many centuries that English grammar has been studied, many different groupings have been suggested, groupings with as few as three and as many as eighteen parts of speech. Actually, it is impossible to work out a perfect system. Even the traditional one of eight parts has its weaknesses. For one thing, there are many instances of overlapping among the eight different groups: a word may have devices characteristic of more than one part of speech. For example, it may show verb inflection and adjective word order. More than one part of speech may also use the same inflection or pattern of word order. In spite of such weaknesses, this eight-part system, because of its familiarity to everyone, is probably the best one.

Of these eight parts of speech, the verb, the noun, the pronoun, the adjective, the adverb, and the interjection carry the main burden of the vocabulary meaning. Prepositions and conjunctions are mainly function words. . . .

HAROLD WHITEHALL

The System of Punctuation

The traditional purpose of punctuation is to symbolize by means of visual signs the patterns heard in speech. Grammarians of the eighteenth century, strongly conscious of pause but little observant of tone and juncture, thought that the comma indicated pause for a time count of one, the semicolon for a time count of two, the colon for a time count of three, and the period for a time count of four. Nowadays, we know that pause is simply pause, that pause is often optional, and that when present it combines with preceding junctures to build up what may be regarded as an audible punctuation of words, word-groups, and sentences when we are speaking. To these combinations of speech phenomena, the common punctuation marks of writing (.), (?), (;), (—), (,) bear a correlation which is at best only approximate. Moreover, modern English punctuation has become an intricate system of conventions, some logical, some indicating separations or connections of context, all of crucial practical importance. Its most important purpose is "to make grammar graphic." As a kind of visual configurational feature of grammar, punctuation cannot be properly understood unless the other grammatical features of the language are also understood.

Punctuation is employed in the following functions:

a. To *link* sentences and parts of words.
b. To *separate* sentences and parts of sentences.
c. To *enclose* parts of sentences.
d. To *indicate omissions.*

We can thus speak of *linking, separating, enclosing,* and *omission* punctuation in the full realization that each function contrasts directly with all the others. It follows, therefore, that when the same marks of punctuation are used in different functions they are very much like words used in different functions: the grammatical meanings of the marks are *different*. The *separating period* (.) is quite distinct in functional use from the *omission period* (.); the *linking dash* (−) is functionally distinct from the *omission dash* (−); the single *separating comma* (,) is functionally distinct from *enclosing commas* (, . . . ,). In an ideal punctuation system, such differences would be clarified by the use of different marks of punctuation. Yet let us be realistic. Man has been speaking for well over 700,000 years. Man has been practicing alphabetic writing only for about 3450 years. Man has punctuated, in the modern sense, for less than 250 years. He has still not mastered an ideal punctuation. In the system as it stands, the distribution of the marks is as follows:

a. For *linking*, use:
  ; the semicolon
  : the colon
  — the linking dash
  - the linking hyphen

b. For *separating*, use:
  . the period
  ? the question mark
  ! the exclamation point
  , the separating comma

c. For *enclosing*, use:
  , . . . , paired commas
  — . . . — paired dashes
  (. . .) paired parentheses
  [. . .] paired brackets
  " . . . " paired quotation marks

d. For *indicating omissions*, use:
  ' the apostrophe
  . the omission period (or dot)
  — the omission dash
  . . . triple periods (or dots)
  . . . . quadruple periods (or dots)

LINKING PUNCTUATION

The semicolon (;), colon (:), and dash (−) are symbolic conjunctions capable of linking subject-predicate constructions without need of conjunctions proper. They differ chiefly in the way they direct emphasis. Semicolons distribute it more or less equally between preceding and following statements; colons throw it forwards towards following statements; dashes throw it backwards towards preceding statements. Since they function as symbolic conjunctions, none of these marks is associated with any distinctive tone pattern of the language. In most cases, indeed, statements preceding any one of them would be read with the final h—l tone-pause pattern characteristic of period punctuation. The hyphen differs from the other linking punctuation marks in that it is used to link parts of the words only. The semicolon, colon, and dash may occur in combination with a final quotation mark, in which case they are always placed *outside* the quotation mark.

The *semicolon* (;) is the symbolic conjunction used to link subject-predicate groups that could otherwise occur as separate sentences, particularly if they are parallel in structure and in emphasis:

> The girl is pretty; you will like her.
> I am out of work; I need financial help.
> I was ill that day; nevertheless, I tried to complete the work.
> He was a close friend of the family; moreover, he had a position open.

It is conventionally used to link word groups containing heavy internal comma punctuation:

> My outfit included a rifle, a shotgun, a water bag, and a bedroll; but I did not forget to include a few good books.
> I liked *The Ordeal of Richard Feverel,* by Meredith; *Oliver Twist,* by Dickens; and Oscar Wilde's fine comedy *The Importance of Being Earnest.*

When the semicolon occurs in conjunction with quotation marks, it is placed *outside* them:

> I was reading Shelley's "Adonais"; I did not wish to be disturbed.

The *colon* (:) is the symbolic conjunction used when emphasis is to be thrown forward upon the word-group or word that follows it:

> It was just as I thought: he had stolen the money.
> My outfit included these necessaries: a rifle, a shotgun, a water bag, and a bedroll.
> I could think of only one word to describe him: cad.

In keeping with its general function of *anticipation,* the colon is conventionally used to introduce the chapter figure of a Bible reference, the page number of a volume reference, the minute figure of a clock reference, and the body of a letter following the salutation:

> Numbers III: 21 (or 3:21)
> American Speech 12: 46–49
> 10:15 A.M.
> Dear Sir:

Like the semicolon, it is always placed *outside* a final quotation mark:

> I found one leading literary tradition in "Adonais": pastoral tone.

The *dash* (–) is the symbolic conjunction to be used when the word-group or word following it is considered to be subsidiary to, a reinforcement or example of, or an unexpected addition to what precedes it. It directs the reader's attention backward:

> A year's work at Harvard—that was what he hoped for.
> A rifle, shotgun, ammunition—these were the essentials of my outfit.
> He comes to dinner, eats your food, smokes your best cigars—then borrows your money.
> He was very crude—crude and utterly crazy.

The dash is conventionally used before the name of the author of a quotation:

> Here lies our sovereign lord, the King.
> Whose word no man relies on;
> Who never spoke a foolish thing,
> And never did a wise one.
>
> —Anonymous

The dash should *not* be used as a kind of coverall punctuation mark for all linking and separating functions.

The *hyphen* (-) links parts of words together. It is most characteristically used to indicate that contiguous words form compounds not marked by stress modification.

> a *well-beloved* woman
> my *commander-in-chief*
> his *better-than-thou* attitude

The conventional uses of the hyphen are these:

a. To indicate that the beginning of a word on one printed line is linked to the rest of the word on the next.

b. To link the elements of compound numbers from twenty-one to ninety-nine:

> *thirty-four* horses
> *sixty-seven* dollars

c. To link the elements of fractions:

> He had a *two-thirds* lead in the election.

Today we tend to write either separately or as single units those words which were formerly hyphenated:

> my *commander in chief*
> a *wellbred* woman

SEPARATING PUNCTUATION

The period separates sentences only. The exclamation mark (!) and the question mark (?), normally used to separate special types of sentences, are also used occasionally to separate parts of sentences. The comma separates *parts* of sentences only. Thus, there is every reason why the period, as sentences separator, should never be confused with the comma, as sentence-part separator, or with the semi-colon, the sentence linker. All the separating punctuation marks are roughly correlated with stress-juncture and tone-pause patterns heard in speech, and it is probable that learning to hear the patterns will direct you towards the appropriate punctuation:

> John was coming(.)
> John was coming(?)
> John was coming(!)
> John was coming(,) and I still had to dress.

When they occur in combination with final quotation marks, all the separating punctuation marks are placed *inside* them. In this respect, they contrast directly with the linking punctuation marks which are placed *outside*.

The period (.) has the one function of separating declarative subject-predicate sentences (including mild commands) from following sentences. It symbolizes the fall from high to low pitch (h–l) followed by breathing pause. Its grammatical meaning is "end of declarative utterance":

> The mountains enclose a valley.
> Please return the books as soon as possible.

The period can occur after statements not in subject-predicate form if they conclude with the h–l tone-pause pattern.

> The more, the merrier.
> To resume.

It is always inserted *before* end quotation marks:

> He said to me, "Mother is coming."

The question mark (?) separates questions and quoted questions from a following context. It symbolizes two quite distinct final tone-pause patterns of actual speech:

a. A fall from high to low tone (h–l) used when a question contains an interrogative word or word order:

>   h_____l
> Why did you go to the theater?

b. A rising high tone, usual when a question does not contain an interrogative word or word order:

>   l_____h
> You went to the theater?

The grammatical meaning of the question mark is "answer needed":

> Are you leaving tonight?
> Is John coming?
> You are in Professor Brown's class?
> "Where is the salt?" he demanded.

It is always inserted *before* end quotation marks:

> He said, "Is this what's wrong?"

The *exclamation point* (!) separates exclamatory sentences or exclamatory words from a following context. It symbolizes various final tone-pause patterns based upon sharply rising or falling tone or a combination of these, or unexpectedly level tone, used in speech when an utterance is surcharged with emotion:

> What a marvelous morning!
> Listen! I hear John coming.

It is always inserted *before* end quotation marks that occur *within* a sentence, but it is placed outside quotation marks at the end of a sentence when the whole sentence is exclamatory:

> "I am finished!" he yelled.
> How horrible was their shout, "We're coming to kill you"!

The *separating comma* (,) originally indicated that a part of a sentence preceding or following it was in some way separated from the remainder. Where it corresponds to anything in speech at all, it generally symbolizes internal grammatical juncture followed by pause in slow-tempo speech. Its use, however, is now highly conventionalized: the comma is often used where speech shows internal juncture unaccompanied by pause but where its omission might lead to misunderstanding. The comma never appears between the main structural elements, the *must* parts, of sentences; i.e., it is never used between the subject and verb, between the verb and a complement, or between two complements, and it is never used before movable modifiers of a sentence if these appear *after* the verb; in short, it is never used to indicate optional internal grammatical junctures. The grammatical meaning of the comma is "dissociation." It is inserted:

a. After each word or word-group in a series terminated by *and, or;* here it may symbolize the high rising tone pattern (h):

> I took bread, butter, tea, and salt with me.
> His cunning, his devious treachery, or his ruthlessness will be enough to make him fight successfully.

b. Between subject-predicate word-groups linked by the coupling conjunctions *and, but, or, not, yet:*

> The book is quite good, and it is relatively inexpensive.
> The food and service were good, yet I was hard to please.

c. After any movable modifier thought of as displaced from a normal end-of-sentence position:

> Instead of the expected twenty, only ten came to the party.
> But: Only ten came to the party instead of the expected twenty.

d. Before any other modifier or modifying word-group thought of as out of its normal sentence position:

> We thought of Goldsmith, poor but genial.
> Talent, Mr. Micawber has; money, Mr. Micawber has not.

e. After an introductory word, word-group, transitional adverb, or vocative expression:

> *This done,* we left the place immediately.
> She didn't like the idea; *nevertheless,* she said she would visit us.
> *Mother,* I have brought my friend to be our guest.

f. After a subject-predicate word-group introducing a direct quotation:

> He exclaimed, "I had no idea that you were in the room."

g. Between elements in sentences and word-groups which might cause confusion if thought of as combined:

> My words are my own; my actions, my ministers'.
> a bright, blue hat contrasted with a bright blue hat

h. Between items in dates, addresses, books and author references, etc.:

> April 1, 1950
> Mary Johnson, Cleveland, Ohio
> *Oliver Twist,* by Charles Dickens

The comma is always inserted *before* end quotation marks:

> "I am tired of your incompetence," he roared.

ENCLOSING PUNCTUATION

Paired commas, paired dashes, and parentheses are used to enclose elements outside the main structure of a sentence. They represent a triple scale of enclosure, in which paired commas enclose elements most closely related to the main thought of the sentence and parentheses those elements least closely related. Brackets are merely a specialized type of parentheses. Quotation marks are used principally to enclose the report of words actually spoken.

Paired commas (, . . . ,) have the following uses:

a. To enclose modifying word-groups of the subject-predicate type which are not regarded as essential to the identification of the word which they modify. Such groups are usually called *non-restrictive*.

> NON-RESTRICTIVE: This invention, *which our army rejected,* became Germany's surprise weapon.
>
> RESTRICTIVE: The invention *which our army rejected* became Germany's surprise weapon.

In the first example, the identification is supplied by *this;* the modifying group *which our army rejected* is thus properly enclosed in paired commas. In the second example, the modifying group is needed to identify *invention.*

b. To enclose interpolated words and word-groups, especially when those are transitional adverbs or groups with the function of transitional adverbs:

> Your ideas, *however,* are scarcely valid.
> Your ideas, *as a matter of fact,* are scarcely valid.
> Your ideas, *I conclude,* are scarcely valid.

Paired dashes (− . . . −) enclose elements less closely related to the main thought of a sentence than those enclosed by paired commas but more closely related than those enclosed by parentheses:

> My friends—at that time mostly workers—took me to task for my social attitudes.

They replace paired commas when the enclosed word-group has heavy comma punctuation of its own:

> The artillery—devastating in its sound, fury, and effect—suddenly opened up on us.

Parentheses enclose material which is obviously outside the main scope of the sentence:

> These words (*we might call them determiners*) are important in English but of little importance in many other languages.

Parentheses are used conventionally to enclose the figures numbering parts of a series, and, in legal contexts, to enclose figures expressing monetary value:

The aims of this course are: (1) to analyze the structure of American English; (2) to examine the resources of its vocabulary; (3) to sketch the history of American English. The signer agrees to pay the sum of one hundred dollars ($100.00).

Brackets ([. . .]) are a special kind of parentheses with the following uses:

a. To insert interpolations in quotations:

As Jarrold said, "It [poetry] is an attempt to express the inexpressible."

b. To insert pronunciations written in the symbols of the International Phonetic Association (IPA):

The usual pronunciation of *bait* is [bet].

They also enclose parenthetical matter already in parentheses.

Quotation marks (". . .") enclose direct quotations from speech:

"You may say that," said my father, "but you don't believe it."

They may be used with caution to enclose references to specific words, slang expressions, hackneyed expressions, familiar and well-worn phrases, and terms you do not like:

My life is one "if" after another.
His car had the "teardrop" shape of that period.
While "on campus," Jones was something of a "rod."
The "liberal arts" curriculum becomes increasingly illiberal.

They are also used to enclose the titles of poems, plays, essays, paintings, etc. (but not the titles of complete volumes or of major works, which are indicated by italics):

I read Shelley's "Alastor" with distinct pleasure.
I particularly admired El Greco's "Toledo."
He was much impressed by the story "Clay" in Joyce's *Dubliners*.

OMISSION PUNCTUATION

Originally, the *apostrophe* (') indicated the omission of a letter no longer pronounced or deliberately suppressed in pronunciation. This is what it still indicates when used with the possessive singular forms of nouns, contracted forms of verb helpers (auxiliaries), and words with an omitted initial letter:

the Lord's Prayer (earlier, the Lordes Prayer)
He's not coming, and he won't come.
a blot on the 'scutcheon

Its conventional uses are as follows:

a. It precedes *s* in the plurals of figures, signs, symbols, and letters:

> My 8's are difficult to decipher.
> There were three x's in this quotation.
> I have difficulty in writing r's.

b. It precedes *s* in plurals of words which have no normal plural form:

> There were too many if's and but's about the matter.

c. In a purely symbolic function corresponding to nothing actual in speech, it indicates possessive plurals of nouns:

> The generals' orders had to be obeyed.
> the college girls' escorts

d. It indicates the possessive singular forms of nouns already ending in *s:*

> Dr. Caius' (or Caius's) words
> Moses' pronouncements

e. It indicates the possessive singular forms of group names:

> Thomas, Manchester, and Scott's *Rhetoric*
> Chase and Sanborn's coffee

f. It indicates the omission of initial centuries in dates:

> the class of '38

The *omission period* or *dot* (.) indicates the omission of several letters, particularly when words are abbreviated:

> Mr. V. S. Johnson
> Ph.D.
> I enjoy the plays of G. B.S.

It is not used after contractions indicated by the apostrophe, after Roman numerals, after numbered ordinals, after nicknames, or after per cent (for *per centum*); it is now often omitted after the abbreviated names of government agencies, labor organizations, and the like:

He'll go.	a five per cent bonus
XXIV	CIC
5th, 6th, 7th	FTC
Dick, Mick, and Ned	

When a sentence ends with an abbreviated word, one period punctuates both the abbreviation and the sentence:

> I was talking to Richard Hudson, Ph.D.

Triple periods or *dots* (. . .) indicate a more or less extensive omission of material at the beginning of, or within, a quoted passage; followed by a period (. . . .) they indicate omission at its end:

> . . . language is . . . the thought itself, its confused cross currents as well as its clear-cut issues. . . .

Triple periods are often used to indicate omissions deliberately left to the reader's imagination:

> He took her slowly in his arms . . . from that moment she was his.

In recent advertising practice, this use is greatly extended in order to create appropriate atmosphere:

> Fly to Britain . . . Europe . . . and beyond.
> Industries are discovering . . . with a rush . . . that the Genie of "Opportunity" is at their beck and call.

The *dash* (—) as used in omission punctuation indicates the deliberate suppression of letters in a person's name in order to avoid positive statement of identification:

> My informant, a certain professor *M*—, vouches for the truth of this report.

In earlier writing it was often used to indicate omissions in oaths, etc.:

> "D—n," he said. "I'll see you hanged yet."

No attempt has been made here to deal with all the minute points of punctuation. Such matters as the use of capitals and italics are treated under the appropriate headings in a dictionary: they are matters of format rather than punctuation although they serve a very real purpose in the transference of spoken to written distinctions. What has been attempted here is to present punctuation proper as a system of symbols each one of which contrasts with all others in function. Ideally, the writer should be able to ignore the grammar book or the dictionary when he is faced with a punctuation problem; what he needs most of all is an understanding of the entire system as it determines the individual application.

OTTO JESPERSEN

Spelling

The traditional way of writing English is far from being so consistent that
it is possible, if we know the sounds of a word, to know how it is to be
spelled, or inversely, from the spelling to draw any conclusions as to its
pronunciation. The following words in their traditional garb and in
phonetic transcription may serve as illustration:

> *though* [ðou]—rhyming with *low*
> *through* [þru]   "   *true*
> *plough* [plau]   "   *now*
> *cough* [kɔf]   "   *off*
> *enough* [i'nʌf]   "   *cuff*

However chaotic this may seem, it is possible to a great extent to explain the rise of all these discrepancies between sound and spelling, and
thus to give, if not rational, at any rate historical reasons for them. A full
account of all these anomalies would, however, require a whole volume;
here we must, therefore, content ourselves with a succinct exposition of
the chief facts that have determined the present English spelling.

The alphabet used in England as well as in most European countries
is the Roman alphabet. Though this is better than many Oriental alpha-
bets, it is far from being perfect as a means of rendering sounds, as it is
deficient in signs for many simple sounds (*e.g.* the initial consonants of
this and *thick*, the final one of *sing*); nor does it possess more than five
vowel-letters, where many languages distinguish a far greater number of
vowels.

At first people could follow no other guide in their spelling than their
own ears: writing thus began as purely phonetical. But soon they began
to imitate the spellings of others, whose manuscripts they copied, their

From *Essentials of English Grammar*, 1933. Reprinted by permission of George Allen
& Unwin Ltd.

teachers and their elders generally. As the spoken forms of words tend continually to change, this would mean that older, extinct forms of speech would continue to be written long after they had ceased to be heard. Such traditional spelling, which is found in all languages with a literary history, has become particularly powerful since the invention of the art of printing; in many respects, therefore, modern English orthography represents the pronunciation prevalent about that time or even earlier.

An equally important factor was the influence of French—later also of Latin—spelling. Norman scribes introduced several peculiarities of French spelling, not only when writing words taken over from that language, but also when writing native English words. Our present-day spelling cannot, therefore, be fully understood without some knowledge of the history of French.

The letters *ch* were used in Old French to denote the sound-combination [tʃ] as in *chaste, chief, merchant;* in English this spelling was used not only in originally French words, but also in native words like *child, much*. In French the stop [t] was later dropped, the sound [ʃ] only remaining; hence *ch* in some late loan-words comes to stand for [ʃ]: *machine, chaise* (which is the Modern French form of the same word that in the old form was taken over as *chair*), *chauffeur*.

In words from the classical languages *ch* denotes the sound [k]: *echo, chaos, scheme*. Schedule is pronounced with [sk] in America, with [ʃ] in England.

The sound-history of French also serves to explain some striking peculiarities concerning the use of the letter *g* in English spelling. Written French *gu* originally served to denote the combination of [g] with a following [u] or [w]; but this combination was later simplified in various ways. In the northernmost French dialects [g] was dropped, and English from those dialects adopted such words as *ward, reward, warden* and *war*. But in other parts of French it was inversely the [u]-sound that disappeared, and a great many words were adopted into English with this simple sound of [g], such as *gallop, garrison;* in some cases English kept the spelling *gu* though French now writes without the *u: guard, guarantee*. In both languages the spelling *gu* came to be extensively used as an orthographic device to denote the sound [g] before *e* and *i*, because in that position g was pronounced [dʒ], thus in *guide, guise;* and in English this spelling was even transferred to a certain number of native words like *guess, guest, guild* (sb.), *guilt, tongue*, though it never obtained in some frequently used words like *get, give, begin, gild* (vb.)

In Old French the letter *g* stood for the sound-combination [dʒ], as Latin g [g] had developed in that way before [e] and [i]; hence spellings like *gentle, giant, age, manage*, etc. Sometimes after a short vowel *dg* was written: *judge, lodge;* thus also in native words like *edge, bridge.*

As with the corresponding voiceless combination [tʃ], the stop in [dʒ] was later dropped in French; hence *g* is in later loan-words pronounced [ʒ]: *rouge, mirage, prestige.*

Another Old French way of writing [dʒ] was *i*, later *j*; hence we have English spellings like *joy, join, journey.* In *bijou j* has the later French value [ʒ].

In OE. the letter *c* was exclusively used for the sound [k], even before *e, i* and *y*, exactly as in Latin. But in French this Latin sound had become first [ts] and later [s] before *e* and *i*; and this value of the letter *c* is consequently found in English, not only in French and Latin words, like *cease, centre, city, peace, pace*—even sometimes where French has *s: ace,* Fr. *as; juice,* Fr. *jus*—but also in some native English words, e.g. *since, hence.* Sc is pronounced in the same way, e.g. *scene, science;* it is written without any etymological reason in *scent* (from French *sentir*).

C is used for the sound [k] in *can, corn, cup, clean, creep* and many similar words, while *k* is written in *kiss, keep, think,* etc., and *y* before *u: queen,* etc. Instead of *ks, x* is written: *six,* etc., even in *coxcomb* and *coxswain* from *cock.*

French influence is responsible for the use of the digraph *ou* for ME. long [uː] as in *couch, spouse* (later Fr. *épouse*); sometimes also for short [u]: *couple, touch.* This was transferred to native words like *house, loud, out, our,* etc. When the long sound was later diphthongized, the spelling *ou* came to be very appropriate. As this diphthongizing did not take place in Scotch, *ou* is there still found for the sound [uː], as in *Dougall, dour, souter,* "shoemaker."

The simple vowel *u* was used for the short vowel as in *up, us, nut, full,* etc., and for the diphthong [iu] or [juː], frequent in French words like *duke, use, due, virtue,* but also found in native words, e.g. *Tuesday, hue, Stuart* (the same word as *steward*).

But at a time when angular writing was fashionable, it became usual to avoid the letter *u* in close proximity with the letters *n, m,* and another *u* (*v, w*), where it was liable to cause ambiguity (five strokes might be interpreted *imi, inu, mu, um, uni, uui,* especially at a time when no dot was written over *i*); hence the use of *o* which has been retained in a great many words: *monk, money, honey, come, won, wonder, cover* (written *couer* before *v, o* and *u* were distinguished), *love,* etc.

A merely orthographic distinction is made between *son* and *sun, some* and *sum.*

In ME. vowels were frequently doubled to show length, and many of these spellings have been preserved, e.g. *see, deer, too, brood,* though the sounds have been changed so that they no more correspond to the short vowels of *set, hot.*

But neither *a* nor *u* were doubled in that way; and instead of writing *ii* it became usual to write *y*. This letter, which in Old English served to denote the rounded vowel corresponding to [i] (= Fr. *u* in *bu*, German *ü* in *über*), has become a mere variant of *i* used preferably at the end of words, while *i* is used in the beginning and interior of words; hence such alternations as *cry, cries, cried; happy, happier, happiest, happiness; body, bodiless, bodily*, etc. But *y* is kept before such endings as are felt more or less as independent elements, e.g. *citywards, ladyship, twentyfold, juryman*. After another vowel *y* is generally kept, e.g. *plays, played, boys;* cf., however, *laid, paid, said* (but *lays, pays, says*: too much consistency must not be expected). In some cases homophones are kept apart in the spelling: *die* (with *dies*, but *dying*, because *ii* is avoided)—*dye, flys,* 'light carriages,' but otherwise *flies* (sb. and vb.).

Further, *y* is written in many originally Greek words: *system, nymph,* etc.

Before a vowel, *y* is used as non-syllabic [i], i.e. [j], e.g. *yard, yellow, yield, yole, yule, beyond*.

Doubling of consonants has come to be extensively used to denote shortness of the preceding vowel, especially before a weak syllable, e.g. in *hotter, hottest* from *hot, sobbing* from *sob*. Instead of doubling *k, ch* and *g* [= dȝ] the combinations *ck, tch* and *dg* (*e*) are written, e.g. *trafficking* from *traffic, etch, edge*.

On account of the phonetic development, however, a double consonant is now written after some long vowels, e.g. in *roll, all, staff, glass*, which had formerly short vowels.

Though since the introduction of printing a great many minor changes have taken place without any great consistency, such as the leaving out of numerous mute *e's*, only one important orthographic change must be recorded, namely, the regulating of *i* and *j*, *u* and *v*, so that now *i* and *u* are used for the vowels, *j* and *v* for the consonant sounds, while, for instance, the old editions of Shakespeare print *ioy, vs, vpon, fiue, fauour* = *joy, us, upon, five, favour*. The old use of *u* for the consonant explains the name of *w: double u*.

Scholars have introduced learned spellings in many words, e.g. *debt, doubt*, on account of Latin *debita, dubito*, formerly written as in French *dette, doute; victuals*, formerly *vittles*. In some cases the pronunciation has been modified according to the spelling; thus [p] has been introduced in *bankrupt*, earlier *bankeroute*, and [k] in *perfect*, earlier *perfit, parfit*. In recent years, with the enormous spread of popular education, combined with ignorance of the history of the language, such spelling-pronunciations have become increasingly numerous.

ROBERT A. HALL, JR.

Our English Spelling System

The real nature of writing in its relation to language is so obvious on a moment's reflection, that it might seem strange that so much misunderstanding could arise about it. Probably the confusion is due to two things: the nature of our English spelling system, and the age at which we start to learn it. People whose languages have a simple, relatively accurate conventional spelling, like Italian, Hungarian, or Finnish, are not confused as to the relation of writing and speech, and are often surprised at the misunderstanding that spellers of English show. But our traditional orthography for English is quite far removed from the reality of speech, and our letters certainly do not stand in a wholly one-to-one relationship with the phonemes of our speech. It takes considerable effort and many years (as we all well know!) to completely master our English conventional spelling; and once we have learned it, it represents a considerable investment. Nobody likes to give up the fruits of any investment, and the more costly it is, the less we want to discard it; and so it is with the spelling of English. Once we have learned it, we have a strong emotional attachment to it, just because we have had considerable difficulty with it and have been forced to put in so much time and effort on learning it.

Furthermore, we learn to speak long before we are able to do any kind of reflective or analytical intellectual work; we learn to speak when we are small children, by a purely unreflecting process of repeated trial and error. But when we go to school and learn to write, we do so consciously and reflectingly. If, in our first school contacts with writing, we were taught a scientifically accurate phonemic spelling, which reflected all the facts of our speech itself, we would have very little trouble and would learn to use such a spelling in a year or two, as do Italian or Hungarian children. But we do not learn an accurate phonemic spelling; we learn our inaccurate, confused traditional English orthography, and we talk about it as we do so. When we were little children learning how to speak, we learned only to speak, not how to analyze our speech. When we are older and learn to spell, we also learn how to talk about spelling and how to analyze it: we are taught to name the letters, to tell how we replace letters by apostrophes or how we drop letters, and so forth. But we still learn nothing whatsoever about how to discuss speech and analyze it in its own terms; the only approach, the only vocabulary we end up with for discussing language is the approach and the vocabulary of spelling. Edith Wharton, in *The Custom of the Country*, says of one of her characters:

> Mrs. Spragg, when she found herself embarked on a wrong sentence, always ballasted it by italicizing the last word.

What Mrs. Wharton meant, of course, was "emphasizing" or "stressing" the last word; but the only term at her disposal was the word *italicizing*, the term that referred to spelling rather than to speech.

This entire situation has given results that are little short of disastrous for the understanding of the true nature of language, throughout the English-speaking world. Very few people have any clear idea of what they actually do when they speak—what organs of their body they use and in what way they use them. Many people find it difficult or downright impossible to conceive of sounds as such, or to hear differences in sound that are not directly related to differences in English spelling. Some even develop emotional blockings on the subject of phonetic analysis, because the strange appearance and use of special symbols in a transcription makes them "feel all funny inside," as one such person put it to me. When it comes to discussing sounds, the only way to identify many sounds in writing for the general reader who knows no phonetics, is to avoid all letters entirely, and to give cumbersome definitions like "the vowel sound of *bit*" or "the initial sound of *thing*"; for, if we were to speak of the *i* of *hit* or the *th* of *thing*, almost everyone would immediately read off those definitions as "the 'eye' (*i*) of *hit*" or "the 'tee aitch' (*th*) of *thing*." Likewise for a discussion of grammar or of syntax, we can recognize grammatical facts which we see reflected in the conventional spelling, like the vowel change in *sing sang sung*; but we find it hard to recognize or discuss those grammatical facts which are not indicated in writing, like the difference between the final consonant sounds of *house* (noun, as in *he has a big house*) and *house* (verb, as in *where can we house them?*), or the change in vowel sound between *you* (stressed, as in *is that you?*) and *you* (unstressed, as in *how do you do?*).

All kinds of misunderstandings and misrepresentations arise as a result of this spelling-induced confusion and ignorance. People often think that spelling a word out is the best way to tell someone how to pronounce it, and think that the names of the letters alone will give a key to the sounds that are involved. I once witnessed a prize example of this confusion when a high-school girl named Carlys (normally pronounced as if spelled *Carleece*, stress on last syllable) was trying to tell my four-year-old boy Philip how to pronounce her name, which he had some difficulty with:

> Philip: Hey, Craleeth!
> Carlys: No, no. Not Craleeth; Carlys. Say that.
> Philip: Craleeth.
> Carlys: No, no, no. Carlys. CAR-LYS.
> Philip: Craleeth.
> Carlys: No! Look; shall I spell it out for you?
> Philip: (not knowing what "spelling it out" meant.: Yes.
> Carlys: See, ay, ahr, ell, wye, ess. Now say it.
> Philip: Craleeth.
> Carlys: ! ! !

Many times we think that, because a word is spelled with a certain letter, we ought to pronounce some sound to correspond to that letter: we pronounce a *t*-sound in *fasten,* we pronounce three syllables in *Wednesday,* we sometimes even try to pronounce the initial *p* in words like *psychology* or *ptarmigan.* This kind of behavior is known as *spelling-pronunciation;* it almost never occurs where a language has a reasonably accurate system of spelling, but always crops up whenever the spelling ceases to represent the language adequately. Our pronunciation of *author* is a case in point. Older English had a word *autor,* meaning "creator, author," which had been borrowed from the French word *autor* of the same meaning, ultimately taken from Latin *auctor.* In the sixteenth century, people came to realize that many words previously spelled with *t* came from Latin or Greek sources in which they were spelled with *th,* such as *theater, thesis.* It came to be a mark of elegance and learning to write *th* instead of *t;* but some people carried their learning too far and wrote *th* even where it didn't belong, as in *author* for *autor.* Then more and more people, seeing the letters *th* in the elegant spelling of *author,* pronounced the *th* with the sound those letters stand for in *thing;* by now, that spelling-pronunciation has become general and we all pronounce *author* with that sound, not with the *t*-sound it originally had. Needless to say, spelling-pronunciation serves no good purpose, and only introduces confusion and misunderstanding into otherwise clear situations, like those of *autor* or *fasten.* That is, once upon a time *autor* was pronounced with a *t*-sound, and everybody was quite happy about it; now, everybody says it with a *th*-sound and is equally happy about it; but nothing has been gained by the change, and there was no need of the uncertainty that prevailed during the period of transition.

"Correct" spelling, that is, obedience to the rules of English spelling as grammarians and dictionary-makers set them up, has come to be a major shibboleth in our society. If I write *seet* instead of *seat, roat* instead of *wrote*, or *hite* instead of *height*, it makes no difference whatsoever in the English language, i.e. in my speech and that of others around me; yet we are all trained to give highly unfavorable reactions to such spellings, and to be either amused or displeased with people who know no better than to "misspell" in such a way. This shibboleth serves, as does that of "correct" speech, as a means of social discrimination: we can class people among the sheep or the goats according as they measure up to the standards we set in spelling. Spelling which is more nearly in accord with speech, and which we might logically expect to be considered better than the conventional spelling, thus comes to be, not praised, but blamed. Spelling "phonetically" becomes equivalent to spelling incorrectly. I once came across a reference to "phonetic" pronunciation, which at first puzzled me, since pronunciation can by definition never be anything but phonetic; it later turned out that the writer was referring to inaccurate pronunciation of a foreign language, such as French *est-ce que vous avez* "have you?" pronounced in a way which he transcribed *ess-ker-vous-avay*. He had come to use the term "phonetic" as equivalent to "incorrect," through the folk use of the term *phonetic spelling* in the meaning of "incorrect spelling."

When we write down the exact words of people whose speech we consider "incorrect," we often purposely misspell their words to indicate their pronunciation and give the reader an idea of what social level they belong to; the realistic novels of Erskine Caldwell, John Steinbeck and others are full of these spelling devices: for instance, *Elviry done tole me she ain' a-gwineta do no sich thing fer nobuddy.* This shocks purists who are attached to "correct" spelling at all costs; but it is spreading more and more as an element of realism, which of course derives its force from the contrast between normal "correct" spelling and pronunciation, and the "incorrect" speech implied by the "incorrect" spelling. A further development of this device is so-called *eye-dialect*, in which misspellings are used to represent normal pronunciations, merely to burlesque words or their speaker. We all pronounce *women* in the same way; but if we spell it *wimmin*, we imply "The person quoted is one who would use a vulgar pronunciation of there were one." Likewise the spellings *licker* instead of *liquor, vittles* instead of *victuals, sez* instead of *says*, and the host of reduced forms such as *I wanna* for *I want to, ya oughta* for *you ought to, watcher gonna do* for *what are you going to do*, or *I hafta* for *I have to.*

This last group of examples may not, at first, seem accurate, because we are often not aware how much we reduce and telescope such combinations in normal speech; but just try observing yourself and see how many times a day you actually use the full, separate forms of the words in such an expression as *what are you going to do,* or *I have to do it.* In fact, *I have to* with a *v*-sound in *have* would be not only unusual, it would be abnormal. But, because of our conventions of spelling, the more realistic and accurate spellings like *I wanna* or *I hafta* are relegated to the comic strips and are made the objects of prejudice, which can be appealed to in whipping up opposition to phonetic transcription or to the writing of, say, the Italian word for "when" as KWAN-*do* instead of the conventional *quando.*

The situation with respect to spelling is much the same as it is with regard to "correct" speech in our society. In each case, an irrational, meaningless standard is set up as a shibboleth for people to conform to, which in many instances puts a premium on lack of realism and on unnaturalness in speech or its representation. In particular, our society's emphasis on the irregularities of English spelling has brought many of us to a point where we cannot distinguish between speech and writing, and where we cannot even conceive of sounds as existing distinct from and prior to letters. Consequently, anyone who goes through our schooling system has to waste years of his life in acquiring a wasteful and, in the long run, damaging set of spelling habits, thus ultimately unfitting himself to understand the nature of language and its function unless he puts in extra effort to rid himself of all the misconceptions and prejudices that our system has foisted on him.

HAROLD WHITEHALL

Writing and Speech

All of us have a grammar. The fact that we use and understand English in daily affairs means that we use and understand, for the most part unconsciously, the major grammatical patterns of our language. Yet because of the effects of education, many of us have come to think of a relatively formal written English and its reflection among those who "speak by the book" as the only genuine English, and to consider its grammar as the only acceptable English grammar. That is by no means true. The basic form of present-day American English is the patterned, rhythmed, and segmented code of voice signals called *speech*—speech is used in everyday conversation by highly educated people (*cultivated speech*), by the general run of our population (*common speech*), or by some rural persons in such geographically isolated areas as the Ozark Plateau, the Appalachian Mountains, or the woodland areas of northern New England (*folk speech*). From the code of speech, the language of formal writing is something of an abstraction, differing in details of grammar and vocabulary and lacking clear indication of the bodily gestures and meaningful qualities of the voice which accompany ordinary conversation. Thus, serious written English may be regarded as a rather artificial dialect of our language. To acquire that dialect, the would-be writer needs to know a good deal about its structural details, and particularly about those in which it differs from the less formal varieties of speech.

Even a moment's reflection will show that the spoken American language is backed by expressive features lacking in the written language: the rise or fall of the voice at the ends of phrases and sentences; the application of vocal loudness to this or that word or part of a word;

From *Structural Essentials of English*. Copyright 1954, © 1956 by Harcourt, Brace & World, Inc. Reprinted by permission of Harcourt, Brace & World, Inc., and Longmans, Green & Co., Ltd.

the use of gesture; the meaningful rasp or liquidity, shouting or muting, drawling or clipping, whining or breaking, melody or whispering imparted to the quality of the voice. Written English, lacking clear indication of such features, must be so managed that it compensates for what it lacks. It must be more carefully organized than speech in order to overcome its communicative deficiencies as compared with speech. In speech, we safeguard meaning by the use of intonation, stress, gesture, and voice qualities. In writing, we must deal with our medium in such a way that the meaning cannot possibly be misunderstood. In the absence of an actual hearer capable of interrupting and demanding further explanation, a clear writer is always conscious of "a reader over his shoulder." All this despite the fact that writing, being permanent, as compared with speech, which is evanescent, allows not only reading but also rereading.

Nor is this all. If written English is somewhat abstract, somewhat artificial, it is also generalized—national, not geographically or socially limited in scope. We must realize that comparatively few of us make use in our day-to-day affairs of a generalized spoken American English that is at all comparable with it. Such a language—a Received Standard Spoken English—exists, but not for the most part in this country where the practical need for it is slight. It exists in England, where the practical need for it is great. In England, many people still start their linguistic careers speaking one or another of the regional dialects, dialects so different from each other in vocabulary and grammar, so quilt-crazy in their distribution, that they form real barriers to generalized, national communication. Yet, in a modern, democratic country, general communication is a necessity. For that reason, Englishmen are willing to accept the notion both of a generalized spoken and a generalized written form of expression on a level above the dialects, and are willing to make the effort of learning them in school and elsewhere. We would be equally willing if our everyday speech happened to resemble this specimen from the English county of Lancaster:

> Nay! my heart misgi'es me! There's summat abeawt this neet's wark as is noan jannock. Look thee here! Yon chap's noan t' first sheep theaw's lifted tax-free fro't' mooar, an' aw've niver been one to worrit abeawt it, that aw hav'nt. But toneet, someheaw, it's noan t'same. There's summat beawn't 'appen—aw con feel it i' my booans. This een, an unconny wind wor burrin' i't'ling, an' not a cleawd i't' sky; an' whin aw went deawn to' t'well for watter, t'bats wor flyin' reawn it in a widdershins ring. Mark my words, there's mooar to coom.

In the United States, our language situation is quite different. Ours is probably the only country on earth in which three thousand miles of travel will bring no difficulty of spoken communication. We do have, of course, regional and social differences of language. The speech of Maine does not coincide in all points with that of Texas, nor the speech of Georgia with that of Minnesota. The speech of cultivated people in urban centers is not precisely that of the general mass of our citizens, nor that of rural residents of limited education in geographically secluded areas. Yet, unless we deliberately choose to emphasize disparities for social or other reasons, our regional and social speech differences create no great barriers to the free exchange of opinions and ideas. They consist of flavoring rather than substance.

Precisely for that reason, pressures for the adoption of a generalized national spoken American English comparable in acceptance and prestige with Received Standard Spoken British have proved largely unavailing. In American life, one may use cultivated or common speech Southern, cultivated or common speech Northeastern, or cultivated or common speech North Middle Western without encountering any great practical disadvantage. Our standards of speech are mainly regional standards, and most of us, in actual fact, speak some kind of a patois in which one or another of the cultivated or common speech regional varieties of American English blends quite happily with elements absorbed from reading and the educational process. We are very fortunate in this—fortunate that American historical and sociological conditions have removed difficulties of spoken communication found in most other parts of the world.

In a lesser sense, however, our good fortune is something of a misfortune. Because an American can understand other Americans no matter what regional or social class they come from, he is apt to underestimate the necessity for a generalized and abstract written American English. Because he finds no pressing reason for standardizing his speech, he is likely to misunderstand the necessity for standardizing his writing. He would like to write as he speaks. Moreover, the differences between the various regional and social varieties of American speech, being slight, are often of so subtle a nature that he tends to find difficulty in discriminating them. Slight as they are, when transferred to writing they are sufficient to make a reader pause, to induce a momentary feeling of unfamiliarity, to interrupt his consideration of the *matter* of expression by unwittingly calling attention to the *manner* of expression. Outside frankly literary writing (particularly the writing of poetry), such pauses, such unfamiliarities, such interruptions will hinder rather than help the writer's communicative purpose. If writing must be generalized, it must be generalized with a good reason: to speak with a local accent is not disadvantageous; to write serious prose with a local accent definitely is.

The moral of all this is clear. To gain command of serious written

English is to acquire, quite deliberately, an abstract and generalized variety of the language differing by nature and purpose from any social or regional variety whatsoever. It is to sacrifice the local for the general, the spontaneous for the permanent. It is to bring to the study of written American English something of the perspective we normally reserve for the study of foreign languages. It is to master a set of grammatical and vocabulary patterns not because they are "correct" but because experience has proved them efficient in the communicative activity of writing.

The word "correct" is deliberately introduced here. The clear distinctions between spoken and written language mentioned in the paragraphs above have been all too often masked by the pernicious doctrine of "correctness." Perhaps that is to be expected. Without the flexible medium of language, a human society in human terms would be impossible. Without language, there could be no continuous record of experience, no diversification of labor, no great social institutions—the humanity of man could never have been achieved. But social activities breed social rituals and social judgments. Because language is *the* basic social instrument, it has inevitably acquired social attitudes so complex and variegated that they have often been allowed to obscure its primary communicative function. For far too many of us, knowledge of language is confused with knowledge of judgments on language that are socially acceptable. Education in the English language has become, for the most part, education in linguistic niceties—a poor substitute for that real linguistic education which ought to show us the major and minor patterns of our language, the way in which they interlock in function, the ways in which they can be manipulated for effective expression. As a result, the instrument of communication which should be every man's servant has become most men's master. This need not be so. Our self-confidence is immediately bolstered, our attitudes towards the study of writing techniques tremendously improved, once we realize that the difficulties of writing English do not spring from faulty nurture, restricted intelligence, or beyond-the-tracks environment but from the necessary change-over from one kind of English to another—that they are neither unpardonable nor irremediable.

No matter what irrationalities surround the details and the perspectives by which English is normally viewed, the fact that it has so admirably served and is still serving the needs of many fine writers guarantees that it is neither an impossible nor an unworthy instrument of human expression. Let us admit that all languages, spoken or written, are man-made things, that their weaknesses as well as their strengths are implicit in their human origin. Let us admit that the world has never known either a faultless language nor one constructed on what to us seems a strictly logical system. The proper approach to written English is first to understand what the medium is; then to concede its limitations and to use its strengths to the best possible effect. Every communicative medium has a set of resistances that the communicator must overcome. Marble is hard; paint relatively unmanageable; music barely descriptive. No small part of any kind of composition is contributed directly by tensions set up between the craftsman's demands on his medium on the one hand and its inherent resistances on the other. To this, the science, craft, and art of expression in written American English is no exception.

PART FOUR

Usage

A reader new to the subject may feel that modern essays on usage are like an adult western. In place of the old reliable melodrama of hero and villain, correct and incorrect, we are offered a confusing, adult reasonableness. In the first essay, Professor Robert Pooley of the University of Wisconsin shows that the family background of the formerly admired rules of grammar and usage is linguistically disreputable. Puzzled whether to use *slow* or *slowly,* we are no longer referred to a rule but to the history of the word and to our own sense of euphony and appropriateness. Professor Charles V. Hartung, in the second essay, surveys the controversy over usage. He describes the virtues and weaknesses of each of four different "doctrines" of English usage, and he then argues that neither "submission to dogmatic authority merely to gain security," nor "compromise of personal conviction so often demanded by consistent adherence to either the doctrine of general usage or the doctrine of appropriateness" is satisfactory. What he recommends is "a disinterested and yet constantly critical evaluation of language as a means to maximum expression." Among other things, this position obviously requires a steady view of change.

One source of puzzlement is the changing status of words and expressions. "Hisn" formed by the analogy with "mine" is not now "correct," but as Robert A. Hall, Jr., observes in the second essay, "today's analogical 'mistakes' are often tomorrow's competing forms, and day-after-tomorrow's 'correct' forms."

Even a dictionary editor cannot reasonably pose as an umpire of usage. His proper job, as Charles Fries argues in the third essay, is to describe rather than to arbitrate. To aid us, the editor classifies his descriptive findings under various labels: *colloquial,*

British, and so on. By attending to his labels we may select a language that will make us sound like an illiterate Yankee, a Southern gentleman, or any one of a dozen other characters. The late Professor John S. Kenyon examines this problem of levels in a slightly different way, and distinguishes between various cultural levels on the one hand and functional varieties of the language on the other. This distinction, he suggests, will help us to know what we are doing when we make linguistic choices in speaking and writing.

At any rate, the choices are ours. That is the point of the next three essays. Professor Allan Hubbell of New York University gives an account of multiple negation in English. If we choose or are brought up to multiply negatives we will sound like an educated Elizabethan or a modern illiterate but not like an educated American. More choices are described to us by Professor Jean Malmstrom of Western Michigan University. Just who uses *ain't* and under what circumstances turns out to be more complicated than we might first have thought. A similar complexity of evidence is the point of her discussion of present-day usage of *kind of.*

Just what are the problems of usage we ought to concentrate on in our schools? Professor Pooley argues that the schools must set a standard, and he offers a list of things we must concentrate on and another list he feels we might as well forget. A man not likely to forget even the smallest point of good expression is the author of the next two essays, the famous English scholar, H. W. Fowler—THE Fowler, of *Modern English Usage.* The dangling or unattached participle is the subject of the first article, and in the second, "Out of the Frying-Pan," Fowler sensibly advises us on how to avoid making bad usage worse. Everywhere in his assured judgments, Fowler makes it clear that muddy prose is somehow worse than a dirty shirt, and that no gentleman—no man of the cultured class—would ever be guilty of either.

That class distinctions in usage exist in a democratic society is disturbing. Anger at such inequality colors the famous economist Thorstein Veblen's argument that the use of "correct" language is merely a way of showing off one's social and economic superiority. Professor Donald Lloyd of Wayne University contends further that fear of being "incorrect" muddies our writing. He urges us to have the courage to write as well as we speak.

ROBERT C. POOLEY

Historical Backgrounds of English Usage

The English language in the Elizabethan period underwent an enormous expansion in its vocabulary. From travelers on the Continent and in the New World, from the scholars of the classical languages in the universities, and from experiments among English writers there poured in a flood of words, most of which became assimilated into the language. Part of the effervescence of the Elizabethan era found its vent in the game of words—not before or since has English witnessed such absorbing interest in words and their meanings, nor such an enormous increase in the number of words. Grammar, on the other hand, attracted little attention and was taken for granted. While the major outlines of English grammar had become fairly fixed by the time of Shakespeare and were essentially the grammar we know today, it was a popular or traditional, rather than a formal, grammar. A study of the usage of Elizabethan dramatists, for example, reveals far greater freedom in number agreement, in double comparatives, and in double negatives than is tolerated in current writing. Elizabethan dramatic literature, in short, is a faithful reproduction of the normal speech of Elizabethan gentlemen, who wrote as they spoke, unhampered by considerations of formal correctness.

The verbal enthusiasm of the Elizabethan era was followed by a natural reaction toward restraint. From the beginning of the seventeenth century there appeared a critical attitude toward English, voiced at first by a few scattered writers who felt that English was an uncouth and disorderly language, lacking the beauty and regularity of Latin and Greek. Gradually the idea of the impurity and irregularity of English came to be commonly accepted, so that by the end of the seventeenth century the interest in language had shifted almost entirely from vocabulary to grammar and syntax. This change of interest was accompanied by a zeal

From *Teaching English Usage*. Copyright 1946 by The National Council of Teachers of English. Reprinted by permission of Appleton-Century-Crofts.

for reform and by a great increase in the numbers of books on the English language. Prior to 1700 there were few books devoted to language criticism; in the first half of the eighteenth century approximately fifty such books appeared, and in the succeeding half century over two hundred were published. These figures reveal the tremendous interest in language which characterized the latter part of the eighteenth century.

The same spirit which brought about the Augustan Age of English literature, the "improving" of Shakespeare and the editing of Milton, accelerated the purifying and correcting of English. That a large part of the critical work in English was beneficial to the language cannot be denied, but unfortunately there was much bad mixed with the good. Many of the writers on language were retired clergymen and country philosophers, who, though possessing some skill in the classics, had no conception at all of the history of English or the methods of linguistic research. Too frequently their statements on English usage were the product of false philology or of personal prejudice. Moreover, the philosophy of the age was inimical to scientific research in language; the prevailing conceptions of language were (1) that language is a divine institution, originally perfect, but debased by man; (2) that English is a corrupt and degenerate off-spring of Latin and Greek. The first theory gave rise to the application of reason and the analogy of the language in an effort to restore English to its pristine glory; the second resulted in corrections of English idioms to make them conform to classical models. The actual usage of English was ignored or despised by all but one or two of the writers of this age.

Thus we find the laudable effort to improve and correct the grammar and syntax of English sadly handicapped by ignorance of linguistic principles on the one hand and misleading philosophies on the other. Yet the prescriptions of the reformers, whether good or bad, were received, approved, and formulated into rules; the rules were gathered into textbooks and were copied from book to book throughout the nineteenth century and may still be found in the books we are now using. In the meantime the English language has continued its organic growth, only slightly influenced by the rules prescribed for it, until today many of the rules bear no more than a faint resemblance to the language customs they are supposed to describe. It is small wonder that English teachers are perplexed in trying to reconcile dead rules with a living language!

The links between the reformers of the eighteenth century and the textbooks of today may be easily traced. One of the most influential of the eighteenth-century writers on language was Bishop Lowth, whose *Short Introduction to English Grammar* appeared in 1762. In 1795 an American named Lindley Murray wrote a grammar, nearly all of which he copied from Lowth. Murray's book enjoyed an enormous popularity; it is estimated that over a million copies were sold in America before 1850. Murray's successors copied freely from his book, so that the direct influence of Lowth persisted well into the latter part of the nineteenth century. The vast expansion of the United States since the Civil War, the accompanying increase in the numbers of textbooks, and the greatly improved theories and methods of education have resulted in textbooks very different in character from those of Lowth and Murray; but whereas in organization and technique the books have made great forward strides, in actual content they still retain much of the theory and practice of the eighteenth and nineteenth centuries.

The teaching of English usage is still further confused by the conflict between the traditional rules, whose origins we have just traced, and the modern science of linguistics, which is giving us entirely new concepts of language and its functions. Linguistics teaches us to look at language from the viewpoints of history, psychology, and sociology, and to understand and interpret modern usage in the light of these factors rather than upon a set of traditional authorities. Some examples of the application of these principles may be interesting to include here.

HISTORY.   Many textbooks contain warnings against the use of the word *slow* as an adverb, pointing out that *slow* is an adjective with a corresponding adverb *slowly*. But when we look back into the history of English, we discover that adverbs were formed in two ways in early English; sometimes by adding *-lic* (the ancestor of *-ly*) and sometimes by just adding *-e*. Thus the descendant of *slow-lic* is *slowly*, a regular adverb, and the descendant of *slow-e* is *slow*, an irregular or "flat" adverb. Both are correct, native English; both have been used in English literature; and both may be used today. The decision as to when to use one or the other is a matter of euphony and appropriateness in the sentence; one need never hesitate to say, "Drive slow!"

PSYCHOLOGY.   Textbooks warn us about placing *only* in the sentence so that it is next to the word it modifies; for example, a sentence like this would be called incorrect by many textbooks: "I *only* had five dollars." Logically it is incorrect, because *only* appears to modify the pronoun *I*, but psychologically it is correct, because custom has established the pattern of the sentence beyond possibility of misunderstanding. If you wanted to say that you were the only one to have five dollars, you would have to say, "I *alone* had five dollars," or "*Only* I had five dollars." The regular pattern, "I *only* had five dollars," has but one meaning, namely, that you possessed no more than five dollars. In this manner the psychology of sentence patterns supersedes logic.

SOCIOLOGY.   The only valid basis for the creation, preservation, or ex-

tinction of a word is its usefulness to society. If the people need a word
it will live; if it is no longer needed it will die. For this reason the Old
English word *a*, which meant *law*, was completely eradicated by the
Scandinavian word *law* because the latter was less open to confusion, and
therefore more useful to society. In similar fashion a modern need is
establishing the foreign word *data* as a singular noun meaning *information* or *collection of facts*, despite the fact that it is a Latin plural. There
is little doubt that a few more years will establish "The *data is* complete,"
not because of logical correctness, but because society finds the word
data useful as a singular noun. These are but a few of the hundreds of
examples which might be cited.

THE DETERMINATION OF "CORRECT" ENGLISH

In the year 1712 Dean Swift wrote a letter to the Earl of Oxford outlining
a plan for the foundation of an English academy similar to the French
Academy for the purpose of regularizing and establishing correct English.
Although his plan was received with interest, it was never acted upon,
and many later attempts to found an academy have failed. The purists
of the later eighteenth century did much of what Swift desired, but
fortunately for the life and vigor of our tongue it has never been submitted to the restraint of a board of authorities. Several theories of
"correctness" in English have therefore been formulated and have influenced writers and teachers of the past and present. One of the most
important of these theories was that enunciated by George Campbell in
1776, that "correctness" rests in good custom, defined as "national," reputable" and "present." This definition was accepted by practically all the
nineteenth-century grammarians (although they frequently did it violence
in specific instances), and may be found in a number of the high-school
composition books of the present day. Another theory, really a modification of Campbell's, proposed by Fitzedward Hall and other nineteenth-
century students of language, is that "good usage is the usage of the best
writers and speakers." This definition is also very widely used in the
textbooks of today, and is probably the expressed or implied standard of
good English in almost every American schoolroom. Both of these definitions, useful as they have been and are, present many difficulties in
application to the teaching of current usage.

The chief difficulty lies in the interpretation of the terms "reputable"
and "the best writers and speakers." For example, nearly all grammar
books list as undesirable English the use of the split infinitive, the dangling participle or gerund, the possessive case of the noun with inanimate
objects, the objective case of the noun with the gerund, the use of *whose*

as a neuter relative pronoun, and many others; yet all of these uses may be found in the authors who form the very backbone of English literature and who are "reputable" and the "best writers" in every sense of the words. If the standard-makers defy the standards, to whom shall we turn for authority? Moreover, the use of literary models tends to ignore the canon of *present* usage, for by the time an author has come to be generally recognized as *standard* his usage is no longer *present*. And among present speakers, who are best? The writer has heard a large number of the most prominent platform speakers of the day, yet he has still to hear one who did not in some manner violate the rules of the books. Are all great writers and speakers at fault, or is it possible that the rules are inaccurate?

The way out of this perplexity is to shift the search for standards away from "authorities" and traditional rules to the language itself as it is spoken and written today. Just as the chemist draws his deductions from the results of laboratory experiments, the biologist from his observation of forms of life, and the astronomer from his telescope, so must students of language draw their deductions from an observation of the facts of language. In establishing the laws of language, our personal desires, preferences, and prejudices must give way to the scientific determination and interpretation of the facts of language. What language we use ourselves may take any form we desire, but the making of rules and the teaching of rules must rest upon objective facts. We must take the attitude of a distinguished scholar who said recently of *due to*, "I don't like it, but there is no doubt about its establishment in English."

If we discard the authority of rules and of "reputable" writers, to what can we turn for a definition of "correct" English? At the outset it must be acknowledged that there can be no absolute, positive definition. "Correct English" is an approximate term used to describe a series of evaluations of usage dependent upon appropriateness, locality, social level, purpose, and other variables. It is a relative term, in decided contrast with the positive nature of (1) *reputability*, the determination of good usage by reference to standard authors; (2) *preservation*, the obligation to defend and maintain language uses because they are traditional, or are felt to be more elegant; (3) *literary*, the identification of good usage with formal literary usage. By discarding these traditional conceptions, and turning to the language itself as its own standard of good usage, we may find the following definition adequate for our present needs. Good English is that form of speech which is appropriate to the purpose of the speaker, true to the language as it is, and comfortable to speaker and listener. It is the product of custom, neither cramped by rule nor freed from all restraint; it is never fixed, but changes with the organic life of the language.

Such a definition is linguistically sound because it recognizes the living, organic nature of language; it is historically sound, for the language of the present is seen to be the product of established custom; it is socially sound in recognizing the purpose of language and its social acceptability in *comfort* to speaker and writer.

Teachers of English will recognize that the acceptance of this or a similar definition of good English necessitates great changes in the presentation of usage in textbooks and in the classroom. Those who are accustomed to rule and authority, to an absolute right and wrong in language, will find great difficulty in making the mental readjustment imperative for a relative rather than an absolute standard of usage. Much of the conventional teaching of grammar and correctness will have to be vastly modified or discarded. There will be much confusion and some distress. But eventually there will grow up in the schools a new theory of good English so closely knit with the language itself that the perplexity now arising from the discrepancies between rule and usage will no longer have cause for existence. But in discarding an absolute right and wrong for a relative standard of appropriateness and social acceptability, we shall have to determine the areas or levels of language usage, to define and illustrate them, and to apply them as standards for the written and spoken English in the schools.

CHARLES V. HARTUNG

Doctrines of English Usage

The teacher of English today may often be tempted to envy the teacher of a generation ago, who could turn to Woolley's handbook or its counterpart and find immediately an unqualified rule to answer questions about debatable usage. But the publication of the Leonard survey, *Current English Usage* (1932), ended the age of certainty for the teacher and ushered in the age of anxiety. There had of course been premonitory signs before the Leonard survey, notably in Krapp's *Modern English* (1909) and in Hall's *English Usage* (1917), but there had not been a systematic and thoroughly documented survey of current opinion. The Leonard survey definitely demonstrated the respectable standing of such locutions as *it is me, will you be at the Browns' this evening,* and *who are you looking for.* As a result the revised editions of prescriptive handbooks began to qualify their absolutism, and the English teacher's life became more complicated. Today the conscientious teacher must keep up with the latest developments in linguistic theory, weigh the results of various polls of English usage, and be constantly attentive to the language customs of his local community and of the wider community reflected in newspaper, radio, and television. There is even one school of opinion which holds that the teacher may well learn several versions of his language and use them appropriately to increase his popularity and effectiveness. Donald Lloyd gives clear and vivid expression to this view:

> We say "he don't" and "ain't," not because we are stupid and stubborn, but because the people we live with and work with and play with—our closest friends—say them. We need, not to exclude these forms from our speech, but to learn to use them in alternation with "doesn't" and "isn't" or "aren't" with easy command in exactly the right circumstances. Then they help us make friends wherever we go. Then they enrich our speech; they do not impoverish it.[1]

English Journal, XLV (1956). Reprinted with the permission of the National Council of Teachers of English and Charles V. Hartung.

This passage is extracted from an eloquent plea to banish prescriptivism from the classroom and is representative of the thinking of probably the most active school of linguists in this country today. Moreover, the relativism expressed here has been characterized as the "modern view of grammar and linguistics" and has been presented as the majority opinion of the Commission on the English Curriculum of the National Council of Teachers of English.[2] For those teachers who may not be familiar with the statement of the view in *The English Language Arts* here is a list of the basic concepts which are there attributed to modern linguists and advocated by the committee on language: (1) Language changes constantly; (2) Change is normal and represents not corruption but improvement; (3) Spoken language is the language; (4) Correctness rests upon usage; (5) All usage is relative. In the same place the point of view of the contemporary linguist is summarized as follows:

> 1. Correctness in modern English usage is not determined by appeals to logic, etymology, or the traditions of earlier days. It cannot be determined by rules of "right" and "wrong." It must be established by the needs of communication in every situation in which language is used.
>
> 2. Since correctness is a relative matter derived from the needs of communication, the teaching of correct English requires the development in pupils of a sensitivity to the requirements of language in all kinds of situations and the gradual development of skill to use English appropriately in each situation.
>
> 3. The teaching of correctness in school and college courses must shift in emphasis from the laying down of negative rules to the development of positive insights. Instead of teaching rules for the avoidance of error, pupils must be taught to observe and understand the way in which their language operates today for the various needs of communication.[3]

This is evidently the doctrine of the new orthodoxy. It comes with good credentials and presents a program that is in many ways attractive. And it has retained enough of the dogmatism of the old orthodoxy (note the words "must" and "requires") to appeal to those in need of authority. The dogmatism of the quoted passage may be partially explained by its polemical purpose, but a more qualified statement would doubtless be more accurate. Even among the linguistic experts cited as the authority for the new doctrine there is not the unanimity that is claimed; for one may find students of language advocating at least four currently respectable points of view from which English usage may be judged. It may serve to clarify the issues if we survey the main points of these four doctrines and make an appraisal of their claims.

Generally speaking, the four main doctrines current among those concerned with judging the propriety of language usage are: (1) the doctrine of rules; (2) the doctrine of general usage; (3) the doctrine of appropriate usage; (4) the doctrine of the linguistic norm. Rarely do those interested in language adhere consistently to any one of these doctrines. Instead there is the usual divergence between theory and practice; some linguists profess one doctrine and practice another. Also there is the usual eclectic compromise. Nevertheless, it is possible to make roughly approximate groupings of schools of opinion according to the degrees of emphasis given to these various doctrines.

THE DOCTRINE OF RULES

From the point of view of the modern school of linguistics the doctrine of rules is, or at least should be, moribund. But even a cursory glance at handbooks and grammars of recent date reveals what a tenacious hold it has on life. And even when the doctrine is disclaimed in theory, we find grammarians following it in spirit and practice. For example, in the preface to R. W. Pence's *A Grammar of Present-Day English,* we find the following statement: "Grammar is not a set of rules thought up by and imposed by some invisible godlike creature." [4] Yet the text itself consists of a set of prescriptions in the spirit of the eighteenth century grammarians and having the effect if not the form of the old rules. Here is an example:

> . . . inasmuch as an interrogative pronoun normally introduces a clause and so may not have the position that a noun of like function would have, the function of an interrogative pronoun may be easily mistaken. Care needs to be exercised to meet the demands of subjective complements of finite verbs and of infinitives. But especial care needs to be taken that the proper objective form is used when an interrogative pronoun coming first functions as the object of a preposition that is delayed.
> 1. Subjective complement
>   *Whom* do you mean? [*Whom* is the object of *do mean.*]
> 2. Object of a preposition
>   Whom were you with last night?
>   [*Whom* is the object of the preposition *with. Not:* Who were you with last night?][5]

In a note some concession is made to the demands of spoken discourse: "Who are you looking for? [Accepted by some in spoken discourse.]" But in the same note we find this comment: "This use of the nominative in informal spoken discourse is regarded by a few as acceptable, although

the fastidious person will probably look upon it as sloppy speech." It is
noteworthy that the text in which this judgment is to be found reached
its seventh printing in 1953. Yet the sentence *Who are you looking for*
is listed as *Accepted* in the Leonard survey printed in 1932.

It would be possible, of course, to multiply examples of the continuing
hold that the doctrine of rules still has on a large proportion of present
day students of language, but it is more to the point to examine the reasons for this hold. Probably the most important reason is that the doctrine has behind it the weight of over a century and a half of almost
undisputed dominance. This is the result of two main sources of authority:
the assumed correspondence of the rules of grammar with basic principles
of reason and the supposed correspondence of the rules with the usage
of the best writers. Some grammarians have assumed that reason has the
prior claim and determines usage; others have placed usage first and
have claimed that rules are inductively derived from the best usage. The
eighteenth century grammarian William Ward gives typical expression
to the view of the first group:

> Use and Custom are considered as the only Rules by which to judge
> of what is right or wrong in Process. But is the Custom which is ob-
> served in the Application of any Language the Effect of Chance? Is
> not such a Custom a consistent Plan of communicating the Concep-
> tions and rational discursive Operations of one Man to another? And
> who will maintain, that this is, or can be, the Effect of unmeaning
> Accident? If then it be not so, it must be the Effect of the Reason of
> Man, adjusting certain means to a certain End: And it is the Business
> of Speculative or Rational Grammar to explain the Nature of the
> Means, and to show how they are applied to accomplish the End
> proposed. If this can be done with sufficient Evidence, the most simple
> of the Elements of Logic will become familiar to those who engage
> in a Course of Grammar, and Reason will go Hand in Hand with
> Practice.[6]

Ward's linking of grammar and logic was a common eighteenth century
practice and carried over into the nineteenth century, receiving the approval of even such a great philosopher as John Stuart Mill. Mill says that
"the principles and rules of grammar are the means by which forms of
language are made to correspond with the universal forms of thought."[7]
The weakness of this thesis was, of course, evident to the language experts of Mill's own time. Henry Sweet and A. H. Sayce brought to bear
their great knowledge of comparative philology to show how little actual
correspondence there is between logic and grammar, and modern linguists
and semanticists have agreed with them. Probably the most judicious
summation of the problem is that of Otto Jespersen:

Most linguists are against any attempt to apply a logical standard to language. Language, they say, is psychology, not logic; or "language is neither logical nor illogical, but a-logical." That is to say, language has nothing to do with logic. To many philologists the very word, logic, is like a red rag to a bull. . . . It would be surprising however if language which serves to express thoughts should be quite independent of the laws of correct thinking.[8]

As Jespersen demonstrates, however, what often has pretended to be logic is no more than Latin grammar disguised, and arguments declaring the correspondence of grammar with logic have often been little more than the forcing of English into Latin syntactical patterns. For example, the rule that the predicative must stand in the same case as the subject is not, as has been claimed, an incontrovertible law of thought but merely a rule of Latin grammar. Many languages of different types violate this so-called incontrovertible law.

The authority that the rules have derived from deductive logic has never been equal to the support given them by the belief that rules are inductively derived from examination of the best usage. George Campbell's dictum that reputable, national, and present usage determines correctness has been cited with approval from the days of Lindley Murray, probably the most popular of eighteenth century grammarians, to the present day. Many writers on language have, in fact, cited Campbell's doctrine as liberalizing in effect, but it is difficult to see how such a belief can be accepted. Campbell so restricted the field of acceptable usage that the doctrine of rules lost little of the force it had held in the writings of such prescriptive grammarians as Bishop Lowth and William Ward. Lowth had, of course, declared the independence of grammar from the usage of even the best writers, whereas Campbell paid lip service to the doctrine of usage. But in practice Campbell, as S. A. Leonard has shown, repudiated the very theory he had set up as a guide. We can see what the doctrine of usage actually became when we examine the following statement from a latter day follower of Campbell:

By good usage is meant the usage generally observed in the writings of the best English authors and in the speech of well-educated people. Dictionaries, grammars, and books on rhetoric and composition record this usage, on the basis of wide observation and study.[9]

This definition follows a pattern dating from the eighteenth century and repeated in scores of nineteenth century handbooks and grammars. The doctrine of usage in the hands of the grammarians has been practically identical with the doctrine of rules.

THE DOCTRINE OF GENERAL USAGE

Joseph Priestley, the eighteenth century scientist and grammarian, was probably the first writer in English to show a consistent regard for the doctrine of general usage. But his views were neglected, and it was not until the rise of scientific linguistics in the late nineteenth century that the doctrine began to make headway against the doctrine of rules. Among the pioneers were W. D. Whitney, Fitzedward Hall, and Alexander Bain. The first full-fledged popular exposition and exemplification of the doctrine, J. Lesslie Hall's *English Usage* (1917), was not published until well into the twentieth century. In contrast with most of his predecessors, who only paid lip service to the doctrine of usage, Hall is consistent and documents his opinion with particular examples. In his article, "Who for Whom," for instance, Hall cites the opinions of contemporary liberal grammarians in favor of *who* as the objective form in questions, and he gives a number of examples from usage, citing Shakespeare, Marlowe, Defoe, Kingsley, and Froude, as well as less well-known writers.

Comprehensive as it is, Hall's work is limited primarily to an examination of written documents, and it was not until Leonard's *Current English Usage* that there was a systematic survey of spoken usage to support Hall's findings. Strictly speaking, the Leonard report is not a survey of the facts of English usage but of opinion about the relative standing of various debatable items. The guiding principle of the survey is indicated succinctly in the statement that "allowable usage is based on the actual practice of cultivated people rather than on rules of syntax or logic." [10] In keeping with this principle, Leonard submitted a number of items of debatable usage to a jury consisting of linguistic specialists, editors, authors, business men, and teachers of English and speech. These judges were to decide the standing of the items according to what they thought the actual usage to be. Four levels of acceptability were indicated: "literary English," "standard, cultivated, colloquial English," "trade or technical English," and "naïf, popular, or uncultivated English." The findings of the report provided evidence to demonstrate the discrepancy between actual usage and the rules of the common school grammar. Among the items indicated as *established,* or acceptable on the cultivated colloquial level by more than seventy-five percent of the judges, were *it is me, who are you looking for, I feel badly,* and many other locutions that had long been proscribed by the handbooks and grammars.

The Leonard report was not a survey of "general" usage but of "cultivated" usage. It is not until the research studies of C. C. Fries that we find a truly inclusive and adequately documented study of general usage.

Eschewing the guidance of the grammars and even of polls of "educated" usage, Fries stated that "it is probably much more sound to decide that the spontaneous usage of that large group who are carrying on the affairs of English speaking people is the usage to be observed and to set the standard." [11] To provide evidence of actual usage. Fries has used letters and transcripts of telephone conversations. Like other modern advocates of the doctrine of usage, Fries has not held to the theory that the standard of general usage should apply in all language situations. In concession to the demands of effective communication and to the practical problems of the teacher in the classroom he has given assent to the doctrine of appropriateness. The problem of the teacher, according to Fries, is to develop in the student the habits that will enable him to use freely the language appropriate to his ideas, the occasion of their expression, and the needs of his hearers. To bring about this end, the teacher needs to become sensitive to the different levels and functional varieties of usage and to develop a program of study designed to meet the particular needs of each class. Although the teacher must take into account the prevailing demand that he equip his pupils with the language habits that have attained the most social acceptability, he needs to develop also an intelligently liberal attitude toward the particular language habits of any group of students.

THE DOCTRINE OF APPROPRIATENESS

In its essentials the doctrine of appropriateness has not changed since the full exposition by George Philip Krapp in his *Modern English* (1909). Krapp introduces his exposition by making a distinction between "good" English and "conventional" or "standard" English. Good English, according to Krapp, is any language which "hits the mark." Since the purpose of language is the satisfactory communication of thought and feeling, any language which satisfactorily performs this function is good English. Standard English is that usage which is recognized and accepted as customary in any particular community. Such locutions as *he don't* or *these kind of people* or *I will* may be standard in one community and not standard in another. Custom is the only relevant determinant of the standard. Krapp's relativism is evident in the following statement:

> What is defended as customary use by a community, or even by a single speaker, to carry the matter to its final analysis, is standard, or conventional, or "right," or "correct," in that community or for that speaker.[12]

In analyzing the concept of "good" English, Krapp arrives at the doctrine of appropriateness. He describes three tendencies in English speech— "popular English," "colloquial English," and "formal or literary English"

—and declares that each of these has its appropriate uses. They are three kinds of arrows by which the speaker attempts to hit the mark of good English. Whether the speaker hits the mark or not depends upon his skill and upon his acumen in sizing up the particular speech situation:

> . . . the degree of colloquialism which one permits, in one's self or in others depends on the subject of conversation, on the intimacy of the acquaintanceship of the persons speaking, and in general on all the attendant circumstances . . . language which may be adequately expressive, and therefore good, under one set of circumstances, under a different set of circumstances becomes inadequately expressive, because it says more or less than the speaker intended, and so becomes bad English. One learns thus the lesson of complete relativity of the value of language, that there is no such thing as an absolute English, but that language is valuable only as it effects the purpose one wishes to attain, that what is good at one time may be bad at another, and what is bad at one time may be good at another.[13]

This doctrine has been somewhat qualified by some of its recent exponents, particularly by Pooley and Perrin, but it has not been changed in its essentials. And it is still subject to the same sort of objection that J. Lesslie Hall made to Krapp's statement of it. Hall pointed out that Krapp's conception of "good" English was unprecedented and varied from the commonly accepted meaning of the term. He also deprecated Krapp's advocacy of "a sort of isolated, neighborhood English" and declared that the consistent carrying out of Krapp's ideas would mean the decline of a *general* and reputable usage for which students of language had been struggling. Consistent application of the doctrine of appropriateness would mean that every newcomer to a community would need to learn a new set of speech habits and that every traveler would need to be sensitive to innumerable local dialects and to cater to the personal language habits of his listeners. This would finally result in the decline of a general standard of cultivated speech understood everywhere and acceptable everywhere. In answer to Hall's objections Krapp might very well have repeated what he had said in *Modern English:* that the completely consistent adherence to the idea of general usage would mean finally a fixed language inadmissive of improvement and that the interplay of standard English and good English makes for a language constantly improving in expressiveness and effectiveness of communication.

THE DOCTRINE OF THE LINGUISTIC NORM

Under the heading of the linguistic norm may be grouped those concepts which emphasize that language is above all responsible to an expressive ideal. Some advocates of the normative approach hold that language should not be subservient to usage and should be judged by consciously derived criteria. I. A. Richards, for instance, has characterized the doctrine of usage as "the most pernicious influence in current English teaching." [14] In attacking the doctrine of usage, Richards does not recommend a return to the doctrine of rules and of what he calls the illegitimate application of logic and philosophy to language. Instead he recommends a self-critical reflection about the conduct of thought in language. Richards' evaluation of modern linguistic theories and his own program are explicitly stated in his latest book:

> There are vast areas of so-called "purely descriptive" linguistics which are a grim danger at present to the conduct of language, to education, to standards of intelligence, to the reserves in theory and in sensibility of the mental tester. . . . The appeal to mere *usage:* "If it's widely in use, it's O.K.," is a case in point. Every useful feature of language was *not in use* once upon a time. Every degradation of language too starts somewhere. Behind usage is the question of efficiency. Inefficient language features are not O.K., however widespread their use. Of course, to the linguistic botanist it is important to preserve all varieties until they have been collected and described. But that is not the point of view of the over-all study of language, its services and its powers. That over-all view is, I am insisting, inescapably NORMATIVE. It is concerned (as every speaker and every listener is always concerned) with the maintenance and improvement of the use of language.[15]

As instances of degradation in language Richards cites the current practice of using *uninterested* and *disinterested* and *imply* and *infer* as synonyms. In each instance the confusion has brought about a loss in precision without a corresponding gain.

Not all adherents to the concept of a linguistic norm have held as strongly as Richards to the principle of consciously critical evaluation of language. Instead such linguistic scholars as Otto Jespersen and Edward Sapir have held that linguistic efficiency is often the result of the spontaneous and intuitive expression of the folk. Probably the best known statement of the belief that language tends constantly toward a norm of maximum expressiveness with least effort is Otto Jespersen's theory of energetics, most recently restated in his *Efficiency in Linguistic Change* (1941).[16] According to Jespersen's theory, linguistic changes involve a constant interplay of opposing demands, one by the individual seeking ease of expression and the other of a social character calling for distinctness of communication. The first tendency is subversive of traditional forms of expression; the second is conservative and tends to keep alive the traditional norm. The interaction between these two demands brings about language changes designed to conserve the energy of the speaker and at the same time to retain the power of exact communication.

Edward Sapir's *Language* contains a discussion of the expression *Who did you see* that may serve to illustrate Jespersen's theory.[17] Sapir declares that the syntax of "whom" in *whom did you see* is logically and historically sound but psychologically shaky. The construction is kept alive by social snobbery but will eventually succumb to the pressure put on it by the uncontrolled speech of the folk. Meanwhile, users of *whom* are torn between an unconscious desire to say *who* and a fear of social penalty. The correctness of *whom* is fundamentally false and within a couple of hundred years the "whom" will probably be as delightfully archaic as the Elizabethan "his" for "its." In his analysis, Sapir cites four reasons for the linguistic shakiness of *whom*. First, *who* is becoming invariable because of its linguistic similarity to such invariable forms as the interrogative and relative pronouns, *which, what,* and *that* and the interrogative adverbs *where, when,* and *how.* Second, interrogative pronouns normally play an emphatic part in the sentence, and emphatic elements are typically invariable. The third powerful reason for the interrogative use of *who* rather than *whom* is its position in the sentence. Normal word order in English places the subject at the beginning of the sentence, before the verb. And the word in the subject position normally takes the subjective form. A fourth difficulty in *whom did you see* is that the *m* sound slows down the movement of the sentence and calls for a deliberate mental and physical effort at odds with the spontaneous speech situations in which the expression is normally used. For these reasons then *whom* is on psychologically shaky grounds and will eventually be replaced by the more natural and expressive *who*. As another instance of the prevalence of psychology over logic in language usage we may cite the rule about the placement of adverbial modifiers. The latest version of Woolley's handbook still carries the following precept and example: "Place such adverbs as *only, merely, just, almost, ever, hardly, scarcely, quite, nearly* next to the words they modify. COLLOQUIAL: *I only want three.* BETTER: *I want only three;* [or] *I want three only.*" [18] It may be that the constructions labeled BETTER are more logically sound, but rhetorically and psychologically they may not be as effective as the COLLOQUIAL version. The intention of the speaker may be to emphasize the reasonableness of his request, not the request itself or the exact amount being requested. If such is his intention, the sooner he introduces the idea of reasonableness into his expression the truer he is to his actual meaning and the more likely he is to get a favorable response. The placement of a modifier depends therefore not on an invariable rule of logic or grammar but on the speaker's full meaning. It is this insistence on precision and fullness of meaning which gives force to the doctrine of the linguistic norm. In its expressive aims it is similar to the doctrine of appropriateness, but whereas the doctrine of appropriateness emphasizes the social situation, particularly the effect on an audience, the doctrine of the linguistic norm holds in balance the intention of the speaker, the nature of the language itself, and the probable effect on the audience.

Because of its over-all point of view the doctrine of the linguistic norm is probably the best vantage ground for the teacher. It provides criteria by which to evaluate both the conservative and the liberalizing forces in language. It does not, to be sure, provide the sense of psychological security and social approval so long associated with the doctrine of rules. But submission to dogmatic authority merely out of a desire to gain security hardly seems a constructive attitude. Nor does it seem desirable to compromise personal conviction in the way so often demanded by consistent adherence to either the doctrine of general usage or the doctrine of appropriateness. The most suitable philosophy of language for the teacher would seem to be one calling for a disinterested and yet constantly critical evaluation of language as a means to maximum expression. And this is the point of view of the doctrine of the linguistic norm.

NOTES

1. "Let's Get Rid of Miss Driscoll," *The Educational Forum* (March 1954), p. 344.

2. *The English Language Arts* (New York: Appleton-Century-Crofts, Inc., 1952), pp. 274–301.

3. *Ibid.*, pp. 278–279.

4. New York: The Macmillan Co., 1947, p. v.

5. *Ibid.*, pp. 204–205.

6. William Ward, *English Grammar* (1765). Quoted by C. C. Fries, *The Teaching of English* (Ann Arbor: The George Wahr Publishing Co., 1949), p. 13.

7. See I. A. Richards, *Interpretation in Teaching* (London: Routledge & Kegan Paul, 1938), p. 280.

8. *Mankind, Nation and the Individual* (London: Geo. Allen, 1946), p. 114.

9. Edwin C. Woolley, *Handbook of Composition,* Revised Edition (Boston: D. C. Heath, 1920), p. 1.

10. Sterling Andrus Leonard, *Current English Usage* (Chicago: The National Council of Teachers of English, 1932), p. 95.

11. *The Teaching of English*, p. 35.

12. New York: Charles Scribners' Sons, 1909, p. 332.

13. *Ibid.*, pp. 327, 329–330.

14. *Op. cit.*, p. 174.

15. *Speculative Instruments* (Chicago: University of Chicago Press, 1955), pp. 123–124.

16. Copenhaven: Ejnar Munksgaard, 1941, pp. 15–16.

17. New York: Harcourt, Brace, 1921, pp. 156–162.

18. *College Handbook of Composition* (Boston: D. C. Heath, 1951), p. 89.

ROBERT A. HALL, JR.

Analogy

Internal borrowing, or *analogy*, is the kind of change that takes place when a child says *foots* instead of *feet*, *oxes* instead of *oxen*, *sticked* instead of *stuck*, or *breaked* instead of *broke*. We usually call such forms as *foots, oxes, sticked, breaked* "mistakes" and all of us—even the most illiterate users of sub-standard English—train our children to say *feet*, not *foots*, and so on. Yet what lies at the root of these "mistakes" is an extremely widespread process, which we call *analogical replacement*. What has happened when the child has said *foots* or *sticked*? Simply this: he has heard and learned a whole host of "regular" formations—plural formations such as *root—roots, hat—hats, book—books, map—maps, box—boxes*, and past formations like *kick—kicked, lick—licked, trick—tricked, rake—raked*, in the hundreds and thousands. He has simply made his new formation of a plural for *foot* or *ox* by abstracting (unconsciously, for the most part) the "regular" ending *-s, -es* and adding it to *foot* or *ox*. Likewise, he has taken the "regular" past ending *-ed* or *breaked* "on the analogy" of other pasts like *kicked, raked*, and so on. He is making what we often call an *analogical new-formation*, by borrowing an element of linguistic form or construction (here the noun-plural suffix *-s -es* or the verb past suffix *-ed*) from one part of our linguistic structure (here the "regular" formations) and adding it to another (here the "irregular" forms). This is a kind of borrowing, just like external borrowing; but the source of borrowing is not somewhere outside but within the language itself, and so we call it internal borrowing.

Analogical changes of this kind are often presented in the shape of proportional formulas, with *x* standing for the new-formation, thus

$$hat : hats = foot : (\text{"}hat \text{ is to } hats \text{ as } foot \text{ is to } x\text{"})$$
$$box : boxes = ox : x$$

$$kick : kicked = stick : x$$
$$rake : raked = break : x$$

Sometimes, objections are made to our statement of analogical replacements in a proportional formula, such as those we have just given; critics say that naive speakers would not be capable of exact enough reasoning to make up a formula of this sort and carry it out. There are two answers to this objection: 1) that what we are giving here is a description of what takes place, not a statement of reasoning that we might necessarily expect from a naive speaker, who speaks normally without abstract analysis and who habitually does perfectly many things he could not possibly describe; and 2) that even naive speakers from time to time are perfectly conscious of the basis for their analogical formations. The great Danish linguistician Otto Jespersen tells the story of a Danish child who should, according to normal Danish usage, have said *nikkede* "nodded" as the past of *nikker* "nod," but said *nak* instead on the analogy of *stak* "stuck," whose present is *stikker*. When the child was corrected, he immediately retorted "*Stikker —stak, nikker—nak,*" showing that he knew perfectly well on what analogy he had made the new past tense form, and stating it in the form of a proportion.

From the point of view of the present language, analogical new-formations like *oxes* or *taked* are "mistakes," forms that would be uttered only by children or others learning the language, or by adults when tired or flustered (that is, as "slips of the tongue"), and that would not be accepted by any native speaker at present. But there are always some forms with regard to which our usage is not fully settled, even that of normal adult native speakers of the language, and for which we may use first one and then another alternative. We have, for instance, the "irregular" plural formation *hoof—hooves,* and the "strong" past tenses *wake—woke, dive—dove;* yet we often hear and make regularized forms for these words: *hoofs, waked, dived.* That is to say, in some respects our usage is *fluctuating;* and in the course of time, we will gradually come to favor one competing form over the other (say, *dived* over *dove*), until at last one is triumphant and drives out the other completely in normal everyday usage.

What we often fail to realize, however, is that some forms which seem fully fixed in our present language were, in earlier times, analogical new-formations, and went through a period of newness, and then of fluctuation, before displacing older forms entirely. Our plurals *days* and *cows* are both analogical replacements of earlier forms which would have sounded quite different if they had developed normally into Modern English. Old English had the singular *dag* "day," plural *dagas,* and *cū* "cow," plural *cȳ* (in which the letter *y* stands for a vowel like that spelled *u* in French or *ü* in German); the Old English plurals, had they developed normally, would have given *dawes* and *kye* (rhyming with *high*) in present-day English. But we do not say *day–dawes* or *cow–kye;* we use the regularized plurals *days* and *cows* instead. This is because around the year 1200, our linguistic ancestors made an analogical new-formation, borrowing the stem *day* from the singular to replace the stem *dawe-* in the plural before the ending *-s*. In the plural of *cow*, there were two successive analogical formations. Around the year 1300, people started to use the plural *kyn*, with the analogical plural ending *-n* (which was then very frequent, but survives now only in *oxen, children, brethren*). The form *kyn* survives at present as an archaism, *kine;* in its turn, it was replaced around 1600 by the plural *cows*, in which the plural ending *-s* was borrowed from the majority of nouns and added to the singular *cow*. There must have been a time when *days* seemed as much of a "mistake" as *foots* does now, and —slightly later—a period when *days* and *dawes* were in competition just as *hoofs* and *hooves* are now. If we extend our time-perspective far enough back, we can see that we use relatively few plural formations which are direct continuations of those in use four or five thousand years ago.

These considerations are of importance when it comes to judging forms like *hisn, hern,* and so forth, or *he done.* When an "ignorant" person borrows the ending *-n* from the possessive pronoun *mine* and adds it to the adjectives *his, her, our, your* and *their,* to make the distinctive possessive pronouns *hisn, hern, ourn, yourn, theirn,* this procedure on his part is not due to ignorance or stupidity. It is due to exactly the same process of analogizing, of regularizing the forms of the language, that we saw in the instances of *cows* or *days,* and that has gone on in producing a great many other forms we now use. The analogy in this instance is, of course:

$$my : mine = his : x$$

and so forth. Likewise, such a past tense as *he done* is traceable to some such analogy as this:

$$he\ has\ kicked : he\ kicked = he\ has\ done : x$$

That such forms as *hisn* or *he done* are not accepted as part of the standard language is not due to any defect in the forms themselves—they are perfectly respectable analogical forms, with as much right to existence as *cows* and *days;* the thing that makes them unacceptable is simply the connotation of social disfavor which has been attached to them.

Very often, internal borrowing (analogy) comes into play when linguistic forms become irregular and grammatical relationships are obscured as a result of changes in phonemes. This is what happened in the case of English *day—dawes;* it has happened in recent centuries in such instances as those of the old plurals *eye—eyen, shoe—shoon, brother—brethren,* which have now been replaced by the more transparent and easily understandable formations *eyes, shoes, brothers* respectively; or in such past tenses of verbs as *help—holp, work—wrought,* now regularized by analogy in the new-formations *helped, worked.* In English noun plurals and verb pasts and past participles, the trend of development is slowly but surely towards analogical leveling of irregularities; even though forms like *gooses, mouses* or *drinked, writed* are simply "errors" or "blunders" now, they may perhaps be perfectly normal by two or three hundred years from now. Today's analogical "mistakes" are often tomorrow's competing forms, and day-after-tomorrow's "correct" forms.

CHARLES C. FRIES

Usage Levels and Dialect Distribution

Even a very superficial examination of the language practices of native speakers of English will reveal many differences in those practices from person to person. A hasty glance at the materials gathered for the *Linguistic Atlas of New England* not only will confirm the impression one receives from casually listening to the speech of those who talk English but will furnish convincing evidence that the differences of usage among native speakers of English are much greater and much more intricate than is usually believed. These differences of English usage occur not only in matters of vocabulary but also in matters of grammar and especially in matters of pronunciation. It is these differences in the practice of those who speak English that give rise to the many discussions concerning our language and often send students and others to our dictionaries for the information necessary to understand these differences. Ever since the publication of Samuel Johnson's *English Dictionary* in 1755 the "dictionary" has been looked to and consulted as the "authority" concerning the acceptability of words and the proper use of word meanings. "What does *the* dictionary say?" occurs as the common question in all our disputes concerning our language—as if there were but one dictionary with ultimate authority and as if the statements recorded in any dictionary were valid for all time. Those who ask "What does the dictionary say?" practically never inquire concerning the publication date of the particular dictionary consulted or the qualifications of those who have produced it. The desire for an easily accessible "authority" on the part of the general public has created an enormous market for many cheap dictionaries, often produced by unscrupulous publishers who have achieved cheapness by reprinting old dictionary materials upon which the copyright has expired —adding, of course, a few of the well-known new words in order to give the appearance of being up-to-date.

Part of the difficulty lies in the common and traditional view of the differences of English usage. Often it is assumed that there exist in any language only two kinds of words, word meanings, and pronunciations: those that are correct and proper and those that are incorrect or mistakes. The "mistakes" are thought to be derived by ignorance and carelessness from the correct or proper uses. It is assumed also that the separation and labeling of the mistakes is a simple process and that grammarians and lexicographers have long ago made the proper decisions and the results of their work need only be preserved and made known to succeeding generations. It is assumed that all dictionaries will incorporate these "accepted" decisions and therefore there is no reason to inquire concerning the qualifications of the editors of a new dictionary or even the means employed to make the assignment of usage labels valid.

NECESSITY OF RECORDING USAGE

From the point of view of modern linguistic science these common naïve assumptions concerning the differences of usage in English must be discarded. They belong to a prescientific period in the study of language—to an age that still believes the earth to be flat and denies the circulation of the blood. The modern dictionary editor who is aware of the principles and methods of the modern scientific study of language and of the accumulations of knowledge concerning our language built up by the patient study of many scholars cannot in honesty follow the easy path of copying the usage labels as they are attached to words and word meanings in former dictionaries. He cannot, as Samuel Johnson often did, condemn words and word meanings in accord with his special prejudices. Johnson, in spite of the fact that his quotations show that the word *excepting* is used by Dryden and Collier, condemns it with the label "an improper word." In similar fashion he attaches the label "low words" to *budge, fun,* and *clever,* although his own quotations give examples of these words from Shakespeare and from Moore, from Addison, Pope, and Arbuthnot.

Constant change—in pronunciation, in grammatical structure, in word meanings, and in the words themselves—is, as far as we know, the normal condition of every language spoken by a living people. The careful study of these changes by the rigorous techniques developed by linguistic science has given us linguistic history. A hundred years of scholarly work has gone into establishing the details of the history of the English language and has forced us to turn away from the methods of "authority" as they are represented in Samuel Johnson's *Dictionary* and its successors. It has demanded the patient recording of the facts of usage as the language is and has been employed by the hosts of speakers of English in this country and in the other countries where English is the language in which the major affairs of the people are conducted. The editor of a modern dictionary is thus confronted with a wide range of constantly changing differences in English usage that cannot be easily separated into correct and proper forms on the one hand and mistakes on the other. These changes in usage render the older dictionaries inaccurate and make necessary continually new examinations of the status of the words and word meanings in English. A dictionary can be an "authority" only in the sense in which a book of chemistry or of physics or of botany can be an "authority"—by the accuracy and the completeness of its record of the observed facts of the field examined, in accord with the latest principles and techniques of the particular science. Older "authorities" in the uses of words are thus superseded by those which incorporate the latest results of the more scientific investigations in the English language.

REGIONAL DIFFERENCES

In the matter of English usage it is not always possible to define precisely the boundaries within which a word or a word meaning is used or recognized. The facilities of travel have so developed in modern times that many speakers of English hear constantly the language of those from other geographical areas. And the radio has brought into even the most secluded communities the speech of all sections of the country. This mixing of speech forms from various geographical areas is not by any means limited to the upper classes.

> "I knowed you wasn't Oklahomy folks. You talk queer kinda—That ain't no blame, you understan'."
> "Ever'body says words different," said Ivy. "Arkansas folks says 'em different, and Oklahomy folks says 'em different. And we seen a lady from Massachusetts, an' she said 'em differentest of all. Couldn' hardly make out what she was sayin'."
>
> (J. Steinbeck, *The Grapes of Wrath*, p. 168.)

In the great mass of differences of usage that appear in the practice of English speakers, however, some words and word meanings and some pronunciations are in common use in special parts of the English-speaking world and appear much less frequently or never in other areas. For these this dictionary marks the geographical areas of special use. Some of the areas thus indicated within this country are New England, the old South, and the Southwest for such words as the following: *selectman, sharpie, levee*[1] (def. 1), *granny* (def. 4), *corn pone, alamo, chaps, chuck wagon* (see the definitions of these words).

British usage differs from the usage of the United States in such words as *lift* (def. 21), *navvy, lorry* (def. 1), *petrol* (def. 1), *gorse* (see the definitions of these words, and the preface by A. W. Read on "British and American Usage," page xxviii).

And Australia has its particular words and word meanings, as *paddock* (def. 3), *swag*[2] (def. 2), *billabong, billy* (def. 3) (see the definitions of these words).

Many words and word meanings are characteristic of certain fields of human activity. Each trade and occupation and sport has its technical vocabulary. Some of this technical vocabulary consists of special words used only in science, art, trade, or sport, such as *Binet test, electrode, binnacle, chiaroscuro, silo, forward pass* (see the definitions of these words).

Much of these technical vocabularies, however, consists of special meanings and uses of words that are employed generally in the language. The *field* in baseball has a special sense, as does *sacrifice, run, hit, out, plate, pitcher*. In the preparation and marketing of alcoholic beverages, the words *proof, dry, mash,* and *smooth* are used with special meanings.

"LEVELS" OF USAGE

Most frequently, however, discussions of language center upon what are often called the "levels" of usage. Some words and word meanings are frequently called "slang." The term "slang" has suffered such a wide extension of its signification and has been applied to so many varieties of words that it is extremely difficult to draw the line between what is slang and what is not. The difference between slang and not-slang does not rest in the meanings of the words themselves. To say that a man is "recalcitrant" is using an acceptable and somewhat learned word; to call him "a kicker" in the same situation is using slang, although the meanings are similar. Some clipped words, as *gent,* are often regarded as slang; others, such as *piano, phone,* and *cello,* are not slang. Slang cannot be defined in terms of either the forms or the strict meanings of the words themselves; it can, however, be characterized in terms of the suggested feelings accompanying certain words—their connotations rather than their denotations. Flippant humor marks the expressions we call slang. Some examples are *Java* (def. 3), *ice* (def. 8), *croak* (def. 4), *hangout, corking* (see the definitions of these words).

Some expressions appear only in poetry. They suggest then those circumstances in which they usually occur. Others are now found only in the written material of books. To mark them *"Poetic"* and *"Literary"* serves to record the special areas in which they are commonly used. Some examples are *gloaming, e'er, lidless* (def. 3), *naught* (def. 2), *scarce* (def. 4) (see the definitions of these words).

Many expressions occur primarily in conversation rather than in formal writing. The occasions for their use are chiefly conversational situations. These are marked *"Colloq."* Even teachers of English frequently misunderstand the application of the label *Colloquial* in our best dictionaries. Some confuse it with *localism* and think of the words and constructions marked "colloquial" as peculiarities of speaking which are characteristic of a particular locality. Others feel that some stigma attaches to the label *"Colloquial"* and would strive to avoid as incorrect (or as of a low level) all words so marked. The word *colloquial,* however, as used to label words and phrases in a modern scientifically edited dictionary has no such meaning. It is used to mark those words and constructions whose range of use is primarily that of the polite conversation of cultivated people, of their familiar letters and informal speeches, as distinct from those words and constructions which are common also in formal writing. The usage of our better magazines and of public addresses generally has, during the past generation, moved away from the formal and literary toward the colloquial.

Some words and expressions occur primarily in the language of those without much conventional education. These expressions are often called "illiterate" or "vulgar English," and are considered "incorrect." As a matter of fact, many of these expressions are survivals from an older period of the language and are "incorrect" only in the sense that they do not occur in the usage of standard English—the practice of the socially accepted, those who are carrying on the important affairs of English-speaking people. Much of the language spoken by the uneducated is the same as that of the polite conversation of cultivated people and also duplicates the expressions of formal literary discourse. The usage labels in a dictionary attempt to mark only those expressions that are peculiar to a particular type or dialect of English. If one ignores the differences that characterize the various geographical areas and the differences of the separate fields of human activity, of trades and vocations and sports, the situation may be roughly represented by the following diagram [p. 278]:

The three circles X, Y, Z represent the three sets of language habits indicated above.

X—formal literary English, the words, the expressions, and the structures one finds in serious books.

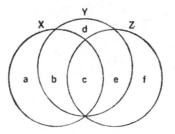

Y—colloquial English, the words, expressions, and the structures of the informal but polite conversation of cultivated people.

Z—illiterate English, the words, the expressions, and the structures of the language of the uneducated.

b, c, and e represent the overlappings of the three types of English.

c—that which is common to all three: formal literary English, colloquial English, and illiterate English.

b—that which is common to both formal literary English and colloquial English.

e—that which is common to both colloquial English and illiterate English.

a, d, and f represent those portions of each type of English that are peculiar to that particular set of language habits.

The following is a list of some of the other usage labels used in this dictionary with typical examples under each of the particular words and expressions to which each label is assigned.

Archaic: impose (def. 8), hugger-mugger (def. 2), glister (def. 1), lief (def. 2), angle[2] (def. 3).

Colloq.: angel (def. 6), brass tacks, fizzle (def. 2), flimflam, goner.

Humorous: celestial (def. 5), human (def. 4).

Obs.: loblolly boy, lust (def. 5), flittermouse, murther, drugget (def. 2).

Obsolesc.: saloon (def. 6), regimen (def. 5).

Rare: image (def. 17), impassionate, faulty (def. 2), instancy (def. 2), genial[1] (def. 3).

Scot.: chap[1] (def. 5), laird, hag[2] (def. 1), icker.

Scot. and N. Eng.: unco, kirk (def. 1), ilk (def. 2), braw, bairn.

South African: laager, kraal (def. 3).

U.S.: chain lightning, challenge (def. 14), biscuit (def. 1), boss (def. 2), quilting bee.

JOHN S. KENYON

Cultural Levels and Functional
Varieties of English

The word *level*, when used to indicate different styles of language, is a metaphor, suggesting higher or lower position and, like the terms *higher* and *lower*, figuratively implies "better" or "worse," "more desirable" or "less desirable," and similar comparative degrees of excellence or inferiority in language.

The application of the term *level* to those different styles of language that are not properly distinguished as better or worse, desirable or undesirable, creates a false impression. I confess myself guilty of this error along with some other writers. What are frequently grouped together in one class as different levels of language are often in reality false combinations of two distinct and incommensurable categories, namely, *cultural levels* and *functional varieties*.

Among *cultural levels* may be included, on the lower levels, illiterate speech, narrowly local dialect, ungrammatical speech and writing, excessive and unskilful slang, slovenly and careless vocabulary and construction, exceptional pronunciation, and, on the higher level, language used generally by the cultivated, clear, grammatical writing, and pronunciations used by the cultivated over wide areas. The different cultural levels may be summarized in the two general classes *substandard* and *standard*.

Among *functional varieties* not depending on cultural levels may be mentioned colloquial language, itself existing in different degrees of familiarity or formality, as, for example, familiar conversation, private correspondence, formal conversation, familiar public address; formal platform or pulpit speech, public reading, public worship; legal, scientific,

This paper from which these excerpts are taken was read before the College English Group of Northeastern Ohio (Modern Language Association) at its annual meeting at Oberlin College, October 25, 1947. Reprinted with the permission of the National Council of Teachers of English.

and other expository writing; prose and poetic belles-lettres. The different functional varieties may roughly be grouped together in the two classes *familiar* and *formal* writing or speaking.

The term *level*, then, does not properly belong at all to functional varieties of speech—colloquial, familiar, formal, scientific, literary language. They are equally "good" for their respective functions, and as classifications do not depend on the cultural status of the users.

The two groupings *cultural levels* and *functional varieties* are not mutually exclusive categories. They are based on entirely separate principles of classification: *culture* and *function*. Although we are here principally concerned with the functional varieties of standard English (the highest cultural level), yet substandard English likewise has its functional varieties for its different occasions and purposes. Thus the functional variety colloquial English may occur on a substandard cultural level, but the term *colloquial* does not itself designate a cultural level. So the functional variety formal writing or speaking may occur on a lower or on a higher cultural level according to the social status of writer or speaker, and sometimes of reader or audience. It follows, for instance, that the colloquial language of cultivated people is on a higher cultural level than the formal speech of the semiliterate or than some inept literary writing.

.   .   .

The best dictionaries, at least in their definitions, give no warrant for the various misuses of *colloquial, colloquially, colloquialism, colloquiality*. I urge the reader to study carefully the definitions in the *Oxford English Dictionary*, with its many apt examples from standard writers, and in *Webster's New International Dictionary, Second Edition*, with its quotations from George Lyman Kittredge. Kittredge's views on the standing of colloquial English are well known. It is said that somebody once asked him about the meaning of the label "Colloq." in dictionaries. He is reported to have replied, "I myself speak 'colloke' and often write it." I cannot verify the story, but it sounds authentic.

It seems to me inevitable that the frequent groupings of so-called "levels" such as "Literary, Colloquial, Illiterate," and the like, will lead the reader to suppose that just as Illiterate is culturally below Colloquial, so Colloquial is culturally below Literary. While I can scarcely hope that my humble remonstrance will reform all future writing on "levels of English," I believe that writers who confuse the meaning of the term *level* must accept some part of the responsibility for the popular misunderstanding of the true status of colloquial English; for I cannot avoid the belief that the popular idea of colloquial English as something to be looked down upon with disfavor is due in part to the failure of writers on the subject to distinguish between *cultural levels of English* and *functional varieties of standard English.*

ALLAN F. HUBBELL

Multiple Negation

"I couldn't find nobody there." This sentence, as anyone who will read this probably knows, contains a double negative, a construction with a fascinating history. Today in all parts of the English-speaking world, its use or avoidance is one of the clearest marks of differentiation between different social groups. Among those who have had comparatively little formal schooling and whose social and occupational status is relatively low, the construction is extremely common. Among the well-educated and more "privileged," it is rare almost to the point of non-existence. In many circles, in fact, a double negative uttered by a presumably educated person would cause the same embarrassed silence as a loud belch in church.

The avoidance of this usage by the more cultivated members of the English speech-community is roughly about three hundred years old. In earlier English, the doubling, tripling, or even quadrupling of negatives was frequent even in the most formal literary styles. King Alfred, for example, in a translation made late in the ninth century, writes a sentence which in modern form would read: "No man had never yet heard of no ship-army." A little later, in the oldest English version of the Gospels, we read: "The five foolish maidens took lamps, but didn't take no oil with them." In the fourteenth century, Chaucer writes of his "gentle knight" that "in all his life he hasn't never yet said nothing discourteous to no sort of person" (four negatives!). As late as Shakespeare's time, the construction was still possible in Standard English, particularly in speech. Thus, in *Romeo and Juliet*, when Mercutio is confronted by Tybalt, he cries out, "I will not budge for no man's pleasure."

In the course of the seventeenth century, however, the multiple negative began to go out of educated use. Undoubtedly the chief cause of its

From *Inside the ACD*, October 1957. © 1957 by Random House, Inc., New York. Reprinted by permission of the publisher.

gradual disappearance was the influence of classical literary Latin, then considered the most nearly perfect language. The fact that Cicero and Caesar did not multiply negatives even in the most emphatic statements of negation weighed heavily with those who aspired to write well. In the latter half of the century, furthermore, there developed a growing distaste for the extravagance and exuberance of Elizabethan English. The piling up of negatives was presumably felt to be one of the extravagances to be shunned.

After 1700 it is rather difficult to find examples of the multiple negative in educated written English. We of course know less about the spoken usage of the eighteenth century and it may be that for a time many avoided doubling negatives in writing but not in speech. But speech too in time conformed and since then Standard English has been quite uniform in this avoidance.

Our school grammars commonly tell us that the double negative is improper because "two negatives make an affirmative," that is, because "I couldn't find nobody there" really means "I could find somebody there." This curious notion appears to have been first set afloat by an eighteenth-century grammarian, Lowth, and it quickly came to be repeated on every side. It rests primarily on an analogy with algebra, where two negative signs cancel one another in certain operations. But ordinary language is not the language of algebra and utterances containing a double negative are regularly interpreted in the sense intended by the speaker and never in an opposite sense. Furthermore, if the reasoning were sound, a triple negative like King Alfred's or like "I won't give you no bubble gum for nothing" would be quite acceptable in modern Standard English. Of course it is not.

Nonstandard English, in this respect as in some others, is intensely conservative and tenacious of past practice. For two hundreds years now, school children have had it dinned (and sometimes beaten) into them that they must not double or triple their negatives. For some of them the instruction is quite superfluous, for they have already learned Standard English at their mothers' knees. The usage of some others comes to be altered. There are those who determine quite early in life that they are going to move up the social ladder and who sense that their inherited speechways will be a bar to advancement. But the usage of a very considerable number is almost unaffected by the school instruction they receive. They leave high school continuing to use a nonstandard variety of the language and, among other things, still multiplying negatives in a fourteenth-century profusion.

Observing this "perverse" adherence to inherited patterns, teachers sometimes think despairingly that there must be some really fundamental fault in their methods. There must be, they feel, some pedagogical device not yet hit upon which could produce much greater results. But to think in this fashion is to misconceive the situation. An individual's linguistic usage is among other things the outward sign of his most deepseated group loyalties. If the usage of the group or groups with which he identifies himself is not that of Standard English, the schools are not likely to have much effect on his practice. For the blunt fact is that only if his loyalties shift will his grammar change. In a democratic society, the schools have an obligation to make a knowledge of the standard language available to everyone. And teachers have an obligation to make this instruction as interesting and meaningful as possible. They should not be surprised, however, if the nonstandard forms of English continue to flourish. They are hardy growths and will be with us for a long time to come.

JEAN MALMSTROM

Ain't Again

The blanket statements in many textbooks that *ain't* is an "illiteracy," "barbarism," or "vulgarism" oversimplify the complex facts of its usage as revealed by the Linguistic Atlas evidence collected in New England, the Middle and South Atlantic States, the North Central States, and the Upper Midwest.[1] *Ain't* has been investigated in its three different contexts: (1) as an alternate present negative form of *be* in sentences like "I am not going to hurt him"; (2) as an alternate present negative form of *have* in sentences like "I haven't done it"; and (3) as an alternate first person singular present negative form of *be* in sentences like "I'm right, am I not?"

In the first context, except in and around New York City, where all the informants use *I'm not*, *ain't* is used in all areas by a few cultivated speakers and many high school graduates. In Atlas terminology, therefore, *ain't* in the first context is "popular" usage; that is, it is characteristic of the speech of persons representing the middle level of education in their respective communities. Further, *ain't* in this context is not "expanding"; that is, its use is not increasing through adoption by cultivated speakers.

In the second context, "I haven't done it," approximately the same kind of distribution is found, except that Eastern speakers who use *ain't* in this context generally use *haven't* also. An old-fashioned form, *hain't*, likewise occurs in this context. Apparently speakers who say both *ain't* and *hain't* usually employ *ain't* to mean *am not* and *hain't* to mean *have not*. In this context, as in the first context, *ain't* is popular usage, not expanding.

In the third context, the Atlas shows that a large majority of the high school graduates in all areas say *ain't I*. Of the cultivated informants, about 20% in New England, about 35% in the Middle and South Atlantic

English Journal, XLIX (1960), and *College English*, XXI (1960). Reprinted with the permission of the National Council of Teachers of English and Jean Malmstrom.

States, and about 73% in the North Central States use *ain't I*, although no college graduate in the Upper Midwest does so. The cultivated speakers who employ *ain't I*, however, almost always use another form also. Generally this form is *am I not*, except in the North Central States where no college graduate uses it. *Aren't I* occurs with some frequency in New England and the Upper Midwest, but rarely elsewhere. *Amn't I* is not used by any Atlas informant. In Atlas terminology, *ain't* in the third context is standard in the North Central States, and strongly popular and expanding elsewhere except in the Upper Midwest.

We must always remember that the Atlas investigates only speech and offers no data on written English. However, since Fries reports no instance of *ain't* in the more than three thousand letters he studied for his *American English Grammar,* we may safely conclude that *ain't* occurs predominantly in speech, not in writing. Therefore its usage may be accurately judged in the light of the Atlas records. We may well remember also that American usage is most adequately described in terms of five dimensions. Socio-educational, situational, methodological, temporal, and regional dimensions all are vital to a comprehensive view.[2] Awareness of these five dimensions is especially enlightening in considering a usage like *ain't I*, which shows regional as well as social and educational differences. Its absence from cultivated speech in the Upper Midwest, where a large proportion of the population is foreign-born and has learned English principally from textbooks, may be an interesting example of the conservative influence of the schools upon the normal patterns of change implicit in the development of any living language.

An exhaustive analysis of elementary, secondary, and college freshman textbooks reveals that only about one text in five discusses *ain't I* apart from the other uses of *ain't*. As a rule, textbooks forbid *ain't* in all its contexts, either stating or implying that it is a social shibboleth. The few texts which discuss *ain't I* separately recognize unanimously that English lacks and needs a first person singular present negative interrogative contraction parallel to *isn't he* (*she, it*) and *aren't we* (*you, they*). These texts usually discuss *am I not, amn't I, aren't I*, and *ain't I* as possible choices available to the speaker who has wandered unwarily into a syntactic trap like "I'm right . . ." and who wishes to end on an interrogative note. The textbooks' comments on these choices vary widely, perhaps because of regional differences in their authors' backgrounds. For instance, *am I not* is said to be "correct," "stilted," or "schoolmarmish." *Amn't I* is said to be "hard to pronounce," "nonexistent," or "Irish." *Aren't I* is called "ungrammatical," "affected," "literary," "British usage gaining favor in the United States," or "British usage condemned by leading American authorities." *Ain't I* is said to be "wrong and usually avoided although accepted by some authorities," "historically and logically justifiable but not standard," "an uncultivated colloquial contraction," "universally condemned but needed in the language," or "the least objectionable use of *ain't*."

Truly, English needs a form like the French *n'est-ce pas* or German *nicht wahr*. Historically, the language has always filled such needs. Today the schools are responsible for the teaching of the nationally standard form of written English and therefore inevitably retard the slow but incessant process of language change. However, as we teachers fulfill our professional duty to the standard written dialect, we may listen with interest to the linguistic grass grow.

NOTES

1. The Atlas facts are presented in full by E. Bagby Atwood in *A Survey of Verb Forms in the Eastern United States* (Ann Arbor: Univ. of Michigan Press, 1953) and by Virginia G. McDavid in her Minnesota dissertation, *Verb Forms in the North Central States and the Upper Midwest* (1956).

2. For a full discussion of these five dimensions of current American English, see Jean Malmstrom, "Linguistic Atlas Findings versus Textbook Pronouncements on Current American Usage," *The English Journal*, 48 (April 1959), pp. 191–198.

JEAN MALMSTROM

Kind of and Its Congeners

Language textbooks for high school students and college freshmen frequently command their readers to use *rather* or *somewhat* instead of *kind of* or *sort of* in a sentence like "It's rather cold." [1] When any evidence accompanies this injunction—and often none does—the authors assert, for instance, that *kind of* and *sort of* are not adverbs and therefore cannot be used adverbially, or that *kind of* and *sort of* are colloquial and therefore are "wrong," "loose," "rustic," or too informal for formal discourse. Generally, no precise definitions of "colloquial," "informal," or "formal" accompany such explanations. Some textbooks particularly condemn *kinda* or *kinder* and *sorta* or *sorter*.

Although the textbooks' consistent pairing of terms may lead students and teachers to believe otherwise, the Linguistic Atlas records show that the partnership of *rather* with *somewhat* and of *kind of* with *sort of* is less than that of Damon with Pythias. The Atlas also offers interesting information on the relative popularity of all four terms in current American speech. The regional surveys conducted for the Linguistic Atlas in New England, the Middle and South Atlantic States, the North Central States, and the Upper Midwest give authoritative information on the speech habits of a representative part of the total population of the continental United States.

These Atlas investigations show that although *rather* occurs everywhere in these areas, especially in the speech of college graduates, nobody says *somewhat*. This fact does not mean that educated Americans do not write *somewhat*. Indeed, Fries in his *American English Grammar* reports its fairly frequent appearance in the letters of his educated writers. The absence of *somewhat* from the Atlas records of American speech serves forcibly to remind us again that written usage is different from spoken

English Journal, XLIX (1960), and *College English*, XXI (1960). Reprinted by permission of the National Council of Teachers of English and Jean Malmstrom.

usage, a fact often slighted by textbook writers and some early students of American usage.

In fact, we may perhaps suspect that the togetherness of *rather* and *somewhat* in textbooks springs from a comment in *Facts about Current English Usage*, the 1938 elaboration by Marckwardt and Walcott of Leonard's 1932 *Current English Usage*. In the discussion of *kind of*, classified under "Doubtful Adverbs," the concluding summary is:

> The judges were nearly equally divided as to the classification of this expression. While it cannot be dismissed as illiterate, it probably is not altogether a safe expression for cultivated *speech*. (Italics added.) Many will prefer *somewhat*.[2]

Facts about Current English Usage, published under the aegis of NCTE, is the most ubiquitous and often the only "usage authority" cited by textbook writers. Its comments, however, are often selectively excerpted. In this instance, the *somewhat* comment, with its casual lack of distinction between writing and speech, has become an almost automatic part of textbook vocabulary. Contrariwise, the classification of *kind of* as an adverb, even though "doubtful" (in acceptability rather than syntactic function) has largely escaped attention.

In addition to the absence of *somewhat*, the Atlas shows that the majority of educated speakers, except in certain isolated relic parts of northeastern New England, prefer *kind of* and *sort of* to *rather*, and that these speakers use *kind of* about twice as often as *sort of*. *Sort of* is heard most frequently in Southern dialect areas, less often in Midland dialect areas, and least often in Northern dialect areas, both on the Atlantic Seaboard and in the Midwest. In spite of the popularity of *kind of* and *sort of* in cultivated speech, Fries records no instances of either in educated writing. We may conclude therefore that these expressions are standard in speech but not in writing. They are indeed colloquial, if we understand that word to mean "characteristic of speech," without the pejorative connotations often attached to it in textbooks.

Another interesting fact revealed by the Atlas is that, normally, *kind of* and *sort of* in sentences like "It's kind of cold" are pronounced without the final fricative /v/. This phonetic fact, reinforced by the textbooks' consistent use of a one-word spelling of *kinda, kinder, sorta,* and *sorter,* may suggest that Americans "feel" these expressions as single words expressing degree. The process of inflectional leveling has been continuous in English for a thousand years; the power of our fixed word-order to establish direction of modification has strengthened as inflections have leveled. In other words, it is not impossible to assume that *kind of* now functions strongly in standard American speech as an "intensifier" or "down-toner"[3] similar to *rather* in standard writing. The conservative influence of the schools, however, may long keep *kind of* waiting at the door of full acceptance in standard writing, especially since the standard *rather* is handily available. Nevertheless, although the power of public education in eradicating nonstandard usages is well attested in the Atlas records, the history of English shows that standard speech forms tend eventually to move into standard writing. Language changes constantly, though slowly, and the great seedbed of change is speech.

NOTES

1. Interestingly, elementary textbooks do not customarily discuss *kind of* and *sort of* in this context.

2. Albert H. Marckwardt and Fred G. Walcott, *Facts about Current English Usage* (New York, 1938), p. 103.

3. A usefully descriptive term borrowed by Fries from C. Stoffel, "Intensives and Down-toners," *Anglistische Forschungen*, Heft 1 (Heidelberg, 1901). See Charles C. Fries, *American English Grammar* (New York, 1940), p. 200.

ROBERT C. POOLEY

Dare Schools Set a Standard in English Usage?

The topic assigned to me is "Dare the School Set a Standard in English Usage?" I shall answer this question Yankee-fashion with another question: Do we dare *not* to set a standard? To this there seems to me to be but one answer: We should not and cannot fail to set a standard. To do so is to abandon the very core of our obligation to the youth we are employed to teach. We are committed by duty and by conscience to bring every student as close as possible to the attainment of a decent standard of English usage by every means at our command. But what is this decent standard and by what terms do we describe it?

One of the commonest misunderstandings of the point of view of the linguistic scholar with regard to English grammar and English usage is that when he observes and reports changes which take place in the English language, he thereby weakens the position of the English teacher and lowers standards. It is extremely important to us all to correct this misapprehension and to recognize why the objective study of our language properly interpreted results in a strengthening of standards rather than in laxity. To do so we shall need to examine more closely what is meant by a standard. It may well be that a misconception of the nature of a language standard is at the root of the misunderstanding.

RANGE OF LATITUDE IN STANDARDS

In all matters concerned with human behavior to which standards may be applied, it will be found that such standards, far from being fixed and unchangeable, are actually only approximations within a fairly wide range of latitude and tolerance. A standard, in human conduct, is a sort of

From *English Journal*, XLIX (1960). Reprinted by the permission of the National Council of Teachers of English and Robert C. Pooley.

gentleman's agreement as to the norm reasonably expected, but behavior superior to this norm and behavior inferior to it are tolerated to a fairly wide degree. When the behavior exceeds the limit of tolerance to the point of becoming noticeable, amusing, embarrassing, or annoying, the standard is violated. But when deviate behavior remains within the range of normally accepted tolerance, the standard may be said to be maintained.

To cite some instances: a gentleman when seated is expected to rise when a lady enters the room. This is the standard. What are the degrees of tolerance? Behavior may and often does range from a ceremonial rising with a bow and offering of a chair to a half-hearted semi-squat movement as a sort of grudging recognition of the standard. The latter behavior is on the edge of tolerance; if it becomes habitual and noticeable the offender may be considered a boor. On the other hand, excessive politeness and ceremonial attached to this simple standard becomes amusing or annoying, and thus violates the standard of behavior. But within the range between these extremes, the standard is considered to be met. Yet within this tolerable range there are troublesome variations. Does a male guest rise when an eight-year-old daughter of the house is introduced? Does a husband rise every time his wife enters the room? At what point in a daughter's age does a father rise for her entrance? Is he a boor if he does not rise when she is fourteen, sixteen, or eighteen? I do not need to elaborate further to illustrate that a standard of behavior such as this has considerable latitude.

Another example may be observed in the so-called "bread and butter" note—the note of thanks sent to one's hostess when one has been a dinner guest or a house guest. Punctilious meeting of this standard requires a note to be written within three days. A formal note sent the day after the engagement may have a tone of rigidity and coldness, as though one were getting a disagreeable task out of the way; failure to respond within a month is a laxity beyond tolerance within the standard. With considerable variation between these extremes is the friendly note of thanks and acknowledgment of courtesies, differing in degree of formality in proportion to the degree of acquaintanceship of the correspondents. It is almost impossible to write exact rules to cover the variety of situations within which this standard must function. Nevertheless, it is a standard whose performance one neglects only at his social peril. Parental instruction, experience, and general good taste determine the readiness to meet this standard; but the standard must be met if one is to remain within the ranks of the socially acceptable.

I have spoken of the two examples above as if they were unchangeable with time. But we are still aware that behavior patterns change with time and that the norms of expected behavior, in other words the standards, shift from one period to another. When I was a young man a formal dinner required a black dinner coat with formal trousers, a black vest, a black tie, and a starched white shirt with jewelled studs and cuff links. I recently attended the Captain's dinner (which was announced as formal) on board a cruise ship of the Norwegian-American line. The passengers were from the ranks of those Americans who may be called the privileged class. Less than a third of the gentlemen were arrayed in the dinner costume of my youth. The black vest has almost disappeared. In its place a cummerbund is worn. Nor need this be black. A number of guests wore dark maroon, deep blue, or plaid cummerbunds, with ties to match. The starched shirt has almost disappeared; soft shirts with studs and links are rare; soft shirts with ordinary buttons are common. Moreover, there were dinner jackets not black, but deep blue, dark maroon, and a few in resplendent plaid. Does this variety and differentiation mean that gentlemen no longer dress for dinner; that anything goes? Not at all; the standard is perfectly clear, but a range of deviation within the standard is now acceptable which a few years back was not.

In contrast, I would remind you that before the turn of the century every hotel, restaurant, and public parlor in which gentlemen gathered was adorned with cuspidors, and most private homes possessed them, even if discreetly concealed. A pattern of behavior once tolerated or taken for granted is today outside the pale; a hostess would be shocked to be asked to produce a cuspidor.

In the realm of social behavior most of us accept the two principles governing standards which I have illustrated; namely, range of tolerance within the standard at any one period of time, and change in the description of the standard from one period to the next. Any wise parent knows that to insist upon the details of a standard as observed a generation before is to breed rebellion at home and ridicule abroad; the essence is to teach the standard as it is observed today by persons of taste, refinement, and social experience. And as part of the teaching the latitude which exists in the performance of any standard should be included. Our aim for our children and ourselves is neither heel-clicking regimentation, nor loutish laxity. Between these undesirable extremes lies a range, not a point, of tolerated behavior within the standard.

Now we return to language, a form of human behavior, to observe that standards of language, unlike those of other behavior, are considered by many to be rigid and fixed with no range of tolerance, and no change of pattern from one period to another. But because language is a form of human behavior, such fixity of standard is an untrue fiction. It cannot be, it never has been, it never will be. At no time in the history of English can the most intolerant investigator find a time or a place where all the polite, educated elite employed exactly the same usages. On the contrary, the investigator finds volume after volume of writing criticizing the "errors" of the great authors and men of distinction of the previous generation. Apparently, to the neutral historical scholar, the only ones who ever spoke purely correct English were the authors of the books condemning their predecessors and contemporaries for gross errors, and of course, no two of them agreed with each other!

Let us face the facts in all seriousness. What we call "good English" is a gentleman's agreement covering a range of acceptable behavior, exactly parallel with the observance of standards in other types of human behavior. This range can be described, it can furnish a pattern of behavior, it can set a standard of the sort that an intelligent scholar of English can accept and use.

STANDARDS FOR CLASSES

It remains to define and describe the standard of English usage we may properly set for our classes, and are indeed obliged by our duty to maintain so far as we are able. I would like to define this standard first in general, universal terms to lay the foundation for particulars. To this end I quote a definition I wrote nearly thirty years ago, which has been adopted by the Council in its curriculum volumes: "Good English is that form of speech which is appropriate to the purpose of the speaker, true to the language as it is, and comfortable to speaker and listener. It is the product of custom, neither cramped by rule nor freed from all restraint; it is never fixed, but changes with the organic life of the language." [1] You will note that this definition allows for a range of latitude within tolerable limits, and provides for the changes which are inevitable in a spoken language. But a definition so broad leaves the classroom teacher with a great many specific decisions to make, and it is to clarify these decisions that the following specific matters are presented.

In proceeding from the most elementary details to the more complex, I do not intend to imply a grade level distribution, for some usage items are easily overcome and others tend to persist into adult life. The order of presentation is roughly that in which the usage matters become significant in the student's command of his language.

The standard we can rightfully set for ourselves, our colleagues in other departments, and our students, for public and private use, contains at present these particulars:

1. The elimination of all baby-talk and "cute" expressions.
2. The correct uses in speech and writing of *I, me, he, him, she, her, they, them.* (Exception, *it's me.*)
3. The correct uses of *is, are, was, were* with respect to number and tense.
4. Correct past tenses of common irregular verbs such as *saw, gave, took, brought, bought, stuck.*
5. Correct use of past participles of the same verbs and similar verbs after auxiliaries.
6. Elimination of the double negative: we don't have no apples, etc.
7. Elimination of analogical forms: *ain't, hisn, hern; ourn, theirselves,* etc.
8. Correct use of possessive pronouns: *my, mine, his, hers, theirs, ours.*
9. Mastery of the distinction between *its,* possessive pronoun, and *it's, it is.*
10. Placement of *have* or its phonetic reduction to *v* between *I* and a past participle.
11. Elimination of *them* as a demonstrative pronoun.
12. Elimination of *this here* and *that there.*
13. Mastery of use of *a* and *an* as articles.
14. Correct use of personal pronouns in compound constructions: as subject (Mary and I), as object (Mary and me), as object of preposition (to Mary and me).
15. The use of *we* before an appositional noun when subject; *us* when object.
16. Correct number agreement with the phrases *there is, there are, there was, there were.*
17. Elimination of *he don't, she don't, it don't.*
18. Elimination of *learn* for *teach, leave* for *let.*
19. Elimination of pleonastic subjects: *my brother he; my mother she; that fellow he.*
20. Proper agreement in number with antecedent pronouns *one* and *anyone, everyone, each, no one.* With *everybody* and *none* some tolerance of number seems acceptable now.
21. The use of *who* and *whom* as reference to persons. (But note, *Who did he give it to?* is tolerated in all but very formal situations. In the latter, *To whom did he give it* is preferable.)
22. Accurate use of *said* in reporting the words of a speaker in the past.
23. Correction of *lay down* to *lie down.*

24. The distinction between *good* as adjective and *well* as adverb, e.g., He spoke *well*.

25. Elimination of *can't hardly, all the farther* (for *as far as*) and Where is he (she, it) *at?*

This list of twenty-five kinds of corrections to make constitutes a very specific standard of current English usage for today and the next few years. Some elements in it may require modification within ten years; some possibly earlier. Conspicuous by their absence are these items which were on the usage lists by which many of us were taught and which survive today in the less enlightened textbooks:

1. Any distinction between *shall* and *will*.
2. Any reference to the split infinitive.
3. Elimination of *like* as a conjunction.
4. Objection to the phrase "different than."
5. Objection to He is one of those boys who *is*.
6. Objection to the reason . . . is because. . . .
7. Objection to *myself* as a polite substitute for *me* as in "I understand you will meet Mrs. Jones and myself at the station."
8. Insistence upon the possessive case standing before a gerund.

These items and many others like them will still remain cautionary matters left to the teacher's discretion. In evaluating the writing of a superior student I would certainly call these distinctions to his attention and point out to him the value of observing them. But this is a very different matter from setting a basic usage standard to be maintained. I think it is fair to say that the items I have listed in the basic table lie outside the tolerable limits of acceptable, current, informal usage; those I have omitted from the base table are tolerated at least, and in some instances are in very general use.

I would like to conclude with a very useful distinction in usage made by one of the distinguished members of our profession, Louis Zahner of Groton School. In the *Atlantic Monthly* for November 1959, he points out the difference between "inventive language," that is, language created to produce a desirable effect, as for example, *to pussyfoot*, or, a *lounge lizard;* and "preventive language," words which defeat meaning by abandoning it: "Isn't it a terrific day:" "He was terrific:" etc. The teacher who loves English will do well to recognize and on occasion praise an unorthodox expression which is creatively effective; but he will condemn with all his force the substitution of meaningless cant for meaningful

Let Geoffrey Chaucer have the last word on standards in English:

> Ye knowe ek, that in forme of speche is chaunge
> Withinne a thousand yeer, and wordes tho
> That hadden pris, now wonder nice and straunge
> Us thinketh hem; and yit they spake hem so,
> And spedde as wel in love as men now do.

NOTE

1. Robert C. Pooley, *Grammar and Usage in Textbooks on English, Bureau of Educational Research Bulletin,* No. 14, University of Wisconsin, August 1933, p. 155.

H. W. FOWLER

Unattached Participles

UNATTACHED PARTICIPLES & adjectives (or wrongly attached). A firm sent in its bill with the following letter:—*Dear Sir,—We beg to enclose herewith statement of your account for goods supplied, & being desirous of clearing our Books to end May will you kindly favour us with cheque in settlement per return, & much oblige.* The reply ran:—*Sirs,—You have been misinformed. I have no wish to clear your books.* It may be hoped that the desire on which they based their demand was ultimately (though not per return) satisfied, but they had certainly imputed it to the wrong person by attaching *being desirous* not to the noun it belonged to (*we*), but to another (*you*). The duty of so arranging one's sentences that they will stand grammatical analysis is much more generally recognized than it formerly was, & it is now not a sufficient defence for looseness of this kind to produce parallels, as can very easily be done, even from great writers of past generations; on this see ILLOGICALITIES. On the other hand it is to be remembered that there is a continual change going on by which certain participles or adjectives acquire the character of prepositions or adverbs, no longer needing the prop of a noun to cling to; we can say *Considering the circumstances you were justified*, or *Roughly speaking they are identical*, & need not correct into *I acquit you* & *I should call them identical* in order to regularize the participles. The difficulty is to know when this development is complete; may I write *Referring to your letter, you do not state* . . . , or must it be *I find you do not state* . . . ? i.e., is *referring* still undeveloped? In all such cases, it is best to put off recognition. A good example of what may prove to have been such a development caught in the act is the phrase *due to*. Every illiterate in the

From H. W. Fowler: *A Dictionary of Modern English Usage*, pp. 674–6. Reprinted by permission of the Clarendon Press, Oxford.

land is now treating *due to* as though *due* had passed into an adverb not needing a noun to agree with, just as *owing,* in *owing to,* has actually done. The prepositional use of *owing to* is more than a century old; but of a similar use of *due to* there is not a vestige in the OED (dated 1897 for D). It is now as common as can be, though only, if the view take in DUE is correct, among the illiterate; that term is here to be taken as including all who are unfamiliar with good writers, & who consequently are unaware of any idiomatic difference between *Owing to his age he was unable to compete,* & *Due to his age he was* &c. Perhaps the illiterates will beat idiom; perhaps idiom will beat the illiterates; our grandsons will know.

The conscious or unconscious assumption that a participle or adjective has acquired the powers of preposition or adverb when it has in fact not done so perhaps accounts for most of the unattached & wrongly attached; but there are many for which no such excuse is possible. Before proceeding to them, let us make a few sentences containing undoubtedly converted participles, sentences in which the seeming participle is not felt to need a noun:—*Talking of test matches, who won the last?; Coming to details, the spoilt ballot-papers were 17; They are illiterate (using the word in its widest sense); Granting his honesty, he may be mistaken; Failing you, there is no chance left; Twelve were saved, not counting the dog; Allowing for exceptions, the rule may stand.* It is natural, & perhaps right, to explain this common type as originally not a participle at all, but a shortening of the gerund preceded by the old preposition *a; talking of = a-talking of,* i.e. in talking or while there is talk of. However that may be, it is only fanatical purists who will condemn such sentences; & a clear acknowledgement of their legitimacy should strengthen rather than weaken the necessary protest against the slovenly uses now to be illustrated. After each extract will be given in brackets first the noun, whether present or not, to which the participle or adjective ought to be attached, & secondly the noun, if any, to which careless grammar has in fact attached it:—*Unlike the other great European capitals which lay themselves out to cater for the tourist, Russian is the only language spoken* (the capital in question; Russian). /*A belief that a Committee of Inquiry is merely an evasion, & that, if* accepted, *the men will be caught out* (Committee; men)./*Experiments have shown that, while* affording *protection against shrapnel, the direct bullet at moderate range would carry fragments of the plate into the body* (plate; bullet)./*Based on your figures of membership, you suggest that the Middle Classes Union has failed* (suggestion; you)./*I would also suggest that, while* admitting *the modernity, the proofs offered by him as to the recent date of the loss of aspiration are not very convincing* (I; proofs)./*A girl fell on a pen, which pierced her eye, &, causing meningitis, she died* (which; she)./ Having muzzled *the House of Lords it is difficult to see at the moment any real obstacle to the successful passage of the Bill* (the Government; ————)./*Whilst* placing *little hope in the present dynasty, it is always possible in the East for some official to rise to power who may change the destinies of his people* (we; official).

H. W. FOWLER

Out of the Frying-Pan

OUT OF THE FRYING-PAN. A very large proportion of the mistakes that are made in writing result neither from simple ignorance nor from carelessness, but from the attempt to avoid what are rightly or wrongly taken to be faults of grammar or style. The writer who produces an ungrammatical, an ugly, or even a noticeably awkward phrase, & lets us see that he has done it in trying to get rid of something else that he was afraid of, gives a worse impression of himself than if he had risked our catching him in his original misdemeanour; he is out of the frying-pan into the fire. A few typical examples will be here collected, with references to other articles in which the tendency to mistaken correction is set forth more at large.

Recognition is given to it by no matter whom it is displayed. The frying-pan was "no matter whom it is displayed by," which the writer did not dare keep, with its preposition at end; but in his hurry he jumped into nonsense; see MATTER, & PREPOSITION AT END./*When the record of this campaign comes dispassionately to be written, & in just perspective, it will be found that* . . . The writer took "to be dispassionately written" for a SPLIT INFINITIVE, & by his correction convinces us that he does not know a split infinitive when he sees it./*In the hymn & its setting there is something which, to use a word of Coleridge, "finds" men.* "A word of Coleridge's" is an idiom whose genesis may be doubtful, but it has the advantage over the correction of being English; *a word of Coleridge* is no more English than *a friend of me.*/*The object is to bring before the public many ancient & modern aspects of the Theatre's Art which have too long been disregarded.* "The theatre's art" is a phrase that, apart from surroundings, no-one would prefer in prose to "the art of the theatre." What the writer has shied at is the repetition of *of* in *of the art of the*

From H. W. Fowler: *A Dictionary of Modern English Usage*, pp. 416, 417. Reprinted by permission of the Clarendon Press, Oxford.

theatre, which is however much more tolerable than this 's INCONGRUOUS. */But the badly cut-up enemy troops were continually reinforced & substituted by fresh units.* The frying-pan was REPLACE in the sense "take the place of"; the fire is the revelation that the writer has no idea what the verb SUBSTITUTE means./*Sir Starr Jameson has had one of the most varied & picturesque careers of any Colonial statesmen.* "Of *any* statesman," idiomatic but apparently illogical, has been corrected to what is neither logical (*of all* would have been nearer to sense) nor English./*The claim yesterday was for the difference between the old rate, which was a rate by agreement, & between the new.* The writer feared, with some contempt for his readers' intelligence, that they would not be equal to carrying on the construction of *between;* he has not mended matters by turning sense into nonsense; see OVERZEAL./*The reception was held at the bride's aunt.* The reporter was right in disliking *bride's aunt's,* but should have found time to think of "at the house of."

The impression must not be left, however, that it is fatal to read over & correct what one has written. The moral is that correction requires as much care as the original writing, or more; the slapdash corrector, who should not be in such a hurry, & the uneducated corrector, who should not be writing at all, are apt to make things worse than they found them.

THORSTEIN VEBLEN

The Higher Learning

. . . lately, since college athletics have won their way into a recognized standing as an accredited field of scholarly accomplishment, this latter branch of learning—if athletics may be freely classed as learning—has become a rival of the classics for the primacy in leisure-class education in American and English schools. Athletics have an obvious advantage over the classics for the purpose of leisure-class learning, since success as an athlete presumes, not only a waste of time, but also a waste of money, as well as the possession of certain highly unindustrial archaic traits of character and temperament. In the German universities the place of athletics and Greek-letter fraternities, as a leisure-class scholarly occupation, has in some measure been supplied by a skilled and graded inebriety and a perfunctory duelling.

The leisure class and its standards of virtue—archaism and waste—can scarcely have been concerned in the introduction of the classics into the scheme of the higher learning; but the tenacious retention of the classics by the higher schools, and the high degree of reputability which still attaches to them, are no doubt due to their conforming so closely to the requirements of archaism and waste.

"Classic" always carries this connotation of wasteful and archaic, whether it is used to denote the dead languages or the obsolete or obsolescent forms of thought and diction in the living language, or to denote other items of scholarly activity or apparatus to which it is applied with less aptness. So the archaic idiom of the English language is spoken of as "classic" English. Its use is imperative in all speaking and writing upon serious topics, and a facile use of it lends dignity to even the most

From *The Theory of the Leisure Class*. Reprinted by permission of The Viking Press, Inc., N.Y., and George Allen & Unwin, Ltd.

commonplace and trivial string of talk. The newest form of English diction is of course never written; the sense of that leisure-class propriety which requires archaism in speech is present even in .the most illiterate or sensational writers in sufficient force to prevent such a lapse. On the other hand, the highest and most conventionalised style of archaic diction is—quite characteristically—properly employed only in communications between an anthropomorphic divinity and his subjects. Midway between these extremes lies the everyday speech of leisure-class conversation and literature.

Elegant diction, whether in writing or speaking, is an effective means of reputability. It is of moment to know with some precision what is the degree of archaism conventionally required in speaking on any given topic. Usage differs appreciably from the pulpit to the market-place; the latter, as might be expected, admits the use of relatively new and effective words and turns of expression, even by fastidious persons. A discriminate avoidance of neologisms is honorific, not only because it argues that time has been wasted in acquiring the obsolescent habit of speech, but also as showing that the speaker has from infancy habitually associated with persons who have been familiar with the obsolescent idiom. It thereby goes to show his leisure-class antecedents. Great purity of speech is presumptive evidence of several successive lives spent in other than vulgarly useful occupations; although its evidence is by no means entirely conclusive to this point.

As felicitous an instance of futile classicism as can well be found, outside of the Far East, is the conventional spelling of the English language. A breach of the proprieties in spelling is extremely annoying and will discredit any writer in the eyes of all persons who are possessed of a developed sense of the true and beautiful. English orthography satisfies all the requirements of the canons of reputability under the law of conspicuous waste. It is archaic, cumbrous, and ineffective; its acquisition consumes much time and effort; failure to acquire it is easy of detection. Therefore it is the first and readiest test of reputability in learning, and conformity to its ritual is indispensable to a blameless scholastic life.

On this head of purity of speech, as at other points where a conventional usage rests on the canons of archaism and waste, the spokesmen for the usage instinctively take an apologetic attitude. It is contended, in substance, that a punctilious use of ancient and accredited locutions will serve to convey thought more adequately and more precisely than would the straightforward use of the latest form of spoken English; whereas it is notorious that the ideas of today are effectively expressed in the slang of today. Classic speech has the honorific virtue of dignity;

it commands attention and respect as being the accredited method of communication under the leisure-class scheme of life, because it carries a pointed suggestion of the industrial exemption of the speaker. The advantage of the accredited locutions lies in their reputability; they are reputable because they are cumbrous and out of date, and therefore argue waste of time and exemption from the use and the need of direct and forcible speech.

DONALD J. LLOYD

Our National Mania for Correctness

Every now and then the editors of the university presses let out a disgruntled bleat about the miserable writing done by scholars, even those
who are expert in literary fields; and from time to time there are letters
and editorials in our national reviews bewailing some current academic
malpractice with the English language. At present, even *PMLA* (the
Publications of the Modern Language Association), traditionally the
repository of some of the worst writing done by researchers, is trying to
herd its authors toward more lucid exposition. And at two recent meetings
of the august Mediaeval Academy, one at Boston and one at Dumbarton
Oaks, bitter remarks were passed about the failure of specialists in the
Middle Ages to present their findings in some form palatable to the general reader, so that he can at least understand what they are writing
about.

Even admitting that a really compelling style is the result of years of
cultivation, much scholarly writing is certainly worse than it needs to be.
But it is not alone in this. Generally speaking, the writing of literate
Americans whose primary business is not writing but something else is
pretty bad. It is muddy, backward, convoluted and self-strangled; it is
only too obviously the product of a task approached unwillingly and
accomplished without satisfaction or zeal. Except for the professionals
among us, we Americans are hell on the English language. I am not in
touch with the general run of British writing by non-professionals, but I
suspect that it is nothing to make those islanders smug, either.

Furthermore, almost any college professor, turning the spotlight with
some relief from himself and his colleagues to his students, will agree
that their writing stinks to high heaven, too. It is a rare student who can
write what he has to write with simplicity, lucidity and euphony, those
qualities singled out by Somerset Maugham; far more graduating seniors

From *The American Scholar*, summer 1952. Reprinted by permission of the publisher.

are candidates for a remedial clinic than can pass a writing test with honors. And freshman writing is forever the nightmare of the teachers of composition, as it would be of their colleagues if the latter could not escape to the simple inanities of their objective tests.

Yet it was not always so. I have on my desk a little manuscript from the fourteenth century written by an unknown author, which I am in the process of editing. When I read it to one of my classes, as I occasionally do, with no more modernization than my own Great Lakes pronunciation and the substitution of a word for one which has become obsolete, it is a simple, clear and engaging document. "Where is any man nowadays that asketh how I shall love God and my fellow-Christians?" it begins. "How I shall flee sin and serve God truly as a true Christian man should? What man is there that will learn the true law of God, which he biddeth every Christian man to keep upon pain of damnation in hell without end? . . . Unnethe [scarcely] is there any lewd man or lewd woman that can rightly well say his Pater Noster, his Ave Maria, and his Creed, and sound the words out readily as they should. But when they play Christmas games about the fire, therein will they not fail. Those must be said out without stumbling for dread of smiting. But if a lewd man should be smited now for each failing that he maketh in saying of his Pater Noster, his Ave Maria, and his Creed, I trowe he should be smited at the full." And so on, to the beautiful poetic line, "Then think it not heavy to dwell with thy mother in her wide house, thou that laist in the strait chamber of her womb." The spelling in the original is hectic, and the capitalization and punctuation sporadic, to say the least.

Yet there was a man who knew what he had to say and set out about saying it, with no nonsense and no fumbling. He aimed for his audience and, judging by the dog-ears and sweat-marks on the book, which is about the size of one of our pocket books, he hit it. Why cannot we do as well in our time? Indeed, the eighteenth century was about the last age in which almost any man, if he was literate at all, could set down his thoughts—such as they were—so that they did not have to be excavated by the reader. We have an abundance of letters, diaries, pamphlets, and other papers from that period, and they are well written. It was the age, we may recall, not only of Boswell and Johnson, but of Pepys and Franklin as well, and of a host of other men whose main legacy to us was a simple, direct, workmanlike style, sufficient to the man and to the occasion, which said what it had to say and said it well. With the end of that century we go into the foggy, foggy darkness, and God knows whether we shall ever find our way out of it—as a people, that is, as a nation of thinking men and women with something to say.

Nevertheless, there is no question what makes our writing bad, or what we shall have to do to better it. We shall simply have to isolate and root out a monomania which now possesses us, which impedes all language study and inhibits all mastery of our native tongue—all mastery, that is, on paper; for as speakers of English, we Americans are loving and effective cultivators of our expression. I recall the gas station attendant who was filling my car. The gasoline foamed to the top of the tank, and he shut off the pump. "Whew!" I said, "that nearly went over." "When you see whitecaps," he replied, "you better stop." "You better had," I said, lost in admiration. But if you had given him a pencil, he would have chewed the end off before he got one word on paper.

The demon which possesses us is our mania for correctness. It dominates our minds from the first grade to the graduate school; it is the first and often the only thing we think of when we think of our language. Our spelling must be "correct"—even if the words are ill-chosen; our "usage" must be "correct"—even though any possible substitute expression, however crude, would be perfectly clear; our punctuation must be "correct"—even though practices surge and change with the passing of years, and differ from book to book, periodical to periodical. Correct! That's what we've got to be, and the idea that we've got to be correct rests like a soggy blanket on our brains and our hands whenever we try to write.

This mania for correctness is another legacy from the eighteenth century, but it did not get a real grip on us until well into the nineteenth. Its power over us today is appalling. Among my other tasks, I teach advanced courses in the English language to students preparing to teach. Most of these are seniors and graduate students, and in the summer especially, there is a sprinkling of older men and women, experienced teachers, who are sweating out a master's degree. They have had courses in "English" throughout their schooling. But of the nature and structure of the English language, the nature of language habits, the relation of speech to writing, and the differences in usage which arise from dialect and from differing occupational and educational demands—of all these, they know nothing at all. Nor do they come to me expecting to learn about these. They want to know two things: what correct usage is and how you beat it into the kids' heads. That there are other considerations important to an English teacher is news to many of them. What they get from me is a good long look at their language.

To trace this monolithic concentration on usage is to pursue a vicious circle, with the linguists on the outside. The literate public seems to get it from the English teachers, and the teachers get it from the public. The attitudes and pronouncements on language of a Jacques Barzun, a Wilson Follett, a Bernard De Voto, or a Norman Lewis ("How Correct

Must Correct English Be?") mean more to English teachers than anything said by the most distinguished professional students of language—such as Leonard Bloomfield, Robert Hall or Charles Carpenter Fries. Correct usage is pursued and discussed, furthermore, without much reference to the actual writing of literary men. Now and again I amuse myself by blue-penciling a current magazine such as the *Saturday Review* or *Collier's* against the rules. I have to report that error is rampant, if variation is to be considered error. The boys just don't seem to pay attention to the rules. Moreover, having seen some of their first drafts, I am pretty sure that what conformity they do display is the work of their wives, secretaries, editors, proofreaders and typesetters, rather than their own. It takes a determined effort to beat the old Adam out of a readable manuscript.

Thus it is only the determined, consciously creative professional who can build his work on the actual language of men. In a recent issue of the *Saturday Review*, I stumbled on a quotation from Wolfgang Langewiesche. "Well, it isn't crowned by no castle, that's for sure," he wrote, "and by no cathedral either." My eyes popped, and I read it again. I liked it. It looked right; it sounded right; it had a fine Chaucerian swing to it. But I bet it cost him some blood and a fifth of Scotch to get it into print. In my own limited publication, I find "a historical" changed to "an historical," all my "further's" changed to "farther" and all my "farther's" to "further," "than us" watered down to "than we," and many, many more. How E. M. Forster got by with "the author he thinks," and got it reprinted in a freshman handbook a few pages along from the prohibition of such locutions baffles me. A phony standardization of usage appears in print, the work of editors unconscious of the ultimate meaning of what they do.

The result of all this is that a wet hand of fear rests on the heart of every nonprofessional writer who merely has a lot of important knowledge to communicate. He writes every sentence with a self-conscious horror of doing something wrong. It is always a comfort to him if he can fit himself into some system, such as that of a business or governmental office which provides him with a model. It is thus that gobbledegook comes into being. I once braced a distinguished sociologist, a student of occupational myths and attitudes, about the convoluted, mainly nominal turgidity of his writing. He apparently admitted verbs into his sentences the way we admit DP's into the United States, reluctantly and with pain. In speech he was racy, confident and compelling, a brilliant lecturer. "It's the only way I can get my work into the periodicals," he told me blandly. "If it's clear and simple, they don't think it's scholarly." With what relief the pedagogues subside into pedagese!

If we really want to get good writing from people who know things, so that we can come to learn what they know as easily as we learn from their talk, we can do it in a generation or so. In school and out, in print and out, we can leave usage to its natural nurse, the unforced imitation of the practices which are actually current among educated people. We can use our English courses in school and college, not to give drill on questionable choices among common alternatives, demanding that one be taken as right and the others as wrong, but to give practice in reading and writing. We can learn to read and write for the idea, and go for the idea without regard for anything else. Then our young people will come to maturity confidently using their pencils to find out what they think and get it down on paper; then our scholars will come to write simply, clearly and brilliantly what they brilliantly know.

In our speech we have arrived, I think, at a decency of discourse which is conducive to effective expression. We listen, with a grave courteous attention, to massive patterns of speaking different from our own because they come from differences in dialect and social status; we listen without carping and without a mean contempt. Furthermore, we participate; we go with a speaker through halts and starts, over abysses of construction, filling in the lacunae without hesitation; we discount inadvertencies and disregard wrong words and we arrive in genial good will with the speaker at his meaning. In this atmosphere, our speech has thrived, and the ordinary American is in conversation a confident, competent expressive being. In writing he is something else again.

No one flourishes in an atmosphere of repression. It is possible, of course, for a person with special aptitudes and a special drive to bull his way past the prohibitions and achieve an individual style. But with the negative attitude that attends all our writing, those whose main interest lies elsewhere are inhibited by fear of "error" and the nagging it stirs up from setting pen to paper, until the sight of a blank white page gives them the shakes. It is no wonder that their expression is halting and ineffective. They cannot fulfill the demands of a prissy propriety and trace the form of an idea at the same time. They thus arrive at adulthood victims of the steely eye of Mr. Sherwin Cody, whose bearded face stares at them from the countless ads for his correspondence school, demanding, "Do YOU make these mistakes in English?" The locutions he lists are not mistakes, and Mr. Cody knows they are not; but his readers do not know it, and they do not know that they don't matter anyway.

For usage doesn't matter. What matters is that we get done what we have to do, and get said what we have to say. Sufficient conformity is imposed upon us by the patterns of our language and by the general practices of its users so that we do not have to run the idea of conformity into the ground by carping about trivial erratics in expression.

Why in this matter of language alone complete conformity should be considered a virtue—except to typists, printers and typesetters—it is difficult to see (unless, perhaps, we are using it as a covert and pusillanimous means of establishing our own superiority). In our other concerns in life, we prize individuality; why in this one matter we should depart from a principle that otherwise serves us well is a puzzle for fools and wise men to ponder, especially since there is no general agreement on what to conform to, and one man's correctness is another's error. Not until we come to our senses—teachers, editors, writers and readers together—and stop riding each other's backs, will the casual, brisk, colorful, amused, ironic and entertaining talk of Americans find its way into print. We should all be happy to see it there.

PART FIVE

Style

A study of language moves naturally into a consideration of style because style in writing, as in any art, is a relation between submission and control. A good writer submits to his medium by learning all that he can about his language and by expressing its deep patterns and idioms; at the same time he controls his medium for particular purposes. These points are illustrated in the first essay of this section as Professor Simeon Potter of the University of Liverpool describes the basic kinds of English sentence patterns and discusses their proper management.

When control is given primary stress in a discussion of writing, a relationship between style and moral character comes into view. This is evident in the second essay by the late English essayist and novelist, George Orwell, the author of *1984*. "What is above all needed," says Orwell, "is to let the meaning choose the word, and not the other way about. In prose the worst thing one can do with words is to surrender to them." Orwell's adjectives for bad writing have moral overtones: slovenly, pretentious, insincere, vague, stale, conventional, correct. The good writer has the courage to speak out and come to the point; he and his style are simple, lively, honest, and direct.

This subject is enlarged in the last essay by Geoffrey Moore, Lecturer in American literature at the University of Hull, into a discussion of the relation between style and national character. Is there an American prose style? After an interesting analysis of samples of modern American prose, Moore concludes that there are really two "nations" in America and two corresponding styles: the educated, literate minority, and the uneducated, semi-literate majority. Looking ahead, Moore wonders wryly if the style of the literate minority in America will survive the tide of careless speech and the mass media. A hopeful answer is implied in the quotation which he placed at the head of his essay. It presumably describes an ideal prose style, one that is "natural, simple, and unaffected . . . , pithy, sinewy, full, strong, compendious and material. . . ." The quoted statement was written three and a half centuries ago in England by John Florio, a student of language and the son of Italian immigrants. In language, as in life, good things come from unexpected places.

SIMEON POTTER

The Sentence

We do not learn to frame sentences instinctively, as we learn to breathe
or to walk. We repeat sentences from memory and we vary them by
analogy. Imagine for a moment that all the sentences you have uttered
during the course of the last two weeks are somewhere accurately
recorded and that you can now scrutinize them at leisure. You will probably find them to be surprisingly varied: long and short; simple, double,
multiple, and complex; statements, commands, wishes, questions, and
exclamations; balanced, periodic, and loose. The words have been largely
of your own choosing, but the sentences have seldom been of your own
making. You have inherited them from the immediate, the distant, and
the long-distant past. You have carried with you in your mind a certain
number of sentence-patterns, few or many according to your individual
linguistic capacity, and into these patterns you have fitted and varied
the words expressing your thoughts and desires.

A child may echo the sounds it hears without being conscious of the
meanings of separate words. Because English is, in the main, an analytic
language (in spite of reviving synthetic tendencies . . .), the sentence
is the most important unit of English speech. The sentence is more important even than the word. Revelling in the exercise of its imitative
faculty, a child will attempt, however imperfectly, to babble whole sentences. A schoolboy may be word-perfect in his recitation of a long and
difficult poem while remaining blissfully ignorant of the poet's intention
and meaning. "If hopes were dupes, fears may be liars," I say to console
a friend. He may like the words and repeat them, and yet neither of us
may pause to reflect upon the astounding personifications implied by
Clough in this oft-repeated line. "Genuine poetry," Mr. T. S. Eliot has

reminded us, "can communicate before it is understood." A lovely sentence may haunt my memory—

> And I shall have some peace there, for peace comes dropping slow,
> Dropping from the veils of the morning to where the cricket sings

—and I may often murmur it to myself without being at all conscious of linguistic form, or function, or even of meaning. Nevertheless, the effective speaker and writer of prose is he who does not merely *catch* his sentence-patterns but who *grips* them and wields them with well-controlled purpose. In addition to possessing a ready command of vocabulary, the good speaker must be endowed with an unerring sense of rhythm. Even the most gifted orator, however, cannot depart too far from the speech patterns accepted by the community in which he lives without running the grave risk of being misapprehended or of being only partially understood. In ordinary affirmations the subject is followed by the predicate, consisting of verb and object or complement. In all the Indo-European languages the sentence is normally bipartite. Basically it is a two-in-one. It is a binary unit. The subject is that to which the speaker wishes to draw the hearer's attention and the predicate is that which the speaker has to say about that subject. If I utter a defective sentence it is probably because, for some reason or other, I have failed to keep these two things clear in my mind. In order to put it right, I have only to ask myself the simple questions: What am I talking about? What have I to say about it? Or, in other words: What is my subject? What do I predicate of that subject? As Edward Sapir has so well said (*Language,* p. 36), "The major functional unit of speech, the sentence . . . is the linguistic expression of a proposition. It combines a subject of discourse with a statement in regard to this subject. Subject and predicate may be combined in a single word, as in Latin *dico;* each may be expressed independently, as in the English equivalent, *I say;* each or either may be so qualified as to lead to complex propositions of many sorts. No matter how many of these qualifying elements (words or functional parts of words) are introduced, the sentence does not lose its feeling of unity so long as each and every one of them falls in place as contributory to the definition of either the subject of discourse or the core of the predicate."

The predicate may indeed have preceded the subject in Proto-Indo-European, as in Modern Welsh, as in parenthetical "said he," or as in H. G. Wells's stylistic mannerism "Came a pause." The sentence-type *Down came the rain,* which is as old as Chaucer, finds its normal place in Modern German. Emphatic *down* comes first, the verb retains second place, and so the subject falls into the final position. It has been computed that the subject precedes the predicate in less than half of King

Alfred's sentences, and if we study the shapes assumed by certain concrete locutions during the last thousand years or so, we detect a gradual shifting towards the modern order: subject, verb and object. Old English *mē gelīciaþ bēc* "To me are pleasing books" becomes modern English *I like books*. The vocables are identical, but the case of the pronoun has been altered from dative to nominative and the grammatical subject has been shifted from the things to the person. Since loving and liking are primarily active feelings, Modern English, it might be claimed, is here more rational than Old English. The modern grammatical subject becomes identical with the logical and the psychological one. Similarly, both *If you like* and *If you please* have derived historically from *If to you it may be pleasing* (*you* being dative of the pronoun and *like* and *please* third person singular of the present subjunctive) very much as in French *s'il vous plaît,* or Dutch *als 't u blieft* or old-fashioned German *wenn es Ihenen gefällt,* where, however, in all three languages, the verb is in the indicative. A still more striking example of the shifting of the grammatical subject to the first place in the sentence, without any resulting change in the position of the pronoun, is seen in *He was given the book* in which *the book* is "retained object." In the corresponding sentence in Old English, however, *the book* is the grammatical subject, *Him wæs gegiefen sēo bōc,* "(To) him was given the book." Similarly Chaucer's *It am I,* in which the grammatical subject is *I* (Old English *Hit eom ic,* Latin *Ego sum*), becomes Modern English *It is I.* In Chaucer's day the subjective character of *I* was still so strong that, in spite of word order, *It am I* sounded just as natural as Old French *Ce suis je.* French has certainly gone further than English in normalizing *C'est moi.* "L'état, c'est moi," said Louis XIV as long ago as in the seventeenth century, not "L'état, c'est je." *It is me* is regarded by many to be too colloquial for literary use. At the same time, the feeling predominates that, apart from grammatical structure, a verb should be followed by the accusative. No one, as Otto Jespersen pointed out, would venture to suggest changing Shelley's emphatic *me* in *Ode to the West Wind*—

> Be thou, Spirit fierce,
> My spirit! Be thou *me*, impetuous one!

No one is shocked by the ungrammatical *Fare thee well* instead of *Fare (go) thou well.*

In the sentence *It's me* the neuter pronoun *it* has no separate meaning. It is a meaningless substitute which brings this simple statement into the usual pattern of subject, and complement. In the casual observations *It is blowing hard, It is cold,* and *It is raining,* you might too readily assume that the neuter pronoun stands for *the wind, the weather,* and *the rain* respectively. "For the rain it raineth every day" sang the clown at the end of *Twelfth Night,* and Robert Louis Stevenson wrote playfully in his verses for children—

> The rain is raining all around
> It falls on field and tree.

After a little reflection you will probably conclude that *it* in *It is raining* is merely a substitute for the subject of the impersonal verb and that it expresses an action or a condition of things without reference to any agent.

Swift defined a good style as the use of proper words in proper places. The proper places will vary considerably according to degrees of emphasis. Usage has left many parts of the sentence relatively free and these we can vary to suit our purpose. Coleridge laid much stress on the importance of word order. He defined poetry, you may remember, as "the best words in the best order." In the words of the greatest poets "there is," Coleridge asserted, "a reason assignable not only for every word, but for the position of every word." In the well-ordered sentence the hearer or the reader will receive no jolt or check. As Herbert Spencer observed, "things which are to be thought of together must be mentioned as closely as possible together." Naturally we place together such words as are more closely associated in meaning. We say "a big brown dog" rather than "a brown big dog," "a handsome young man" and not "a young handsome man," and "a kind old gardener" and not "an old kind gardener." So, too, we place together those phrases which are most closely associated in our minds. "Delighted to make your acquaintance" we say upon being introduced and not, as in German, "Delighted your acquaintance to make."

The classification of sentences is not a difficult matter. Sentences are of three kinds according to *form:* simple ("I know it"), compound ("I know it and I am proud of it"), and complex ("I know that he will come"). They are of four kinds according to *function:* statement ("I know it"), command-wish ("Long live the King!"), question ("Are you coming?"), and exclamation ("How good you are!"). The verb generally comes before the subject in wishes and questions. As we pass from a simple to a complex sentence we do not, as in some other languages, change the order of the words: "I hope (that) he will come. He will, I hope, come. Presumably he will come." But in German we are bound to say: "Ich hoffe, er wird kommen. Ich hoffe, dass er kommen wird. Hoffentlich (vermutlich) wird er kommen."

Sentences may be further categorized according to *style* as loose, balanced, and periodic, although this division is of its very nature somewhat vague and ill defined. All three types of sentence are good and a master of English will weave them skilfully into the varied fabric of style. In the so-called *loose* sentence the writer or speaker states fact after fact just as these occur to him, freely and artlessly. Daniel Defoe opens *The Life and Adventures of Robinson Crusoe* with a long, loose, rambling sentence which nevertheless grips our attention at once: "I was born in the year 1632, in the city of York, of a good family, though not of that country, my father being a foreigner of Bremen, who settled first at Hull: he got a good estate by merchandise, and leaving off his trade, lived afterward at York, from whence he had married my mother, whose relations were named Robinson, a very good family in that country, and from whom I was called Robinson Kreutznoer; but, by the usual corruption of words in England, we are now called, nay, we call ourselves, and write our name Crusoe, and so my companions always called me." The style is conversational. We seem to hear the author talking quietly to us in the first person and telling us the story of his life. This imaginary autobiography seems at once factual and real. As the writer tells us about the time and the place of his birth, about his parentage and his name, he adds clause to clause pleasantly. The sentence might well have ended after the first clause, "I was born in the year 1632"; or it might have ended in at least thirteen other places after that. On the other hand, it might have gone on and on for many pages. There is no ambiguity, no obscurity, and no tautology. The reader receives no mental check. All is easy and natural. But behind this apparent artlessness there is art concealed, and behind this easy and natural prose—Defoe was writing in the year 1719—lay more than ten centuries of linguistic change and development. There is probably no surer way of appreciating the maturity and concreteness of Defoe's prose than by translating it into some foreign tongue.

In the *periodic* sentence the climax comes at the close. The reader is held in suspense until at last he hears what he has long been waiting for, and only then is he able to comprehend the meaning of the sentence as a whole. It is a style cultivated to good effect by the orators of classical antiquity, Demosthenes and Cicero, as well as those of modern times, Burke and Gladstone. When, in *The Laws of Ecclesiasticall Politie*, Richard Hooker reflected upon what might be the subsequent fate of man if the ordinances of nature should fail, he expressed himself in a stately and sonorous prose far different from Defoe's: "Now if nature should intermit her course, and leave altogether though it were but for a while the observation of her own laws; if those principal and mother elements of the world, whereof all things in this lower world are made, should lose the qualities which now they have; if the frame of that heavenly arch erected over our heads should loosen and dissolve itself; if celestial spheres should forget their wonted motions, and by irregular volubility turn themselves any way as it might happen; if the prince of the lights of heaven, which now as a giant doth run his unwearied course, should as it were through a languishing faintness begin to stand and to rest himself; if the moon should wander from her beaten way, the times and seasons of the year blend themselves by disordered and confused mixture, the winds breathe out their last gasp, the clouds yield no rain, the earth be defeated of heavenly influence, the fruits of the earth pine away as children at the withered breasts of their mother no longer able to yield them relief: what would become of man himself, whom these things now do all serve?" The language is highly rhythmical and the imagery is Biblical, reminiscent of Isaiah, the Psalms, and the Book of Job. The word-picture is painted with consummate art. After a long and steady climb upward over successive terraces of conditional clauses, the reader descends swiftly with the final rhetorical question.

As an example of a shorter but no less effective period we might consider the sentence in his *Autobiography* in which Edward Gibbon describes the birth of the idea of his great *History:* "It was at Rome, on the 15th of October 1764, as I sat musing amidst the ruins of the Capitol, while the barefooted friars were singing vespers in the temple of Jupiter, that the idea of writing the decline and fall of the city first started to my mind." In Rome, ruinous and Christian, late in the afternoon in the fall of the year, the inspiration came to the historian. The word-picture is brief, but it is artistically perfect. The rhythm is stately and entirely satisfying. The reader is held in suspense to the end.

Had he wished, and had he been less of an artist, Gibbon might have said exactly the same things in a different way, arranging them in their logical and grammatical order: "The idea of writing the decline and fall of the city first started to my mind as I sat musing amidst the ruins of the Capitol at Rome on the 15th of October 1764, while the barefooted friars were singing vespers in the temple of Jupiter." What has happened? It is not merely that a periodic sentence has been re-expressed as a loose one. The emphasis is now all wrong and the magnificent cadence of the original is quite marred. All is still grammatically correct, but "proper words" are no longer in "proper places." The passage has quite lost its harmonious rhythm.

The *balanced* sentence satisfies a profound human desire for equipoise and symmetry and it has long been at home in English as in Hebrew, Greek, and Latin, and many other languages both ancient and modern. It may express two similar thoughts in *parallelism* or two opposing ones in *antithesis*. Such proverbial sayings as *Like master like man, More haste less speed, First come first served,* and *Least said soonest mended* probably represent a primitive Indo-European sentence-type which survives in many lands.

"Children sweeten labours," wrote Francis Bacon, "but they make misfortunes more bitter: they increase the cares of life, but they mitigate the remembrance of death." Speaking at the Guildhall, London, on October 9, 1805, just one fortnight after the Battle of Trafalgar, William Pitt declared: "England has saved herself by her exertions and will, I trust, save Europe by her example." No less memorable was the balanced sentence uttered in the House of Lords by Edward Viscount Grey of Fallodon on August 3, 1914, on the eve of Britain's entry into the First World War: "The lamps are going out all over Europe: we shall not see them lit again in our lifetime."

English sentence-patterns show infinite variety and *loose, periodic*, and *balanced* are only relative terms. The best writers shape their sentences in such a way as to give just the right degree of emphasis, and this they must achieve, in written language, by word order alone. Now it is certainly not surprising that in a language like ours, with such a long history behind it, some patterns have become blended, mixed, or, to use the technical term, "contaminated," and that some of these "contaminations" have been sanctioned by usage. "I am friendly with him" and "We are friends" ("He and I are friends") have become contaminated and so have produced "I am friends with him." It is an idiom or manner of expression peculiar to English. "I am friends with him" cannot be translated literally into French, German, or Italian, though it is as old as Shakespeare. "I am good friends with my father," says Prince Hal (I *Henry the Fourth*, III. iii. 202), "and may do any thing." "But whom say ye that I am?" (*St. Matthew*, xvi, 15) is frequently quoted from the King James Bible as an example of an ungrammatical accusative *whom* used as the complement of the verb *to be*. Is it, then, an error? Perhaps no direct yes or no can be given in answer to this question. The sentence is a good example of a blending of "Who say ye that I am?" and "Whom say ye me to be?" That is all. The English poets, even the very greatest of them, have occasionally indulged in such contaminations of sentence-structures, refusing to be bound by strict rules. "I should have liked to have been there," someone will say. Clearly this is a blending of "I should like (I wish now as I look back) to have been there" and "I should have liked (but unfortunately I was unable) to be there." "They each did their best" is likewise a mixture of "They all (all of them) did their best" and "Each of them did his best."

If it is true that we repeat sentences from memory and vary them by analogy, and that we do not really frame sentences in any other way, then we should perhaps look upon all analogous creations with a kind and indulgent eye. "Do like I do" is no worse than Elizabethan "Do like as I do." "Do like me" and "Do as I do" mark a desirable distinction, but it would be well to recognize that the distinction is more stylistic than grammatical. "What are you doing of?" is the Cockney's analogous creation, based upon "What are you doing?" and "What are you thinking of?" "I would say" and "I should like to say" are blended and so we hear "I would like to say," an undesirable form which is helped on its way to acceptance by the general tendency, especially in North America and in Ireland, to ignore the (relatively recent) traditional distinctions between *shall* (*should*) in the first person and *will* (*would*) in the second and third. "It looks as though" is now on everyone's lips—"It looks as though there will be a general election (or anything else for that matter) soon." "It looks to me," said Burke in 1790 (*Reflections on the Revolution in France*) "as if I were in a great crisis." The verb to-day would be in the past subjunctive (or subjunctive equivalent) if people were conscious of the precise implication: "It appears as would or might be the case if." But "It looks as though" has come to be a mere substitute for "apparently, probably, by all appearances," and it is now invariably followed by the future tense. "You and I will decide between us" has influenced "Let you and me decide" which becomes "Let you and I decide" on the lips of the heedless, who no longer think of "Let us decide" as "Allow us to decide" supplanting "Decide we," the old jussive. Whatever the grammarians may say, there is abundant evidence in many languages for the use of the superlative degree in a comparison of only two persons or things. Nevertheless, "Which (selective) is the stronger of the two?" is more satisfactory than "Who is the strongest of the two?" If we say "He was one of the kindest men that has ever lived" we break that favourite rule of the prescriptive grammarians which states that the verb in a relative clause should agree with its nearer antecedent. Doubtless we are thereby confusing "He was the kindest man that ever lived" and "He was one of the kindest men that have ever lived." We may confuse "The reason why printing is slow is that paper is scarce" and "Printing is slow because paper is scarce" and, as a result, we say "The reason why printing is slow is because paper is scarce." If we are observant and alert, we shall probably hear many interesting "contaminations," such as these, both tolerable and intolerable, every day of our lives.

Another interesting thing we shall observe is the way in which natural emphasis overrides strict logic in word order. "He only died last week" may be denounced by modern precisians on the ground that it flouts one of those rules of proximity whereby the modifying adverb should be placed as near as possible to the word, phrase or clause it modifies. "He died only last week" or "It was only last week that he died" should stand.

Stress, intonation, and pause, however, make everything clear, or even clearer, when *only* is detached. "He only died last week" implies no ambiguity and no misplaced emphasis. Shakespeare himself wrote in Sonnet xciv—

> The summer's flower is to the summer sweet
> Though to itself it only live and die

—and not "Though only to itself" or "Though to itself alone," the latter cadence seeming certainly preferable to my modern ear. Mr. Vernon Bartlett once opened a wireless talk on world affairs with the words: "I am not an expert on China. I have only been there twice in my life." Natural emphasis and intonation were just right: the hearer's attention was arrested at once. "I have been there only twice in my life" would have sounded unnatural and pedantic in comparison. Language, after all, is more psychological than logical. So, too, in regard to the placing of the preposition, we should do well to divest ourselves of the notion that it is "an inelegant word to end a sentence with" and that, just because it is called a *pre-position,* it must therefore "be placed before." In Old English (*ūs betwēonan* "between us") as in Latin (*pāx vōbiscum* "peace be with you"), there were *postpositions* and the tradition has been kept alive through centuries of English poetry: "the table round" (Shakespeare); "stoutly struts his dames before" (Milton); "my heart within" (Scott); "the willowy hills and fields among" (Tennyson); "I will go to France again, and tramp the valley through" (Flecker). The final preposition became a butt for the nineteenth-century grammarians, who averred that the most careful writers avoided it and that the Authorized Version of the Bible contained not one instance of it. As a matter of fact, the curious reader will not go far in the Book of Genesis before encountering an example in Chapter xxviii: "I will not leave thee, until I have done that which I have spoken to thee of." It is a remarkable fact that even Dryden, that acknowledged master of English prose, criticized Ben Jonson's conversational style adversely on the ground that it showed the "common fault" of putting the preposition at the end, a fault which, Dryden added, "I have but lately observed in my own writings." Indeed, when revising his *Essay of Dramatic Poesy,* Dryden went so far as to rewrite the sentences in which an end preposition occurred and his illustrious example was followed by others. To-day we accept the final preposition as permissible and desirable in such natural and spontaneous expressions as "What are you thinking of?" and "I sometimes wonder what the world is coming to." Phrasal verbs, consisting of verbs joined with adverbs and prepositions, are now in such frequent use that, in order to avoid the prepositional ending entirely, a speaker would sometimes be driven to perpetrate an intolerably artificial sentence. Against such a clumsy sentence, according to Sir Ernest Gowers (*Plain Words,* p. 74), Mr Winston Churchill is said to have added the marginal comment: "This is the sort of English up with which I will not put." Sir Ernest goes on to tell the story of a nurse who contrived to get no fewer than four prepositions together at the end of a sentence when she asked a child: "What did you choose that book to be read to out of for?" And did the child understand? If stress, rhythm, intonation, and pause were right, yes. The nurse "said what she wanted to say perfectly clearly, in words of one syllable, and what more can one ask?" You may have observed, by the way, that *out* in "read to out of for" is really an adverb or, if you will, that *out-of* is a prepositional compound consisting of adverb and preposition. At any rate, the dividing line between prepositions and adverbs is often shadowy and vague.

The English sentence, then, is something of a paradox. Word order has become more significant than hitherto, far more important than in Old, Middle, or Tudor English, and yet it has retained enough of its elasticity to give to the skilful speaker all the scope and power he needs. We English have inherited our sentence-patterns, but we have abundant freedom to vary words, phrases, and clauses within those inherited patterns. We shall be effective as speakers and as writers if we can say clearly, simply, and attractively just what we want to say and nothing more. If we really have something worth saying, then we are bound by the nature and necessities of our language to say it as simply as ever we can. If we have something very abstruse and complex to say, then, of course, we cannot say it simply, but we shall endeavour to say it as clearly as the theme permits. We shall vary our style, our vocabulary and our speech-level to suit the occasion and, at the same time, we shall never lose sight of the needs and capacities of our hearers. If, following the wise counsel of Aristotle, we keep these three things constantly in mind—our subject-matter, our purpose, and our audience—all will be well.

GEORGE ORWELL

Politics and the English Language

Most people who bother with the matter at all would admit that the English language is in a bad way, but it is generally assumed that we cannot by conscious action do anything about it. Our civilization is decadent and our language—so the argument runs—must inevitably share in the general collapse. It follows that any struggle against the abuse of language is a sentimental archaism, like preferring candles to electric light or hansom cabs to aeroplanes. Underneath this lies the half-conscious belief that language is a natural growth and not an instrument which we shape for our own purposes.

Now, it is clear that the decline of a language must ultimately have political and economic causes: it is not due simply to the bad influence of this or that individual writer. But an effect can become a cause, reinforcing the original cause and producing the same effect in an intensified form, and so on indefinitely. A man may take to drink because he feels himself to be a failure, and then fail all the more completely because he drinks. It is rather the same thing that is happening to the English language. It becomes ugly and inaccurate because our thoughts are foolish, but the slovenliness of our language makes it easier for us to have foolish thoughts. The point is that the process is reversible. Modern English, especially written English, is full of bad habits which spread by imitation and which can be avoided if one is willing to take the necessary trouble. If one gets rid of these habits one can think more clearly, and to think clearly is a necessary first step toward political regeneration: so that the fight against bad English is not frivolous and is not the exclusive concern of professional writers. I will come back to this presently, and I hope that by that time the meaning of what I have said here will have become clearer. Meanwhile, here are five specimens of the English language as it is now habitually written.

These five passages have not been picked out because they are especially bad—I could have quoted far worse if I had chosen—but because they illustrate various of the mental vices from which we now suffer. They are a little below the average, but are fairly representative samples. I number them so that I can refer back to them when necessary:

> (1) I am not, indeed, sure whether it is not true to say that the Milton who once seemed not unlike a seventeenth-century Shelley had not become, out of an experience ever more bitter in each year, more alien [sic] to the founder of that Jesuit sect which nothing could induce him to tolerate.
>
> Professor Harold Laski (Essay in *Freedom of Expression*)

> (2) Above all, we cannot play ducks and drakes with a native battery of idioms which prescribes such egregious collocations of vocables as the Basic *put up with* for *tolerate* or *put at a loss* for *bewilder*.   Professor Lancelot Hogben (*Interglossa*)

> (3) On the one side we have the free personality: by definition it is not neurotic, for it has neither conflict nor dream. Its desires, such as they are, are transparent, for they are just what institutional approval keeps in the forefront of consciousness; another institutional pattern would alter their number and intensity; there is little in them that is natural, irreducible, or culturally dangerous. But *on the other side*, the social bond itself is nothing but the mutual reflection of these self-secure integrities. Recall the definition of love. Is not this the very picture of a small academic? Where is there a place in this hall of mirrors for either personality or fraternity?
>
> Essay on psychology in *Politics* (New York)

> (4) All the "best people" from the gentlemen's clubs, and all the frantic fascist captains, united in common hatred of Socialism and bestial horror of the rising tide of the mass revolutionary movement, have turned to acts of provocation, to foul incendiarism, to medieval legends of poisoned wells, to legalize their own destruction of proletarian organizations, and rouse the agitated petty-bourgeoisie to chauvinistic fervor on behalf of the fight against the revolutionary way out of the crisis.   Communist pamphlet

> (5) If a new spirit *is* to be infused into this old country, there is one thorny and contentious reform which must be tackled, and that is the humanization and galvanization of the B.B.C. Timidity here will bespeak canker and atrophy of the soul. The heart of Britain may be sound and of strong beat, for instance, but the British lion's roar at present is like that of Bottom in Shakespeare's *Midsummer Night's Dream*—as

gentle as any sucking dove. A virile new Britain cannot continue indefinitely to be traduced in the eyes or rather ears, of the world by the effete languors of Langham Place, brazenly masquerading as "standard English." When the Voice of Britain is heard at nine o'clock, better far and infinitely less ludicrous to hear aitches honestly dropped than the present priggish, inflated, inhibited, school-ma'amish arch braying of blameless bashful mewing maidens!   Letter in *Tribune*

Each of these passages has faults of its own, but, quite apart from avoidable ugliness, two qualities are common to all of them. The first is staleness of imagery; the other is lack of precision. The writer either has a meaning and cannot express it, or he inadvertently says something else, or he is almost indifferent as to whether his words mean anything or not. This mixture of vagueness and sheer incompetence is the most marked characteristic of modern English prose, and especially of any kind of political writing. As soon as certain topics are raised, the concrete melts into the abstract and no one seems able to think of turns of speech that are not hackneyed: prose consists less and less of *words* chosen for the sake of their meaning, and more and more of *phrases* tacked together like the sections of a prefabricated henhouse. I list below, with notes and examples, various of the tricks by means of which the work of prose-construction is habitually dodged:

DYING METAPHORS. A newly invented metaphor assists thought by evoking a visual image, while on the other hand a metaphor which is technically "dead" (e.g. *iron resolution*) has in effect reverted to being an ordinary word and can generally be used without loss of vividness. But in between these two classes there is a huge dump of worn-out metaphors which have lost all evocative power and are merely used because they save people the trouble of inventing phrases for themselves. Examples are: *Ring the changes on, take up the cudgels for, toe the line, ride roughshod over, stand shoulder to shoulder with, play into the hands of, no axe to grind, grist to the mill, fishing in troubled waters, on the order of the day, Achilles' heel, swan song, hotbed.* Many of these are used without knowledge of their meaning (what is a "rift," for instance?), and incompatible metaphors are frequently mixed, a sure sign that the writer is not interested in what he is saying. Some metaphors now current have been twisted out of their original meaning without those who use them even being aware of the fact. For example, *toe the line* is sometimes written *tow the line.* Another example is *the hammer and the anvil,* now always used with the implication that the anvil gets the worst of it. In real life it is always the anvil that breaks the hammer, never the other way about: a writer who stopped to think what he was saying would be aware of this, and would avoid perverting the original phrase.

OPERATORS OR VERBAL FALSE LIMBS. These save the trouble of picking out appropriate verbs and nouns, and at the same time pad each sentence with extra syllables which give it an appearance of symmetry. Characteristic phrases are *render inoperative, militate against, make contact with, be subjected to, give rise to, give grounds for, have the effect of, play a leading part (role) in, make itself felt, take effect, exhibit a tendency to, serve the purpose of, etc., etc.* The keynote is the elimination of simple verbs. Instead of being a single word, such as *break, stop, spoil, mend, kill,* a verb becomes a *phrase,* made up of a noun or adjective tacked on to some general-purpose verb such as *prove, serve, form, play, render.* In addition, the passive voice is wherever possible used in preference to the active, and noun constructions are used instead of gerunds (*by examination of* instead of *by examining*). The range of verbs is further cut down by means of the *-ize* and *de-* formations, and the banal statements are given an appearance of profundity by means of the *not un-* formation. Simple conjunctions and prepositions are replaced by such phrases as *with respect to, having regard to, the fact that, by dint of, in view of, in the interests of, on the hypothesis that;* and the ends of sentences are saved by anticlimax by such resounding commonplaces as *greatly to be desired, cannot be left out of account, a development to be expected in the near future, deserving of serious consideration, brought to a satisfactory conclusion,* and so on and so forth.

PRETENTIOUS DICTION. Words like *phenomenon, element, individual* (as noun), *objective, categorical, effective, virtual, basic, primary, promote, constitute, exhibit, exploit, utilize, eliminate, liquidate,* are used to dress up simple statement and give an air of scientific impartiality to biased judgments. Adjectives like *epoch-making, epic, historic, unforgettable, triumphant, age-old, inevitable, inexorable, veritable,* are used to dignify the sordid processes of international politics, while writing that aims at glorifying war usually takes on an archaic color, its characteristic words being: *realm, throne, chariot, mailed fist, trident, sword, shield, buckler, banner, jackboot, clarion.* Foreign words and expressions such as *cul de sac, ancien régime, deus ex machina, mutatis mutandis, status quo, gleichschaltung, weltanschauung,* are used to give an air of culture and elegance. Except for the useful abbreviations *i.e., e.g.,* and *etc.,* there is no real need for any of the hundreds of foreign phrases now current in English. Bad writers, and especially scientific, political, and sociological writers, are nearly always haunted by the notion that Latin or Greek words are grander than Saxon ones, and unnecessary words like *expedite, ameliorate, predict, extraneous, deracinated, clandestine, subaqueous,* and hundreds of others constantly gain ground from their Anglo-Saxon opposite numbers.* The jargon peculiar to Marxist writing (*hyena, hangman, cannibal, petty bourgeois, these gentry, lackey, flunkey, mad dog, White Guard,* etc.) consists largely of words and phrases translated from Russian, German, or French; but the normal way of coining a new word is to use a Latin or Greek root with the appropriate affix and, where necessary, the -ize formation. It is often easier to make up words of this kind (*deregionalize, impermissible, extramarital, non-fragmentary* and so forth) than to think up the English words that will cover one's meaning. The result, in general, is an increase in slovenliness and vagueness.

MEANINGLESS WORDS. In certain kinds of writing, particularly in art criticism and literary criticism, it is normal to come across long passages which are almost completely lacking in meaning.† Words like *romantic, plastic, values, human, dead, sentimental, natural, vitality,* as used in art criticism, are strictly meaningless, in the sense that they not only do not point to any discoverable object, but are hardly ever expected to do so by the reader. When one critic writes, "The outstanding feature of Mr. X's work is its living quality," while another writes, "The immediately striking thing about Mr. X's work is its peculiar deadness," the reader accepts this as a simple difference of opinion. If words like *black* and *white* were involved, instead of the jargon words *dead* and *living,* he would see at once that language was being used in an improper way. Many political words are similarly abused. The word *Fascism* has now no meaning except in so far as it signifies "something not desirable." The words *democracy, socialism, freedom, patriotic, realistic, justice,* have each of them several different meanings which cannot be reconciled with one another. In the case of a word like *democracy,* not only is there no agreed definition, but the attempt to make one is resisted from all sides. It is almost universally felt that when we call a country democratic we are praising it: consequently the defenders of every kind of régime claim that it is a democracy, and fear that they might have to stop using the word if it were tied down to any one meaning. Words of this kind are often used in a

---

* An interesting illustration of this is the way in which the English flower names which were in use till very recently are being ousted by Greek ones, *snapdragon* becoming *antirrhinum, forget-me-not* becoming *myosotis,* etc. It is hard to see any practical reason for this change of fashion: it is probably due to an instinctive turning away from the more homely word and a vague feeling that the Greek word is scientific.

† Example: "Comfort's catholicity of perception and image, strangely Whitman-esque in range, almost the exact opposite in aesthetic compulsion, continues to evoke that trembling atmospheric accumulative hinting at a cruel, an inexorably serene time-lessness. . . . Wrey Gardner scores by aiming at simple bull's-eyes with precision. Only they are not so simple, and through this contented sadness runs more than the surface bittersweet of resignation." (*Poetry Quarterly.*)

consciously dishonest way. That is, the person who uses them has his own private definition, but allows his hearer to think he means something quite different. Statements like *Marshal Pétain was a true patriot, The Soviet press is the freest in the world, The Catholic Church is opposed to persecution*, are almost always made with intent to deceive. Other words used in variable meanings, in most cases more or less dishonestly, are: *class, totalitarian, science, progressive, reactionary, bourgeois, equality*.

Now that I have made this catalogue of swindles and perversions, let me give another example of the kind of writing that they lead to. This time it must of its nature be an imaginary one. I am going to translate a passage of good English into modern English of the worst sort. Here is a well-known verse from *Ecclesiastes*:

> I returned and saw under the sun, that the race is not to the swift, nor the battle to the strong, neither yet bread to the wise, nor yet riches to men of understanding, nor yet favour to men of skill; but time and chance happeneth to them all.

Here it is in modern English:

> Objective consideration of contemporary phenomena compels the conclusion that success or failure in competitive activities exhibits no tendency to be commensurate with innate capacity, but that a considerable element of the unpredictable must invariably be taken into account.

This is a parody, but not a very gross one. Exhibit (3), above, for instance, contains several patches of the same kind of English. It will be seen that I have not made a full translation. The beginning and ending of the sentence follow the original meaning fairly closely, but in the middle the concrete illustrations—race, battle, bread—dissolve into the vague phrase "success or failure in competitive activities." This had to be so, because no modern writer of the kind I am discussing—no one capable of using phrases like "objective consideration of contemporary phenomena"—would ever tabulate his thoughts in that precise and detailed way. The whole tendency of modern prose is away from concreteness. Now analyze these two sentences a little more closely. The first contains forty-nine words but only sixty syllables, and all its words are those of everyday life. The second contains thirty-eight words of ninety syllables: eighteen of its words are from Latin roots, and one from Greek. The first sentence contains six vivid images, and only one phrase ("time and chance") that could be called vague. The second contains not a single fresh, arresting phrase, and in spite of its ninety syllables it gives only a shortened version of the meaning contained in the first. Yet without a doubt it is the second kind of sentence that is gaining ground in modern English. I do not want to exaggerate. This kind of writing is not yet universal, and outcrops of simplicity will occur here and there in the worst-written page. Still, if you or I were told to write a few lines on the uncertainty of human fortunes, we should probably come much nearer to my imaginary sentence than to the one from *Ecclesiastes.*

As I have tried to show, modern writing at its worst does not consist in picking out words for the sake of their meaning and inventing images in order to make the meaning clearer. It consists in gumming together long strips of words which have already been set in order by someone else, and making the results presentable by sheer humbug. The attraction of this way of writing is that it is easy. It is easier—even quicker, once you have the habit—to say *In my opinion it is not an unjustifiable assumption that* than to say *I think.* If you use ready-made phrases, you not only don't have to hunt about for words; you also don't have to bother with the rhythms of your sentences, since these phrases are generally so arranged as to be more or less euphonious. When you are composing in a hurry—when you are dictating to a stenographer, for instance, or making a public speech—it is natural to fall into a pretentious, Latinized style. Tags like *a consideration which we should do well to bear in mind* or *a conclusion to which all of us would readily assent* will save many a sentence from coming down with a bump. By using stale metaphors, similes, and idioms, you save much mental effort, at the cost of leaving your meaning vague, not only for your reader but for yourself. This is the significance of mixed metaphors. The sole aim of a metaphor is to call up a visual image. When these images clash—as in *The Fascist octopus has sung its swan song, the jackboot is thrown into the melting pot*—it can be taken as certain that the writer is not seeing a mental image of the objects he is naming; in other words he is not really thinking. Look again at the examples I gave at the beginning of this essay. Professor Laski (1) uses five negatives in fifty-three words. One of these is superfluous, making nonsense of the whole passage, and in addition there is the slip—*alien* for *akin*—making further nonsense, and several avoidable pieces of clumsiness which increase the general vagueness. Professor Hogben (2) plays ducks and drakes with a battery which is able to write prescriptions, and, while disapproving of the everyday phrase *put up with,* is unwilling to look *egregious* up in the dictionary and see what it means; (3), if one takes an uncharitable attitude towards it, is simply meaningless: probably one could work out its intended meaning by reading the whole of the article in which it occurs. In (4), the writer knows more or less what he wants to say, but an accumulation of stale phrases chokes him like tea leaves blocking a sink. In (5), words and meaning have almost parted company. People who write in this manner usually have a general emotional meaning—they dislike one thing and want to express solidarity with another—but they are not interested in the detail of what they are saying. A scrupulous writer, in every sentence that he writes, will ask himself at least four questions, thus: What am I trying to say? What words will express it? What image or idiom will make it clearer? Is this image fresh enough to have an effect? And he will probably ask himself two more: Could I put it more shortly? Have I said anything that is avoidably ugly? But you are not obliged to go to all this trouble. You can shirk it by simply throwing your mind open and letting the ready-made phrases come crowding in. They will construct your sentences for you—even think your thoughts for you, to a certain extent—and at need they will perform the important service of partially concealing your meaning even from yourself. It is at this point that the special connection between politics and the debasement of language becomes clear.

In our time it is broadly true that political writing is bad writing. Where it is not true, it will generally be found that the writer is some kind of rebel, expressing his private opinions and not a "party line." Orthodoxy, of whatever color, seems to demand a lifeless, imitative style. The political dialects to be found in pamphlets, leading articles, manifestoes, White Papers and the speeches of undersecretaries do, of course, vary from party to party, but they are all alike in that one almost never finds in them a fresh, vivid, homemade turn of speech. When one watches some tired hack on the platform mechanically repeating the familiar phrases—*bestial atrocities, iron heel, bloodstained tyranny, free peoples of the world, stand shoulder to shoulder*—one often has a curious feeling that one is not watching a live human being but some kind of dummy: a feeling which suddenly becomes stronger at moments when the light catches the speaker's spectacles and turns them into blank discs which seem to have no eyes behind them. And this is not altogether fanciful. A speaker who uses that kind of phraseology has gone some distance toward turning himself into a machine. The appropriate noises are coming out of his larynx, but his brain is not involved as it would be if he were choosing his words for himself. If the speech he is making is one that he is accustomed to make over and over again, he may be almost unconscious of what he is saying, as one is when one utters the responses in church. And this reduced state of consciousness, if not indispensable, is at any rate favorable to political conformity.

In our time, political speech and writing are largely the defense of the indefensible. Things like the continuance of British rule in India, the Russian purges and deportations, the dropping of the atom bombs on Japan, can indeed be defended, but only by arguments which are too

brutal for most people to face, and which do not square with the pro-
fessed aims of political parties. Thus political language has to consist
largely of euphemism, question-begging and sheer cloudy vagueness.
Defenseless villages are bombarded from the air, the inhabitants driven
out into the countryside, the cattle machine-gunned, the huts set on fire
with incendiary bullets: this is called *pacification*. Millions of peasants are
robbed of their farms and sent trudging along the roads with no more
than they can carry: this is called *transfer of population* or *rectification of
frontiers*. People are imprisoned for years without trial, or shot in the back
of the neck or sent to die of scurvy in Arctic lumber camps: this is called
elimination of unreliable elements. Such phraseology is needed if one
wants to name things without calling up mental pictures of them. Consider for instance some comfortable English professor defending Russian
totalitarianism. He cannot say outright, "I believe in killing off your opponents when you can get good results by doing so." Probably, therefore,
he will say something like this:

"While freely conceding that the Soviet régime exhibits certain features which the humanitarian may be inclined to deplore, we must, I
think, agree that a certain curtailment of the right to political opposition
is an unavoidable concomitant of transitional periods, and that the rigors
which the Russian people have been called upon to undergo have been
amply justified in the sphere of concrete achievement."

The inflated style is itself a kind of euphemism. A mass of Latin words
falls upon the facts like soft snow, blurring the outlines and covering up
all the details. The great enemy of clear language is insincerity. When
there is a gap between one's real and one's declared aims, one turns as
it were instinctively to long words and exhausted idioms, like a cuttlefish
squirting out ink. In our age there is no such thing as "keeping out of
politics." All issues are political issues, and politics itself is a mass of lies,
evasions, folly, hatred, and schizophrenia. When the general atmosphere
is bad, language must suffer. I should expect to find—this is a guess which
I have not sufficient knowledge to verify—that the German, Russian and
Italian languages have all deteriorated in the last ten or fifteen years, as
a result of dictatorship.

But if thought corrupts language, language can also corrupt thought.
A bad usage can spread by tradition and imitation, even among people
who should and do know better. The debased language that I have been
discussing is in some ways very convenient. Phrases like *a not unjustifiable
assumption, leaves much to be desired, would serve no good purpose, a
consideration which we should do well to bear in mind,* are a continuous
temptation, a packet of aspirins always at one's elbow. Look back through
this essay, and for certain you will find that I have again and again com-

mitted the very faults I am protesting against. By this morning's post I have received a pamphlet dealing with conditions in Germany. The author tells me that he "felt impelled" to write it. I open it at random, and here is almost the first sentence that I see: "[The Allies] have an opportunity not only of achieving a radical transformation of Germany's social and political structure in such a way as to avoid a nationalistic reaction in Germany itself, but at the same time of laying the foundations of a co-operative and unified Europe." You see, he "feels impelled" to write—feels, presumably, that he has something new to say—and yet his words, like cavalry horses answering the bugle, group themselves automatically into the familiar dreary pattern. This invasion of one's mind by ready-made phrases (*lay the foundations, achieve a radical transformation*) can only be prevented if one is constantly on guard against them, and every such phrase anaesthetizes a portion of one's brain.

I said earlier that the decadence of our language is probably curable. Those who deny this would argue, if they produced an argument at all, that language merely reflects existing social conditions, and that we cannot influence its development by any direct tinkering with words and constructions. So far as the general tone or spirit of a language goes, this may be true, but it is not true in detail. Silly words and expressions have often disappeared, not through any evolutionary process but owing to the conscious action of a minority. Two recent examples were *explore every avenue* and *leave no stone unturned,* which were killed by the jeers of a few journalists. There is a long list of flyblown metaphors which could similarly be got rid of if enough people would interest themselves in the job; and it should also be possible to laugh the *not un-* formation out of existence,* to reduce the amount of Latin and Greek in the average sentence, to drive out foreign phrases and strayed scientific words, and, in general, to make pretentiousness unfashionable. But all these are minor points. The defense of the English language implies more than this, and perhaps it is best to start by saying what it does *not* imply.

To begin with it has nothing to do with archaism, with the salvaging of obsolete words and turns of speech, or with the setting up of a "stand-ard English" which must never be departed from. On the contrary, it is especially concerned with the scrapping of every word or idiom which has outworn its usefulness. It has nothing to do with correct grammar and syntax, which are of no importance so long as one makes one's meaning clear, or with the avoidance of Americanisms, or with having what is called a "good prose style." On the other hand it is not concerned with fake simplicity and the attempt to make written English colloquial. Nor

---

* One can cure oneself of the *not un-* formation by memorizing this sentence: *A not unblack dog was chasing a not unsmall rabbit across a not ungreen field.*

does it even imply in every case preferring the Saxon word to the Latin one, though it does imply using the fewest and shortest words that will cover one's meaning. What is above all needed is to let the meaning choose the word, and not the other way about. In prose, the worst thing one can do with words is to surrender to them. When you think of a concrete object, you think wordlessly, and then, if you want to describe the thing you have been visualizing you probably hunt about till you find the exact words that seem to fit it. When you think of something abstract you are more inclined to use words from the start, and unless you make a conscious effort to prevent it, the existing dialect will come rushing in and do the job for you, at the expense of blurring or even changing your meaning. Probably it is better to put off using words as long as possible and get one's meaning as clear as one can through pictures or sensations. Afterward one can choose—not simply *accept*—the phrases that will best cover the meaning, and then switch round and decide what impression one's words are likely to make on another person. This last effort of the mind cuts out all stale or mixed images, all prefabricated phrases, needless repetitions, and humbug and vagueness generally. But one can often be in doubt about the effect of a word or a phrase, and one needs rules that one can rely on when instinct fails. I think the following rules will cover most cases:

(i) Never use a metaphor, simile, or other figure of speech which you are used to seeing in print.

(ii) Never use a long word where a short one will do.

(iii) If it is possible to cut a word out, always cut it out.

(iv) Never use the passive where you can use the active.

(v) Never use a foreign phrase, a scientific word, or a jargon word if you can think of an everyday English equivalent.

(vi) Break any of these rules sooner than say anything outright barbarous.

These rules sound elementary, and so they are, but they demand a deep change of attitude in anyone who has grown used to writing in the style now fashionable. One could keep all of them and still write bad English, but one could not write the kind of stuff that I quoted in those five specimens at the beginning of this article.

I have not here been considering the literary use of language, but merely language as an instrument for expressing and not for concealing or preventing thought. Stuart Chase and others have come near to claiming that all abstract words are meaningless, and have used this as a pretext for advocating a kind of political quietism. Since you don't know what Fascism is, how can you struggle against Fascism? One need not swallow such absurdities as this, but one ought to recognize that the present political chaos is connected with the decay of language, and that one can probably bring about some improvement by starting at the verbal end. If you simplify your English, you are freed from the worst follies of orthodoxy. You cannot speak any of the necessary dialects, and when you make a stupid remark its stupidity will be obvious, even to yourself. Political language—and with variations this is true of all political parties, from Conservatives to Anarchists—is designed to make lies sound truthful and murder respectable, and to give an appearance of solidity to pure wind. One cannot change this all in a moment, but one can at least change one's own habits, and from time to time one can even, if one jeers loudly enough, send some worn-out and useless phrase—some *jackboot, Achilles' heel, hotbed, melting pot, acid test, veritable inferno,* or other lump of verbal refuse—into the dustbin where it belongs.

1946

GEOFFREY MOORE

American Prose Today

> It is a natural, simple, and unaffected speech that I love, so written as it is spoken, and such upon the paper as it is in the mouth, a pithy, sinewy, full, strong, compendious and material speech, not so delicate and affected as vehement and piercing. . . .   FLORIO's *Montaigne*

"We have really everything in common with America—except, of course, the language." Oscar Wilde's witticism still has some truth, although, like mother-of-pearl, it changes colour according to the angle of view. It is true that some British readers have, or pretend to have, difficulty with some American writing. Different terms for the same thing can sometimes be puzzling; unfamiliar idioms, reference to objects or institutions unknown in England, and a slicker, wilder sense of humour even more so. Fashionables, particularly literary fashionables, affect remarks like "I couldn't quite follow all the jokes—that peculiar dialect, is it *Bronx?*" (see G. S. Fraser, "The Aesthete and the Sensationalist," *Partisan Review*, April, 1955). And there are even a dogged few of the Old Guard who cry "Beaver!" whenever they recognise an Americanism, and send a fiery letter to their favourite fourpenny. However, the majority of the English are by now hopelessly lost. It's not merely that "O.K." is widely used among the working-class and lower-middle-class and that errand boys and young clerks say "I don't get you" and "I haven't seen him in years." But —oh, more horrible still—even our distinguished worthies use American words and phrases, and in their written style, moreover. H. W. Horwill once made a list, including "proposition," "up against" (it), "disgruntled," and "out to" (increase efficiency) which had been used by such unimpeachably British personages as Sir Winston Churchill, the Archbishop of York, Sir Michael Sadler, and Sir William Holdsworth. In fact, the process has gone so far that even those purists who would rather die than be discovered committing an Americanism unconsciously use words of American origin in normal usage. Leafing through a dictionary of American English, one finds, on almost every page, words which are now commonly accepted in England as English—"in the neighbourhood of" (say,

From *New World Writing*, No. 8. Reprinted by permission of the author.

a million pounds), "landslide" (for the English "landslip"), "to take a cut" (in wages). Even "boarding-house," "business man," "graveyard," "law-abiding," "overcoat," and "telegram" are American importations; and there are a great many more, some of them now abandoned in their country of origin.

The influence of American usages, most of them new, but some from an English older than that now current in Britain, may be put to detailed proof by reference to the dictionary of Sir William Craigie and Professor Hulbert and that of Professor M. M. Mathews, and, among numerous others books, to H. L. Mencken's cocksure but massively documented *The American Language* and its *Supplements*. But most readers would, I think, be willing to accept, without proof, the statement that, in certain respects, American English has a dynamic which British English no longer possesses. It can be found in that popular and picturesque style common to detective stories and Hollywood movies (so popular in fact that English writers like Peter Cheyney and James Hadley Chase have worked hard to supply a pastiche of it). It can be found in the vivid American phrases of each new generation, from "what makes him tick" and "to blow one's top" to "out of this world" and "strictly from hunger" (when I was at school it was "Sez you")—embarrassing clichés already, of course, but nonetheless vivid. It can be found more pervasively, however, in less sensational words which, for over a hundred and fifty years, have been forcing their way into general Anglo-American usage—words like "belittle," "demoralizing," and "lengthy."

But, say we accept these facts, what do they tell us? Merely that a great new nation, in an expanding and optimistic frame of mind, has been striking out in all directions, coining new words and phrases, and using accepted ones in new contexts. It is, after all, only what we might have expected. What is more interesting is to inquire whether this great new nation has by now developed a distinctive prose, expressive of its spirit. We do not quarrel these days about whether there is not an American literature. There plainly is, and we can point to its various aspects and analyse, within reason, its characteristics. But is there such a thing as an American prose? I refer here to nonfiction, the prose of exposition, the ordinary literary means of communication.

The sophist might answer: Yes, American prose is prose written by Americans. But, we persist: Is it different from English prose, and, if so, how? Or, alternatively: Is there "an American style"? The answer might be that there are a number of American styles and that they owe their nature to the circumstances of American development. Not merely racial, or religious, or social differences, but, as Mr. Wallace Stevens once said, physical ones too, have made the attitude of the people different, and the attitude of a people is reflected in its prose. Add to this the spirit which founded the United States, the early struggles, the theocratic art-banishing society of New England, the early establishment of a unique kind of democracy, the distrust of aristocratic virtues (elegance, propriety, mannered grace, intellect) and the acceptance of brotherhood-become-chumminess, and you have a taste of the brew which might be expected to make American prose different from British. From the first, the American moved about a lot and so, despite the difference in accent between, say, South Carolina and New Hampshire, usage was sufficiently standard that he could be understood in any part of the country. In England, however, as Mr. Harold Whitehall has pointed out, the inhabitants of, for example, Howden in Yorkshire used to find it very difficult to under-stand the inhabitants of Dewsbury, forty miles away. And so, largely on the basis of aristocratic speech, Britain developed a *lingua franca*, Re-ceived Standard English, the rules of which could be laid down and accepted as gospel. H. W. Fowler could write a *Modern English Usage,* but no American ever either dared to write, or felt the necessity of writ-ing, a *Modern American Usage.* Mr. Horwill, an Englishman, did, of course, produce one, but that was for the aid of the British. However, there seems, by this time, to have developed a generally accepted and, as it were, legitimate body of American usage which can be called Stand-ard without fear of offending Americans' own susceptibilities. At least I take it to be so and, with this in mind, I should like to examine various examples of modern "expositional" American prose in an effort to dis-cover whether they have the "independence and vigour" which, in 1954, *The Times Literary Supplement* found so marked in American creative writing. Although this will involve commenting on usage, I do not pro-pose to single out American usages which are now perfectly acceptable in Britain.

POLITICAL PROSE

My purpose was to sketch the genesis and set in some crude historical perspective the present troubled world scene, and then to attempt to defrost a tiny segment of the opaque window through which we see others and others see us—and to do it briefly, having listened to many lectures myself!

This is from the foreword to Adlai Stevenson's *Call to Greatness.* Two things are immediately noticeable: first, the modest tone, and, second, the use of an original figure of speech which has been drawn naturally and unaffectedly from American experience. Almost all Americans, except those who live in the extreme Southern states, find it necessary at some time during the winter to "defrost," either manually or by aid of a device built into their cars, a driving window which has been made opaque by frost or frozen snow. The style might be described as "literary" (e.g., "genesis," "present troubled world scene"), yet it gives an impression of ease. It has the ring of sincerity and makes us feel that we can trust a man who is at once so unpretentious and yet so quietly convinced that he can clarify our vision of world affairs.

Having come to the above conclusion about this passage, I was surprised, on re-reading it, to find that it is actually ungrammatical. I say "surprised" since, as a teacher, my eye is, if anything over-alert to such things. The fault is in the first line, in which, to make grammatical sense, there should be an "of" after "genesis." It gives a very awkward ring to the sentence, however, and the writer, being American, was led to reject it. An Englishman would probably either have put it in or re-worded the sentence. It is, I think, a good example of how even the most educated and highly literate of Americans have, when they feel like it, a cavalier attitude toward the niceties of grammar. I have noticed that in the *non solum, sed etiam* construction, for example, Americans rarely put in the "also."

HISTORICAL PROSE

(a) *As the sectional tension increased, the sense of irrepressible differences, long buried in the national consciousness, began to burst into the clear. The growing pressure on the North had finally persuaded many Northerners that the slavery system embodied a fundamental threat to free society.*

(b) *August gave way to September, September to October, and the clamor grew increasingly furious. Jackson men paraded the streets in the glare of torches, singing campaign songs, carrying hickory poles, gathering around huge bonfires blazing high into the night.*

These two extracts are both from Arthur M. Schlesinger, Jr.'s *The Age of Jackson*. Together they make a point better than one alone, and that point is that the methods and the vocabulary of the journalist have invaded the writing of history. (cf., *Time*, April 22, 1955, "Warm in the April sunshine, London's upper-crust horseplayers crowded the club enclosure at Kempton Park Race Track. Peeresses in Dior tweeds appraised each other. . . ." etc.) The tone is different. *Time's* is not merely colourful; it is impertinent. Mr. Schlesinger is not writing sensationally, he is merely trying to "bring the scene to life." Although he is in no sense perverting the facts, he is nonetheless "popularising" history. And since he is not merely a famous historian, but also an academic one, approved of academically, the method is worth remarking on. It is not entirely new. Strachey was, of course, a populariser and, so to pick an example from a number of others, was Philip Guedalla; but the texture of these English writers was finer grained, more glittering. Mr. Schlesinger's style, although it is not bad, is without flair, bouncy yet workaday ("as sectional tension increased," "embodied a fundamental threat"), with an occasional, rather disconcerting vernacular phrase (e.g., "into the clear"). It is the style of a man who has not thought much about language. The four parts of Mr. Schlesinger's first sentence create four different effects. The first gives us the sense of *pulling*, the second of energy contained under *pressure*, like steam in a kettle, the third *buries* this steam kettle, the fourth allows it to "burst into the clear" which seems superficially to fit with the idea of "irrepressible differences," but is vaguely disconcerting until we realize that the stress is on "into the clear," which is a hunting term. There is, in other words, a confusion of different kinds of language. This is for me a most interesting discovery, since I did not pick Mr. Schlesinger invidiously, but in a spirit of enquiry, knowing him to be one of the most outstanding of the younger American historians.

CRITICAL PROSE

(a) *Such an art when it pretends to measure life is essentially vicarious; it is a substitute for something that never was—like a tin soldier, or Peter Pan. It has all the flourish of life and every sentimental sincerity. Taken for what it is, it is charming and even instructive. Taken solemnly, as it is meant to be, the distortion by which it exists is too much for it, and it seems a kind of baby-talk.*

(b) *. . . aesthetic value has been defined as conformity to or expression of a culture. This is the side of formism most prevalent today. A work of art has aesthetic value in proportion as it gives expression to its age. This definition tends to run over into a culture relativism very congenial to contemporary art historians, and in marked contrast to the universality of aesthetic values emphasized in the first formulation of aesthetic value for formism above as representation of the universal.*

(c) *There is nothing to do different from what we already do: if poets write poems and readers read them, each as best they can—if they try to live not as soldiers or voters or intellectuals or economic men, but as human beings—they are doing all that can be done. But to expect them (by, say, reciting one-syllable poems over the radio) to bring back that Yesterday in which people stood on chairs to look at Lord Tennyson, is to believe that General Motors can bring back "the tradition of craftsmanship" by giving, as it does, prizes to Boy Scouts for their scale-models of Napoleonic coaches; to believe that the manners of the past can be restored by encouraging country-people to say*

Grüss Gott *or* Howdy, stranger *to the tourists they meet along summer lanes.*

The first extract is from R. P. Blackmur's essay on the verse of E. E. Cummings in *The Double Agent;* the second is from Stephen C. Pepper's *The Basis of Criticism in the Arts;* and the third from Randall Jarrell's *Poetry and the Age.* The field of criticism in the United States is so rich that I should have preferred to take at least two or three more examples —from Edmund Wilson, say, or Van Wyck Brooks, or the late F. O. Matthiessen. However, these three samples do at least reveal three important aspects of American criticism. The second passage is of the kind which is so often the target for British writers—jargon criticism. I could have quoted more extreme examples (from Kenneth Burke, for instance) for there is a great deal of this kind of thing, particularly in academic or semi-academic writing, of which there is so much more in the United States than anywhere else. I think of it sometimes as a Germanic derivation. "The side of formism," "cultural relativism," and the garbled mumble of the end of the final sentence—this is the antithesis of clarity. Perhaps it is the result of Coleridge's example; he learnt from Germany too. Perhaps it is the overseriousness and earnestness of the American commentator. Perhaps it is a little of the unconscious desire to blind the vulgar with science. Perhaps it is an attempt to order a frighteningly vast world of thought and feeling. Perhaps it is—as Marius Bewley suggested of Kenneth Burke—that these "methodological" critics have developed their jargon and their unreadable style in order to isolate them "against the shock of the work of art itself." But, whatever the reason, the effect is both exasperating and perturbing.

The Blackmur passage, on the other hand, is a good illustration of what we mean when we say that someone's writing "has style." The language is both elegant and precise, the manner judicious but not portentous, flavored by just the right amount of everyday reference ("tin soldier, or Peter Pan" and "baby-talk"). It is the writing of an acute sensibility. We cannot help feeling the force of the conviction behind the sentiments, not only because of what they say but because of the manner of their expression. The language is faintly Jamesian ("all the flourish of life and every sentimental sincerity"). The final effect is of a man who respects literature too much to make it merely a stamping-ground for pseudo-scientific theories.

Mr. Jarrell, in his conversational ease, his common sense and his liveliness, is representative of the younger generation of American critics. He will not allow his individual perception and spirit to be subdued by the acceptances of academic style and theory. His is a style of wit and irony, which can sometimes approach the self-consciously brilliant but is anchored to earth (and this is why it is so effective for most readers) by the essential rightness of the sentiments. The style is more noticeably idiosyncratic than Mr. Blackmur's. It is perceptive, impressionistic, and opinionated. But in the last resort it obtains its effect by laying the cards on the table and saying, as it were, "Now, after all. . . ." Only a man with a wide cultural background and a sureness of judgement based on good taste can afford to do this. Finally, the style achieves a vividness and concreteness by reference to manners and institutions well known in American life.

HUMOROUS PROSE

(a) *I have a lot of other notes jotted down about why I hate women, but I seem to have lost them all, except one. That one is to the effect that I hate women because, while they never lose old snapshots or anything of that sort, they invariably lose one glove. I believe that I have never gone anywhere with any women in my whole life who did not lose one glove. I have searched for single gloves under tables in crowded restaurants and under the feet of people in darkened movie theatres. I have spent some part of every day or night hunting for a woman's glove. If there were no other reason in the world for hating women, that one would be enough. In fact, you can leave all the others out.*

(b) *I first heard pure Slurvian fluently spoken by a co-worker of mine who told me that his closest friend was a man named Hard (Howard). Hard was once in an automobile accident, his car, unfortunately, cliding with another, causing Hard's wife, Dorthy, who was with him, to claps. Dorthy didn't have much stamina but was a sweet women—sweet as surp.*

The first passage is from James Thurber's *Let Your Mind Alone!*, the second is from John Davenport's "Slurvian Self-Taught." They seem to me to show two sides of American humour, both driving perhaps from the frontier tradition. Despite its urbanity, the Thurber piece is in the tradition of Mark Twain, the father of the American natural style and one of the first to use the device of exaggeration (the "tall tale") successfully as a literary mode. As Mark Twain in his descriptive passages and essays used the simple, common "conversational" style and idiom of his day, so Mr. Thurber uses the natural "conversational" style of our day. I perhaps ought to explain what I mean by "conversational." By this I understand the vernacular of the ordinary educated person translated into literature (notice the direct "I," and "in my whole life"). While, therefore, it is "a conversational style," it is not exactly as it would be in spontaneous speech. "Invariably," for example, and "I have" would sound a little mannered if actually spoken by one friend to another. Actual speech usage would be too clumsy for a writer whose effects are as subtly obtained as Mr. Thurber's. The humour, which I find irresistible, arises from exaggerating a fairly common situation. The writer is half-serious, half-joking, and the hit-on-the-funny-bone effect is helped by the direct and simple language, and by the masterly sense of timing. The last sentence is both a parting shot and an ending which gathers up the whole of the essay.

The second extract is deadpan, and achieves its effect by being written as if it were a sort of anecdotal reminiscence by a professional investigator of linguistics. This level is allowed to merge into the level of overt humour, as in the last sentence of the passage quoted. It could not, I feel, have been written by anyone but an American, because no one but an American could have the knowledge of and feeling for the vernacular (slurred or otherwise) which this writer displays. The sense of timing which both writers exploit so magnificently seem to be a part of the American temperament (to ask why arouses some interesting anthropological and sociological speculations). It is displayed outside literature by such comedians as Jack Benny and Fred Allen. The former, particularly, builds easily on the natural cadences of American speech, in which there runs a faint but constant undercurrent of humour.

JOURNALISTIC PROSE. In a democratic country, in which almost everyone can read and in which everyone is supposed to have equal opportunities for education, or for anything else, one might expect to find a "typical" or "representative" American style, in the kind of publication which is read by the majority. According to figures taken from the polls of the Princeton Institute of Public Opinion and Mr. J. K. Wood's *Magazines of the United States,* although only approximately 20 per cent of Americans read books at all, 83 per cent regularly read newspapers and magazines.

1. NEWSPAPERS

(a) *Secretary of Agriculture Ezra Taft Benson has called on western Kansas farmers to begin a day of "prayer and supplication to ask God in heaven to send rain." Well, that's one way of stopping the good Kansas dirt from blowing over to Russia. It's certainly not the best way. The secretary has made a tour; he's impressed. But first and foremost the secretary is a politician, not a conservationist. It will take a little more than politics to keep that western Kansas dirt on the ground.*

This passage from a student newspaper editorial seems clear and direct —"conversational," "natural," in fact, yet not altogether or ingenuously so. The tone is cocky. "Secretary of Agriculture Ezra Taft Benson" is borrowed from *Time's* style, which was presumably invented to give the impression that everybody's time, including *Time's*, was limited. Yet the saving of one three-letter word and two commas is not worth the ungracefulness of the usage. One feels that the writer is breathing down one's neck. A cliché slips in ("first and foremost"). "Impressed" gives one a feeling of inadequately describing Mr. Benson's possible reactions. Noticeable American usages are "called on," which has a Town Meeting ring, and "politician," which in England means someone in politics but in the United States is a bad word.

> (b) *Reed's number one problem is working capital. So in order to get money for equipment and to meet his payroll until he gets to rolling, he is incorporating the business and plans to sell stock. The telephone switchboard will be installed soon and within the next few weeks he plans to have a grand opening.*

This is from an article in the *St. Louis Post-Dispatch,* and is sub-colloquial. It reads like a cross between the vernacular and the language of radio copy-writers—more the latter. Few in conversation talk about their "number one" problem, but writers of "commercials" do. "Meet his payroll" and "get to rolling" are examples of those vivid coinages which arise out of a forceful expanding society in which the tone of general prose is set by the majority, who have no ear for subtlety of language. They are designed to give an impressionistic picture to people whose range of communication, understanding, and imagination is narrow. This kind of prose does not work through the intelligence but through the emotions. The repetition of "get" and "plan" emphasizes the narrowness of the vocabulary. Within its limits it is a most effective kind of communication, and sufficiently hard-punching to penetrate the dullest mind capable of reading words on a page. It is an example of American pragmatism. It is probably inevitable in a democratic society in which the mass media have superseded the printed page as the chief means of communication. It reflects the speech and the habits of mind of the majority of people and it would be sentimental, ineffectual, and entirely unrealistic (not to say reactionary) for one to regret that this particular form of speech ever invaded prose. But one does.

> (c) *The Pakistan grain storage contract presents a flagrant case of official negligence and mismanagement. Any monkey business with government contracts can and should be a matter of public concern. So we have this relatively small item of grain elevators grown into a national story.*
>
> (d) *For the present, and with all due consideration of both Soviet*

aims and motivations, it appears as if the Soviets are prepared to give ground at least in part and at least at one point—Austria. After stalling and sabotaging the Austrian treaty in more than 260 treaty meetings stretching over nearly a decade, they have now reached agreement with Austria on the terms of liberation which, barring new Soviet demands, the West is likely to accept.

These two passages are from editorials, the first in the *Kansas City Star* for May 4, 1955, the second from *The New York Times* for May 2, 1955. The most noticeable thing about the first is the way in which it combines an elevated and judicious style with colloquialisms. "Presents a flagrant case" in the first passage consorts oddly with "monkey business." The grave "can and should be a matter of public concern" is immediately followed by the colloquial "So we have this . . . ," as one might say, to a friend, "So we have this fellow (or car, or problem) on our hands." This lack of taste, of consistency of tone, of feeling for what is appropriate in the context may arise from the comparative lack of literary training in American, particularly Middle Western, schools. *The New York Times* passage is a much better piece of writing and much more of a piece. It is much less "literary" than a leader in the London *Times* would be, but more pompous. To some extent, "stalling," which is vivid and vernacular, conflicts with the high editorial style ("all due consideration").

2. MAGAZINES

(a) *The only comment on the American economy that can be made with perfect assurance is that nobody really understands it. On the whole, this is a good thing. An economy capable of being thoroughly understood would probably prove treacherous. Of course, there are always a few professionals who like to believe that they understand the American economy, and these people turn up at Congressional hearings to explain why the market acts the way it does, but it is quite obvious that they are just groping their way along, the same as everybody else.*

This is from the editorial page of *The New Yorker* entitled "Talk of the Town," the nearest thing to the essay one can find in the United States today. It is highly intelligent and professionally polished, yet intimate and engaging in its manner. The man who wrote this passage did have an ear, and he did have taste. The short second sentence picks up an echo both of the New York Yiddish colloquialism "This is a good thing?" and the British (*1066 and All That*) "a Good Thing," and yet is simply effective without these probably unintended connotations. The third sentence is disarming. It is as sensitively balanced as a line of verse. "Treacherous" strikes one as being just the right word; no other will do. It is meaningful, connotative, and funny, yet not fancy. "Of course," "these people," and "the same as everybody else" keep the level down, an important thing in a milieu in which ceremony or over-refinement are quickly smelled out. This kind of prose mirrors the most attractive kind of American personality, that of a man who is polite but not deferential, droll, easy in manner, and responsive.

> (b) *Barsov went. At his own request, the U.S. authorities flew him to Linz. "Are you sure you want to go back?" they asked him at the end. He was.*
>
> *The Soviets had a propaganda bonanza in Barsov; they pointed to him as an example of what happens to those who desert the Soviets and trust the West.*

This quotation from an article in the *Reader's Digest* is an example of "bright" snappy journalism. The clipped style ("Barsov went," "He was.") probably owes something to the Walter Winchell manner of radio reporting. The American slang word "bonanza" (a rich strike) is a good choice since it adds, like a raccoon's tail to a streamlined car, a human touch to prose which is in danger of becoming cold through its professional terseness. This prose is tailored for "modern people" who, after a day in the office or the factory, believe that the best way to relax is by not mentally taxing themselves. It has, therefore, a "cat on the mat" simplicity and clarity, otherwise a number of readers (who knows how many?) would consider themselves too tired even to try to grasp its import. This kind of prose must also have a reasonable quota of direct speech and be sharply paragraphed, for unrelieved indirect speech and normal paragraphing would be too dull and difficult to lure the fickle attention of the new kind of reader. Such devices are, of course, used in other publications too, both inside and outside the United States. In Britain, for example, the *Daily Express*, which is much influenced by the fashions of the United States, is an extreme example of bright journalism.

Mention of the *Reader's Digest* brings up the matter of condensing and rewriting which is practiced in a much more open, thoroughgoing, and ruthless way in the United States than anywhere else, mainly in the interests of efficient marketing. Morally, the practice is highly questionable, but I will confine myself to its effect on prose in magazines. It is said that the *Reader's Digest* not only condenses articles and novels already published, but that to a considerable extent it commissions articles, has them rewritten to exactly the right style and length, and then, by agreement, places them in selected magazines, so that it will seem in any given month that there is a choice from the nation's periodicals. In the case of *The New Yorker*, a magazine of a different breed, I have also often heard the complaint that articles and even stories pass through the editorial mill to such an extent that some are completely rewritten. How much this is true I have no way of telling since the workings of *The New Yorker* are clothed in comparative mystery. I judge that it is probably exaggerated, owing to the nature of the contributors, for one thing. Where an ordinary working journalist might have few misgivings about having his prose tampered with, the respected critics and writers whose work appears in *The New Yorker* might be expected to have more to say. At any rate, there is a noticeable difference, as might be expected, between the style of a book-piece by Anthony West, or Edmund Wilson, and an article on television by Philip Hamburger, or between a short story by Eudora Welty and one by John Cheever. Whatever editing there is is probably not only less extreme but different in kind from that of the *Reader's Digest. Reader's Digest* prose is excellent up to a point—clear, uninvolved and pithy; but it is no vehicle for conveying ideas of any subtlety. Nuances of language it will not bear; that is not its purpose. Subtle, imaginative language and original figures of speech—if they are ever present in the contributions—must be smoothed into prose which can be easily grasped by the meanest intelligence. The magazine must be an efficient machine, and it is. But a steady diet of its prose has the same effect on the mind as a steady diet of pap on the teeth. *The New Yorker*, on the other hand, communicates at a level of intelligence and imagination which is probably higher than that of any other general magazine written in English. Both the *Reader's Digest* and *The New Yorker* probably have an ideal reader in mind, but they are very different kinds of people. The *Reader's Digest* aims at the Everyman of the Twentieth Century, the lowest common denominator of reader. Given that purpose the *Reader's Digest* editors do an extremely efficient job. Considering the editorial policy of maximum human interest and maximum optimism, the success with which the editors manipulate their material this side of sentimentality is extraordinary. What is important in this comparison, however, is, I believe, the difference in intention. The editors of the *Reader's Digest* seem, like the writers for *Time*, to be working in a region below their own natural range. The editors of *The New Yorker*, on the other hand, seem to be aiming at men and women like themselves. It is this, I imagine, which is responsible for the difference in tone, depths, and degree of idiosyncrasy between the prose of the two magazines.

> (c) *The speaker rustled his notes, clinked a pocketful of keys and stared at the ceiling while he fumbled for words. Then his wife's voice cut through the jangle: "Put your keys down, honey." Meekly, irascible*

*Columnist Westbrook Pegler obeyed. For once the foaming temper was
in check. Mellow with memory, onetime Sportswriter Pegler had turned
out for the Tucson, Ariz. Press Club dinner, greeting the new baseball
season.*

   Peg. . . .

This passage is, of course, from *Time* (April 11, 1955). The formula
is familiar and highly successful: first, the dramatic opening, the deliberate
holding back of the name. Who can this Milquetoast be? To our surprise,
it is none other than irascible Columnist Westbrook Pegler, who, having
been introduced in a cloud of unknowing, soon becomes, in the democratic fashion, our friend, "Peg." This richly staged introduction, as
designing as an advertiser's banquet, achieves its purpose admirably,
again within the imaginative scope and vocabulary of the lowest common
denominator of readers, although the level is, one suspects, rather higher
than that of the *Reader's Digest*. It is the most lavish example so far of
the presentation of factual material in an emotional way. It was prophesied
by Tocqueville as a concomitant of the Age of Democracy. Everyone can
read, but few can or want to read properly. Even to say "properly" is
suspect in this time of the triumph of the mindless. Must democracy
inevitably lead to the relaxing of standards and pandering to increasingly
jaded palates? It is a nice question. The "average reader" cannot be
expected to use his brain because he wants "relaxation" after his day's
work, or because he has no time to spare, or because he wasn't taught
properly in High School. So the writers of *Time* labour (and they probably have some fun doing it, too) to present him with ever more brightly
written and attractively presented material. If they did not, their public
would go off and read *Newsweek*, no doubt.

ADVERTISING PROSE

   (a) *Yes, only Viceroy has this filter composed of 20,000 tiny filter
   traps. You cannot obtain the same filtering action in any other cigarette. . . . That's why more college men and women smoke Viceroys
   than any other filter cigarette. . . .*

This passage, taken from an advertisement by the makers of Viceroy
cigarettes in a student newspaper, is typical of nationwide current advertising technique for cigarettes, and of the kind of prose used in such
advertisements.

   The copywriters have apparently now reached their nadir, for they
are using the same formula in print as on the radio. Perhaps this is significant in terms of the relationship of speech to literature in the United

States, but I doubt it. The method is one of insidious hammering, as if with a little rubber hammer which the torturer wields tirelessly, so that, in the end, one's whole body is in tune with the nagging rhythmic blows. Four (at least four) things are constant: first, the meaningless and tiresome "yes," worn like a charm to scare away the advertising man's bogey (lack of smoothness, lack of a "friendly" yet authoritative, selling ring); second, the appeal to "science"; third, the "You cannot . . . in *any other cigarette*" (which varies in some cases to "No other cigarette made . . . etc.); and, fourth, the repetition on the same, though slightly modulated note ("That's why . . . than any other filter smoke"). Writers on the traditional ballad tell us that their anonymous authors used the device of "incremental repetition" in order that a rhythmic, memorable pattern might be retained in the minds of an audience which lived in an oral tradition. Here is incremental repetition today, serving other ends in another society.

WHY SWELTER? JUST A TWIST OF THE WRIST CHANGES
HOT MISERY . . . TO COOL COMFORT!
LIVE AND WORK IN G-E "COMFORT-CONDITIONED AIR"!

Simply dial out swelter with this great new General Electric Room Air Conditioner! You can sleep dry and cool tonight in G-E "Comfort-Conditioned Air"—air that's always cool, dry and filtered to reduce dust, dirt and pollen.

WHY NOT CALL ON YOUR GENERAL ELECTRIC DEALER NOW?

The most noticeable thing about this passage, which is taken from an advertisement in *Life*, is its colourful and highly sensory use of language. This, coupled with the exclamatory style, creates an effect of pseudo-momentousness. Nothing more, possibly, in the way of emotive effect, could have been crammed into the headline. The advertising copywriters are, as I believe Mr. Hayakawa once pointed out, the folk-poets of modern commercial civilisation. They know all the tricks of language that a poet or a story writer knows, but they put them to the service, not of art, but of commercial persuasion. As Tocqueville said, "Democracy not only infuses a taste for letters among the trading classes, but introduces a trading spirit into literature." The writer of this copy ("Just a Twist of the Wrist") had an ear for the fundamental rhythms of the English language, a language which naturally and easily falls into patterns of rhyme, alliteration and onomatopoeia. These are patterns which can be found as easily in literature as in ordinary speech, from "A faire felde ful of folke / Fonde I there bytwene," of William Langland to "The breezes blew, the white foam flew, / The furrow follow'd free" of Coleridge, from Cockney rhyming slang to the "What's cookin', good-lookin'" of the American high school boy.

"Dial it out" is another example of verbal ingenuity devoted to the end of persuading. The effect is concentrated and dramatic. One can see oneself just dialling away "swelter," (i.e. the state of sweltering) by that "twist of the wrist." The use of "swelter" here, incidentally, is an interesting illustration of the extreme grammatical flexibility of the English language in communicating sensations, and also of the streamlining tendency of American English.

Another interesting convention is "Comfort-Conditioned Air." Perhaps the copywriter, like Fleming with his moulds, made the discovery by sheer accident. At any rate, it seems to be a reversal of the familiar "Air-Conditioned Comfort." And the wonder of it is that it means something. The poet, fiddling with words, struck rich ore (a bonanza). The effect of it was so heady that when he came to compose the whole line he made the very air, now "cool, dry and filtered," the property of General Electric. What kind of air have you there, Mr. Jones? I have G.E. Comfort-Conditioned Air in here, Mr. Smith.

One last point calls for mention and that is the use of "great," which, second to "beautiful," seems to be the most overworked word in the English language. If this air-conditioner is "great," what then was the invention of the aeroplane or the propounding of the Theory of Relativity?

I trust that my own tone, in commenting on these examples, has not at times seemed like those of the Reverend John Witherspoon. The Reverend John's is mild in comparison with later British commentators who were apt to report on the misuse of language in the United States with shouts of glee, thus arousing the animosity and eventually the triumphant counter-cries of H. L. Mencken. A pre-Revolutionary (immigrant) American, the Reverend John hoped for a specifically American style, to be watched over by some "center of learning and politeness." In the meantime he thought it his duty to point out the various misuses of the English language in America, which he listed under the headings of: (1) Americanisms, (2) vulgarisms in England and America, (3) vulgarisms in America alone, (4) local phrases or terms, (5) common blunders arising from ignorance, (6) cant phrases, (7) personal blunders, and (8) technical terms introduced into the language.

On subjects like America and Prose one's mind cannot be made a blank. One has impressions, and my impression, before examining the samples I have chosen, was that in spite of some obvious examples of excessive rhetoric, of ineptness in handling words, of crudeness, of a peculiarly American kind of inflation, American prose as a whole had more naturalness than the English and at its best a transparent sincerity and simplicity worthy of American ideals. I did not, however, choose my quotations to prove this point. I threw my net as wide as I could, examined the pieces as objectively as possible, and relied on my findings to provide me with some conclusions which might or might not prove what I had previously accepted.

I find, on the whole, that my preconceptions are borne out only in so far as the best topical commentary, the best political writing, the best criticism and, above all, the best humorous writing is concerned. Elsewhere, there are great variations. Of course, the reader might object that he could have chosen a whole set of other samples which would alter the emphasis, or alternatively, that the quotations were far too short for judgment. This might be true, but short of conducting a statistical survey I do not see what else could be done. Perhaps, before our time runs out, one of the great Foundations will have provided funds for such an enterprise. But since language cannot be gauged like physical reactions, and the value of the comments depends on the taste of the investigator, it would be a difficult task. In the meantime, and in the light of my own crude sampling, I offer, diffidently, some general conclusions.

In the first place, it seems to me that American "expositional prose" is much weaker than American creative prose. Only in the case of people of acute sensibility, at the highest level, do we find a kind of prose which, by its tasteful natural diction, its use of figures drawn from American life, and its ease of manner can be held up as an example of the use of English which is both good and distinctively American. The American temperament seems better fitted to explore the creative possibilities of language, and one can find all kinds of examples to support this from the ebullience but relative crudeness of Thomas Wolfe to the fine-grained yet almost overwhelmingly rhetorical "immediacy" of William Faulkner. In the hands of the modern American short story writer, particularly, American prose is both beautiful and exciting to read. Life leaps from the page: sights, colours, smells, all the multifarious aspects of common and uncommon human existence make an impact which British creative prose rarely achieves. But the cultural climate of the United States in the 20th century has apparently not been conducive to the development of a widespread and distinctively American instrument for conveying facts, ideas, and comment at the general level. Feelings and emotions get in the way, for one thing. There is too commonly an inability to express a logical sequence of thought with "ease, grace, precision," what I have called "having no ear" for the English language. One reason for this lies, I am sure, in the deep-seated American feeling that "style" is something ornamental, part of a way of life that is variously called "British" or "aristocratic." It does not matter that the reaction, which is an emotional one, is understandable. What matters is that it is bad for American prose. To quote Sir Arthur Quiller-Couch again:

> The editor of a mining paper in Denver, U.S.A., boldly the other day laid down this law, that niceties of language were mere "frills": all a man needed was "to get there," that is, to say what he wished in his own way. But just here . . . lies the mischief. You will not get there by hammering away on your own untutored impulse. You must first be your own reader, chiselling out the thought definitely for yourself: and, after that, must carve out the intaglio more sharply and neatly, if you would impress its image accurately upon the wax of other men's minds.

But there is another reason, I believe, for the comparative lack of literary ability in all but the exceptional in the United States and this lies in the tendency to "educate for life" and to relegate literature to an inferior place. A questionnaire sent out in 1949 for *Harper's Magazine* by Norman Lewis revealed what Mr. Lewis called a "linguistic liberalism" among those people in the United States who "use the English language as a direct means of earning a livelihood." This meant accepting such expressions as "His work is different *than* mine," "I encountered *less* difficulties than I had expected" (attributed to Mr. Arthur Schlesinger, Jr.), and "The reason I'm worried is *because* I think she's ill." If we substitute "sloppy English" for "linguistic liberalism" we are, I think, nearer the mark. Yet, as against ninety-three American College Professors of English who rejected the first expression, there were sixty-two who accepted it as worthy of currency in educated speech. Forty-nine out of the one hundred and fifty-five even accepted the barbarous second example, and the astounding total of eighty-nine out of one hundred and fifty-five the third. This perhaps partly explains why college students' essays are such examples of bad prose. But what is far more perturbing than uneducated usage in educated exposition is the sheer muddle of the language, the lack of an ability, in the college group, to express ideas lucidly and coherently. Yet even those who seem on the page to be semi-literate morons can make good sense when they speak, be ready in comment, even advance ideas. One's conclusion cannot but be that American conditions, educational and otherwise, have militated against clear and graceful literary expression. Yet Abraham Lincoln, that self-educated man, could express himself simply, cogently, and with style. Could he have learnt it had he grown up in America today? Where would he find models? Well, he could find them for one thing in Mr. Stevenson's prose, or Mr. Thurber's. He could read *The New Yorker*, or the *Atlantic*, or *Harper's*. The compilers of college textbooks of exposition certainly seem to strive to put good examples of prose before their readers. One wonders what the 40 per cent of college professors of English who say "His work is different *than* mine" do with them. Point out their queer usage perhaps?

It seems, then, that "independence and vigour," which the United States has in abundance, may produce good novels and stories but does not make a good climate for expositional prose which, unlike creative writing, touches everybody. In fact, the outstanding exceptions which I have noted would be classified by some as outside the mainstream of American culture. It almost seems as if there were, as Disraeli said of 19th century English society, "two nations" in America, but instead of these two nations being the rich and the poor they are the educated and the uneducated, the literate and the semi-literate. One remembers some of Tocqueville's prophecies:

> The most common expedient employed by democratic nations to make an innovation in language consists in giving some unwonted meaning to an expression already in use. This method is very simple, prompt, and convenient; no learning is required to use it aright, and ignorance itself rather facilitates the practice; but that practice is most dangerous to the language.

There will always, I feel, be Americans to whom these practices will be abhorrent. They will uphold the standards of American prose to the end. But to whom will they make their communication, except to each other?

All this raises, no doubt, most interesting questions, some as basic as one could wish for, such as: Does literacy matter? It is true that one can be intelligent without being literate. But Western Civilisation is built upon such principles and traditions as demand literacy. To deny it is to deny Western Civilisation as an idea and to prepare the way for barbarism. Yet some years ago a Californian professor seriously suggested, not merely that the oral might eventually entirely supersede the written communication, but that it was a good thing that it should do so. Perhaps in the end it will be so. Perhaps the triumph of the mass media and the encouragement of "speech" rather than literature in schools has started a tide which cannot be turned. And what, when it is upon them, will the publishers and manufacturers of typewriters do then, poor things? If they are, like the rest of us, still here, that is.

Aids to Study and Topics for Writing

PART ONE

Dictionaries, Words, and Meanings

WHITEHALL: THE DEVELOPMENT OF THE ENGLISH DICTIONARY

Aids to Study

1. Consult your desk dictionary for its remarks on the size of the English vocabulary. Count the number of entry words on a few typical pages, multiply the average number of entries per page by the number of pages in the dictionary, and get an estimate of the size of its vocabulary. What factors can you think of which might influence the sizes of the various dictionaries?

2. Just out of curiosity, how large do you imagine your own vocabulary is? By sampling pages in your dictionary, figure out what percentage of the entry words (a) you *know* and *use*, either in speaking or writing, and (b) you *recognize* when others use them or when you're reading. How accurate do you think such an estimate might be? What are the weaknesses in this way of estimating size of vocabulary?

3. Vocabulary: Consult your dictionary for these words, and then work out the answers.

   a. *gloss*, n.—What is its technical meaning for language? What is its relation to *glossary*, to the verb *to gloss*, and to the phrase *to gloss over*?

   b. *magnum opus*—Why didn't Whitehall put it in italics? Was he right or wrong?

   c. *inkhorn terms*— What were they? How did the meaning develop? And what is *aureate diction*? What's the difference between the two?

   d. *superscript letters*— What are they?

   e. *encyclopedic dictionaries*— What are they? Is this the best way to spell *encyclopedic*? How do you decide?

   f. *lexicography*— What is it? Where did the word come from?

4. Dictionaries of "hard words" seem a rather sensible sort of book, since most of the time it's the "hard words" we use the dictionary for. But there are some problems. Make up two lists, ten words each, one of "hard" words, one of "easy" words. Put three nouns, three verbs, two adjectives, and two adverbs in each list. Now, without consulting a dictionary, write definitions for all twenty words. Which list is easier to handle? Why? Can you see why we need more than dictionaries of "hard words"?

5. On p. 7, Whitehall lists seven characteristics of modern American dictionaries. Check your own desk dictionary against the list. Is anything missing? Does yours have things not in Whitehall's list?

6. Whitehall says very little about one great series of modern American dictionaries. Which dictionaries are these? Why do you suppose they were not treated fully in his essay? (Note the source of his essay.)

7. Most of the great American dictionaries have been commercial successes.

What sorts of weaknesses would you expect a dictionary aimed at "the market" to show?

Topics for Writing

1. Consult an encyclopedia or a biographical dictionary for information about Joseph Worcester and Noah Webster. Write a factual essay comparing their characters, careers, and accomplishments.
2. Whitehall says that the typical American dictionary differs from British dictionaries "because the conditions of American life and culture differ from those of English life and culture." Write an essay in which you explore similar factors that might make different demands on dictionaries for these two countries.

MATHEWS: MEANINGS AND ETYMOLOGIES; DICTIONARIES CONTAIN SURPRISES

Aids to Study

1. What principle do the editors of your desk dictionary claim to have used in determining the order of listing of meanings? Examine a number of entries to see how they have followed the stated principle.
2. What is *etymology?*
3. If you have a desk dictionary other than *Webster's New World Dictionary,* compare its entry for *anecdote* with the entries from other dictionaries quoted by Professor Mathews. How do they differ?
4. Here are some questions suggested by Professor Mathews; try to answer them by looking up the etymologies of the italicized words:
   a. Why should an *acrobat* walk on his tiptoes?
   b. The name of what animal is preserved in *arctic?*
   c. Should a *diploma* be flat or folded once in the middle?
   d. Should *athletes* be given prizes?
   e. Where would you expect a *hippopotamus* to live?
   f. Why should a *volume* be round?
   g. Should you give a *parasite* food or a night's lodging?
   h. Why would it be impossible to collect *poll tax* from the headless horseman who appears in Irving's "Legend of Sleepy Hollow"?
   i. Which of the following animals would you expect a *polecat* to like best: duck, chicken, pig, turkey?
   j. In what school subject should a *glamour* girl excel?
   k. If a goat could act on the stage would he do better in *tragedy* or in *comedy?*
   l. How tall would you expect a *pygmy* to be?
   m. In ancient times where did people think the voice of a *ventriloquist* came from?
   n. Should a *pugnacious* animal fight with its teeth or its claws?
   o. Would you expect a *planet* to stay in the same spot?
   p. What was the occupation of the first *pedagogues?*

q. Would you expect an *alligator* and a *lizard* to resemble each other?

r. How should a *candidate* dress when out electioneering?

s. In Latin *rostrum* meant the beak of a bird. What does it mean now? Does your dictionary tell how it came to have its present meaning?

t. Would you feel flattered if someone called you a *dunce?* Look up the etymology of the word in a large dictionary.

u. From what animals were the first *bugles* made?

v. What objects were the first to be *considered?*

w. From what old law-court phrase does *culprit* come?

5. Here's an entry from the *OED.* Compare it with your desk dictionary's entry. This is only one of several noun and verb entries for *cant* in the *OED.* After reading through this entry, say what you think Emerson means by the word *cant* in the epigraph for "Dictionaries Contain Surprises."

Cant (kænt), *sb.*[3] [This and its accompanying vb. presumably represent L. *cant-us* singing, song, chant (Pr. and NFr. *cant*, Fr. *chant*), *cantā-re* NFr. *canter*) to sing, chant; but the details of the derivation and development of sense are unknown.

Cantare and its Romanic representatives were used contemptuously in reference to the church services as early as 1183, when according to Rigord (*c* 1200) *Gest Philip. August.* (1818) II, the Cotarelli of the Bourges country 'sacerdotes et viros religiosos captos secum ducentes, et irrisoriè *cantores* ipsos vocantes, in ipsis tormentis subsannando dicebant: *Cantate nobis, cantores, cantate;* et confestim dabant eis alapas, vel cum grossis virgis turpiter cædebant'. So far as the evidence shows, the vb. appears in Eng. first applied to the tones and language of beggars, 'the canting crew': this, which according to Harman was introduced *c* 1540, may have come down from the religious mendicants; or the word may have been actually made from Lat. or Romanic in the rogues' jargon of the time. The subsequent development assumed in the arrangement of the verb is quite natural, though not actually established. Some have however conjectured that *cant* is the Irish and Gaelic *cainnt* (pronounced kaᵗnᵗtᵗ, or nearly kant ʃᵗ) 'language'. And as early as 1711 the word was asserted to be derived from the name of Andrew Cant or his son Alexander Cant, Presbyterian ministers of the 17th c. This perhaps means that the surname of the two Cants was occasionally associated derisively with canting. The arrangement of the sb. here is tentative, and founded mainly on that of the vb., which appears on the whole earlier.]

† **I.** (Sporadic uses, from L. *cantus* or its representatives; not directly related to II.)

† **1.** Singing, musical sound. *Cant organ:* app. a technical term in music. *Obs.*

1501 Douglas *Pal. Hon.* I. xlii, Fabourdoun, pricksang, discant, countering, Cant organe, figuratioun, and gemmell. **1704** Swift *T. Tub Wks.* 1760 I. 100 Cant and vision are to the ear and the eye the same that tickling is to the touch. **1708** *Brit. Apollo* No. 79. 2/2 That shrill Cant of the Grasshoppers.

† **2.** Accent, intonation, tone. *Obs.*

1663 *Aron-bimn.* 110 It depends not upon the cant and tone, or the wording of the Minister. **1763** *Ann. Reg.* 307/2 If these lines want that sober cant which is necessary to an epitaph.

II. The speech or phraseology of beggars, etc., and senses connected therewith.

3. 'A whining manner of speaking, esp. of beggars'; a whine.

1640 Cleveland in Wilkins *Polit. Ballads* I. 28 By lies and cants, [they] Would trick us to believe 'em saints. **1705** Hickeringill *Priest-cr.* IV. (1721) 227 With a Cant like a Gypsie, a Whine like a beaten Spaniel.

4. The peculiar language or jargon of a class:

a. The secret language or jargon used by gipsies, thieves, professional beggars, etc.; *transf.* any jargon used for the purpose of secrecy.

1706 in PHILLIPS. **1707** J. STEVENS tr. *Quevedo's Com. Wks.* (1709) 226 They talk'd to one another in Cant. **1715** KERSEY, *Cant*, Gibberish, Pedler's French. **1734** NORTH *Exam.* II. v. ¶ 110. 383 To avoid being understood by the Servants, they framed a Cant, and called the Design of a general Rising the Lease and Release. **1865** DICKENS *Mut. Fr.* xvi. 127 The ring of the cant.

b. The special phraseology of a particular class of persons, or belonging to a particular subject; professional or technical jargon. (Always *depreciative* or *contemptuous*.)

1684 T. BURNET *Th. Earth* I. 214 There is heat and moisture in the body, & you may call the one 'radical' and the other 'innate' if you please; this is but a sort of cant. **1712** ADDISON *Spect.* No. 421 ¶ 3 In the Cant of particular Trades and Employments. **1750** JOHNSON *Rambl.* No. 128 ¶ 4 Every class of society has its cant of lamentation, which is understood by none but themselves. **1839** DICKENS *Nich. Nick* xxxiv, All love—bah! that I should use the cant of boys and girls—is fleeting enough. **1841–4** EMERSON *Ess.* xiii. *Poet Wks.* (Bohn) I. 156 Criticism is infested with a cant of materialism. **1861** HOLLAND *Less. Life* viii. 119 Repeating the cant of their sect and the cant of their schools.

† **c.** The peculiar phraseology of a religious sect or class. (Cf. 5 b.) *Obs.*

1681 DRYDEN *Abs. & Achit.* 521 Hot Levites..Resum'd their cant, and with a zealous cry Pursued their old beloved theocracy. **1696** C. LESLIE *Snake in Gr.* (1698) Introd. 46 Really to understand the Quaker-Cant is learning a new Language. **1709** SACHEVERELL *Serm.* 15 Aug. 15 Diabolical Inspiration, and Non-sensical Cant. **1711** *Spect.* No. 147 ¶ 3 Cant is by some people derived from one Andrew Cant who, they say, was a Presbyterian minister.. who by exercise & use had obtained the Faculty, alias Gift, of talking in the Pulpit in such a dialect, that it's said he was understood by none but his own Congregation, and not by all of them.

d. Provincial dialect; vulgar slang.

1802 MAR. EDGEWORTH *Irish Bulls* (1832) 226 The cant of Suffolk, the vulgarisms of Shropshire. **1852** GLADSTONE *Glean.* IV. lxxxii. 122 The coarse reproduction of that unmitigated cant or slang.

e. *attrib.*

1727 SWIFT *Let. Eng. Tongue* Wks. 1755 II. I. 185 To introduce and multiply cant words is the most ruinous corruption in any language. **1824** W. IRVING *T. Trav.* I. 273 Slang talk and cant jokes. **1841** BORROW *Zincali* (1843) II. 150 The first Vocabulary of the 'Cant Language'..appeared in the year 1680 appended to the life of 'The English Rogue'.

5. A form of words, a phrase:

† **a.** A set form of words repeated perfunctorily or mechanically. *Obs.*

1681 *Sejanus* in *Bagford Ballads* (1878) 758 *note*, A young Scribe is copying out a Cant, Next morn for to be spoke in Parliament. **1704** STEELE *Lying Lover* I. i. 7 Sure..you talk by Memory, a Form or Cant which you mistake for something that's gallant. **1712** ADDISON *Spect.* No. 291 § 6 With a certain cant of words.

b. A pet phrase, a trick of words; *esp.* a stock phrase that is much affected at the time, or is repeated as a matter of habit or form. (Formerly with *a* and *plural*.) *arch.*

1681 *Country-man's Compl. & Advice to King*, Gods! to be twice cajol'd by cants and looks. **1691** WOOD *Ath. Oxon.* II./450 Enamour'd with his obstreporousness and undecent cants. **1692** BENTLEY *Boyle Lect.* 200 That ordinary cant of illiterate..atheists, the fortuitous or casual concourse of atoms. **1710** HEARNE *Collect.* (1886) II. 365 The late happy Revolution, (so he calls it, according to the common Cant). **1769** *Junius Lett.* xxvi. 119 *note*, Measures, and not men, is the common cant of affected moderation. *c* **1815** JANE AUSTEN *Northang. Ab.* (1833) I. v. 22 It is really very well for a novel ..is the common cant.

c. *attrib.*

1712 ADDISON *Spect.* No. 530 ¶ 3 Enlivened with little cant-phrases. **1753** *Stewart's Trial* App. 130 It was a cant word through the country, That the tenants might sit, since the worst of it would be paying the violent profits. **1774** GOUVR. MORRIS in Sparks *Life & Writ.* (1832) I. 23 The belwethers ..roared out liberty, and property, and a multitude of cant terms. **1790** PALEY *Horæ Paul.* (1849) 396 There is such a thing as a peculiar word or phrase cleaving, as it were, to the memory of a writer or speaker and presenting itself to his utterance at every turn. When we observe this we call it a cant

word or a cant phrase. **1855** Prescott *Philip II* (1857) I. v. 79 To borrow a
cant phrase of the day, like 'a fixed fact'. **1868** Helps *Realmah* xvii. (1876)
465 He..can—to use the cant phrase—afford to support the dignity of the
peerage.

6. As a kind of phraseology:

a. Phraseology taken up and used for fashion's sake, without
being a genuine expression of sentiment; canting language.

1710 Berkeley *Princ. Hum. Knowl.* § 87 All this sceptical cant follows
from our supposing, etc. **1783** Johnson in *Boswell* 15 May, My dear friend,
clear your mind of cant..you may *talk* in this manner; it is a mode of talking
in society; but don't *think* foolishly. **1809** Syd. Smith *Wks.* (1867) I. 174
The pernicious cant of indiscriminate loyalty. **1870** Lowell *Study Wind.* 157
Enthusiasm, once cold, can never be warmed over into anything better than
cant. **1875** Smiles *Thrift* ii. 20 In fact there is no greater *cant* than *can't.*
1883 J. Parker *Tyne Ch.* 320 There is a cant of infidelity as certainly as
there is a cant of belief.

b. *esp.* Affected or unreal use of religious or pietistic phraseology;
language (or action) implying the pretended assumption of good-
ness or piety.

1709 Strype *Ann. Ref.* I. lv. 609, I set down this letter at large, that men
may see the cant of these men. **1716** Addison *Freeholder* No. 37 (J.) That
cant and hypocrisy, which had taken possession of the people's minds in the
times of the great rebellion. **1789** Mrs. Piozzi *Journ. France* I. 256 Hypo-
critical manners, or what we so emphatically call cant. **1849** Robertson
Serm. Ser. I. x. (1866) 182 Religious phraseology passes into cant. **1875**
Hamerton *Intell. Life* vi. iii. 211 He had a horror of cant, which..gave him
a repulsion for all outward show of religious observances. **1879** Froude
Cæsar i. 6 The whole spiritual atmosphere was saturated with cant.

c. *attrib.*

1747 Carte *Hist. Eng.* I. 601 To make up what was wanting in the justice
of their cause..by a cant and sophistical way of expression.

7. One who uses religious phrases unreally.

1725 *New Cant. Dict., Cant,* an Hypocrite, a Dissembler, a double-tongu'd,
whining Person. **1824** Mrs. Cameron *Pink Tippet* iii. 16 Lest she should
be called a cant. **1873** E. Berdoc *Adv. Protestant* 132 He was not a cant, but
really felt what he said.

6. Among the several dictionaries discussed in Professor Mathews's essays,
where do you suppose you would find (a) the best information about
current American pronunciation of a word; (b) the latest information about
current U.S. meanings of a word; (c) the fullest historical account of a
word?

7. Use an unabridged dictionary, preferably the *OED,* to see if you can
answer the following questions posed by Professor Mathews:

a. How did Arabian girls use *alcohol* 2000 years ago?

b. In what way is it said that a certain nobleman's love of gambling led
to the presence of *sandwich* in the English language?

c. The nickname of what Admiral is said to be preserved in the word *grog?*

d. In Matthew 3:4 it is said that John the Baptist ate locusts and wild
honey. Did the *locusts* he ate belong to the animal or the vegetable
kingdom?

e. When you *curry favor* with someone, what part does a chestnut-colored
horse play in your activity?

f. Where would you look to find the *signature* of a plant? How were
doctors formerly guided by these signatures?

g. What habit of the *moose* gave the animal its name?

h. What does it mean *to tell out of school?*

  i.   In what condition is one who has a *bee in his bonnet?*
  j.   What should one do who is asked to *tell it not in Gath?*
8.   Where did the *juke box* get its name?

  Topics for Writing

1.   Here are the *OED* entries for *huckster*. Compare them with your desk
dictionary's entries and then write an essay in which you describe the
development of the word's meaning.

> **Huckster** (hɒ·kstəɪ), *sb.* Forms: 3 *Orm.* huccster, 4–5 hukstar,
> 4– huckster; also 4–5 hok(e)ster(e, hoxter, 5 howkster, hukstere,
> hukkester, huk-, hwkstare, (hoggester), 5–6 hook-, hukster, 5–7
> hucster, 5–9 huxter, 6 hocster, houkester, huckester, huckstar, 9
> *dial.* huikster. [See Huck *v.* Although the series *huck, hucker, huck-*
> *ster,* corresponds formally with *bake, baker, baxter, brew, brewer,*
> *brewster,* etc., in which the verb is the starting-point, the late date
> of *huck* as compared with *huckster,* and the continental parallels
> of the latter, make difficulties. MDu. had *hokester, hoekster,* early
> mod.Du. *heukster,* 'huckster' fem.; also MDu. *hoeker,* early mod.
> Du. *heuker* masc. = MLG. *hoker,* mod. Ger. *höker,* 'higgler,
> hawker, retailer, market-man, costermonger'; none of these, how-
> ever, appear to be known as early as our *huckster.*
>
> The origin of the Du. and Ger. words themselves is unsettled; Ger., besides
> *höker,* has *höke, höcke,* MHG. *hucke,* MLG. *hoke,* to be referred, according
> to Kluge, prob. to *hocken* to squat, sit on the 'hunkers'; but Verwijs and Ver-
> dam state grounds for connecting MDu. *hoeker, hoekster* rather with Du. *hoek*
> a corner. The history is thus altogether obscure.]
>
> **1.** A retailer of small goods, in a petty shop or booth, or at a
> stall; a pedlar, a hawker. **a.** Applied to a woman.
>
> *a* 1300 *Sat. People Kildare* xviii. in *E. E. P.* (1862) 155 Hail be ȝe hoke-
> sters dun bi þe lake..He is sori of his lif þat is fast to such a wif. 14.. *Nom.*
> in Wr.-Wülcker 692/42 *Hec auxiatrix,* a huxter. *c* 1475 *Pict. Voc.* Ibid.
> 793/29 *Hec aucionatrix,* a hoxter. 1851 MAYNE REID *Scalp Hunt.* ix. 70 The
> women, light-hearted hucksters.
>
> **b.** Without distinction of sex. (The ordinary use.) *locally* in
> specific senses: see quots. 1858–77.
>
> *c* 1200 ORMIN 15817 Forr þatt teȝȝ turrndenn Godess hus Inntill huccster-
> ess boþe. 1387 TREVISA *Higden* I. lx. (Rolls) II. 171 þey beeþ..in gaderyne
> of catel hoksters [*v.r.* hucksters] and tauerners. *c.* 1440 *Promp. Parv.* 252/2
> Hwkstare,..*auxionator,* auxionatrix. 1483 *Gild Bakers Exeter* in *Eng. Gilds*
> 337 To make serche..att all hoggesters houses with-yn the Juris-diccion of
> the said Cite. 1534 MORE *Treat. on Passion* Wks. 1304/1 A substanciall mer-
> chaunt and not an hukster. 1591 PERCIVALL. *Sp. Dict., Regatonear,* to sell
> pedlerie ware, to play the hucster. 1641 BEST *Farm. Bks.* (Surtees) 29 Wee
> buy our molten tallowe..of the hucksters and tripe-wives. 1705 HICKERINGILL
> *Priest-cr.* II. vi. 62 The throwing down of a Hucksters Apples by a Fisher-
> Boy. 1858 SIMMONDS *Dict. Trade, Huckster,* an inferior dealer or minor
> trader; a hawker or itinerant vendor of goods with a pack, box, or tray. 1877
> *Holderness Gloss., Hucksthers,* dealers in farm produce, who attend the mar-
> kets to purchase from the producers for the purpose of retailing it out again
> to small customers. 1889 *Spectator* 28 Dec., From the great shops in Regent
> Street and Bond Street to the smallest huxters' in the slums, there are Christ-
> mas presents in the windows.
>
> **c.** As term of reproach: A regrater, an engrosser of corn, etc.;
> a broker, a middleman.
>
> [*a* 1400 *Burgh Laws* lxvi. in *Sc. Stat.* I. 346/1 Hukstaris þat byis and sellis
> agane to wynning sal nocht by ony thing before þat undern be rungyn in
> wynter and mydmore in somer.]
>
> 1573–80 BARET *Alv.* H 707 An Huckster: a regrater: a seller by retaile: a
> wifler, *propola.* 1580 HOLLYBAND *Treas. Fr. Tong, Dardanier,* an huckster,
> he that kepeth corne till it be deare. 1595 DUNCAN *App. Etymol.* (E. D. S.),
> *Mango,* interpolator, a hukster, a regrator. 1612 T. TAYLOR *Comm. Titus* i. 11

Such as by fraud and base arts play the hucksters to enhanse the price. **1630** LENNARD tr. *Charron's Wisd.* (1658) 49 It is the great Intermedler and Huckster, by which we traffick. **1700** T. BROWN tr. *Fresny's Amusem. Ser. & Com.* 78 Marriage Hucksters, or Wife-Brokers.

2. *transf.* and *fig.* A person ready to make his profit of anything in a mean or petty way; one who basely barters his services, etc., for gain; a mercenary; an overreacher of others.

1553 GRIMALDE *Cicero's Offices* I. (1558) 18 No hucsters of warre warremen as we bee. **1645** MILTON *Colast. Wks.* (1851) 350 Wee have it..as good cheap, as any hucster at law, newly set up, can possibly afford. **1673** *Vain Insolency Rome* 5 With what craft, and artifice, the Romish Hucksters endeavour to seduce the people of our Church of England..to the Communion of Rome. **1842** ROGERS *Introd. Burke's Wks.* (1842) I. 9 Mr. Hamilton, who managed the whole matter in the true spirit of a political huckster, had the meanness to accept this offer. **1868** MISS BRADDON *Charlotte's Inher.* I. i. 7, I am no huckster, to sell my daughter to the best bidder.

† **3.** *Phase. In huckster's hands (handling):* in a position in which it is likely to be roughly used or lost; beyond the likelihood of recovery. *Obs.*

1581 RICH *Farewell* D iv b, We will returne to his wife, who was lefte in hucsters handelyng (as you haue heard). *a* **1592** GREENE *Alphonsus* I. Wks. (Rtldg.) 226/2 The crown is lost, and now in hucksters' hands. **1687** R. L'ESTRANGE *Answ. Diss.* 21 They are gotten into Hucksters Hands, and there's No coming off without a Scratch'd Face. *a* **1700** B. E. *Dict. Cant. Crew* s.v., *In Huckster's Hands,* at a desperate Pass, or Condition, or in a fair way to be lost. **1738** SWIFT *Pol. Conversat.* 68 Madam, he shall ne'er have it [a Handkerchief] again; 'tis in Huckster's Hands.

4. *Comb.,* as *huckster-booth; huckster-like* adj., adv.

1591 SPENSER *M. Hubberd* 925 The Ape wanting his huckster man, That wont provide his necessaries. **1665** GLANVILL *Scepsis Sci.* Pref. (R.), Nor will I huckster-like discredit any man's ware, to recommend mine own. **1866** BLACKIE *Homer & Iliad* I. 101 The huckster-booths of the Lawnmarket. **1870** *Standard* 13 Dec., He only mulcted nations, and did not hucksterlike fine every little open town he came across.

Hence **Hucksterdom,** *nonce-wd.* [see -DOM.].

1886 *Pall Mall Budget* 8 July 28/2 From the hucksterdom of his environment.

Hu·ckster, *v.* [f. HUCKSTER *sb.*]

1. *intr.* To bargain, haggle. *lit.* and *fig.*

1592 [see HUCKSTERING *ppl. a.*]. *a* **1665** J. GOODWIN *Filled w. the Spirit* (1867) 319 Be ingenuous and noble towards God, and not stand picking and huckstering with your hearts to know how you must do to escape hell fire. **1775** BURKE *Sp. Conc. Amer. Wks.* III. 57 Despotism itself is obliged to truck and huckster. **1855** MOTLEY *Dutch Rep.* IV. i. II. 522 The estates..irritated the Prince of Orange by huckstering about subsidies. **1861** SALA *Dutch Pict.* xxi. 336 A dunghill of vanity for chapmen to huckster over.

2. *trans.* To traffic in, in a petty way; to retail or expose for sale (esp. in small quantities); to bargain over. Also, to adulterate. *lit.* and *fig.*

1642 T. HILL *Trade of Truth* 37 This graduall Huckstering up the purity of truth. **1670** MILTON *Hist. Eng.* III. *Wks.* (1847) 502/2 Some who had been called from shops and warehouses..to sit in supreme councils and committees..fell to huckster the commonwealth. **1677** GALE *Crt. Gentiles* III. 19 Such as hucstered and made merchandise of Christ. **1770** BURKE *Pres. Discont. Wks.* 1842 I. 129 The sealed fountain of royal bounty, which had been infamously monopolized and huckstered. **1879** FARRAR *St. Paul* (1883) 541 The deceitful workers who had huckstered and adulterated the word of God. **1898** *Humanitarian* XI. 357 A man..huckstering cheap lollypops to the small fry of the Board Schools.

2. Consult as many dictionaries as you can for the meanings and etymologies of the noun *record*. Write an essay in which you explore and explain its development.

ROBERTSON AND CASSIDY: CHANGING MEANINGS AND VALUES OF WORDS

Aids to Study

1. What further examples of the "etymological fallacy" can you think of? Check them in an unabridged dictionary to see what happened to their meanings.

2. Consult the *OED* for the following words: *affair, awful, minister, gentle, shade, sergeant, shears, scissors, cad, boor, gossip, hussy.* What processes of semantic change does each illustrate?

3. Here is the *OED* entry for *frock*. What seems to have caused each of the changes it shows in historical development?

> **Frock** (frǫk), *sb.* Forms: 4–5 frokke, 5 frogge, 4–6 frok(e, *Sc.* or *north.* frog, 6–7 frocke, 6– frock. [a. F. *froc* (recorded from 12th c.); of uncertain origin.
>
> Cf. Pr. *floc* frock, med. L. *froccus, floccus.* Some scholars regard the *fl*-forms as the original, and identify the word with L. *floccus*, OF. *floc* FLOCK *sb.*[2] Others regard *froc* as adopted from a Teut. word, OHG. *hroch* (once), OS. *hroc* (once), OFris. *hrokk* (rare); but in these forms it is believed by many Germanists that the *hr-* is a misspelling without phonetic significance, the usual forms being OHG. *roch* (mod. Ger. *rock*), OFris. *rokk*, OE. *rocc.*]
>
> **1.** A long habit with large open sleeves; the outer and characteristic dress of a monk. *Rarely,* a cassock (of an Anglican clergyman). Hence, the priestly office which it indicates. Cf. UNFROCK *v.*
>
> 1350 *Durh. MS. Cha. Roll,* In xj pannis..præter ij frokkes. 1362 LANGL. *P. Pl.* A. v. 64 Of a freris frokke were the foresleuys. *c* 1440 *Promp. Parv.* 179/2 Froke, monkes habyte..*cuculla.* 1466 *Paston Lett.* No. 549 II. 270 For a cope called a frogge of worsted for the Prior of Bromholm xxvi *s.* viii *d.* 1548 UDALL *Erasm. Par. Luke* xix 3–4 An other poynteth to some one of the pharisaical sort, clad in a blacke frocke or cope. 1683 TEMPLE *Mem.* Wks. 1731 I. 465 A French Monk, who some time since had left his Frock for a Petticoat. 1762 H. WALPOLE *Vertue's Anecd. Paint.* I. iii. 51 As the frock of no religious order ever was green, this cannot be meant for a friar. 1810 SCOTT *Lady of L.* III. iv, The Hermit by it stood, Barefooted, in his frock and hood. 1887 W. GLADDEN *Parish Problems* 333 It was the utterance of such words as these that cost the great Carmelite preacher [Father Hyacinthe] his frock.
>
> **2.** An upper garment worn chiefly by men; a long coat, tunic, or mantle.
>
> 13.. *E. E. Allit. P.* B. 1742 þe kyng comaunded anon to clepe þat wyse, In frokkes of fyn cloþ. 1375 BARBOUR *Bruce* x. 375 With blak froggis all helit thai The Armouris at thai on thame had. *c* 1425 WYNTOUN *Cron.* VIII. xxxviii. 57 Ilkane a gud Burdowne in hand, And royd Frogis on þare Armyng. *c* 1460 *Towneley Myst.* (Surtees) 241, I wold be fayn of this frog [Christ's coat] myght it fall vnto me. 1500–20 DUNBAR *Poems* li. 3 To giff a doublett he is als doure, As it war off ane futt syd frog. 1527 *Lanc. Wills* I. 6 And also that he geiff to Richard Fene a jakett called my frocke. 1611 BIBLE *Ecclus.* xl. 4 From him that weareth purple and a crown, vnto him that is clothed with a linnen frocke. 1649 G. DANIEL *Trinarch., Hen.* V, clxxix, Another girds his Frock, wᵗʰ a sure Thonge. 1700 DRYDEN *Sigism. & Guisc.* 144 Yet (for the wood perplexed with thorns he knew) A frock of leather o'er his limbs he drew. 1848 W. H. KELLY tr. *L. Blanc's Hist. Ten Years* II. 559 Kings at arms covered with long frocks of cloth of gold.
>
> *fig.* 1604 SHAKS. *Ham.* III. iv. 164 (Qo. 2) That monster custome..to the vse of actions faire and good..giues a frock or Liuery That aptly is put on to refraine night.
>
> **b.** *Frock of mail:* a defensive garment, armour. Cf. *coat of mail.*
>
> 1671 MILTON *Samson* 133 Samson..Made arms ridiculous, useless the.. frock of mail Adamantean proof. 1835 BROWNING *Paracelsus* III. 715, I have addressed a frock of heavy mail, Yet may not join the troop of sacred knights.

fig. 1841–4 EMERSON *Ess., Politics* Wks. (Bohn) I. 244 The gladiators in the lists of power feel, through all their frocks of force and simulation the presence of worth.

3. A loose outer garment worn by peasants and workmen; an overall; more fully *smock-frock.*

a 1668 DAVENANT *News from Plymouth* IV. i, *Cable.* Come your affair, Squire of the Frock! Briefly Dispatch! Where is this courteous Damsel? *Porter.* At my House, Sir. 1698 FRYER *Acc. E. India & P.* 95 Flesh-coloured Vests, somewhat like our Brickmakers Frocks. 1724 DE FOE *Mem. Cavalier* (1840) 237, I had pistols under my grey frock. 1777 WATSON *Philip II* (1839) 525 Three officers..disguised like the peasants of that country with long frocks. 1840 R. H. DANA *Bef. Mast* xxxvi. 136 The duck frocks for tarring down rigging. 1883 C. WALFORD *Fairs* 153 Dealers in haubergs, or waggoners' frocks.

b. A wearer of a smock-frock; a poor person.

1612 W. PARKES *Curtaine-Dr.* (1876) 25 The rich and the poore, euen from the furd gown to the sweating frock. 1625 B. JONSON *Staple of N.* v. ii, *Porter.* Sir, I did give it him. *P. sen.* What..A frock spend sixpence!

c. A woollen 'guernsey' or 'jersey' worn by sailors; *esp.* in *Guernsey* or *Jersey frock.*

1811 W. THOM *Hist. Aberd.* vi. 150 Besides stockings, they make frocks, mitts, and all sorts of hosiery. 1825 JAMIESON, Frock, a sort of worsted netting worn by sailors, often in lieu of a shirt. 1856 EMERSON *Eng. Traits, Voy. Eng.* Wks. (Bohn) II. 13 The sailors have dressed him in [a] Guernsey frock. 1867 SMYTH *Sailor's Word-bk.*, Frog, an old term for a seaman's coat or frock. *Ibid., Jersey frocks,* woollen frocks supplied to seamen.

4. The outer garment, for indoor wear, of women and children, consisting of a bodice and skirt; a gown, dress.

The word is now applied chiefly to the garment worn by children and young girls, cf. *short frock;* that worn by women is commonly called a *dress; gown* is also current, though (exc. in the U.S.) less generally. (But in the language of fashionable society the use of *frock* for 'dress' has within the last few years been revived.)

1537 *Bury Wills* (Camden) 134, I wyll my goddowter and seruant, shall haue my wosted kyrtell..and my froke. 1550 CROWLEY *Way to Wealth* 325 Let youre wiues therefore put of theire fine frockes and Frenche hoodes. 1613 DRAYTON *Poly-olb.* xviii. 284 And on her loynes a frock with many a swelling pleate. 1705 *Lond. Gaz.* No. 4117/4 Cloathed with a red Damask Coat, with blue Flowers, and over it a white Holland Frock. *Ibid.* No. 4149/4 James Smith, upwards of 4 years of Age, in a hanging Sleeve Coat, and a painted Frock..is missing. 1755 JOHNSON s. v. *Frock,* A kind of gown for children. 1818 *La Belle Assemblée* XVII. No. 108. 87/2 The newest ball-dress is composed of a frock of tulle, over a rose-coloured slip of satin. 1833 HT. MARTINEAU *Three Ages* III. 108 Striving to patch up once more the girl's frock and the boy's coat. 1867 TROLLOPE *Chron. Barset* II. xlv. 9, I don't think I've ever been in London since I wore short frocks. 1882 MISS BRADDON *Mt. Royal* II. vii. 143 Fishky..looked lovely in her white satin frock and orange-blossoms. 1884 *Girl's Own Paper* 28 June 618/3, I think 'frock' seems to be applied to the morning costume, and 'dress' to that of evening only. 1889 BARRIE *Window in Thrums* 172 There could never be more than a Sabbath frock and an everyday gown for her.

5. A coat with long skirts. In mod. quots. = FROCK-COAT.

1719 DE FOE *Crusoe* II. vi, A light coat like a frock. 1748 SMOLLETT *Rod. Rand.* (1812) I. 387 A gentleman dressed in a green frock came in. 1770 RICHARDSON *Anecd. Russian Emp.* 325 A light blue frock with silver frogs. 1839–40 W. IRVING *Wolfert's R.* (1855) 162, I observed the Duke of Wellington..He was alone, simply attired in a blue frock. 1855 THACKERAY *Newcomes* I. 128 Dine in your frock..if your dress-coat is in the country. 1876 BESANT & RICE *Gold. Butterfly* III. 194 The coat..a comfortable easy old frock, a little baggy at the elbows.

b. A coat of a similar 'cut' used as a military uniform; *spec.* see quot. 1881.

1753 HANWAY *Trav.* (1762) I. VII. xcii. 422 He..appears..always in his regimentals, which are a blue cloth frock with silver brandenburgs. 1881 WILHELM *Milit. Dict.*, Frock, in the British service, the undress regimental coat of the guards, artillery, and royal marines. 1890 *19th Cent.* Nov. 842 The stable jacket will retain its freshness, as its owner drills in his 'service frock'.

6. *attrib.* and *Comb., frock-body; frock-like* adj.; † frock-clothes,

-dress (*rare*), dress of which a frock-coat is a part: so frock-suit;
† frock-man = 3 b; frock-uniform, undress uniform (see 5 b).

   1862 F. WILFORD *Maiden of our own day* 97, I can make this °frock-body
while you are making the skirt. **1769** *Public Advertiser* 1 June 3/2 Silk Cloths
..for Gentlemens Dress and °Frock Cloaths. **1854** J. BUCHANAN in *Harper's
Mag.* Jan. (1884) 256/1, I was invited 'in °frock dress' to the dinner. **1886**
W. J. TUCKER *E. Europe* 183 From beneath his vest there hung..the °frock-
like 'gatya' (drawers) of the Magyar peasant. **1657** REEVE *God's Plea for
Nineveh* II. 46 If ye fight for the wall, let not the °frokman take the right
hand of you in worth. **1810** WELLINGTON in Gurw. *Desp.* VI. 591 We..shall
be highly flattered by your company..whether in full or in °frock uniforms.

   Hence **Fro·ckhood**, the state of being dressed in a (short) frock;
† **Fro·ckified** *ppl. a.*, clad in a (monk's) frock.

   1708 MOTTEUX *Rabelais* IV. xlvi. (1737) 186 A frockify'd Hobgoblin. **1861**
WYNTER *Soc. Bees* 124 How many Billies and Bobbies, revelling in all the
glorious ease of frockhood, have you not reduced to the cruel purgatory of
breeches.

4. What are some of the possible causes of semantic change?
5. Vocabulary: Consult your desk dictionary for these:
    a. *pejorative*— What's a good synonym? Is there a verb made from *pejora-
        tive*? What subjects, other than semantic change, can you use the word
        pejorative in or on?
    b. *thingumabob, gadget, jigger, gimmick*: Where did these come from and
        how did they develop?
    c. *starve*— When did it cease to mean *die of any cause*? (Consult the
        OED.) How can the lexicographer decide that the change has taken
        place?
    d. *hussy*— How did it develop its present meaning?
    e. *monstrous*— What has happened to this word's meaning, and why?
    f. *twist*, n.— This dance craze hit the country in full force in 1961. Is it in
        the dictionaries? Account for the semantic development. What else does
        twist mean as a noun?

        Topics for Writing
1. Here is the *OED* entry for *genius*. Compare it with other dictionary discus-
    sions of the word, and then write an essay in which you discuss all its
    changes of meaning since it first entered the language. Try to offer explana-
    tions for each of these changes.

   Genius (dʒīˑniŏs). Pl. genii (dʒīˑniˌəi), geniuses, († genius's).
[a. L. *genius*, f. °*gen-* root of *gi-gn-ĕre* to beget, Gr. γίγνεσθαι to
be born, come into being.
   In Lat. the word has mainly the sense 1 below (the extended sense 2 occurs
post-classically), and a fig. sense approaching 3. As a word of learned origin
it is found in the Rom. langs.: F. *génie* (whence Ger. *genie*), It., Sp., Pg.
genio, which have approximately the same senses as in Eng. To some extent
the sense-development in Rom. has been affected by confusion with *ingenium*
(see ENGINE): cf. for example F. *génie civil* 'civil engineering'.]
   1. With reference to classical pagan belief: The tutelary god or
attendant spirit allotted to every person at his birth, to govern his
fortunes and determine his character, and finally to conduct him
out of the world; also, the tutelary and controlling spirit similarly
connected with a place, an institution, etc. (Now only in *sing.*)

In the first two quots. *Genius* is the proper name of an allegorical person who in the *Rom. de la Rose* represents the native moral instincts of mankind as setting bounds to the range of sexual passion.

[**1390** GOWER *Conf.* I. 48 O Genius min owne clerke Come forth and here this mannes shrifte. *c.* **1400** *Rom. Rose* 4768 They..Whom genius cursith, man and wyf, That wrongly werke ageyn nature.] **1513** DOUGLAS *Æneis* IX. iv. 49 Gif that euery mannis schrewit desyre Be as his God and Genyus in that place. **1536** BELLENDEN *Cron. Scot.* (1541) Proheme Cosmogr. xii, Thair is na thing may be so odius To man, as leif in miserie and wo Defraudand god of nature genius. [Cf. Ter. *Phorm.* I. i. 10 and Hor. *Ep.* II. ii. 188.] **1596** DRAYTON *Leg.* iv. 51 The pale Genius of that aged floud. **1605** SHAKS. *Macb.* III. i. 56 Vnder him My Genius is rebuk'd, as it is said Mark Anthonies was by Cæsar. **1612** DRAYTON *Poly-olb.* 1. 10 Thou Genius of the place..Which liued'st long before the All-earth-drowning Flood. *c* **1630** RISDON *Surv. Devon* § 225 (1810) 237 Genii of the spring. **1647** R. STAPYLTON *Juvenal* 63 Any thing wherein the spirit or soule delighted, was called sacred or peculiar to the genius, especially feasting and marriage. **1663** DRYDEN *To Author* 55 in Charleton *Stone-heng,* Watch'd by the Genius of this Royal place. **1701** ROWE *Amb. Step-Moth.* I. i. 51 Let their Guardian Genii still be watchful. **1745** COLLINS *Ode Col. Ross* i, Britannia's Genius bends to earth. *c* **1800** K. WHITE *Childhood* II. 260 Kind genii of my native fields benign. **1831** CARLYLE *Sart. Res.* (1858) 87 It was his guiding Genius (*Dämon*) that inspired him; he must go forth and meet his Destiny. **1843** DICKENS *Christm. Carol* i, It seemed as if the Genius of the Weather sat in mournful meditation on the threshold. **1863** *Scotsman* 12 Aug., We are now able..to thank our stars that the genius of red tape was so strong even in France. **1871** FARRAR *Witn. Hist.* iii. 99 Christians..who would die rather than fling into the altar-flame a pinch of incense to the Genius of the Emperors. **1887** BOWEN *Virg. Æneid* v. 95 His sire's familiar, or genius haunting the shore.

† b. After Lat. use: This spirit viewed as propitiated by festivities; hence, one's appetite. *Obs.*

1605 B. JONSON *Volpone* I. i. B 2 a, What should I do, But cocker vp my Genius, and liue free To all delights, my fortune calls me to? **1693** DRYDEN *Juvenal* iv. 105 To your glad Genius sacrifice this Day; Let common Meats respectfully give way.

c. (*A person's*) *good, evil genius:* the two mutually opposed spirits (in Christian language *angels*) by whom every person was supposed to be attended throughout his life. Hence applied *transf.* to a person who powerfully influences for good or evil the character, conduct, or fortunes of another.

1610 SHAKS *Temp.* IV. i. 27 The strongest suggestion, Our worser Genius can **1613** PURCHAS *Pilgrimage* (1614) 365 A tradition of two Genii, which attend every man, one good, the other evill. **1653** H. MORE *Antid. Ath.* III. xiv. (1712) 130 The Pythagoreans were of opinion that every man has two Genii, a good one, and a bad one. **1660** J. S. *Andromana* III. v. in Hazl. *Dodsley* XIV. 244 My better genius, thou art welcome as A draught of water to a thirsty man. **1702** ROWE *Tamerl.* IV. i. 1689 Thou..art an evil Genius to thyself. **1770** LANGHORNE *Plutarch* (1879) II. 1006/2 Men had their evil genii, who disturbed them with fears, and distressed their virtue. **1868** FREEMAN *Norm. Conq.* (1876) II. vii. 24 It needed the intervention of his better genius in the form of Godwine.

† d. In astrological use the word survived, with some notion of its original sense, passing into a symbolical expression for the combination of sidereal influences represented in a person's horoscope. *Obs.*

1643 MILTON *Divorce* I. x, But what might be the cause, whether each one's allotted Genius or proper star, or [etc.]. **1657** H. PINNELL *Philos. Ref.* 67 The other part therefore of Man, or this sydereall body is called the Genius of Man, because it proceedeth from the Firmament; it is called *Penates*, because it is in our power and born with us, the shadow of the visible body, *Lar domesticus,* the good or bad household or private Angell.

e. The quasi-mythologic personification of something immaterial (e.g. of a virtue, a custom, an institution), esp. as portrayed in painting or sculpture. Hence *transf.* a person or thing fit to be taken as an embodied type of (some abstract idea).

1597 SHAKS. *2 Hen. IV,* III. ii. 337 Hee was the very Genius of Famine. **1875** B. HARTE *Tales Argonauts, Baby Sylvester,* A golden lizard, the very genius of desolate stillness, had stopped breathless upon the threshold of one cabin.

2. A demon or spiritual being in general. Now chiefly in pl. *genii* (the *sing.* being usually replaced by GENIE), as a rendering of Arab. جِنّ *jinn*, the collective name of a class of spirits (some good, some evil) supposed to interfere powerfully in human affairs.

c 1590 GREENE *Fr. Bacon* ix. 71 Whereas the pyromantic genii Are mighty, swift, and of far-reaching power. 1646 BUCK *Rich. III* Ded., To the common-rout, they..are another kind of Genius, or *ignis fatuus.* 1653 LD. VAUX *Godeau's St. Paul* 321 The worship of Angels or Geniuses [*printed* Genieuses]. 1655 STANLEY *Hist. Philos.* II. (1701) 83/1 They mock even the Genius of Socrates as a feigned thing. 1681 H. MORE *Exp. Dan.* ii. 25 The activity therefore of the Aerial Genii or Angels may be understood by these Winds. 1688 MRS. BEHN tr. *Van Dale's Hist. Orac.* (1718) 150 Evil Genii, and Spirits condemn'd to eternal punishment. 1756–82 J. WARTON *Ess. Pope* (1782) II. x. 178 It seemed one of those edifices in Fairy Tales, that are raised by Genii in a nights time. 1779 FRANKLIN *Wks.* (1889) VI. 261 Albumazar..was visited nightly by genii and spirits of the first rank. 1832 W. IRVING *Alhambra* I. 251 The genii, who watch over the place, were obedient to my magic power. 1879 GLADSTONE *Glean.* I. i. 32 The whole narrative really recalls the most graceful fictions of wise genii and gentle fairies.

3. † **a.** Of persons: Characteristic disposition; inclination; bent, turn or temper of mind. *Obs.*

1581 SIDNEY *Apol. Poetrie* (Arb.) 62 A Poet, no industrie can make, if his owne Genius bee not carried vnto it. 1599 B. JONSON *Ev. Man out of Hum.* II. i. (1600) D 4 a, I cannot frame me to your harsh vulgar phrase, tis agaynst my Genius. 1663 GERBIER *Counsel* 36 Those things whereunto their Genius doth tend. 1686 *Observ. Chinese Char.* in *Misc. Cur.* (1708) III. 215 There have been various ways thought of for Expressing Significancy, according to the several Genii of the Persons that were the Inventors. 1690 EVELYN *Mem.* (1857) III. 318 Its being suitable to my rural genius, born as I was at Wotton, among the woods. 1697 tr. *C'tess D'Aunoy's Trav.* (1706) 83 He immediately discovered the Queens Genius, and easily made himself her Confident. 1713 DERHAM *Phys. Theol.* v. i. 312 There is the same Reason for the variety of Genii, or Inclinations of Men also. 1761 HUME *Hist. Eng.* III. lxi. 319 Men of such daring geniuses were not contented with the ancient and legal forms of civil government. 1780 JOHNSON *Let. to Mrs. Thrale* 10 July, Every man has his genius..my genius is always in extremes. 1781 J. MOORE *View Soc. It.* (1790) I. xvi. 188 The intriguing genius of Pope Julius. 1804 W. TENNANT *Ind. Recreat.* (ed. 2) II. 162 Operations requiring no effort..and on that account peculiarly suited to the genius of the indolent Bengalese.

b. With reference to a nation, age, etc.: Prevalent feeling, opinion, sentiment, or taste; distinctive character, or spirit.

1639 FULLER *Holy War* v. xix. (1640) 260 The warre-genius of the world is altered now-a-dayes, and supplieth number with policie. *c* 1645 HOWELL *Lett.* (1650) II. 74 Before I wean my self from Italy, a word or two touching the genius of the nation. 1665 BOYLE *Occas. Refl.* 189 My Acquaintedness with the Genius of the Age had sadly taught me that I was to alter my Method. 1701 SWIFT *Contests Nobles & Comm.* Wks. 1755 II. I. 44 The people of England are of a genius and temper never to admit slavery among them. 1711 ADDISON *Spect.* No. 29 ¶ 9 A Composer should fit his Musick to the Genius of the People. 1754 HUME *Hist. Eng.* (1761) I. ix. 196 The barbarous and violent genius of the age. 1791 BURKE *App. Whigs* Wks. 1842 I. 531 The genius of this faction is easily discerned. 1845 STEPHEN *Comm. Laws Eng.* (1874) I. 81 Owing perhaps to some peculiar averseness in the early genius of the country from change in its legal institutions. 1855 PRESCOTT *Philip II,* I. I. i. 2 This flexibility was foreign to the genius of the Spaniard.

personified. 1871 MORLEY *Voltaire* (1886) 4 The rays from Voltaire's burning and far-shining spirit..struck upon the genius of the time, seated dark and dead like the black stone of Memnon's statue.

c. Of a language, law, or institution: Prevailing character or spirit, general drift, characteristic method or procedure.

1647 N. BACON *Disc. Govt. Eng.* I. xlix. (1739) 85 The right genius of this Law will also more evidently appear by the practice of those times. 1699 BENTLEY *Phal.* 244 The Genius and Constitution of Tragedy. 1705 ADDISON *Italy* 183 They are chiefly to be ascrib'd to the very Genius of the Roman

Catholick Religion. **1755** JOHNSON *Dict.* Pref., Such [words] as are readily adopted by the genius of our tongue. **1765** HARRIS *Three Treat.* Advt., Those Treatises, being written in Dialogue, from their Nature and Genius admit not of Interruption. **1776** ADAM SMITH *W. N.* I. viii. (1869) I. 77 The genius of the British Constitution. **1791** BURKE *Th. Fr. Affairs* Wks. VII. 15 They will examine into the true character and genius of some late events. **1814** T. BELL *View Coven.* Wks. 270 The Decalogue changed as it were its genius. *a* **1850** CALHOUN *Wks.* (1874) III. 219 The genius of our constitution is opposed to the assumption of power. **1875** JOWETT *Plato* (ed. 2) II. 17 He expresses the very genius of the old comedy. **1875** STEWART & TAIT *Unseen Univ.* i. § 36 (1878) 54 The whole genius of Christianity would appear to point towards a total submission.

   d. With reference to a place: The body of associations connected with, or inspirations that may be derived from it. (Cf. 1 and 7.)

   [**1681** DRYDEN *Prol. Univ. Oxf.* 25 By the sacred genius of this place.] **1823** LAMB *Elia.* Ser. II. *Tombs in Abbey,* Is the being shown over a place the same as silently for ourselves detecting the genius of it? **1844** DISRAELI *Coningsby* IV. xv, In Palestine, I met a German student who was accumulating materials for the History of Christianity, and studying the genius of the place. **1844** STANLEY *Arnold* I. iii. 101 Whatever peculiarity of character was impressed on the scholars whom it sent forth, was derived not from the genius of the place, but from the genius of the man.

   † **e.** Of material things, diseases, etc.: The natural character, inherent constitution or tendency.

   1675 GREW *Anat. Trunks* II. vi. § 6 Convolvula's do not wind by any peculiar Nature or Genius. **1697** DRYDEN *Virg. Georg.* I. 80 The Culture suiting to the sev'ral Kinds Of Seeds and Plants; and what will thrive and rise, And what the Genius of the Soil denies. **1725** POPE *Odyss.* IX. 152 Here all products and all plants abound, Sprung from the fruitful genius of the ground. **1728–30** – in Spence *Anecd.* (1858) 9 In laying out a garden, the first thing to be considered is the genius of the place: thus at Riskins.. Lord Bathurst should have raised two or three mounts; because his situation is all a plain. **1747** BERKELEY *Tar-water in Plague* Wks. III. 483 Fevers.. change their genius in different seasons.

   4. Natural ability or capacity; quality of mind; the special endowments which fit a man for his peculiar work. (Now only with mixture of sense 5.)

   1649 MILTON *Eikon.* 241 To unsettle the conscience of any knowing Christian is a thing above the genius of his Cleric elocution. **1662** EVELYN *Chalcogr.* 74 Hugens.. so worthily celebrated for his.. universal Mathematical Genius. **1725** T. HEARNE *Pref. to R. Brunne's Chron.* I. 27 For no Study can be more pleasant to Persons of a genius than that of our National History and Antiquities. **1729** FRANKLIN *Ess.* Wks. 1840 II. 263 Different men have geniuses adapted to a variety of different arts and manufactures. **1759** ROBERTSON *Hist. Scot.* I. i. 68 His genius was of that kind which ripens slowly. **1768** W. GILPIN *Prints* 125 Dorigny seems to have exhausted his genius upon it. **1831** BREWSTER *Newton* (1855) I. xii. 322 The peculiar genius of Newton has been displayed in his investigation of the law of universal gravitation. **1840** THIRLWALL *Greece* VII. 71 A design certainly suited to Alexander's genius. **1853** LYTTON *My Novel* II. x, The Squire, whose active genius was always at some repair or improvement.

   b. Natural aptitude, coupled with more or less of inclination † *to, for* (something). (Now only with mixture of sense 5.)

   1643 SIR T. BROWNE *Relig. Med.* I. § 6, I have no Genius to disputes in Religion. **1707** J. ARCHDALE *Descr. Carolina* II, I advise, That such Missionaries be well skill'd in Chymistry, and some natural Genius to seek the Virtues in Herbs, Metts and Minerals. **1727** DE FOE *Syst. Magic* I. i. (1840) 7 One having a genius to this, another to that kind of knowledge. **1788** PRIESTLEY *Lect. Hist.* v. 1. 381 A genius for science by no means depends upon climate. **1798** FERRIAR *Illustr. Sterne* ii. 38 He had no great genius for poetry. **1818** JAS. MILL *Brit. India* II. v. viii. 684 He had no genius, any more than Clive, for schemes of policy including large views of the past. **1844** MRS. BROWNING *Crowned & Buried* xxvii, He had The genius to be loved. **1871** SMILES *Charac.* vi. (1876) 183 Their genius for borrowing, in the long run, usually proves their ruin. **1878** R. W. DALE *Lect. Preach.* ii. 38 Mr. Gladstone has an extraordinary genius for finance. **1889** LOWELL *Latest Lit. Ess., Walton* (1891) 80 Walton had a genius for friendships.

   5. (Only in *sing.*) Native intellectual power of an exalted type, such as is attributed to those who are esteemed greatest in any department of art, speculation, or practice; instinctive and extraordinary capacity for imaginative creation, original thought, invention, or discovery. Often contrasted with *talent*.

This sense, which belongs also to F. *génie*, Ger. *genie*, appears to have been developed in the 18th c. (It is not recognized in Johnson's Dictionary.) In sense 4 the word had come to be applied with especial frequency to the kind of intellectual power manifested by poets and artists; and when in this application 'genius', as native endowment, came to be contrasted with the aptitudes that can be acquired by study, the approach to the modern sense was often very close. The further development of meaning was prob. influenced by association with senses 1 and 2, which suggested that the word had an especial fitness to denote that particular kind of intellectual power which has the appearance of proceeding from a supernatural inspiration or possession, and which seems to arrive at its results in an inexplicable and miraculous manner. This use, which app. originated in England, came into great prominence in Germany, and gave the designation of *Genieperiode* to the epoch in German literature otherwise known as the 'Sturm und Drang' period. Owing to the influence of Ger. literature in the present century, this is now the most familiar sense of the Eng. word, and usually colours the other senses. It was by the Ger. writers of the 18th c. that the distinction between 'genius' and 'talent', which had some foundation in Fr. usage, was sharpened into the strong antithesis which is now universally current, so that the one term is hardly ever defined without reference to the other. The difference between *genius* and *talent* has been formulated very variously by different writers, but there is general agreement in regarding the former as the higher of the two, as 'creative' and 'original', and as achieving its results by instinctive perception and spontaneous activity, rather than by processes which admit of being distinctly analyzed.

1749 FIELDING *Tom Jones* XIV. i, By the wonderful force of genius only, without the least assistance of learning. **1755** W. SHARPE (*title*), Dissertation on Genius. **1756–82** J. WHARTON *Ess. Pope* (1782) II. viii. 21 It were to be wished that no youth of genius were suffered to look into Statius. **1783** BLAIR *Rhet.* iii. I. 41 Genius always imports something inventive or creative. **1801** FUSELI in *Lect. Paint.* i. (1848) 348 By Genius I mean that power which enlarges the circle of human knowledge; which discovers new materials of Nature, or combines the known with novelty. **1849** MACAULAY *Hist. Eng.* ii. I. 259 The genius of Halifax bore down all opposition. **1853** DE QUINCEY *Autobiog. Sk. Wks.* L. 198 *note*, Talent and genius..are not merely different, they are in polar opposition to each other. Talent is intellectual power of every kind, which acts and manifests itself..through the will and the active forces. Genius..is that much rarer species of intellectual power which is derived from the genial nature—from the spirit of suffering and enjoying—from the spirit of pleasure and pain..It is a function of the passive nature. **1858** CARLYLE *Fredk. Gt.* IV. iii. I. 407 Genius..means transcendant capacity of taking trouble, first of all. **1866** R. W. DALE *Disc. Spec. Occ.* vii. 241 The word hardly knew what music was, till the genius of Handel did homage to the Messiah. **1883** FROUDE *Short Stud.* IV. II. iii. 195 A man of genius..is a spring in which there is always more behind than flows from it.

6. Applied to a person. † **a.** With qualifying adj.: One who has *great, little*, etc. 'genius' (sense 4) or natural ability. Also, one who has a 'genius' (sense 3) or disposition of a specified kind. *Obs.*

[**1647–1697**: see 6 b.] **1731** A. HILL *Adv. Poets* 18 Vulgar Genii, sowr'd by sharp Disdain. **1768** W. GILPIN *Prints* 237 With a little genius nothing sways like a great name. *Ibid.* 240 A trifling genius may be found, who will give ten guineas for Hollar's shells.

b. A person endowed with 'genius' (in sense 5). (Now only *geniuses* in pl.)

The earlier examples, in which the word is accompanied by a laudatory adj., probably belongs strictly to 6 a.

1647 W. BROWNE tr. *Gomberville's Polexander* IV. IV. 294 Those great Genius's, on whom most Kings disburthen themselves of the government of their Estates. **1697** DRYDEN *Virg., Past.* Pref. (1721) I. 91 Extraordinary Genius's have a sort of Prerogative, which may dispense them from Laws. **1711** ADDISON *Spect.* No. 160 ¶ 1 There is no Character more frequently given to a Writer, than that of being a Genius. I have heard many a little Sonneteer called a *fine Genius*. **1755** AMORY *Mem.* (1769) I. 91 Such admirable genii as Burnet and Butler. **1762–71** H. WALPOLE *Vertue's Anecd. Paint.* (1786) II. 90 Under the direction of that genius [Inigo Jones] the

King erected the house at Greenwich. **1793** BEDDOES *Math. Evid.* 61 Why are not geniuses for arts or sciences born among savages? **1800** LAMB *Lett.* (1888) I. 141 All poems are good poems to George; all men are fine geniuses. **1806** H. SIDDONS *Maid, Wife, & Widow* I. 173 Isaac was a good-dispositioned, industrious boy, but no genius. **1873** H. ROGERS *Orig. Bible* ix. (1875) 382 Certain transcendent geniuses—the Bacons, the Newtons, the Shakespeares, the Miltons.

    7. *phr.* ‖ **genius loci** [L. = 'genius of the place'], the presiding deity or spirit (see sense 1); but often used in the sense of 3 d.

    1771 SMOLLETT *Humph. Cl., To Dr. Lewis* 8 Aug., The pleasure-grounds are, in my opinion, not so well laid out according to the *genius loci.* **1835** W. IRVING *Crayon Misc., Newstead Abbey* (1863) 286 A white marble bust of the *genius loci,* the noble poet, shone conspicuously from its pedestal. **1878** L. W. M. LOCKHART *Mine is Thine* xix. II. 50 The *genius loci* may be solemn and pensive, but we laugh at him.

    8. *attrib.* and *Comb.,* as *genius school; genius-gifted, genii-haunted* adjs.; *genius-born a.,* born of genius; † *genius-chamber,* bridal chamber (see GENIAL *a.*[1]).

    1894 MILN *Strolling Players in East* xxi. 194, I represented..the sweet meek maiden who was the °genius-born daughter of Shakespeare's pen. **1513** DOUGLAS *Æneis* IV. i. 36 War nocht also to me is displesant °Genyus chalmer or matrimone to hant. *a* **1851** Mrs. SHERWOOD *Life* i. (1854) 17 My °genius-gifted and benevolent father. **1817** Mrs. HEMANS *Mod. Greece* Poems (1875) 29 Or Tigris rolls his °genii-haunted wave. **1882** SEELEY *Nat. Relig.* (1883) 166 The point of close resemblance between the °genius school in art, and the anti-legal school in morals.

    Hence (*nonce-wds.*) **Ge·niused** *a.* [-ED[2]], endowed with genius; **Ge·niusess** [-ESS], a female genius; **Ge·niuskin** [-KIN], a little genius.

    1772 NUGENT tr. *Hist. Friar Gerund* I. 145 She was not a common woman, but a geniusess and an elegant writrix. **1880** S. LANIER *Poems* (1884) 108 Led by the soaring-genius'd Sylvester. **1882** H. C. MERIVALE *Faucit of B.* II. i. xvii. 21 He failed..to catch a single idea out of those words with which my geniuskin of song had inspired me.

2. Choose a word—perhaps a current slang word—and, using all the dictionaries available to you, write an essay in which you describe its development in English.

MENCKEN: EUPHEMISMS

Aids to Study

1. Americans seem always to be embarrassed about toilets. Make lists of some of the euphemisms you've heard for a toilet and for the room in which it stands.

2. Euphemisms about sex often seem more suggestive than do matter-of-fact explicit, scientific words. Look up this sense of *suggestive* to make sure you understand it, and then try to decide why the statement might be true.

3. What reasons can you find to explain all the various classes of euphemisms Mencken cites?

4. Is a euphemism a bad thing?

5. What process or processes of semantic change seem to be involved in the creation of euphemisms? Cite some examples to illustrate your conclusions.

Topics for Writing

1. Trades seem to want to be considered professions. Pick a trade not mentioned by Mencken and look for euphemisms in its names for itself and its activities. Write an essay in which you describe what you find.

2. *Druggist* and *pharmacist* have had curious careers in English. Write an essay in which you reconstruct their histories from the *OED* entries below. Has euphemism had any bearing on their use?

> **Druggist** (drŏ·gist). Also 7 drouguist. [a. F. *droguiste* (1549 in Hatz.-Darm.), f. *drogue* drug: see -IST.] One who sells or deals in drugs.
> In Scotland and United States the usual name for a pharmaceutical chemist. *Chemist and druggist:* see CHEMIST 4.
> **1611** COTGR., *Drogueur*, a druggist, or drug-seller. **1639** J. W. tr. *Guibert's Physic.* I. 10 Two pennyworth of Sene..which they may have at the Apothecaries or drouguists. **1652** GAULE *Magastrom.* 360 Two chymists had agreed upon a cheat, that one of them should turn druggist, and sell strange roots and powders. **1709** ADDISON *Tatler* No. 131 ¶ 3 That this new Corporation of Druggists had inflamed the Bills of Mortality and puzzled the College of Physicians with Diseases, for which they neither knew a Name or Cure. **1799** *Med. Jrnl.* II. 123 Mr. Brown, Wholesale Chemist and Druggist. **1802** *Ibid.* VIII. 247 Compounding and vending medicines in the shop of a druggist or an apothecary.

> **Pharmacist** (fä·ɹmăsist). [f. PHARMACY + -IST: cf. *botanist.*] A person skilled or engaged in pharmacy; one who prepares or dispenses medicines; a druggist or pharmaceutical chemist.
> **1834** LYTTON *Pompeii* I. ii, Unskilful pharmacists! pleasure and study are not elements to be thus mixed together. **1875** H. C. WOOD *Therap.* (1879) 437 He used two samples of the alkaloid prepared by different pharmacists. **1898** *Rev. Brit. Pharm.* 29 The Pharmacopœia, generally a stickler in legality, speaks of 'pharmacists', which, strictly speaking, chemists and druggists are not.

3. Mencken himself makes vigorous use of the language: he speaks of "the advance of human taxidermy," and he describes morticians' "expectant hauling of the ill." Reread his discussion of *mortician* and the other euphemisms connected with that trade, and then write an essay in which you show how Mencken manages to make clear his amusement and disgust while appearing merely to present a factual discussion.

4. Advertising is obviously a good place to look for euphemisms. Analyze the ads for cigarettes, patent medicines, detergents, or some other group of products, and write an essay in which you discuss the euphemisms you find and try to explain the reasons for their existence.

SCHLAUCH: SEMANTIC REJUVENATION

Aids to Study

1. What do these words and phrases mean as Miss Schlauch uses them: *jejune, context, the original metaphoric synthesis, evinced,* and *rejuvenation?*

2. What does your desk dictionary tell you about the meaning of *ambiguity?* Note how the double force of old and new meanings works in the poetry Miss Schlauch cites.

3. How do Miss Schlauch's remarks about the usefulness of knowing older and etymological meanings square with the conclusions of Professors Robertson and Cassidy?

4. Schlauch speaks (p. 52) of "*sophisticated* writers." Sledd (p. 98) also

uses the word. What does it mean in these contexts? What does it have to do with good manners?

5. In the Dickinson poem, what are *essential* oils? Does *necessary* carry all the meaning of *essential*?

6. What is *"attar* from the rose"?

Topics for Writing

1. Under what circumstances should you ignore what "the dictionary says"? Use some examples and write an essay on this subject.

2. What is the term used on your campus for a short, unannounced quiz? For a class which didn't meet because the teacher didn't appear? For un-excused absences? For a course said to be ridiculously easy? Write an essay in which you discuss the origins of some of these terms, using dictionaries where they will help you and what you have learned about semantic change where they will not.

3. Here is a poem by John Donne. Study its diction carefully and write an essay in which you discuss the semantic rejuvenation you find.

A Valediction: forbidding mourning.
As virtuous men passe mildly away,
    And whisper to their soules, to goe,
Whilst some of their sad friends doe say,
    The breath goes now, and some say, no:

So let us melt, and make no noise,
    No teare-floods, nor sigh-tempests move,
T'were prophanation of our joyes
    To tell the layetie our love.

Moving of th'earth brings harmes and feares,
    Men reckon what it did and meant,
But trepidation of the spheares,
    Though greater farre, is innocent.

Dull sublunary lovers love
    (Whose soule is sense) cannot admit
Absence, because it doth remove
    Those things which elemented it.

But we by a love, so much refin'd,
    That our selves know not what it is,
Inter-assured of the mind,
    Care lesse, eyes, lips, and hands to misse.

Our two soules therefore, which are one,
    Though I must goe, endure not yet
A breach, but an expansion,
    Like gold to ayery thinnesse beate.

If they be two, they are two so
　　As stiffe twin compasses are two,
Thy soule the fixt foot, makes no show
　　To move, but doth, if the 'other doe.

And though it in the center sit,
　　Yet when the other far doth rome,
It leanes, and hearkens after it,
　　And growes erect, as that comes home.

Such wilt thou be to mee, who must
　　Like th'other foot, obliquely runne;
Thy firmnes makes my circle just,
　　And makes me end, where I begunne.

JOHNSON: PREFACE TO THE DICTIONARY

Aids to Study

1. Discuss Johnson's attitude toward the English spelling of his time.
2. Read the *Oxford English Dictionary's* etymologies for *enchantment, incantation,* and *entire,* given below. Do Johnson's etymological discussions seem to be accurate?

> **Enchantment** (en,tʃɑ·ntmĕnt). Forms: 4–7 enchaunt(e)ment, 5–8 inchaunt(e)ment, 3– enchantment. [a. OF. *enchantement,* f. *enchanter* to ENCHANT: see -MENT.]
>
> † **Inca·nt,** *v. Obs.* [ad. L. *incantā-re* to chant, make incantation, charm, enchant, bewitch, f. *in-* (IN-²)+*cantāre* to sing, chant.] a. *intr.* To use incantation or enchantment. b. *trans.* To enchant, charm. Hence Inca·nting *vbl. sb.* and *ppl. a.*
> 　　1546 BALE *Eng. Votaries* I. (1550) 35 All vayn and craftye scyences.. exorcising, incanting, & conjuring. 1658 BROMHALL *Treat. Specters* I. 38 They ..have lesse incanting amongst them then formerly. 1665 SIR T. HERBERT *Trav.* (1677) 306 With incanting voices,..poesy, mirth, and wine, raising the sport commonly to admiration.
>
> † **Incantate,** *v. Obs.* rare⁻⁰. [f. ppl. stem of L. *incantāre:* see prec.] = prec.
> 　　1623 COCKERAM II, To Charme, Incantate.
>
> **Incantation** (inkæntē¹·ʃən). [a. F. *incantation* (13th c. in Godef. *Compl.*), ad. L. *incantātiōnem,* n. of action from *incantāre:* see INCANT.]
>
> **Entire** (entəiᵒ·ɹ), *a., adv.* and *sb.* Forms: α. 4–6 enter(e, 5–6 entier(e, -tyer(e, (4 entre, 4–7 enteer(e), 7 entyre, 6–entire. β. 4 intier, 5–6 intere, 5–7 intyre, 6 Sc. inteir, 6–9 intire. [a. OF. *entier, entir* = Pr. *entier, entieyr,* Cat. *enter,* Sp. *entero,* It. *intero,* Pg. *inteiro:*-L. *inte·gr-um,* f. *in* not + °*tag-* root of *tangĕre* to touch.
> 　　The L. *integer* was used in the lit. senses 'whole, unbroken sound', and in the fig. of 'untainted, upright'; these senses remained in early French and consequently in Middle English, but with very few exceptions only the lit. senses have survived to the present time.]

3. Vocabulary:
　　a. The *genius* of our tongue (p. 57)—What does he mean by *genius?* Will

your desk dictionary help you? Examine the *OED* entry (pp. 366–71); what does it record about this use of the word?

b. *cognation* (p. 58)—How does it differ from *descent*?

c. *appendant* (p. 60)—How do *appendant* clauses differ from *dependent* ones? Is *appendant* still a useful word? How can you tell?

d. *truncated* (p. 62)—If the examples were *truncated*, what happened to them?

e. *extenuation* (p. 63)—What is it?

f. *auxiliaries* (p. 63)—Who or what are these?

g. *intumescence* (p. 66)—What has this to do with the tide?

4. Make a list of ten other words from Johnson's preface which are unfamiliar to you. Which ones are words apparently no longer in common use? How can you be sure? Which are words whose meanings have changed appreciably from Johnson's day to ours?

5. Johnson decided to limit his researches into the older English language to the Renaissance and after (p. 61). How accurate do you think his remarks on this matter are, especially those in the famous paragraph beginning, "But as every language has a time of rudeness . . ."?

6. Here are four entries from Johnson's dictionary (reprinted by permission of the New York Public Library, Rare Book Division) Compare them closely with the entries in your desk dictionary. What differences do you detect in Johnson's method?

To Baste. *v. a.* participle paſſ. *baſted*, or *baſten*. [*baſtonner*, Fr. *Bazata*, in the Armorick dialect, ſignifies to ſtrike with a ſtick; from which perhaps *baſton* a ſtick, and all its derivatives, or collaterals, may be deduced.]

1. To beat with a ſtick.

> Quoth ſhe, I grant it is in vain
> For one's that *baſted* to feel pain,
> Becauſe the pangs his bones endure,
> Contribute nothing to the cure.   *Hudibras.*
>   Tir'd with diſpute, and ſpeaking Latin,
> As well as *baſting*, and bear bating.   *Hudibras.*
>   *Baſtings* heavy, dry, obtuſe,
> Only dulneſs can produce;
> While a little gentle jerking
> Sets the ſpirits all aworking.   *Swift.*

2. To drip butter, or any thing elſe, upon meat as it turns upon the ſpit.

> Sir, I think the meat wants what I have, a *baſting*.
>   *Shakeſp. Romeo and Juliet.*

3. To moiſten meat on the ſpit by falling upon it.

> The fat of roaſted mutton falling on the birds, will ſerve to *baſte* them, and ſo ſave time and butter.
>   *Swift's Directions to the Cook.*

4. To ſew ſlightly. [*baſter*, Fr. to ſtitch.]

CANT. *n. ʃ.* [probably from *cantus*, Lat. implying the odd tone of voice uſed by vagrants; but imagined by ſome to be corrupted from *quaint.*]

1. A corrupt dialect uſed by beggars and vagabonds.
2. A particular form of ſpeaking peculiar to ſome certain claſs or body of men.

> I write not always in the proper terms of navigation, land ſervice, or in the *cant* of any profeſſion. *Dryden.*

> If we would trace out the original of that flagrant and avowed impiety, which has prevailed among us for ſome years, we ſhould find, that it owes its riſe to that *cant* and hypocriſy, which had taken poſſeſſion of the people's minds in the times of the great rebellion. *Addiſon. Freeholder,* N° 37.

> Aſtrologers, with an old paltry *cant*, and a few pot-hooks for planets, to amuſe the vulgar, have too long been ſuffered to abuſe the world. *Swift's Predictions for the Year* 1701.

> A few general rules, with a certain *cant* of words, has ſometimes ſet up an illiterate heavy writer, for a moſt judicious and formidable critick. *Addiſon. Spectator,* N° 291.

3. A whining pretenſion to goodneſs, in formal and affected terms.

> Of promiſe prodigal, while pow'r you want,
> And preaching in the ſelf-denying *cant*. *Dryden's Aurengz.*

4. Barbarous jargon.

> The affectation of ſome late authours, to introduce and multiply *cant* words, is the moſt ruinous corruption in any language. *Swift.*

5. Auction.

> Numbers of theſe tenants, or their deſcendants, are now offering to ſell their leaſes by *cant*, even thoſe which were for lives. *Swift.*

To **CANT.** *v. n.* [from the noun.] To talk in the jargon of particular profeſſions, or in any kind of formal affected language, or with a peculiar and ſtudied tone of voice.

> Men *cant* endleſsly about *materia* and *forma*; hunt chimeras by rules of art, or dreſs up ignorance in words of bulk or found, which may ſtop up the mouth of enquiry.
> *Glanville's Scepſis Scientifica.*

> That uncouth affected garb of ſpeech, or *canting* language rather, if I may ſo call it, which they have of late taken up, is the ſignal diſtinction and characteriſtical note of that, which, in that their new language, they call the godly party. *Sanderſon.*

> The buſy, ſubtile ſerpents of the law,
> Did firſt my mind from true obedience draw;
> While I did limits to the king preſcribe,
> And took for oracles that *canting* tribe. *Roſcommon.*

> Unſkill'd in ſchemes by planets to foreſhow,
> Like *canting* raſcals, how the wars will go. *Dryden's Juven.*

OATS. *n. f.* [aten, Saxon.] A grain, which in England is generally given to horfes, but in Scotland fupports the people.

It is of the grafs leaved tribe ; the flowers have no petals, and are difpofed in a loofe panicle : the grain is eatable. The meal makes tolerable good bread. *Miller.*

The *oats* have eaten the horfes. *Shakefpeare.*

It is bare mechanifm, no otherwife produced than the turning of a wild *oatbeard*, by the infinuation of the particles of moifture. *Locke.*

For your lean cattle, fodder them with barley ftraw firft, and the *oat* ftraw laft. *Mortimer's Hufbandry.*

His horfe's allowance of *oats* and beans, was greater than the journey required. *Swift.*

THING. *n. f.* [ðınʒ, Saxon ; *ding*, Dutch.]
1. Whatever is ; not a perfon. A general word.

Do not you chide ; I have a *thing* for you.
——You have a *thing* for me ?
It is a common *thing*—
——Ha ?
——To have a foolifh wife. *Shakefp. Othello.*

The great mafter he found bufy in packing up his *things* againft his departure. *Knolles's Hift. of the Turks.*

The remnant of the meat-offering is a *thing* moft holy.
Lev. ii. 3.

Says the mafter, you devour the fame *things* that they would have eaten, mice and all. *L'Eftrange.*

A *thing* by neither man or woman priz'd,
And fcarcely known enough to be defpis'd. *Dryden.*

I fhould blufh to own fo rude a *thing*,
As it is to fhun the brother of my king. *Dryden.*

Wicked men, who underftand any *thing* of wifdom, may fee the imprudence of worldly and irreligious courfes. *Tillotfon.*
2. It is ufed in contempt.

I have a *thing* in profe, begun above twenty-eight years ago, and almoft finifhed : it will make a four fhilling vo-lume. *Swift.*
3. It is ufed of perfons in contempt, or fometimes with pity.

See, fons, what *things* you are ! how quickly nature
Falls to revolt, when gold becomes her objeȼt ?
For this the foolifh over-careful fathers
Have broke their fleeps with thought, their brains with
care. *Shakefpeare's Henry* IV.

Never any *thing* was fo unbred as that odious man. *Congr.*

The poor *thing* fighed, and with a bleffing expreffed with the utmoft vehemence turned from me. *Addifon.*

I'll be this abjeȼt *thing* no more.
Love give me back my heart again. *Granville.*

4. It is uſed by *Shakeſpeare* once in a ſenſe of honour.
   I lov'd the maid I married ; never man
   Sigh'd truer breath : but that I ſee thee here,
   Thou noble *thing !* more dances my wrapt heart. *Shakeſp.*

Topics for Writing

1. One of the best ways to appreciate Johnson's difficulties is to try to write definitions yourself. Write full definitions for each of these, without consulting any dictionary (do this one in class, so that you won't be tempted to seek help!) :

a. book (n.)	e. elegant
b. burial	f. solicit
c. collect (v.)	g. to
d. gladden	h. two

   Now consult your desk dictionary, evaluate your performance, and write an essay in which you discuss the difficulties which turned up.

2. Write an essay in which you describe Johnson's purposes when he began his dictionary and contrast them with his more sober appraisal of what he had accomplished when it was done.

3. Study the four entries above from Johnson's own dictionary. Write an essay in which you compare them with the entries for the same words in either your desk dictionary or *Webster's Third New International Dictionary.* What are the differences in the lexicographers' purposes, methods, and results?

MACDONALD: THE STRING UNTUNED

Aids to Study

1. Consult your desk dictionary for these terms, often used as "warning labels" in dictionaries: *slang, colloquial, erroneous, incorrect, illiterate.* Find examples of words to which you would attach these labels if you were a lexicographer. Now check your choices against your desk dictionary and against Merriam-Webster-III (MW-III).

2. Macdonald says that MW-III is the only English dictionary now in print which is comparable to the *Oxford English Dictionary.* But there are important differences between them. List as many of these as you can. Then consult Mitford Mathews's essay, pp. 23ff., for the *OED* entry for *deer,* and compare it in detail with the MW-III entry below on p. 379.

3. On pp. 74–5 of Macdonald's essay is a list of new political terms which MW-III defines. How many are in your desk dictionary? Look in the daily newspaper for some even newer political terms which are not in *any* dictionary. How would you define them?

4. What is a *structural linguist?* Are there other kinds of linguists? What is a *polyglot?*

deer \ˈdi(ə)r, ˈdiə\ *n, pl* **deer** *also* **deers** [ME, deer, animal, fr. OE
dēor beast; akin
to OHG *tior* wild
animal, ON *dȳr*,
Goth *dius* wild
animal, Lith *dvèsti*
to breathe, expire,
Skt *dhvaṁsati* he
falls to dust, per-
ishes — more at
DUST] **1** *obs* **:** ANI-
MAL; *esp* **:** a quad-
ruped mammal
⟨rats and mice and
such small ~ —
Shak.⟩ **2 a :** any
of numerous ru-
minant mammals
that constitute the
family Cervidae,
that have two large
and two small
hoofs on each foot
and antlers borne
by the males of

fallow deer

nearly all and by the females of a few forms, that are represented
by numerous species and individuals in most regions except
most of Africa and Australia, and that constitute an important
source of food in many places for man and the larger carniv-
orous animals — see CARIBOU, ELK, MOOSE, MUSK DEER, REIN-
DEER; VENISON **b :** any of the small or medium-sized members
of the family as distinguished from certain esp. large forms
(as elk, moose, or caribou) **3 :** DEERSKIN **4 :** a grayish yel-
lowish brown that is lighter and slightly yellower than olive
wood and lighter than acorn — called also *bobolink, camel's
hair*

5. Vocabulary:
   a. What would a "*Jim Crow* flavor" (p. 70) be?
   b. What kind of approach is a "*normative* approach"?
   c. Is *schoolmarm* a word to use without quotation marks or italics? How
      would you decide?
   d. What is a *nonce* word? Find some examples in your desk dictionary.
   e. What does *tergiversating* mean?
   f. Is *scholar's knee* (p. 81) a good synonym for *gnostimania*? What is
      Macdonald's point?
   g. What's the matter with *irregardless* (p. 83)?
   h. What is "the unresolved *bimonthly* and *biweekly* problem" (p. 89),
      and how do you think it might best be resolved?
6. Macdonald doesn't like the use of the *schwa* (ə) or "upside-down *e*."
   Why not? Does your desk dictionary use it? What difficulty would you encounter in using a conventional English letter to represent that sound in
   recording pronunciations?
7. Consult your desk dictionary for the meanings of the word *masses*. What is
   Macdonald's objection to MW-III's treatment of it? Is he justified?
8. What is usually meant by "encyclopedic material" in a dictionary? Why does
   Macdonald object to its omission in MW-III? What are MW-III's reasons for
   omitting it? Considering the purposes of a dictionary, who do you think
   has the better argument?

Topics for Writing

1. Write an essay in which you discuss the purposes for which *you* need a
   dictionary, and describe a kind of dictionary which would be ideal for

those purposes. Then discuss existing dictionaries to see which ones, if any, meet these needs best.

2. Here are MW-II's, MW-III's, and *OED's* entries for *disinterested* and *uninterested*. Write an essay in which you explore the history of the current confusion of these words and decide what you think a modern dictionary ought to say about them. Do you believe your desk dictionary treats them soundly? How will what you have learned affect your own use of these words, if at all?

dis·in′ter·est·ed (-ĕs·tĕd; -ĭs·tĭd; 119; *cf.* INTERESTED), *adj.*
1. Lacking or revealing lack of interest; indifferent; uninterested. *Now Rare.*
2. Not influenced by regard to personal advantage; free from selfish motive; not biased or prejudiced; as, a *disinterested* decision or judge; *disinterested* sacrifices.
Syn. and **Ant.** — See FAIR.

un·in′ter·est·ed (ŭn·ĭn′tĕr·ĕs·tĕd; *see* INTERESTED), *adj.*
Not interested; as: **a** *Obs.* Impartial; disinterested. **b** Not having an interest, esp. a property interest (in something); not personally concerned. **c** Not having the mind or feelings engaged; inattentive; apathetic; indifferent; — now the usual sense. — **un·in′ter·est·ed·ly,** *adv.* — **-ed·ness,** *n.*

disinterested *adj* **1 :** lacking or revealing lack of interest : INDIFFERENT, UNINTERESTED, APATHETIC, UNCONCERNED **2 :** not influenced by regard to personal advantage : free from selfish motive : not biased or prejudiced ⟨a ~ decision⟩ ⟨~ sacrifices⟩ **syn** see INDIFFERENT

un·interested \″+\ *adj* [¹*un-* + *interested,* past part. of *interest*] **:** not interested: as **a :** having no interest and esp. no property interest in **:** not personally concerned **b :** not having the mind or feelings engaged **:** INATTENTIVE, APATHETIC **syn** see INDIFFERENT

Disi·nterested, *ppl. a.* [f. prec. vb + -ED ¹; or f. DIS- 10 + INTERESTED.]

† **1.** Without interest or concern; not interested, unconcerned. *? Obs.*

a 1612 DONNE βιαθανατος (1644) 99 Cases, wherein the party is dis-interested. 1684 *Contempl. State of Man* i. x. (1699) 113 How dis-interested are they in all Worldly matters, since they fling their Wealth and Riches into the Sea. 1767 *Junius Lett.* iii. 18 A careless disinterested spirit is no part of his character.

2. Not influenced by interest; impartial, unbiased, unprejudiced; now always, Unbiased by personal interest; free from self-seeking. (Of persons, or their dispositions, actions, etc.)

1659 O. WALKER *Oratory* 115 The soul..sits now as the most disinterested Arbiter, and impartial judge of her own works, that she can be. 1705 STANHOPE *Paraphr.* III. 435 So should the Love to our Neighbour be..Not mercenary and designing, but disinterested and hearty. 1726 *Adv. Capt. R. Boyle* 273 Any disinterested Person would make the same Judgement; your Passion has blinded yours. 1800 MRS. HERVEY *Mourtray Fam.* II. 82, I fairly own I was not disinterested in wishing you here. 1865 LIVINGSTONE *Zambesi* xxii. 446 His disinterested kindness to us..can never be forgotten.

Uni·nterested, *ppl. a.* [UN-¹ 8.]

† **1.** Unbiassed, impartial. *Obs.*

a 1646 J. GREGORY *Posthumà, Episc. Puerorum* (1649) 107 By this uninterested disguis the more to justifie the Celebrations. 1660 R. COKE *Power & Subj.* 49 Nor do I think that any uninterested casuist will deny [etc.].

† **2.** Free from motives of personal interest; disinterested. *Obs.*

1661 (*title*), A Relation of the business..concerning Bedford Levell,.. by a person uninterested. 1704 N. N. tr. *Boccalini's Advts. fr. Parnass.* III. 191 What think you of uninterested Men, who value the Publick Good beyond their own private Interest? 1767 COWPER *Let. Wks.* 1837 XV. 17 You know me to be an uninterested person.

3. Unconcerned, indifferent.

1771 *Ann. Reg.* II. 253/1 He is no cold, uninterested, and uninteresting advocate for the cause he espouses. 1774 *Trinket* 54 In this amiable society can my heart be uninterested? 1823 BYRON *Juan* x. lxxiii, In the same quaint, Uninterested tone. 1850 THACKERAY *Pendennis* lvii, An almost silent but not uninterested spectator.

Hence Uni·nterestedly *adv.*, -ness.

1691 T. H[ALE] *Acc. New Invent.* 55 As to that Uninterestedness so pretended to by them. 1891 H. HERMAN *His Angel* 108 He looked upon the.. crowds..uninterestedly.

3. Write a *précis* (look it up!) of Macdonald's review, stating as clearly as possible his objections to the editorial policies of MW-III, as well as his commendations.

4. Write an essay in which you apply Macdonald's standards to Dr. Johnson's descriptions of his own methods. How well does Dr. Johnson measure up to Macdonald's demands?

SLEDD: THE LEXICOGRAPHER'S UNEASY CHAIR

Aids to Study

1. Sledd discusses the question of *motives* (p. 94). Does Macdonald question the MW-III lexicographers' motives?

2. State as clearly as possible "the ideal of the standard and standardizing dictionary" to which Sledd refers (p. 94). On what assumptions does this ideal rest?

3. Sledd says that the question "how rational choice among the resources of a language is possible for the man who does not know what those resources are" is unanswerable. What does this mean? What kind of dictionary does it imply that we need?

4. "A dictionary without quotations is like a table of contents without a book" (p. 95). Explain the possible arguments for and against this assertion.

5. What is the matter with *Life* magazine's logic (p. 96)?

6. State arguments for and against the use of the *colloquial* label in a dictionary. List ten words you believe might properly bear that label in a modern dictionary, and state your reasons. In what sort of contexts do they usually appear? Does your desk dictionary label them? Does MW-III?

7. Sledd objects to *alright* as a spelling. What's the matter with it? Would Dr. Johnson have objected too? Compare MW-II, MW-III, and your desk dictionary on this point. How do you think *you* ought to spell it?

8. Vocabulary:
   a. What's a *quibble,* and how did the word develop? Is it only a noun?
   b. What kind of labels do you find on *kye* and *kine* in your desk dictionary? In MW-III? In *OED?*
   c. What is *stridulation?* List some synonyms.
   d. What's the objection to *shook-up* as Standard English?
   e. Does to *rob* someone mean the same thing as to *roll* someone?
   f. What are "*keening* critics"? Does the word have any etymological or semantic relationship to the adjective *keen?*

g. What is the meaning of *popular* in the phrase "popular reviews"? Would *unpopular* be a proper antonym?

h. Examine the etymology and current meaning of *diacritical* (p. 100). What are *diacritics?*

i. *Matters linguistic* and *linguistic matters* seem to mean roughly the same. But *within the dictionary proper* (p. 100) and *within the proper dictionary* don't. Why not? Does your desk dictionary help? What's the difference between the two adjectives?

j. How large is a *plethora* (p. 100)?

k. What are *synonymies* (p. 101)?

Topics for Writing

1. Macdonald objects to some of the prefatory material in MW-III as "impenetrable lexical jargon." Some of it *is* difficult and technical. Sledd quotes from the preface a passage explaining technique of definition. Rewrite the passage in simpler, clearer language, omitting no idea. Make sure that all the terms are clearly defined.

2. One of the central arguments reviewers have had involves "the notion that the lexicographer should be a lawgiver not a historian." Write an essay in which you weigh the arguments on both sides of this question. Which *should* he be? Is there a good single answer? Can he avoid being both?

EVANS: BUT WHAT'S A DICTIONARY FOR?

Aids to Study

1. Evans says (p. 111), ". . . the trouble is due to the fact that . . ." Is this good standard English usage? What do the dictionaries say on this point?

2. "The broad general findings of the new science" are stated in full on pp. 103–4. Compare them closely with Johnson's and Macdonald's views of language, stated and implicit. For example, did Dr. Johnson believe that each language is unique?

3. Evans says that all usage is relative. Relative to *what?*

4. "Words in themselves are not dignified, or silly, or wise, or malicious. But they can be used in dignified, silly, wise, or malicious ways by dignified, silly, wise, or malicious people" (p. 111). How sensible is this statement? Why?

Topics for Writing

1. If you were about to buy an unabridged dictionary and could buy either MW-II or MW-III, which one would you buy? Write an essay in which you discuss your decision, especially in the light of the three reviews you have read.

2. Write an essay in which you distinguish between the ideal qualities of a desk dictionary and those of an unabridged dictionary. Study your desk

dictionary carefully to see what sorts of compromises the editors have had to make in order to save space. Did they make the right ones?

PART TWO

The History of English

SCHLAUCH: FAMILY RELATIONSHIPS AMONG LANGUAGES

Aids to Study

1. Study the several Germanic versions of "Yes, Mother, I have three." Then write as many statements as you can to describe the similarities among them. Remember that *sounds* are more important than *spellings*.
2. Look up the word for *father* in as many English-foreign language dictionaries as possible. From the list of words can you pick out family relationships among languages? Do the same thing with the word *foot*.
3. Study the Romance-language versions of "Yes, Mother, I have three." Make a list of descriptive statements about the similarities, being as complete as possible. Now compare and contrast the statements you've made for the Romance languages with those you've made for the Germanic languages. Where do the differences lie?
4. Why is *Indo-European* a better term for the parent language than *Aryan* or *Indo-Germanic*? Consult a map for the locations of all the members of the Indo-European group.
5. What are *runes*? What, if any, is their relationship to the letters of our alphabet? What unfamiliar letters did you find in Professor Schlauch's essay? What sounds do they seem to stand for?
6. Draw up a chart showing the groups of languages Professor Schlauch discusses. Put Indo-European at the top and then show by lines—as in a family tree—how the several groups are related.
7. Look at the chart you made for number 6 above. Does it show accurately how many Latin and French words English has? What kinds of relationship does this sort of chart omit?

Vocabulary

1. *tang* (p. 115)—What, precisely, does it mean? Where did we get the word?
2. *polyglot* (p. 116)—Does its etymology account for its present meaning, or has semantic change also been at work?
3. *phonology* (p. 118)—What are its meanings?
4. *morphology* (p. 118)—Note that it has several meanings. What is the meaning peculiar to the subject of language?

Topics for Writing

1. Write an essay in which you explore the similarities between English vocabulary words and those of a modern foreign language. Explain your method as you go.
2. Professor Schlauch speaks (p. 119) of Vulgar Latin. Is she saying the same thing about that kind of Latin that we say when we refer to Vulgar English? Consult the dictionaries and your own experience, and then write an essay in which you explore this curious word *vulgar*.

HOOK AND MATHEWS: CHANGES IN THE ENGLISH LANGUAGE

Aids to Study

1. Consult your desk dictionary for the dates usually given to the "Old English" and "Middle English" periods. How do you suppose these dates are arrived at?
2. What sort of influence has Latin had on English since the two languages first made contact?
3. What kinds of contribution did the Norsemen make to the English language?
4. What effects did the Norman Conquest have on English?
5. Mark the heavy stress in each of the following words:
   a. heritage, royal, countess, majesty
   b. cadet, caprice, ballet, fiancee
   Which group do you believe English adopted first? Check the *OED* for the date of the earliest citation of each.
6. Where do you put the heavy stress on *cigarette*? Do you ever hear any other stress pattern for the word?
7. In view of what you've learned in numbers 5 and 6 above, formulate a statement to explain what happens to the stress of French words when they enter English.
8. Compare the French and popular American-English pronunciation of these words: *liqueur, lingerie, bonbon, coiffure, menagerie*. How did the English pronunciation develop? Can you state a principle which describes what happens to the pronunciations of foreign words when English borrows them?
9. What does your desk dictionary say its policy on "correctness" is?
10. Make a list of reasons for various kinds of linguistic change in English.

Vocabulary

1. What is grammatical *case* (p. 122)?
2. Get a good definition of *phonetic*.
3. We use the word *grammar* in a lot of different ways. Make a list of precise meanings, with examples of your own. What is *grammar*? What is *a grammar*? What's the difference?

4. What other English words besides *ox* preserve the *-en* plural today? What other unusual plural forms for nouns in English can you think of?

Topics for Writing

1. Write an essay in which you list some of the grammatical differences you can see between your English and Chaucer's.
2. Select at random a page in your desk dictionary and make a list of the languages of origin mentioned in the etymological entries. How many different languages appear? Which ones occur most often? Write an essay in which you report on your experiment and the conclusions it leads you to draw.
3. What current words—perhaps from the daily newspaper—has American English borrowed recently from foreign languages? How many of them are in your desk dictionary? Write an essay in which you report your findings.

BAUGH: THE ENRICHMENT OF THE LANGUAGE DURING THE RENAISSANCE

Aids to Study

1. What language or languages did Elyot rely on most often to furnish him with new words for English? How useful is your desk dictionary in answering this question?
2. What are some of the fields of knowledge for which late Middle English lacked terminology? Why?
3. Renaissance defenders of pure "English" English were of course fighting a losing battle. How pure was English in 1550? What languages had already contributed generously to its vocabulary?
4. Professor Baugh remarks that we cannot tell which words of a group of borrowings will last, which will disappear. What kinds of causes—however incomplete—do you think might help make these choices for us?
5. English has always had many native resources for making new words—especially by compounding. How do you account for the fact that the Renaissance chose to borrow so much more often than it availed itself of these native resources?

Vocabulary

1. What are *vernaculars*? Is there any pejorative sense of the word in modern English?
2. Elyot says (p. 135) that *maturity* "is translated to the acts of man." Is it still? Check it in an unabridged dictionary.
3. Elyot uses the word *braverie* (p. 135) in a curious way. Consult the *OED* for the meaning Elyot used. Then, consult your desk dictionary: Is this still a good meaning for *bravery*? How about the adjective *brave*?
4. *Amazed* (p. 136), as used by Edward Phillips, had a slightly different

meaning from that we generally give it. What was it? What would Professor Schlauch think of an effort today to use it in that sense?

5. "Strange termes" (p. 136) didn't mean just *unusual* ones. What *did* Elyot mean? Chaloner (p. 136) uses it in this sense too. Look up the etymology of *outlandish* (p. 137). How has it changed its meaning?

Topics for Writing

1. Some Renaissance people were for borrowing, some against it. But we *did* borrow. Write an essay in which you explore the reasons why we almost *had* to borrow. Be sure to discuss the possible alternatives to borrowing.
2. Read the daily newspaper carefully for a few days and make a list of foreign words we seem to be in the process of borrowing. Then, illustrating your discussion with these words, write an essay in which you show under what circumstances we continue to borrow words from foreign languages rather than rely on the resources of our own.

MARCKWARDT: THE LANGUAGE OF THE COLONISTS

Aids to Study

1. What dates do most historians use to include the American Colonial period? How much of the country was settled, how much even explored by the end of that period? Was your own state settled by then?
2. Where, in England, did the main groups of colonists come from? Which groups probably spoke the London dialect?
3. How do puns and rimes from Shakespeare's plays help us discover the sounds of his language?
4. Make a list of the vowels in Shakespeare's English which are different from our modern ones.
5. What differences in stress does Professor Marckwardt describe in comparing Elizabethan and modern American English?
6. What was Shakespeare's practice with second person pronouns? How did it differ from ours?

Vocabulary

1. What's an "*inacomodate* condition," (p. 157)?
2. Where did the expression "to dress meat" come from? Do we still use it?
3. *Queasy*—What's its history?
4. How did Bradford pronounce *boatswain*? Look into the history of the word and its pronunciation.

Topics for Writing

1. Rewrite in good modern English the passage from William Bradford's *History* (pp. 157–8). Then write an essay in which you discuss the differences, besides those Professor Marckwardt cites, between your version and Bradford's. How many of these can you explain reasons for?

2. Look locally—in place names, names of animals, trees, and the like—for evidence of the first settlers' arrival. Were English-speaking settlers the first Europeans to arrive? If not, what signs can you see that others were there first? Write an essay in which you report some of your findings.

3. What signs of Indian influence on English do you find in your state or local area? Write an essay in which you describe and explain these linguistic relics.

PART THREE

The Structure of English

GLEASON: LANGUAGE

Aids to Study

1. What is the difference between *expression* and *content* in language?

2. From your knowledge of a foreign language, find a good example of difference in content between that language and English. Are differences in idioms, such as those between French and English versions of "I'm hungry" and "He's eighteen years old," illustrations of differences in content?

3. Vocabulary is arbitrary. Write the word *pain* on a slip of paper. If it were found by a Frenchman, what would it mean? What other words can you think of which illustrate the same point?

4. Vocabulary "is the least stable and even the least characteristic of the three components of language." Explain why this should be so, illustrating from the things you have learned about words and their changes in meaning in sections one and two.

5. In learning a second language, says Professor Gleason, vocabulary is the easiest matter, yet students fear it most. Read (or perhaps your instructor will read to you) Mark Twain's essay, "The Wonderful German Language." Does the American humorist agree with the fearful students or with the linguists about what offers the greatest difficulty in learning a language?

Vocabulary

1. What is a phoneme? What is a morpheme? What is the significant difference between them?

2. Get good definitions for *phonology, morphology, syntax,* and *rhetoric.* What's the difference between *syntax* and *rhetoric?* Between *grammar* and *syntax?* Between *grammar* and *rhetoric?*

3. What are the semantic problems you encounter in dealing with terms like *rhetoric, syntax,* and *grammar?*

4. What would a science be if it were *autonomous?*

Topics for Writing

1. Explain in an essay what it is about language that linguists are interested in.
2. Make up some nonsense words, and explain why they take the form they do. *Can* you really make up words with absolute freedom as to the sounds you employ?
3. Obviously, Professor Gleason's way of looking at language is different from the view that most of us have as laymen. Write an essay in which you list some of the things you or your parents and friends always thought were true about language, but which linguistics controverts.

ROBERTS: PHONEMES

Aids to Study

1. Go carefully through Roberts's list of phonemes on pages 175 and 176. Pronounce all the words, especially in context: that is, put them in sentences, sometimes at the beginning, sometimes in the middle, sometimes at the end. Do the same with the examples on pp. 176–7. Then make a list of phonemes—and of sample words in which they occur—wherein your speech seems to differ from Roberts's California speech.
2. Compare your lists with those of others in your class who were born and raised in the same town or county or state as you. Do you find consistent dialectal differences in phonemes?
3. Now practice transcribing these words exactly as you normally pronounce them. Be sure to put them in sentences so that you can hear them as you normally say them.

   a. king
   b. rather
   c. possible
   d. follow
   e. Canadian
   f. something
   g. often
   h. surprised
   i. Tuesday
   j. Wednesday
   k. February
   l. absorb

4. Practice making a few simple phonetic transcriptions, being certain that you record the actual sounds you usually make. Transcribe your full name, the way you would say it in response to a question. Transcribe these words: *clothes, interesting, machinery, roof, psychology, execute, executive, screams.* Transcribe this sentence, exactly as you would normally say it: "How do you get to the bookstore from here?"
5. Check your pronunciations—as you've transcribed them—with those in your desk dictionary. Any disagreements?
6. Transcribe these words the way you normally say them:

   a. tenth
   b. length
   c. strength
   d. finger
   e. singer
   f. debt
   g. doubt
   h. pneumatic
   i. graph
   j. news
   k. few
   l. blue

m. cot	o. cat	q. bomb	s. merry
n. caught	p. balm	r. Mary	t. marry

7. How many of the vowels and diphthongs Roberts describes do you actually have? Which ones are you missing? Do you know anyone—a speaker of a different dialect—who has these sounds?

Topics for Writing

1. Write an essay in which you consider some of the advantages and disadvantages in a system of spelling reform for English which might propose to use some or all of the phonemic alphabet in place of our conventional one.
2. If you are currently studying a foreign language, write an essay in which you describe and discuss the phonemic differences between that language and English. Why are such phonemes—like the French *r* and *u*—hard for you to learn?

ROBERTS: INTONATION

Aids to Study

1. Define each of the three features of intonation: stress, pitch, and juncture.
2. Using Professor Roberts's symbols for *primary, secondary, tertiary,* and *weak* stress, mark the stresses in these utterances as you would normally say them:
   a. an ice cream cone; a handsome man; a handyman
   b. a ball point pen display
   c. There's the cigarette machine.
   d. There's nobody in the house.
   e. Please don't talk to the elevator operator.
3. Using the line symbols employed by Professor Roberts, mark the pitch patterns in the following utterances, and describe the differences in meaning which may be obtained by the use of different patterns for each utterance.
   a. What time is it
   b. You're going home now
4. Mark the junctures in the following dialogue, using the symbols Professor Roberts uses, and making certain that the junctures reflect the way you actually speak the words.
   a. "Why don't you come over to my house?" John asked.
   b. "Because I've got to go to the store, where Mother said she'd wait for me," I answered.
5. Now, using Roberts's phonemic alphabet (pp. 175–6), transcribe the passage in number 4. Don't forget to put the phonemic transcription between slants.

Vocabulary

1. Compare Roberts's definition of *intonation* with that in your desk dictionary. What else can *intonation* mean?

2. Is a *gross* difference (p. 178) a bad thing?
3. Where's your *glottis* (p. 179)? What does it do? What's the plural?
4. Transcribe *separate* as it occurs in your reading of each of the following sentences:
   a. We have separate lockers.
   b. She had to separate two eggs.
   Where did *separate* get that first *a* in its spelling?

Topics for Writing

1. Most of you have never encountered a discussion of intonation before, yet you've all noticed how it can change the meanings of sentences whose words are identical. Write an essay in which, through some examples of your own, you explore the relationship between various intonational signals and conventional English punctuation. Are there any systematic relationships—for example between commas and one kind of juncture, or between a particular pitch curve and a question mark?
2. Write an expository essay, using your own examples, in which you define and explain English juncture.

WHORF: LINGUISTICS AS AN EXACT SCIENCE

Aids to Study

1. Whorf compares (p. 194) the effects of linguistic phenomena on talkers with the effects of gravitation. What's the point?
2. Explain Whorf's "linguistic relativity principle." How does this idea correspond to Professor Gleason's remarks on the differences in *structures of content* among languages?
3. Make up an English nonsense word you've never heard before and test it against the formula for one-syllable words in English.
4. Test these words against the formula: *gout, bill, snarf, duz, glib.*
5. Linguistics is also called a *social science.* What assumptions underlie such a statement? How do these fit with what Professor Whorf says about linguistics as an *exact* science?
6. Why does Professor Whorf think scientific study of language is important? Can you think of other arguments, either for or against his conclusions?

Vocabulary

1. How serious is an *innuendo* (p. 193)? Is it worse than an *allegation?*
2. Whorf speaks (p. 194) of "an *illusion* that talking is quite *untrammeled* and *spontaneous*. . . ." What has he said when he used those three words?
3. *Jargon* (p. 195) is a common enough term. Does it have a technical meaning for linguistics? What other words could Whorf have used here?
4. *Wiseacres* (p. 195) looks oddly like slang. What does your dictionary say of it? What is its etymology? What does the word mean?

5. What's a *welter* of data (p. 197), and what, if anything, does that sort of *welter* have to do with a *welterweight?*

Topics for Writing
1. Whorf's list (p. 193) of terms for scientific talking has some good examples. Write a *synonymy*—an essay in which you illustrate and distinguish among these terms: *analyze, compare, deduce, reason, infer, postulate, theorize, test, demonstrate.* Look at some of the synonymies in your desk dictionary for models, but then make your essay as full and exact as you can.
2. Whorf's formula for one-syllable words is intended to illustrate the precision of language. Make an experiment and write an essay in which you report on the results of your efforts to formulate one of the following:
   a. When do we use the *inflected* comparative and superlative of adjectives, and when do we use the periphrastic (*more, most, less, least*)?
   b. We have three forms for the so-called *-s* ending for noun plurals, /-z/, /-əz/, and /-s/.
      Formulate the rules for our use of each.
   c. Foreigners learning English always have trouble with the definite article *the*. Formulate rules for when we use it and when we omit it.

FRIES: A CLASSIFICATION OF GRAMMATICAL PHENOMENA

Aids to Study
1. In the quotation (pp. 204–5) from Mencken's "Vulgate" version of the opening lines of the Declaration of Independence, what grammatical problems do you see besides the double negatives? List these, and with the aid of a dictionary, account for the odd forms and the substandard syntax.
2. What about the vocabulary in the passage Mencken rewrote? How much of it is still slang? How much of it is not in your desk dictionary at all? Can you account for the omissions? Would you change any of these labels to conform to more nearly current standards?
3. What's the difference between the *dative* and *accusative* cases in Latin? Does English preserve formal distinctions between them? Are there inflections to distinguish them in nouns? In pronouns? How did the term *objective case* arise in English?
4. Look closely at the dialogue in the comic strips in your daily newspaper. What substandard or Vulgar English do you find there? Do Professor Fries's remarks about comic writers' use of such language seem to be borne out?
5. What are the three types of device English uses to express grammatical ideas? Find new examples of each.

Vocabulary
1. What is *vulgate*, anyway? What has it in common with the *Vulgate Bible?*
2. What's a *preterit?* Is this a better term to use than *past tense?*

3. What are *demonstratives* (p. 205), and how would you use them *attributively?* Compose some examples.

4. *Concord*—Does your desk dictionary record Fries's specialized meaning for this word (p. 205)?

5. Write a "dictionary definition" of *function word,* and then compare yours with your desk dictionary's definition.

6. Does your desk dictionary record a special grammatical or linguistic meaning for the term *frequency?* Should it? Why?

7. Is there any difference between *word order* and *syntax?* Explain.

Topics for Writing

1. Mencken's "Vulgate" version of those lines from the Declaration of Independence sounds dated. Rewrite them using more nearly current vulgate language. Now, without consulting the original, rewrite them in the best expository prose you can muster. Then, compare both versions with the original document's wording, and discuss the differences. What kinds of things did you change in your two versions, and what are the chief differences between your "good" version and the historical original?

2. What advantages can you see to stripping away semantics and concentrating on "grammatical" meaning when you're examining grammar? Write an essay in which you explore the problem.

3. Of all the material you have previously considered part of the study of grammar what does Fries seem to include, and what does he seem to exclude? Answer the question in an essay.

BROWN, BROWN, AND BAILEY: GRAMMAR IN A NEW KEY;
GRAMMATICAL DISTRIBUTION

Aids to Study

1. Distinguish between "vocabulary" elements and "grammatical" elements, and give some examples of each.

2. Write out some English sentences which employ the grammatical symbols used in the sentences on page 212. Simply fill in the vocabulary elements.

3. What are the arguments the authors use to urge the study of grammar?

4. Examine the uses of the word *round* on page 219. What *are* the other devices that make clear *round's* part of speech in each sentence?

5. Write a number of short sentences using *like* in as many different parts of speech as possible. How do we know what is meant?

6. Prepositions often live double or triple lives in English. Find some which exhibit functional shift, and illustrate the variety of their lives.

Vocabulary

1. What do the authors mean by "grammatical distribution"?

2. What does your dictionary say about *function words* (p. 222)? *Do* can be

a function word. What does your dictionary have to do to define it? Does it define the uses in this and the preceding sentence?

3. Make several lists which illustrate how affixes of various kinds can distinguish between nouns and adjectives, adjectives and adverbs, verbs and nouns, and verbs and adverbs.

Topics for Writing

1. Write a short essay in which you discuss what *grammar* seems to be to Brown, Brown, and Bailey. Would Gleason agree, or does his definition include more?

2. Brown, Brown, and Bailey report (p. 214) that *ambiguities* are "serious obstacles to good writing." Schlauch, on the other hand, in discussing *semantic rejuvenation,* said there were virtues in ambiguity. Write an essay in which you explore and illustrate some of the strengths and weaknesses of grammatical and lexical ambiguity.

3. Consult a dictionary for grammatical definitions of each of the eight traditional parts of speech listed on p. 222. Then write an essay in which you discuss the logic of these definitions. Demonstrate which ones are based on *form,* which on *function,* and which on *meaning.* Then discuss the logical weaknesses of using such terms to describe English grammar.

WHITEHALL: THE SYSTEM OF PUNCTUATION

Aids to Study

1. Punctuate these utterances, following the suggestions Professor Whitehall makes:
   a. I've ordered books stationery and a new typewriter ribbon
   b. She turned and asked Do you want me to come with you or would you prefer to go alone
   c. Stop I cried and I was never more angry in my life or I'll

2. Punctuate the following passage:
   If I were you I told him I'd have nothing more to do with them Their remarks their appearance their very names the whole business seems if you'll take my advice too silly to fool with

3. Make a phonemic transcription of the passage in number 2 above, and then mark stress, pitch, and junctures. Now, what relationships do you see between intonation and punctuation?

4. What sort of assistance does your desk dictionary afford you in problems of conventional punctuation?

5. What intonation curves—combinations of pitch, stress, and juncture—seem to fit with each of the groups of punctuation described on p. 224?

Vocabulary

1. Whitehall says (p. 224) that dashes function as *symbolic conjunctions.* What does this mean?

2. *Heavy* punctuation means "a lot of it." Where does this meaning of heavy come from? Consult an historical dictionary and trace the development of that sense of the word *heavy*.

3. *Convention* and *conventional* turn up quite often in this essay. Check your dictionary for the several senses of each. What do you suppose has caused the pejorative overtones some senses have?

Topics for Writing

1. Write an essay in which you explain the relationship between intonation and punctuation as they affect the distinction between restrictive and non-restrictive modifiers.

2. Your instructor will read the following passage to you. Punctuate it as you hear it read; then compare your punctuation with that of your classmates. Try to account for the difference. You all heard the same reading:

> among that large class of young persons whose reading is almost entirely confined to works of imagination the popularity of Byron was unbounded they bought pictures of him they treasured up the smallest relics of him they learned his poems by heart and did their best to write like him and to look like him many of them practised at the glass in the hope of catching the curl of the upper lip and the scowl of the brow which appear in some of his portraits a few discarded their neckcloths in imitation of their great leader for some years the Minerva press sent forth no novel without a mysterious unhappy Lara-like peer the number of hopeful undergraduates and medical students who became things of dark imaginings on whom the freshness of the heart ceased to fall like dew whose passions had consumed themselves to dust and to whom the relief of tears was denied passes all calculation this was not the worst there was created in the minds of many of these enthusiasts a pernicious and absurd association between intellectual power and moral depravity from the poetry of Lord Byron they drew a system of ethics compounded of misanthropy and voluptuousness a system in which the two great commandments were to hate your neighbour and to love your neighbour's wife

You may see how Lord Macaulay punctuated it by consulting his essay on Moore's *Life of Byron*.

JESPERSEN: SPELLING; HALL: OUR ENGLISH SPELLING SYSTEM

Aids to Study

1. Make a list of one- and two-syllable English words which use the letter *a* as a vowel, and then transcribe the words phonetically. How many different sounds do you find for the English letter *a*?

2. Now make a list of transcriptions of words which all have the stressed vowel /a/. Then spell these words conventionally. How many different spellings are there for the sound /a/?

3. Do the same thing for the sound /iy/. How many different ways does English spell /iy/?

4. Consult your desk dictionary for the origin of the word *ye* in phrases like *Ye Olde Tea Shoppe*. What other spelling curiosities are traceable to writing and printing?

5. George Bernard Shaw is usually credited with inventing this "logical" English spelling of a common word: *ghoti–gh* as in *rough, o* as in *women,* and *ti* as in *motion; ghoti:* a perfectly reasonable spelling of *fish.* See what similar horrors of English spelling you can invent, the sort that a foreigner trying to spell English phonetically might conceivably propose.

6. What reasons can you think of to explain why Americans put so much emphasis on correct spelling?

7. Find in literature some examples of *eye-dialect.* What, actually, does the writer do: vary the spelling to conform to standard English sounds, vary it to conform to substandard or geographical dialect sounds, or both?

8. Jespersen uses some IPA characters which Roberts does not employ in his system for transcribing English phonemes. What are Roberts's transcriptions for Jespersen's [dʒ], [ʃ], and [ʒ]?

9. List all the English alphabetical symbols for consonants—*letters,* not *phonemes.* Now, after each one list all the possible *phonemic* values each can have in English, with an example of each. For example, *e* can be /e/ as in *met,* /iy/ as in *detour, etc.*

10. What are *spelling-pronunciations?* Find some more examples to add to those Jespersen gives.

Vocabulary

1. What's a *shibboleth* (p. 241), and where did we get the word?

2. What's a *ptarmigan?* How *do* we pronounce it? Where did we get the spelling?

3. *Foisted* is a curious word. What's its history? Does it carry a usage label? *Should* it?

Topics for Writing

1. List twenty nouns ending in *y* in the singular. Then try to draw up a generalization which will explain how these words form their plurals.

2. Do the same thing for ten words whose singulars end in *-o.* You may need more than one generalization.

3. What does Professor Hall seem to think we ought to do about our spelling system? If you are a poor speller, are you comforted by his remarks? Write an essay in which you explore the problem.

4. In view of what Jespersen and Hall say about the oddities of English spellings, how do you think spelling should be taught—by rule, generalization, memorization of single words, mnemonic devices, or what? Write an essay in which you consider the problem and offer some reasonable solutions.

5. Transcribe the conversation between Philip and Carlys (p. 240) in phonemic symbols. Then write an essay in which you explain the misunderstanding. How do you treat Carlys's last speech in phonemic symbols?

WHITEHALL: WRITING AND SPEECH

Aids to Study

1. List some of the chief differences between writing and speech.
2. How does the British linguistic situation differ from the American? Consult
   your desk dictionary for its remarks on British pronunciation. What *is* Received Standard British English, and who speaks it?
3. What does Whitehall think *correctness* is?
4. "Education in the English language has become, for the most part, education in linguistic niceties. . . ." What are some of these?
5. In what aspects of the language do you discover the greatest difficulties
   when you change from speech to writing?

Vocabulary

1. *Rhythmed* (p. 243) is a curious word. Does your desk dictionary suggest
   that *rhythm* regularly exhibits functional shift as verb or adjective? What
   limitation, if any, would you place on its use in this form and function?
2. Whitehall speaks of "the code of speech" (p. 243). What's the difference
   between a *code* and a *cipher*?
3. What sense of *medium* is meant on p. 244? What's the plural of the word?
   Have you ever heard or seen another plural? How would you decide which
   one to use in a given speech or writing situation?

Topics for Writing

1. What sort of things must one do in a course in English composition, according to Professor Whitehall's last paragraph? How has your own school work
   in English composition tried to meet these needs? Write an essay in which
   you describe and evaluate your own work in English composition to date.
2. Write an essay in which you discuss and evaluate some of the arguments in
   favor of a standardized written American English.
3. Write an essay in which you discuss and illustrate some of the strengths
   and limitations of written English which Whitehall refers to on page 244.

PART FOUR

Usage

POOLEY: HISTORICAL BACKGROUNDS OF ENGLISH USAGE

Aids to Study

1. What are *number agreement, double comparatives,* and *double negatives?* What sort of problems do they present today? Are deviations in them from standard practices *never* tolerated in Standard English?
2. What are the arguments and what sort of evidence is there to lead us to reject the conceptions "(1) that language is a divine institution, originally perfect, but debased by man; (2) that English is a corrupt and degenerate off-spring of Latin and Greek"?
3. What other "flat" adverbs—besides *slow*—can you find in English? Does the existence of flat adverbs help to explain some substandard usages in English? How?
4. Why should anyone object to *due to?*
5. What do you think of *comfort* as a criterion of good English? Does it run counter to any attitudes you have held about language?
6. How does variation in pattern of intonation further complicate the sentence "I only had five dollars"?

Vocabulary

1. If "the philosophy of the age was inimical to scientific research in language" (p. 252), precisely what effect did it have?
2. What does Pooley mean by *organic growth* (p. 252), and what other kinds of growth might there be? What's significant in the *organic* part of it?
3. What's a *dangling participle* (p. 254)?
4. What's a *gerund,* and how does one dangle? Give an example.
5. What's the difference between *gender* and *sex?* What, in language, is *natural* gender?
6. What kind of *canon* is a *canon* of usage (p. 255)?

Topics for Writing

1. Read Shakespeare's *Love's Labour's Lost,* IV.ii. What kinds of peculiar usage are being made sport of here? Write an essay in which you discuss your findings.
2. Examine an old grammar—perhaps one from the library or one used by your parents when they were in school, or possibly even the one you used in high school. What assumptions does it make about usage? Write a de-

tailed review essay, in which you place the book according to the various historical attitudes Pooley describes.
3. Write an essay in which you define and describe the group of "the best writers and speakers" whom you think you should model usage on in your own composition classes. How do you decide?

HARTUNG: DOCTRINES OF ENGLISH USAGE

Aids to Study
1. What are the chief objections to the doctrine of rules? Are there any arguments which a modern linguist might use in *favor* of it?
2. Contrast the doctrine of general usage with the doctrine of appropriateness.
3. Discuss the advantages the doctrine of the linguistic norm has over the other three doctrines.
4. What kinds of purpose are best served by each of these four doctrines? Is a combination of some of them unsound or inconsistent?

Vocabulary
1. What is *prescriptivism* (p. 258), and what does it contrast with?
2. What is *absolutism* (p. 257) generally, and what does it mean for usage?
3. What is *relativism* (p. 258) as applied to doctrines of usage?
4. What is the difference between *normative* (p. 265) and *average?* What is a *norm?*
5. Explore the usage problem involving *different from, than,* and *to.* Where will you use each of them and why?
6. What should you do about *awful* as an adverb?

Topics for Writing
1. Using Fries's *American English Grammar,* Bryant's *Current American Usage,* dictionaries of usage like Fowler, Nicholson, Horwill, and Evans and Evans, plus the dictionaries available to you, explore the attitudes toward usage of *shall* and *will* in English, and write an essay in which you show how the several doctrines have affected these attitudes. Conclude by stating and supporting what seems to you to be the most satisfactory attitude.
2. Write an essay in which you perform the same sort of investigation on the usage of genitives before gerunds: is it *his* going or *him* going that you're against?
3. What about *folks?* Write an essay in which you evaluate it as a usage problem, and discuss the attitudes of the several doctrines toward it.

HALL: ANALOGY

Aids to Study

1. Think of some more examples of "mistakes" resulting from *internal borrowing* or *analogy*. For example, what is the past tense of the verb *sneak?*
2. What are the reasons that some analogical forms are respectable while others are unacceptable?
3. What are the plurals of *mongoose, moose, stadium?* Why should you hesitate over some of these? What about *data* and *agenda?* Write down the singular and plural forms *you* would use, and then see what your desk dictionary records for all these words.
4. Look up *analogy* in your desk dictionary, and compare the meanings marked *Philology* or *Linguistics* with the one labeled *Logic*. How does this distinction bear on the problems of grammar and usage we've been treating thus far in this book?
5. Consult a historical dictionary for the curious analogical development of the verb *ring*.
6. Words like *beautifuler* and *bestest* are formed on analogy. With what, and how?
7. What archaic plurals like *kine* can you think of? Have all of them been replaced by a regular plural? Check your desk dictionary to see.

Vocabulary

1. What principal parts do you use for the verb *dream?* What does your desk dictionary say about the problem? How has the process of analogy worked here?
2. How do you account for the humorous noun *invite* (instead of *invitation*)? How does analogy figure in its existence?
3. What are the current plurals for these words: *curriculum, status,* and *stimulus?* Is analogy at work on any of them?

Topics for Writing

1. Analogy has forced many of our former strong verbs into the weak verb pattern. Besides *dive* and *dream* and the others Hall cites, what ones can you think of that are currently under some strain? Which ones do adults most often form on the weak pattern? Write an essay in which you survey the subject.
2. What, in logic, is a *false analogy?* Does the same thing exist in linguistic change? Explore this question in an essay.

Aids to Study

1. Where do the greatest differences in English usage occur: in grammar, in pronunciation, or in vocabulary?
2. What reasons can you offer to account for your answer to question one?
3. What's the difference between a *usage label* and a *field label* in a dictionary? What sorts of limitation will each place on the acceptable use of the word?
4. Make a list of the usage labels used in your desk dictionary. Where will you hear or see or use words bearing each of these labels?
5. What are the chief geographical dialects of the United States? What does your dictionary tell you about them?
6. How accurate a term does the word *levels* appear to be in describing usage?
7. Fries warns us about some unscrupulous dictionary publishers (p. 273). Examine your own desk dictionary for this information: who was the publisher? The editor? What's the date of earliest copyright for this edition? What's the base dictionary if yours is an abridgment? When was it published? When was it last revised? What do the various "printing" dates signify?
8. What kinds of distinctions does your dictionary use between *slang, pop.,* and *colloq.* (if it uses all three) as usage labels? Do you agree with the decision? Look up some words which you feel ought to be marked with one or another of these labels. Did the editors agree? If not, what causes the difference of opinion? Are there any instances where your dictionary is clearly behind the times?

Topics for Writing

1. Compare Fries's attitudes toward *authority* in dictionaries with Macdonald's and Dr. Johnson's.
2. Make up a list of words you believe are peculiar to your own geographical dialect. Discuss their meanings and their distribution, and then comment on your dictionary's labeling of these terms.
3. Pick a geographical dialect different from your own and try to describe it. Take into account sounds, unusual syntactic structures and forms, and words and meanings which seem to you odd and therefore peculiar to that dialect. Report your findings in an essay.

Aids to Study

1. The G. & C. Merriam Co.'s decision not to use the *colloquial* label in Webster's *Third New International Dictionary* caused quite a furor. (See the essays by Macdonald and Evans). Consult MW-III to see what the editors'

reasons were. Is *colloquial* a word in the process of semantic degeneration?
2. Compare Kenyon's views with Hartung's (pp. 257–268). Do any of Hartung's doctrines of usage coincide with Kenyon's categories? Would the two men be at odds over usage, or would they agree?

Vocabulary
1. What's the difference between "*slovenly* and *careless vocabulary*" (p. 279)?
2. Consider the usage problems of *those/these* with *kind of/sort of:* are these problems of functional variety or of cultural level or both? How do you decide?

Topics for Writing
1. Kenyon says (p. 279) that cultural levels may be summarized in the two general classes *substandard* and *standard*. Notice his criteria for each, collect specific usage practices to document your conclusion, and write an essay in which you describe your own cultural level of English. How can you tell which level seems to dominate?
2. Listen to the speech and (with his permission) read some of the papers written by your roommate or a classmate. Keep full notes on usages you encounter which seem noteworthy either way, and then write an essay in which you describe the cultural levels of his English.
3. Watch your own speech and writing for a week or so, and then write an essay in which you describe and cite evidence for your practices of *familiar* or *formal* writing or speaking. What sorts of things change in the functional varieties of your English as the situations change?

HUBBELL: MULTIPLE NEGATION

Aids to Study
1. When did the multiple negative cease to be acceptable in good English?
2. What arguments does Hubbell use against the "logical" prohibition of multiple negatives?
3. Why does Hubbell think the double negative continues to be a problem, despite all the teaching aimed against it?
4. How *can* we teach Standard English, according to the author? Does he agree with the views on this subject expressed by Fries?
5. Is the use of the double negative a problem of cultural level or functional variety, or both? What is the evidence to support your view?

Vocabulary
1. Is *can't hardly* a double negative? How will you decide?
2. *Not infrequent, not unlikely,* and *not uncommon* have two negative elements each. How do they differ from what we usually call double negatives?
3. *Can't help but* and *couldn't help but* are sometimes cited as double negatives. Is that what they are? What sort of labels would you give them?

Topics for Writing

1. In his final paragraph, Hubbell concludes that "group loyalties" are the only really effective forces in making people change their language habits. Is there evidence to support this statement in changes in your own language practices since you entered college? Document your answer in an essay.
2. Write an essay in which you explore the usage situations and appropriate labels if any for this expression: *We haven't but one hour left.*

MALMSTROM: AIN'T AGAIN; KIND OF AND ITS CONGENERS

Aids to Study

1. What reasons can you offer for the existence of the forms *aren't I, am I not,* and *amn't I?* Why hasn't one of them displaced *ain't* in all circumstances?
2. How has analogy operated in the problem of *ain't?*
3. Why should some speakers differentiate between *hain't* and *ain't?*
4. Is the use of *ain't* a problem of cultural level or functional variety, or both? Explain.
5. How does *kinda* evolve from *kind of?* Transcribe some phrases to illustrate your answer.

Vocabulary

1. Some uses of *ain't* are called (p. 285) *popular* usage. What does *popular* mean in this context?
2. Some textbooks call *aren't I* an *affected* usage. What do they mean?
3. What are *congeners?*
4. What is an *injunction* of the sort mentioned on p. 288?

Topics for Writing

1. What evidence can you find to show that English really needs a form "like French *n'est-ce pas* or German *nicht wahr*"? What harm do school teachers seem to have done in preventing the growth of one? Write an essay on these points, and try to advise a teacher or parent what he should demand.
2. Discuss the "power of public education in eradicating nonstandard usage."
3. Make a survey of dictionaries and usage books and write an essay in which you attempt to estimate the present state of *kind of* and *sort of.*

POOLEY: DARE SCHOOLS SET A STANDARD IN ENGLISH USAGE?

Aids to Study

1. Why should the existence of a reasonable range of latitude in standards be so much frowned on in connection with language, when almost no one seriously insists on an unvarying single standard in other forms of social behavior? What possible causes can you suggest?

2. How do you suppose *them* ever came to be used as a demonstrative?
3. Make a generalization or a series of generalizations to describe Standard English use of *a* and *an* and the distribution of each.
4. Make a series of generalizations to describe the use and abuse of *well* and *good* in post-verbal positions.
5. Pooley suggests that "some elements in [the list on pp. 294–295] may require modification within ten years; some possibly earlier." Which ones show signs of this need already? (Pooley's essay was published in 1960.)

Vocabulary

1. Not many verbs in English will move in front of the subject to form questions. *Drive we to the store?* sounds odd and archaic. *Dare,* however, will work in the front positions as in the title of Pooley's essay. What other verbs will work that way?
2. How does analogy affect the development of the forms *theirselves* and *hisself?*
3. How would you explain to a foreigner the best way to master acceptable practices in distinguishing *its* and *it's?*

Topics for Writing

1. Write a set of rules for the use of the personal pronouns Pooley lists in item two, page 294.
2. Write an essay in which you state the problems involved in the past tenses and past participles of the verbs listed in items four and five, page 295. What causes these verbs to be problems, and what do you think might be the best current lines to take in dealing with them?
3. Write an essay in which you explore the causes for confusion of some forms of *lie* and *lay.* Describe the problem as exactly as possible, and formulate some generalizations which could be used to teach acceptable practice.
4. Write an essay in which you explore and describe usage in your social group as regards number agreement with the antecedent pronouns *one, anyone, everyone, each, no one, everybody,* and *none.*
5. Chaucer's language (p. 296) has changed a good bit. Write an essay in which you explore the changes in meaning, in form, and in syntax apparent in the quoted passage. For example, "wonder nice and strange" needs several comments: what is the modern form of *wonder* for such positions? What does *nice* mean now? What did *nice* and *strange* mean then?—and so forth.

FOWLER: UNATTACHED PARTICIPLES; OUT OF THE FRYING-PAN

Aids to Study

1. What does Fowler mean (p. 298) by "In all such cases, it is best to put off recognition"? What sort of attitude toward usage would you call this? Which one of Hartung's "doctrines" does it seem to belong to?

2. You're Fowler's generation's grandsons: has *idiom* beaten the illiterates or not (p. 299)?

3. Rewriting is one of the best ways to learn; recast each of Fowler's examples, beginning with *Unlike the other great European capitals* . . . (pp. 299–300).

4. Rewrite, in better form, each of Fowler's examples in "Out of the Frying-Pan" (pp. 301–2).

Vocabulary

1. What does *per return* mean? Would you use it? Explain.
2. What is the current view of the acceptability of *due to* as a preposition?
3. What is *idiom*, as Fowler uses it, page 299?
4. What is a *fanatical purist* (p. 299)? What does he stand for?

VEBLEN: THE HIGHER LEARNING

Aids to Study

1. How do "archaism and waste," the leisure class "standards of virtue," reflect themselves in linguistic practice?

2. What is the flavor of "Biblical English"? Is this what Veblen means by "the highest and most conventionalized style of archaic diction"?

3. "A discriminate avoidance of neologisms is honorific . . ." Put this clause into language suitable for an essay *you* might write. Is Veblen seriously choosing such words? How would you decide?

4. How do Veblen's remarks in his final paragraph bear on the current furor over gobbledegook and jargon in business, the law, education, social science, and the like?

Vocabulary

1. Consult your desk dictionary for the meanings of *classic*.
2. What is "a skilled and graded *inebriety*"? Does your desk dictionary have the word?
3. What's the distinction, if any, between *obsolete* and *obsolescent* (p. 303)?
4. *Elegant* has been a very modish word in English. What does it mean now, and how would you describe its overtones?
5. What has *honor* to do with *honorific*?
6. Is there any difference in meaning between *cumbrous* (p. 305) and *cumbersome*?

Topics for Writing

1. How do Veblen's views of English spelling fit with Jespersen's and Hall's? Discuss their views in an essay.
2. For a man opposed to conspicuous consumption, Veblen uses a good many big words. Paraphrase his essay; put his ideas as clearly as you can in your own words.

LLOYD: OUR NATIONAL MANIA FOR CORRECTNESS

Aids to Study

1. ". . . we Americans are hell on the English language." ". . . their writing stinks to high heaven too." Does Professor Lloyd write Standard English? How will you decide?
2. Our "mania for correctness" is the cause to which the author attributes our loss of the eighteenth-century facility for writing. What other possible causes can you think of?
3. What does the author mean by the phrase "to beat the old Adam out of . . . ." (p. 309).
4. Lloyd appears to want us to write as we speak. If we did so, do you think it would be literally true that "usage doesn't matter"?

Vocabulary

1. What is *pedagese*? Is it in your desk dictionary? *Should* it be there? What usage label ought it to have?
2. What does *convoluted* mean?
3. *Lewd* has undergone considerable semantic change since the Middle Ages. Consult the dictionaries for its history: what did it mean in the document Lloyd quotes (p. 307)? What does it mean now? Can you account for the change?
4. *Hectic* is a word we use a great deal. Lloyd talks about *hectic* spelling: is this an unusual sense of the word? Do you see semantic change at work?
5. What's so bad about *monolithic* concentration? What is a *monolith*, and how do you account for the pejorative overtones in *monolithic*?
6. If you *brace a sociologist* (p. 309), what do you do?

Topics for Writing

1. How do Lloyd's views square with those of Professor Fries? Write an essay in which you discuss the problems.
2. Study Lloyd's essay carefully, noting particularly his diction and syntax. If you were to be his editor, what changes would you ask him to make, and why? How do your own attitudes toward usage influence your decisions? Explain it all in an essay.
3. "[Teachers] want to know two things: what correct usage is, and how you beat it into the kids' heads" (p. 308). You have now had a good look at the language. What *should* Lloyd's graduate students want to know? Explore the subject in an essay.
4. Discuss the fears *you* have had about language and your use of it, and describe the effects your reading and writing and discussing the language—as this book has invited you to do—have had on those fears.

POTTER: THE SENTENCE

Aids to Study

1. What limitations are there to the number and variety of sentence patterns you may be able to employ?
2. What are the three kinds of sentence-*forms?* What are the four kinds of sentences classified as to *function?*
3. How would you classify the *style* of these sentences from Ernest Hemingway's *A Farewell to Arms:*

> Now in the fall the trees were all bare and the roads were muddy. I rode to Gorizia from Udine on a camion. We passed other camions on the road and I looked at the country. The mulberry trees were bare and the fields were brown. There were wet dead leaves on the road from the rows of bare trees and men were working on the road, tamping stone in the ruts from piles of crushed stone along the side of the road between the trees. We saw the town with a mist over it that cut off the mountains. We crossed the river and I saw that it was running high. It has been raining in the mountains. We came into the town past the factories and then the houses and villas and I saw that many more houses had been hit. On a narrow street we passed a British Red Cross ambulance. The driver wore a cap and his face was thin and very tanned. I did not know him. I got down from the camion in the big square in front of the Town Major's house, the driver handed down my rucksack and I put it on and swung on the two musettes and walked to our villa. It did not feel like a homecoming.

And these, from Joseph Conrad's *The Heart of Darkness:*

> The *Nellie,* a cruising yawl, swung to her anchor without a flutter of the sails, and was at rest. The flood had made, the wind was nearly calm, and being bound down the river, the only thing for it was to come to and wait for the turn of the tide.
>
> The sea-reach of the Thames stretched before us like the beginning of an interminable waterway. In the offing the sea and the sky were welded together without a joint, and in the luminous space the tanned sails of the barges drifting up with the tide seemed to stand still in red clusters of canvas sharply peaked, with gleams of varnished sprits. A haze rested on the low shores that ran out to sea in vanishing flatness. The air was dark above Gravesend, and farther back still seemed condensed into a mournful gloom, brooding motionless over the biggest, and the greatest, town on earth.

4. Macdonald and Evans are writing for intelligent, literate lay audiences, and their subject is the same—MW-III. Yet the differences in tone and style—in syntax, diction, figure of speech and the like—are great. List and comment on some of these differences.

Vocabulary

1. What is an *analytic* language (p. 315)?
2. What's the difference—if any—between *bipartite* and *binary* as Potter uses them (p. 316)?
3. Defoe's use of the words *leaving off* have a curiously old flavor (p. 319). Consult some dictionaries and your own word sense. Would *obsolete* or *archaic* be the proper label for that use of the phrase?
4. What kind of prose is *sonorous* prose (p. 319)?
5. Make up some illustrative examples for the words *antithesis* and *antithetical*.
6. What's a *jussive* (p. 322)?
7. Is there such a word as *precisians* (p. 322)? How will you decide?
8. What did the grammarians do who *averred* (p. 323)?

Topics for Writing

1. Potter quotes a number of remarks about style in writing. He speaks also of classifying *sentences* as to *style:* loose, balanced, and periodic. Try your hand at a definition of style. What sorts of things must you discuss in such a definition?
2. Pick one of the essayists in this volume who seems to have a distinctive style—Hall, or Veblen, or Whorf, or Lloyd, for example—and write an essay in which you discuss the style of the essayist. Analyze and classify his sentence structure, describe his diction, and comment on his syntax.
3. Dr. Johnson is one of the great English stylists. Write an analytical and descriptive essay in which you distinguish and illustrate the qualities of that famous style.
4. Potter says a number of useful things about style. Write an essay in which you attempt a definition of style: what is it, and how best can we describe it?

ORWELL: POLITICS AND THE ENGLISH LANGUAGE

Aids to Study

1. Orwell speaks (p. 325) of "the half-conscious belief that language is a natural growth and not an instrument which we shape for our own purposes." Is this the issue the linguists were raising? Is this the usage quarrel over again? Or would someone like Lloyd agree with Orwell?
2. How much truth is there in Orwell's statement (p. 325) that "an effect can become a cause," and how well does it apply to language?
3. Rewrite Laski's sentence (p. 326, no. 1) so that it avoids all the objectionable qualities Orwell discusses.
4. What is stale about the imagery of the *Tribune* letter (p. 326, no. 5)?
5. Pick out one of the longer essays in this collection and examine it closely for signs of dying metaphors. What examples can you find, and how would you put life into them?

6. Revise the best essay you've written so far this year by rigorously applying Orwell's rules (p. 335). For example, *remove* or replace every "metaphor, simile, or other figure of speech which you are used to seeing in print." Replace long words with short ones. This kind of tinkering with your prose can show you what revision really can accomplish.

Vocabulary
1. How do you play *ducks and drakes* (p. 326), and what's Hogben's point?
2. How did *hackneyed* get its modern meaning? Just what *is* a hackneyed figure? How does it differ from a *stereotype?* From a *cliché?*
3. Where *does* "toe the line" come from (p. 327)?
4. Orwell calls (p. 328) the following words *unnecessary*. Find the short equivalents: *expedite, ameliorate, predict, extraneous, deracinated, clandestine, subaqueous*.
5. What do *romantic* and *sentimental* (p. 329) mean? Are they of no real use?
6. What does Orwell mean (p. 335) by *outright barbarous?*

Topics for Writing
1. Try to rewrite the Communist pamphlet's sentence so that the loaded language disappears. What sorts of genuine ideas are left? Try to state accurately what the writer wanted to get across. Is there a better way? Discuss and illustrate the whole problem in an essay.
2. Almost no one is safe when we start examining prose for signs of pretentious diction. Pick any of these essayists except Veblen and search his essay for big words which could just as well be replaced by smaller, more common ones.
3. Social scientists are said to exhibit a good many symptoms of pretentious diction, particularly in the terminology peculiar to their subject matter. Linguists are social scientists. What signs of this flaw do you find in the linguistic terminology in this book? How much of it could be disposed with? Explore this problem in an essay.
4. "The inflated style itself is a kind of euphemism" (p. 333). Explore this idea in an essay.

MOORE: AMERICAN PROSE TODAY

Aids to Study
1. Moore remarks that Americans never felt the need for a Fowler, a *Modern American Usage*. But, under various titles, such books have been written. Look at the ones by Margaret Nicholson, and Bergen and Cornelia Evans, and the most recent one, *Current American Usage* (N.Y., 1962) by Margaret Bryant. What kinds of things do they talk about?
2. What's the *non solum, sed etiam* construction?
3. Moore draws some conclusions about Midwestern schools from his reading of Midwestern newspapers. Are these warranted conclusions?

Vocabulary
1. What does Florio, translating Montaigne, mean by a *"compendious* and *material* speech" (p. 337, epigraph)?
2. Would you label *slicker* (p. 337) as *informal,* or *colloquial,* or *slang?* Or is it perfectly standard in this use?
3. Why should the Old Guard cry *"Beaver!"* and what's a *fourpenny* that it can receive mail?
4. What's a *dynamic* (p. 338)? Is this something Orwell would have censured?
5. What's a *pastiche* (p. 338), and where will it appear?
6. Should *chumminess* (p. 339) have quotes around it?
7. Why does Moore put *expositional* in quotes (p. 339)? What other word could he have used?
8. What does Moore mean when he says he didn't "pick Mr. Schlesinger *invidiously*" (p. 341)?
9. What's an idiosyncratic style (p. 343)?
10. *Deadpan* is a word we use a great deal. Should it have a usage label? What does your desk dictionary say? Do you agree?
11. "It's a nice question" (p. 349). What does *nice* mean here?
12. If you were grading papers, would you correct Moore's *learnt* (p. 353)?

Topics for Writing
1. Study the style of writing in the editorial and local news pages of your local newspaper (don't count wire service stories) and then write an essay in which you discuss the qualities of syntax, diction, and figure which seem typical. How, if at all, do they differ from the kinds of expository prose Moore seems to like best?
2. Student newspapers are usually much criticized by their readers. Study a few issues of your own, and try to extend Moore's method to cover this kind of American prose. What are its hallmarks, and what does it need most? Write an exploratory essay.
3. Attack or defend Moore's final paragraphs. *Are* we in as bad a plight as he suggests?
4. Look closely at Moore's own style. What are its peculiarly British qualities? What are its virtues? Its defects? How does it differ from *The New Yorker* prose he seems to like best of the American samples he cites? Write an essay on it.